Palgrave Studies in Cross-disciplinary Business Research, In Association with EuroMed Academy of Business

Reflecting the growing appetite for cross-disciplinary business research, this series aims to explore the prospects of bringing different business disciplines together in order to guide the exploration and exploitation of scholarly and executive knowledge. Each book in the series will examine a current and pressing theme and consist of a range of perspectives such as management, entrepreneurship, strategy and marketing in order to enhance and move our thinking forward on a particular topic.

Contextually the series reflects the increasing need for businesses to move past silo thinking and implement cross-functional and cross-disciplinary strategies. It acts to highlight and utilize the emergence of cross-disciplinary business knowledge and its strategic implications across economic sectors, geographic regions and organizational types.

Published in conjunction with the EuroMed Academy of Business, books will be published annually and incorporate new scientific research works developed specifically for the book or based on the best papers from their conferences. Over the last decade EuroMed have developed a cross-disciplinary academic community which comprises more than 30,000 students and scholars from all over the world.

Each submission is subject to a proposal review and a double blind peer review. For further information on Palgrave's peer review policy please visit this website: https://www.palgrave.com/gp/book-authors/your-career/early-career-researcher-hub/peer-review-process For information on how to submit a proposal for inclusion in this series please contact Liz Barlow: liz.barlow@palgrave.com.

For information on the book proposal process please visit this website: https://www.palgrave.com/gp/book-authors/publishing-guidelines/submit-a-proposal

Demetris Vrontis · Alkis Thrassou ·
Leonidas Efthymiou · Yaakov Weber ·
S. M. Riad Shams · Evangelos Tsoukatos
Editors

Business in Uncertainty

Evolution, Transformation and Adaptation Across Disciplines and Typologies

palgrave
macmillan

Editors
Demetris Vrontis
GNOSIS Mediterranean Institute for Management Science, School of Business
University of Nicosia
Nicosia, Cyprus

Leonidas Efthymiou
Department of Management
School of Business
University of Nicosia
Nicosia, Cyprus

S. M. Riad Shams
Newcastle Business School
Northumbria University
Newcastle upon Tyne, UK

Alkis Thrassou
GNOSIS Mediterranean Institute for Management Science, School of Business
University of Nicosia
Nicosia, Cyprus

Yaakov Weber
College of Management Academic Studies
School of Business Research Center
Rishon LeZion, Israel

Evangelos Tsoukatos
EuroMed Research Business Institute
Nicosia, Cyprus

ISSN 2523-8167 ISSN 2523-8175 (electronic)
Palgrave Studies in Cross-disciplinary Business Research, In Association with EuroMed Academy of Business
ISBN 978-3-031-65586-9 ISBN 978-3-031-65587-6 (eBook)
https://doi.org/10.1007/978-3-031-65587-6

Cover illustration: Daniele Levis Pelusi via Unsplash.com

This Palgrave Macmillan imprint is published by the registered company Springer Nature Switzerland AG
The registered company address is: Gewerbestrasse 11, 6330 Cham, Switzerland

Contents

Editors and Contributors

About the Editors

Demetris Vrontis is the Vice Rector for Faculty and Research and a Professor of Strategic Marketing Management at the University of Nicosia, Cyprus. He is the President of the EuroMed Academy of Business and the Managing Director of Gnosis Mediterranean Institute for Management Science, which serve as important and influential regional hubs in the area of Business and Management. He is the Founder and Editor in Chief of the EuroMed Journal of Business, an Associate Editor of the International Marketing Review, an Associate Editor of the Journal of Business Research, a Consulting Editor of the Journal of International Management and an Associate Editor of the Journal of Strategic Marketing. He has published widely in over 300 refereed journal articles, 50 books and 80 chapters in books, and he has presented papers to over 80 conferences around the globe. He is a certified Chartered Marketer and a Chartered Business Consultant.

Alkis Thrassou is a Professor at the University of Nicosia (Cyprus, EU) and holds a Ph.D. from the University of Leeds (UK). He is the Director of Gnosis Mediterranean Institute for Management Science, the Chief Editor of Palgrave Intersections of Business and the Sciences, the Managing Editor of Palgrave Studies in Cross-disciplinary Business Research, an Associate Editor of EuroMed Journal of Business, and a

Senior Research Fellow of the EuroMed Academy of Business. He has edited and published in numerous internationally esteemed scientific journals and books, and his works have been cited in thousands of scientific publications. He further retains strong ties with industry, acting also as a consultant, and holding the prominent professional qualifications of Chartered Marketer (FCIM), Chartered Construction Manager (FCIOB) and Chartered Management Consultancy Surveyor (MRICS).

Leonidas Efthymiou is Associate Professor in Organisation, Tourism and Hospitality Studies at the University of Nicosia, and adjunct faculty at Unicaf University. He previously worked at Intercollege, Pearson Education and the University of Leicester. He has also taught online for Universities in Europe, Africa and the United States. He also travels frequently to Africa, in his capacity as Instructional Designer. He has co-edited and published several books, articles, media reports, policy papers and encyclopaedia articles. His research output lies at the intersection of employment, digitisation and education. Leonidas received a number of awards, including the best PhD Thesis award, by the Academy of Management in 2011, Boston Massachusetts. He trained at the universities of Leicester (Ph.D., M.Sc.), Derby (BA) and the Higher Hotel Institute Cyprus (Dip. Hons).

Yaakov Weber is professor emeritus that teaches courses on Strategic Management, Mergers and Acquisitions Management, Strategic Alliances, Corporate Strategy, Cross Cultural Management, and Global Strategic Management. He lectured in various universities in United States (for example NYU), Western and Eastern Europe and China, in graduate schools of business administration as well as executive programs, in private and public organizations as well as Industrial Associations for CEOs and Directors He also participating and conducting international Ph.D. seminars, in Ph.D. committees as well as referee in international Ph.D. exams. Prof. Weber's studies were published in top leading international academic journals, such as Strategic Management Journal. Journal of Management, Management Science, Journal of Business Research, California Management Review, and Human Relations, among others. His papers received more than 8500 citations in leading journals and books. Several papers were selected by various academic collections and were described as represent "the most significant new material" and, "most important works published in Sociology" (in 1996). Other papers are

"2nd most cited in last 5 years (2010–2015) and "most read" (2011–2015), or "most download", in leading journals. He served as associate editor and in editorial boards of several journals and act as a referee for numerous leading journals. He served as Guest Editor for special issues in leading journals, such as California Management Review, Human Resource Management, Journal of World Business, and more. Recently Prof. Weber is the winner of the Outstanding Author Contribution Award. His recent book that was invited by Financial Times, A Comprehensive Guide for Mergers and Acquisitions, was published in 2014. This and his other books, can be seen in AMAZON. Also, currently, coeditor of 3 book series at EMERALD, Rutledge, and Palgrave Macmillan. Prof. Weber is Co-Founder and Co-President of the EuroMed Business Research Institute (www.emrbi.org), the EuroMed Academy of Business and the EuroMed Research Centre. Prof. Weber has been senior consultant to CEOs, top executives and directors in leading domestic and international companies such as Coca-Cola, Dead-Sea Works, Society of Israel Plastics & Rubber Manufacturers, largest International Engineering company in Israel, Health-care Organizations, The USA-Israel Chamber of Commerce, large and small organizations in Chemical industry, High-Tech industry and many others in various industries as well as to the largest international consulting firm in Israel. His recent large project of international consulting was to an international merger in Moscow, Russia. Prof. Weber conducted numerous workshops to top executives in many countries. Recently he conducted workshop to the senior executives of one of the 4 largest investment companies in China.

S. M. Riad Shams is a senior lecturer in marketing and Ph.D. Programme Leader at the Newcastle Business School, Northumbria University. He has extensive academic and industry experience. Riad has co-authored a core textbook, 'Marketing Management: Past, Present and Future' (which is currently in its 4th edition) for postgraduate and advanced undergraduate teaching. He delivered an invited keynote at the SIDREA International Conference in January 2020, which was sponsored by the Sapienza University of Rome. He has published seventeen books, and contributed articles to top-tier marketing and business journals. Riad obtained a second place in the Cambridge-Kent-Czinkota Competition for Excellence in International Business Research – 2019, and entered into the Kent Business School's Honours Board. He received the Emerald Literati Award (Outstanding Paper) in 2019, the Emerald Literati Award

(Outstanding Reviewer) in 2018, and the EuroMed Research Award in 2014. As per Google Scholar, Riad is the fifth most cited author in social business research, and sixth most cited author in sustainable marketing research.

Evangelos Tsoukatos is associate professor of Management at the Helleninc Mediterranean University and adjunct faculty at: the University of Nicosia, Cyprus and the Hellenic Open University. He holds a Ph.D in Management Science from the Lancaster University Management School (LUMS), UK, a B.Sc. in Mathematics from the "Aristotelion" University of Thessaloniki, Greece, a Postgraduate Diploma and M.Sc. in Operational Research from LUMS, UK. Dr Tsoukatos holds the position of Vice President – Operations and Development at the EuroMed Research Business Institute. He authored and edited books and journal special issues and has heavily published internationally in scholarly journals and presented in academic conferences. For his published research, he has gained wide recognition from his peers. He is Associate Editor of the EuroMed Journal of Business (EMJB) and editorial board member in a number of international scholarly journals.

Contributors

Sofia Bakirli is an Academic Quality and Subject Coordinator at the European Business School in Munich. She holds a B.A. in Educational Psychology, an M.Sc. in International Human Resources, and a PG certificate in Adult Learning and is currently Ph.D. Candidate in Business Administration at the European University of Cyprus.

Vaida Balbieriūtė is a junior researcher with an interest in exploring the intersection of business strategy, media management, and leadership studies. Vaida has established a substantial and, at the same time, varied professional profile in media, marketing, and public sector administration, having worked in international environments in Europe and Asia within traditional and digital media agencies with leading business strategy professors. Most recently, she focused on higher education policy and strategy at Vilnius University, as well as marketing strategy at city investment agency Klaipėda ID.

Elisavet Bouloumpasi holds a Degree in Food Science and Technology and a master degree in Enology and Viticulture, both from the Aristotle University of Thessaloniki, Greece. She is also Ph.D. student, Department of Food Science and Technology, Faculty of Agriculture, Aristotle University of Thessaloniki, Greece. She is an Adjunct lecturer in the Department of Agricultural Biotechnology and Oenology since 2010 and has over 20 years' laboratory experience in implementing analytical and microbiological methods for the analysis of food and beverages. She has produced 30 scientific publications in well recognized journals with a significant number of citations.

Meliz Bozat is currently pursuing her Ph.D. at the University of Nicosia, in the School of Business and she is a researcher for GNOSIS Mediterranean Institute for Management Science. She received her bachelor's degree from the University of Nicosia in Tourism Leisure and Events Management with the best graduate award. Afterwards, she worked in many reputable casinos, in Cyprus as a reception and public relations supervisor, and also in a five-star hotel, arranging events to enhance her skills in the tourism and events field. After a few years of work experience in the tourism and events field, she studied for an M.B.A. in Events Management at Bournemouth University and graduated with Merit. She also has a work experience in casinos in the UK, as a marketing assistant, public relations and reception supervisor. In 2021, she has decided to enhance her academic skills with a Ph.D. and contribute to the literature. Meliz's research interests include tourism and hospitality, destination marketing, events management, marketing of new technologies, AI, robotics, also consumer behaviour, sustainable development and innovation. In addition, her Ph.D. topic focuses on consumer behaviour, technology and the hotel industry.

Federica Cavallo is Research Fellow e Ph.D. in Business Management at Department of Management, Economics, Mathematics and Statistics, University of Salento (Lecce). Her research interests include web marketing, social media communication, wine and agrifood business and tourism. She has authored several publications and presented papers at scientific conferences.

Sherwin Ignatius Chia is a Senior Lecturer and the Head of the Human Resource Management Programme at the S R Nathan School of

Human Development in Singapore University of Social Sciences. Sherwin's research focuses on the effects of self-regulation as well as job resources and job demand. He is also interested in cultural psychology and careers. He is passionate about teaching and loves experimenting new ways to bring theories to life in the classroom. Sherwin received his Ph.D. from the Nanyang Business School in Nanyang Technological University. Prior to rejoining Singapore University of Social Sciences, Sherwin led an innovative corporate social responsibility education programme at IBM Singapore and served as the head psychologist for the Centre of Leadership Development at the Ministry of Defence of Singapore.

Paraskevi Dekoulou is an Assistant Professor in Media Management at the Department of Journalism and Mass Communications, Aristotle University of Thessaloniki (Greece). She teaches media management and economics, strategic digital marketing and marketing communications, cultural management and entrepreneurship. At the same time, she is an Adjunct Professor in Marketing at the National and Kapodistrian University of Athens (Greece). She holds a Ph.D. Degree in Media Management from Aristotle University of Thessaloniki, she received a Master in Business Administration and an M.Sc. in Media Management from Stirling University, and a bachelor's degree (Hons) in Journalism and Mass Media Communications from Aristotle University of Thessaloniki. She has taught a wide array of marketing and management modules at both private and public academic institutions in Greece and Cyprus. Her main research interests include media management, strategic marketing, marketing communications, consumer behavior and corporate social responsibility. Her research work has been presented in international academic conferences and published in international academic journals. Moreover, she has been highly involved in coordinating the implementation of numerous EU funded projects, such as Interreg Euromed, Erasmus + and EEA Grants.

Niccolò Fiorini is a postdoctoral researcher at the University of Siena, Department of Business and Law. He obtained a Ph.D. in Economics, Markets and Institutions (EMI) from the IMT School for Advanced Studies in Lucca, a master's degree cum laude in management and governance and a bachelor's degree cum laude in economics and business from the University of Siena, and a first-level master's degree in "GINTS – Management of Financial Institutions and New Information

Technologies" from the Department of Business and Law of the University of Siena. He was a visiting Ph.D. student at the Judge Business School of the University of Cambridge, Clare Hall College, UK (January – June 2015), and Erasmus student at the WHU – Otto Beisheim School of Management in Koblenz, Germany (September – December 2010). From January to July 2018, he carried out a period of Higher Education and Research at the Fraunhofer Institute IAO in Stuttgart. His research interests are marketing, technology transfer, entrepreneurship, Industry 4.0, Business Models, and ecosystems.

Simone Gibellato as a Project Manager specializing in the fields of bio-construction, sustainable agriculture, and social innovation, his main aspiration is to promote the conceptualization and implementation of innovative projects based on the values of circular economy and sustainability, integrating them into new organizational models. This preference has led him to develop an interest in project management in the areas of technology transfer and international cooperation. He is currently pursuing a Ph.D. in Circular Economy Innovation, focusing on Grassroots and Responsible Innovations. His research skills primarily concentrate on qualitative methodologies through the analysis of various case studies.

Manlio Del Giudice is a Full Professor of Management at the University of Rome 'Link Campus'. He built his academic and scientific career outside of Italy for more than 12 years, in a wide number of world-renowned. He has served as editor-in-chief of the top-tier Journal of Knowledge Management. His research studies comprise more than 160 publications in high-ranking peer to peer journals (3* e 4*). His main research interests deal with knowledge management, technology transfer, foresight management, innovation and technology management.

Stergios Gkitsas (Ph.D. candidate, MA, BA) is an elementary school teacher and head of the school where he works. He is also a Ph.D. candidate at the School of Primary Education of Aristotle University of Thessaloniki. He has published several papers in international journals such as Nutrients and Environmental Education Research. He has also published several papers in international conference proceedings. His research focuses on issues of sustainability, water footprint, and education.

Johana Hajdini is a Ph.D. candidate at the Department of Management and Business Administration at University G. d' Annunzio of Chieti-Pescara, Italy. Her research interests include marketing and consumer behavior with a specific focus to healthcare organizations. She is currently interested in researching technological transformation of healthcare organizations from a multi-perspective. She has attended several national and international level conferences and co-authored book chapters. She has also served as a reviewer for international journals, such as International Marketing Review and EuroMed Journal of Business.

Lea Iaia, Ph.D. Senior Researcher of Management in the Computer Science Department at the University of Turin. Her research interests regard the marketing and communication processes with specific reference to the use of digital marketing and social media by organisations. Besides, Lea interests include information technology, innovation and technology management, and sustainability. She won several awards for her research work and academic effort. She has authored book chapters and several publications at leading journals, such as Annals of Tourism Research, Technological Forecasting and Social Change, Journal of Business Research, International Marketing Review, Corporate Social Responsibility and Environmental Management.

Irene (Eirini) Kamenidou, Ph.D., M.Sc., B.Sc., B.Sc., BA is a Professor of Marketing at the International Hellenic University of Greece and a visiting professor at the Hellenic Open University. She has published articles in several academic journals such as Journal of Business Research, International Marketing Review, EuroMed Journal of Business, Sustainability, Nutrients, and International Journal of Environmental Research and Public Health. Her research interests focus on marketing (agricultural, food, tourism, retailing, health, social), consumer behavior and sustainability. She has served as Dean at the School of Business and Economics of the Eastern Macedonia and Thrace Institute of Technology.

Aikaterini Karampatea holds a B.Sc. in Chemistry (Auth) and Oenology (Diplôme National d'Oenologue and Master (uB)) and a Ph.D. in Vine, Wine and Beverage Sciences (UniWA). She is Research Fellow at the Department of Agricultural Biotechnology and Oenology of IHU. She has experience on analytical and winemaking techniques and consulting as she owns an oenological laboratory (Oenopolis). She has participated in research and educational programs and has published articles in international scientific journals and national and international conferences. She is a member of Oenologues de France and Association of Greek Chemists. She is also a wine judge and participated in more than 20 international wine competitions.

Spyridon Mamalis, Ph.D., M.Sc., M.Sc., B.Sc. is a Professor of Marketing in the International Hellenic University of Greece, Department of Management Science and Technology and also is a visiting professor at the Hellenic Open University. Also, he is the Head of the Department of Agricultural Biotechnology and Oenology Development. He has served as the president of the Geotechnical Chamber of Greece. He has published 7 books, 53 peer reviewed articles in international journals and 87 articles in international conference proceedings. Finally, he has been the leader of more than 8 projects financed by EU.

Esposito Marialuisa is an accountant who engages in professional consultancy for businesses on both national and international fronts, specializing in business advisory, planning and control, budget analysis, and evaluation. She holds a degree in Administration and Finance from Luigi Bocconi Commercial University and has gained experience as a controller at Prysmian Group and BNP Paribas in Milan.

Bruno Marsigalia is an Assistant Professor of Business Economics at the G. Marconi University of Rome, where he holds the chairs of Business Economics, Management Control and Economics of Sustainability and Responsibility. His research area covers the topics of business financial statements, business valuation, management control techniques, business crisis, financial transactions, national and international accounting standards, and valuation of intangible assets.

Alberto Massacci is a postdoctoral researcher at the University of Siena, Department of Business and Law. He obtained a Ph.D. in Economics in the Tuscan Doctoral program jointly held by the University of Siena, Florence and Pisa. He holds a master's degree cum laude in Finance and a bachelor's degree in economics and business from the University of Siena. He was visiting researcher at the Madison University (WI—USA) and the University of Graz (AT). He is currently working on Agritech, a project financed by the Italian National Recovery and Resilience Plan (PNRR) aimed at fostering the digital and sustainable transition in the agrifood

Industry. His research interests lie in the area of Marketing, Entrepreneurship, Business Models, Tourism and Sustainability. Additionally, He has gained professional and research experience in Finance and Real Estate.

Michela Matarazzo, Ph.D. is a Full Professor of Management at the G. Marconi University of Rome, where she serves as Coordinator of the Master Degree Course in Economics and Management of Sustainability and as Director of the first level Master in Global Marketing and International Trade. She holds a Ph.D. in Business Economics at the University of Naples "Federico II". She has been an elected board member for two terms (2013–2015 and 2016–2018) at the Società Italiana Management, track co-chair at the Società Italiana Marketing (International Marketing, 2016–2018 and 2019–2021) and at the Euromed Conference (Innovation Management, 2016–2018). From 2019 she is track co-chair at the Euram Conference (Growth strategies and internationalization for SMEs, SIG Entrepreneurship). Her research interests include international business with a special focus on consumer behaviour, country image, international corporate reputation, SMEs' internationalization and market entry modes, also in relation to the digital contexts. She has authored and co-authored more than 100 publications, including, conference papers, book chapters, journal articles, among which International Marketing Review (3*) and Journal of Business Research (3*) and 3 books on firms' internationalization and on cross-border M&As.

Simona Mihail-Yiannaki holds the position of Associate Professor in Finance and serves as the Chairperson of the Department of Accounting, Economics, and Finance. Since 2023, she has been the program coordinator for the M.Sc. Data Analytics in Accounting and Finance at European University Cyprus. Simona is also a Visiting Professor in Asset Management at Lumsa University in Italy and Pforzheim University in Germany, where she teaches Research Methods in Finance to M.Sc. students. Furthermore, she actively manages EUC-PEAK, the Entrepreneurship Center of the EUC Business School.

Ifigeneia Mylona is an Assistant Professor in Marketing and Communications at the Department of Management Science & Technology of International Hellenic University. She is a member of staff of the M.Sc. in Digital Marketing, M.Sc. in Information Systems and M.B.A. in Tourism of International Hellenic University. She studied Communications with

Politics at the University of Leeds in England. She continued with post-graduate studies in Communication Policy (MA in Communication Policy Studies) at the University of City in London. She has acquired her Ph.D. at the School of Drama, Film and Visual Arts at Kent University (Canterbury, England).

Valerio Natale is currently a Research Fellow in Management at the Department of Business and Legal Studies of the University of Siena. His research topic is new digital solutions and new marketing strategies in the Life Science sector. He has a master's degree in management and governance, obtained from the same university. After graduating he worked for a multinational in Vilnius (Lithuania) in the accounting sector. Subsequently, he became a Research Assistant, and currently a Research Fellow, in the same department. He carried out two periods abroad for the European research project OpenInnoTrain, one month in Porto (Portugal) and two months in Vaasa (Finland). His overall research topics concern new technologies applied in various fields and sectors of management.

Stephen Oduro, Ph.D. (International Management), is Assistant Professor at the Free University of Bozen-Bolzano (UNIBZ), Italy. His research interests include but are not limited to international marketing, Small Business Management, sustainability & corporate social responsibility, and meta-analysis, and he has published in leading journals, including the Journal of Product and Brand Management, Technovation, Marketing Intelligence and Planning, and European Journal of Innovation Management. Stephen is a member of the European Academy of Management and Societa' Italiana Marketing (SIM).

Yianna Orphanidou is a faculty member of the Department of Management specializing in Hospitality and Tourism at the University of Nicosia. She holds a B.A. (HONS) in Hospitality Management and an M.Sc. in Hospitality and Tourism Education from Surrey University (UK), and currently, she is pursuing her Ph.D. at the University of Nicosia. Her academic prowess is complemented by a wealth of practical experience in the dynamic realm of Tourism and Hospitality Management. She has actively contributed to over 20 funded European, International, and National projects, showcasing her commitment to cutting-edge research and technological advancements in the field and she published numerous journal articles. Her multifaceted involvement extends beyond academia, as she holds pivotal roles in various Tourism and Hospitality professional organizations, serving as a board director. Her research endeavors are marked by a keen focus on tourism sustainable development and the intricacies of hospitality human resources. Her scholarly pursuits delve into the intricate balance between environmental responsibility and the growth of the tourism sector, as well as the nuanced management of human capital in the hospitality industry.

Stavros Pavlidis (Ph.D. PD., Ph.D., B.Sc.) is a federal employee at the Region Unit of Eastern Macedonia and Thrace and an adjunct professor at the International Hellenic University, School of Management and Economics, Dept. of Management Science and Technology. His research focuses mainly on agricultural and food marketing. He has published many articles in international journals and conference proceedings.

Marco Pironti was a Visiting scholar at the Center for Computational Research & Management Science, MIT, Boston (MA), at the Institute of Management, Innovation and Organization, Haas School of Business, Berkeley and at the CEBIz of Columbia University and Visiting Professor at Westminster Business School (UK). He is a Professor of Innovation Management and Entrepreneurship at the University of Torino – Computer Science Department, Dean of ICxT Interdepartmental Innovation Center and member of Scientific Committee of Ph.D. program in Innovation for the Circular Economy. He is an author of more than 100 articles and other publications. His main research interests are relating to strategy, innovation management and business modelling & planning. He was the Deputy Mayor of Innovation, Smart City and ICT Systems of the City of Torino.

Tommaso Pucci is Associate Professor in Management researcher at the University of Siena, Department of Business and Law. He graduated in Economics (cum laude) at the Faculty of Economics of the University of Florence (Italy). He got a Ph.D. in Economics and Management of Enterprises and Local Systems. Since 2009, he has been carrying out research and teaching activities at the Department of Business and Law (University of Siena) as adjunct professor and research fellow. Since 2019 he has been associate professor of management in the Department of Business and Law (University of Siena). His research interests are Management, R&D and Innovation Management, Science Parks, Industrial Districts and other Incubator Organizations for Business Start-up, Network Organizations,

Management and Marketing of "Made in Italy" products, International Business.

Joana Ramanauskaitė is an associate professor at the Sustainable Management Research Group at School of Economics and Business, Kaunas University of Technology. Her research interests are in corporate sustainability, sustainability transition, quality management. She is also a member of the Sustainability Transitions Research Network (STRN). Joana lectures in courses of sustainable development and quality management since 2019. The researcher participates in international research projects funded by Erasmus+ and Research Council of Lithuania.

Veronica Scuotto is an Associate Professor in Entrepreneurship and Innovation at the University of Naples Federico II, after joined the University of Turin (Italy), working at the Pôle Universitaire Léonard de Vinci in Paris (France) and then the University of the West of Scotland (UK). She obtained the Italian National qualification as Full Professor in 2020. She was awarded the high cite researcher 2023 by Clarivate. She has published several articles featured in high-ranking peer-to-peer journals (3* and 4*). She is the managing editor of the journal of intellectual capital and part of several editorial boards.

Adriana Skendi is an Adjunct Assistant Professor in the Department of Agricultural Biotechnology and Oenology, IHU holding a Ph.D. in Food Science and Technology and an M.Sc. in Food Quality Management. She also holds a second degree in Business Administration and is engaged as a postdoctoral researcher in different projects. Her scientific interest is the study of polysaccharides and antioxidants and their structural and technological aspects in food structure, quality and consumer acceptance. She has great expertise in developing analytical methods for detection/quantification of mycotoxins and phenolics. She is a co-author of several scientific publications and a reviewer for scientific journals.

Eglė Staniškienė a professor at the Department of Management, School of Economics and Business, Kaunas University of Technology (KTU), Ph.D. in Social Sciences. Research interests include sustainable development, corporate social responsibility, responsible consumption and sustainable production, employee well-being, quality system management and interdisciplinary research. Currently, E. Staniškienė is a member of the expert council of the Lithuanian Responsible Business Association

(LAVA) dealing with SDG12. E. Staniškienė is Co-president COPERNICUS Alliance, European Network on Higher Education for Sustainable Development. She has published more than 60 scientific publications, participated in more than 20 national and international projects. E. Staniškienė is an expert of the United Nations Economic and Social Council (ECOSOC), she participated in Group Meeting on "Socially just transition towards sustainable development: The role of digital technologies on social development and well-being of all" (at United Nations Economic and Social Council (ECOSOC) (2020) She uses and develops her scientific competence in the study process and in cooperation with business and public sector organizations. Lecturing includes courses on Sustainable Development, Quality Management, Quality and Sustainable Development Management, the Circular Economy and others.

Živilė Stankevičiūtė, Ph.D. in Management, is professor at Sustainable Management research group, School of Economics and Business, Kaunas University of Technology, Lithuania. Her doctoral dissertation on Sustainable Human Resource Management has been recognised internationally: she got Baltic University Programme Annual Award for the Best Ph.D. defended in 2015. Her research interests are: Sustainable Human Resource Management, Employee Wellbeing, Digital Transformations, Corporate Social Responsibility, Sustainable Development. She is a member of National Expert Council for sustainable development goals at Lithuanian Responsible Business Association (LAVA) dealing with SDG8. Lecturing includes courses on Sustainable Development, Contemporary Human Resource Management Theories and Concepts, People Analytics. She has expertise in the field of partnership with business while conducting research projects and providing the practical implications based on research quantitative and qualitative data. In 2019 and 2020, she got Kaunas University of Technology Award as a Most Active Young Researcher. In 2022 and 2023, she was awarded for her outstanding contribution to the development of junior researchers.

Aikaterini Stavrianea is an Assistant Professor at the National and Kapodistrian University of Athens, Department of Media and Communication and an Adjunct lecturer at the Hellenic Open University. She holds her B.A. from the National and Kapodistrian University of Athens, her M.Sc. in Integrated Marketing Communications from Northwestern University (Chicago, IL.) and her Ph.D. from Athens University of Economics and Business. She has published many articles in international journals and conference proceedings. Her research interests mainly focus on customer experience, consumer behavior and marketing communications.

Živilė Stravinskaitė is a manager. She has been interested in emotional intelligence for many years. During her Master's studies, she became attracted to organisational life cycles. She is convinced that a manager's ability to identify where an organisation is in its lifecycle can help to determine what actions they need to take and what leadership style to choose to help the organisation thrive. She has applied these competencies in her research and in her practical management work.

Mathupayas Thongmak is an associate professor of Information Systems in the Management Information Systems department of Thammasat Business School, Thammasat University in Bangkok, Thailand. She holds a Ph.D. in Computer Engineering from the Faculty of Engineering, Chulalongkorn University. Her research interests include adoption and diffusion of IS/ IT, education/ learning relating to IS/IT, social media & marketing, software quality, digital piracy, and green ICT. Her research has appeared in various journals, including Journal of Computer Information Systems, International Journal of Electronic Commerce Studies, Online Journal of Applied Knowledge Management, Electronic Green Journal, Knowledge Management & E-Learning, Journal of E-Learning and Higher Education, International Journal of Information Technologies and Systems Approach, International Journal of Software Engineering and Knowledge Engineering, and Education for Information. She has reviewed multiple journals, including Sage Open, Engineering Journal, Children and Youth Services Review, Electronic Commerce Research and Applications, International Journal of Electronic Commerce Studies, Knowledge Management & E-Learning, Recent Patents on Computer Science, and Telematics and Informatics.

Erika Vaiginiene is an associate professor at Vilnius University Faculty of Economics and Business Administration. She is an experienced researcher-consultant with a demonstrated history of working in the higher education industry. She has more than 20 years of work experience in higher education, in different positions (Professor; Head of Strategic Management office; Deputy for Research, Innovation and Quality Assurance; Acting Director of Business School (6 months)). Her research and consulting areas cover the topics of higher education, entrepreneurship and innovation management, change management and foresight development. She is a member of CEEMAN, AOM, EMRBI and FEN. Erika holds a Ph.D. in Social Science in Business Administration and Management. She is a certified change manager. She has strong skills in quantitative and qualitative research methodologies, the development of valid survey questionnaires, and foresight methodologies.

List of Figures

List of Tables

CHAPTER 1

Profiling Business in Uncertainty: Evolution, Transformation, and Adaptation Across Disciplines and Typologies

Demetris Vrontis, Alkis Thrassou, Meliz Bozat, and Leonidas Efthymiou

1.1 Introduction

In today's fast-paced business world, dealing with uncertainty is a major challenge. As pointed out by Coase in 1937, uncertainty can hinder organisational integration, a struggle that lasts till the present day, and reconfirmed by recent studies in contemporary management. Recent

D. Vrontis · A. Thrassou · M. Bozat
GNOSIS Mediterranean Institute for Management Science, School of Business, University of Nicosia, Nicosia, Cyprus
e-mail: vrontis.d@unic.ac.cy

A. Thrassou
e-mail: thrassou.a@unic.ac.cy

M. Bozat
e-mail: bozat.m1@live.unic.ac.cy

D. Vrontis et al. (eds.), *Business in Uncertainty*, Palgrave Studies in Cross-disciplinary Business Research, In Association with EuroMed Academy of Business, https://doi.org/10.1007/978-3-031-65587-6_1

events like the war in Ukraine, natural disasters, and COVID-19 emphasise the need for businesses to adapt to uncertain conditions (Thrassou et al., 2022; Vrontis et al., 2022). A series of crises have led to the concept of 'permacrisis', a term describing an era of continuous critical events, which coexist and reinforce each other (Overland & Loginova, 2023; Vainik et al., 2023). In the light of permacrisis, governments and industries are ought to innovate for stability and public well-being (Daglio & Tahlak, 2023; Giousmpasoglou, 2023).

To manage uncertainty, organisations employ strategic management techniques like risk reduction and strategic adaptation (Goher et al., 2023). Strategic management in uncertain environments is crucial for resilience and competitiveness, requiring dynamic capabilities and resource planning (Haarhaus & Liening, 2020). Concepts like the RBV and OA help organisations adapt and innovate within uncertainty (Darvishmotevali et al., 2020; Freeman et al., 2021). Additionally, the emergence of Industry 4.0 (Buhalis et al., 2024) brings new challenges summarised in the VUCA paradigm, emphasising the need for agile leadership and technological ability (Raja, 2021). Despite the challenges, strategic management concepts like RBV, OA, and VUCA offer valuable tools for navigating uncertainty and fostering resilience and innovation in today's business landscape (Haarhaus & Liening, 2020).

Within this context, this chapter presents an in-depth overview of theoretical frameworks and strategic management concepts, assisting businesses in exploring the nature of business uncertainty and presenting approaches to effectively managing uncertain conditions. Especially, in today's ever-evolving business environments, offering insights and strategies for organisations is essential for businesses' capability to thrive within uncertainty. The chapter commences by highlighting the inevitable changes in organisations and how these changes introduce uncertainty which instantly affects the decision-making processes of an organisation. The section then explores various types of uncertainty, particularly environmental uncertainty is emphasised as it presents both opportunities and threats to the overall performance of an organisation. The next part of the

L. Efthymiou (✉)
Department of Management, School of Business, University of Nicosia, Nicosia, Cyprus
e-mail: efthymiou.l@unic.ac.cy

book chapter is about the new paradoxical term that was introduced into the third decade of the twenty-first century while severe and recurring catastrophic events occurred such as pandemics, wars, and climate change and more. This section highlights the persistent challenges that governments face in times of emergent and long-standing issues and significance of transformative responses from global organisations. This phenomenon can be achieved through adaptation and innovation to provide a stable business environment while also generating public value.

Furthermore, a key theoretical framework for uncertainty management is discussed, which communicated strategies for risk management and uncertainty management. The chapter also emphasises the importance of differentiating between risk and uncertainty as the role of uncertainty in decision-making has received considerable attention in the field of international business which also influences multinational companies. Then, a section delineates the role of strategic management in environmental uncertainty, seeking effective strategies in response to environmental uncertainties. Therefore, developing dynamic capabilities to manage resources in an efficient way is crucial because when uncertainty level escalates, organisations need to adapt swiftly through suitable decision-making process, especially when taking into account the impact of technological advancements and globalisation.

Moreover, the analysis focuses on adaptation and resilience, which refer to an organisation's capacity to withstand crisis and adapt to new environments. It can be achieved and sustained through organisational innovation in adjusting environmental changes and minimise the impact of threats and risks. Towards the end, the chapter investigates strategic management concepts in uncertain environments, such as the resource-based view (RBV), which focuses on enhancing internal strengths and capabilities of an organisation to maintain a competitive advantage. Additionally, the concept of organisational agility (OA) is discussed, highlighting the organisations' ability to adapt in complicated environments which indicates the importance of organisations being able to sense and respond to environmental changes rapidly. Furthermore, the chapter explores the VUCA (Volatile, Uncertain, Complex, Ambiguous) framework, which describes the dynamic shifts in the external environment and their impact on organisations due to the fourth industrial revolution. It discusses how organisations can adopt the VUCA world by fostering innovation, adaptability, and resilience.

Finally, drawing on the findings of the critical review, a conceptual framework has been developed and presented in Fig. 1.2, followed by implications and future research with suggestions.

1.2 Literature Review

Introduction to Business Uncertainty

Organisations must embrace inevitable changes to ensure their survival and success, yet these changes also unavoidably introduce uncertainty to the organisation. As Coase pointed out in 1937, uncertainty stances as a substantial barrier to organisational integration, and businesses struggle with uncertainty while formulating plans and making decisions, experiencing shifts in the nature and extent of uncertainties over time (occasionally undergoing gradual shifts or sudden changes) resulting in decision-makers' perspectives and choices being affected. However, encountering uncertainty doesn't necessarily imply market failure, but organisations must seek safe markets that are unaffected by current circumstances, which prompts them to make decisions contrary to their usual choices. Within the realm of international business, several forms of uncertainty exist, originating from distinct sources such as environmental factors and based on their nature as either exogenous or endogenous. Simply, environmental uncertainty relates to the degree to which external environments exhibit '*shifts in technologies, changes in customer preferences, and fluctuations in product demand or the supply of materials*'.

In brief, environmental uncertainty embraces political, economic, governmental, cultural, and discontinuous uncertainties, including formal and informal elements within a country's environment. Hence, it can be asserted that environmental uncertainty primarily occurs due to unpredictable or random actions, which can contribute to an organisation's performance in a positive (opportunities) or negative (constraints and threats) way. For instance, if the market is stable and predictability is high, organisations face minimal immediate risk; however, the presence of unpredictable environmental conditions, poses uncertainty and thus risks to organisations. In times of higher uncertainty, Giones et al. (2020) suggest it's crucial to find the balance between how entrepreneurs act and how managers think by being more economical, which involves applying ideas relevant to the incidence, intensity, and formality of business plans to enhance readiness and resilience. Therefore, managers find it challenging to strategically incorporate innovative ideas into their decisions, whereas low environmental uncertainty aids firms in defining their business strategy. At this point, it is essential to differentiate between the concepts of risk and uncertainty when considering business strategy, as risk, measured with probabilitics, may lead solely to negative effects, while uncertainty, fundamentally unquantifiable, holds the potential for positive outcomes; the unknowns are unknowns (Lima et al., 2022). Altig et al. (2022) emphasise that recent instances of uncertainty, such as the 9/11 terrorist attacks, the Global Financial Crisis, the Brexit referendum, and the COVID-19 pandemic of 2020, emphasise the necessity for sound and adaptable measures of uncertainty. Therefore, decision-makers must develop a thorough understanding of uncertainty management, to effectively navigate the process with minimised impact.

Due to these uncertainties, there has been a growing interest in achieving and maintaining resilience across diverse disciplines, as well as the capacity to absorb disturbance (Granig & Hilgarter, 2020). The resilience of organisations provides the capacity to endure crisis phases and adapt to new environments, leveraging the experience to gain a competitive advantage (Bartuseviciene et al., 2023). To achieve and maintain resilience, scholars and practitioners consider organisational innovation as an essential factor because innovation enables organisations to adjust to environmental changes and mitigate the impact of threats and risks (Aldianto et al., 2021). It appears that innovation is crucial for competitive strategy during crises, but empirical evidence is needed to understand how an organisation establishes a foundation for resilient organisations by enhancing its innovation processes (Pratono, 2022). Therefore, organisations increasingly find the need to modify, alter, or reshape their business models (BM) in response to emerging trends such as the sharing economy, gamification, rapidly changing demographics, urbanisation, and technological advancements, which seem to influence organisations and a high degree of uncertainty caused by trends that necessitate organisations to adjust their business models to remain competitive (Granig & Hilgarter, 2020).

Permacrisis

At the commencement of the third decade of the twenty-first century, the world found itself in a constant state of crisis (Overland & Loginova,

2023). Due to the events that encapsulate the realities of the 21st decade, such as the global climate crisis, compounded by the worldwide COVID-19 pandemic, the war in Ukraine in 2022, and the implementation of Brexit, all led to the emergence of the paradoxical term 'perma-crisis' (Giousmpasoglou, 2023; Vainik et al., 2023). In essence, the term permacrisis refers to recurring and severe catastrophic events like wars, epidemics, pandemics, food insecurity, climate changes, humanitarian crises, and widespread regional conflicts (Hosseini, 2023). However, the term permacrisis appears paradoxical since the word 'permanent' implies enduring or lasting without change, while the word 'crisis' suggests a pivotal moment, indicating a situation that unfolds with either positive or negative consequences (Vainik et al., 2023). Hence, this scenario highlights the significance of governments as they have to address emerging challenges alongside long-standing issues which are mentioned above, compelling them to adapt and innovate to transform their societies and economies for stability, ultimately striving to generate public value during challenging circumstances (Daglio & Tahlak, 2023). Ultimately, perma-crisis is considered a phenomenon, characterised by gradual progression, consistently producing adverse effects, transitioning from one phase to another, resulting in a stagnation effect on key areas of social development during periods of uncertainty but permacrisis mainly involves a series of interconnected crises occurring simultaneously (Deviatnikova, 2023). For this reason, Giousmpasoglou (2023) argues that permacrisis should be seen as a chance to transform organisations globally while emphasising the moral responsibility of various industries' stakeholders to establish a sustainable working environment for future generations in a truly global context (Vrontis et al., 2023, 2024).

Uncertainty Management

Uncertainty management demands employing strategies that enable organisations to either reduce (risk management) or cope with (strategic management) uncertainty; as decreasing uncertainty serves as a natural motivator influencing organisations' behaviour, while the ability to cope with uncertainty is empowering for the adaptation of appropriate strategies in an effective addressing of the specific type of uncertainty that organisations encounter. As briefly mentioned in the previous section, the term uncertainty is often used interchangeably with the term risk but in business management, the term uncertainty is favoured over risk due to its use in practice as a synonym for threat and hazard, thereby eliminating ambiguity (Goher et al., 2023; Lima et al., 2022). Secondly, uncertainty management, unlike risk management, offers a broader perspective for the identification of uncertainties and focuses on the management of the source of the threat rather than solely addressing the threat itself (Goher et al., 2023). Ultimately, involvement in business activities is essentially accompanied by a certain level of uncertainty, demanding constant decision-making among various alternatives which implies that uncertainty dominates every stage of an organisation's existence, establishing risk as an integral component of the organisation itself (Settembre-Blundo et al., 2021). Therefore, the role of uncertainty in decision-making has received substantial attention in the field of international business (IB) studies since the 1920s and it has been shown to affect multinational companies (MNCs). In early literature, the basic uncertainty management process has three main stages as summarised in Fig. 1.1 (Goher et al., 2023).

In the initial phase, referred to as planning and identification, various uncertainties are outlined, with each uncertainty described using diverse tools such as literature reviews, brainstorming, interviews, surveys, and SWOT analysis (**S**trengths, **W**eaknesses, **O**pportunities, and **T**hreats) depending on the organisation's preference; then ultimate identification is determined by expert judgement and experience (Goher et al., 2023). In the second phase of uncertainty management, an evaluation of uncertainty is conducted to prioritise and achieve the determined goal, by utilising a blend of qualitative and quantitative methods (Goher et al., 2023). The final stage involves responding to uncertainties by assisting decision-makers in managing both opportunities and threats as it requires reducing threats and maximising opportunities, leading to the mitigation of uncertainties during implementation within the organisation's capacity (Goher et al., 2023). However, in this modernised era, these traditional management regulations predominantly hinder innovative ideas due to the inherent uncertainty linked with research and

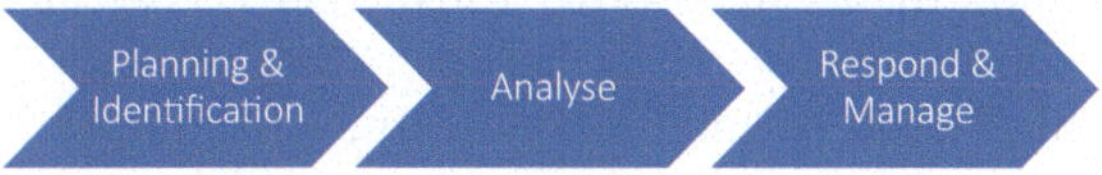

Fig. 1.1 Basic uncertainty management process

development tasks, contrasting with the formalised systems envisioned to govern such activities (Henri & Wouters, 2020). Therefore, even though many studies on decision-making within MNCs have integrated uncertainty, the IB literature lacks precise differentiations among various dimensions of uncertainty and frequently handles the concept inconsistently. However, as previously mentioned briefly, worldwide occurrences like the COVID-19 pandemic, the implementation of Brexit, and the conflict in Ukraine have triggered exceptional crises (Giousmpasoglou, 2023; Vainik et al., 2023). These crises have posed challenges to business environments and made it difficult to operate, irrespective of an organisation's size, structure, location, or resources which led to the introduction of a new term, 'permacrisis', to characterise the ongoing era affecting humanity as a whole (Giousmpasoglou, 2023).

Importance of Strategic Management in Environmental Uncertainty

The initial conceptualisation of environmental uncertainty, dealing with uncertainty has been characterised by Thompson as the '*essence of the administrative process*' since 1967 and contemporary practitioners and scholars are increasingly seeking effective approaches to manage environmental uncertainty (Haarhaus & Liening, 2020, p. 4). When there are environmental changes, organisations need to quickly modify their routines to enable themselves to acquire or develop new resources and integrate them to create new abilities (Hitt et al., 2021). Ultimately, employing effective strategies helps decision-makers in dealing with environmental uncertainties while maintaining consistently high performance and enhancing their competitive position (Darvishmotevali et al., 2020). This implies that organisations must have or quickly develop dynamic capabilities to manage their resources in a more adaptable and efficient manner (Hitt et al., 2021). The rationale behind this is that as the level of uncertainty increases, organisations require dynamic capabilities to explore, take action, learn, and adapt as dynamic capabilities, originating from subordinate functions and processes, provide practical insights essential for developing these higher-order capabilities (Haarhaus & Liening, 2020).

However, high levels of uncertainty emerge when rationales are insufficient as experiential foundations for knowledge can be driven by multiple factors such as customers, suppliers, competitors, and wholesalers encompassing predictable elements (Darvishmotevali et al., 2020), but also unpredictable elements with technology, markets and competitors being most well-known sources due to their continuous and rapid changes (Chen & Tian, 2022; Darvishmotevali et al., 2020). Hence, the growing uncertainty over the years highlights the growing necessity to understand the factors driving uncertainty, particularly when focusing on technological uncertainty, which is the most significant contributor to environmental uncertainty along with globalisation and highly disruptive business models (Darvishmotevali et al., 2020; Haarhaus & Liening, 2020). Within this perspective, it is worth noting that traditional management approaches and techniques are highly perceived as limited in their ability to handle an unpredictable environment because traditional methods include approaches like hierarchical command-and-control structures, long-term planning, forecasting, and organisation-as-a-machine metaphors, which fall short in capturing the uncertainty and complexity of today's business environment as nonlinear interactions and feedback effects make it impossible to predict specific long-term outcomes of managers' actions (Haarhaus & Liening, 2020).

1.3 Strategic Management Concepts in Uncertain Environments

Resource-Based View

As conventional concepts are lacking in mitigating the effects of uncertain environments, organisations must prepare themselves for upcoming environmental uncertainties that involve establishing organisational resilience to formulate effective responses to specific situations and, ultimately, undertaking transformative actions to leverage disruptive surprises that may pose a threat to the survival of organisations (Haarhaus & Liening, 2020). Therefore, a key focus in the domain of strategic management is the organisation's adoption of the resource-based view (RBV), which extends from the dynamic capability approach (Freeman et al., 2021). This perspective covers both tangible and intangible assets, along with the organisation's operational capabilities, aiming to enhance the efficient and effective utilisation of existing resources while simultaneously establishing and sustaining a competitive advantage (Freeman et al., 2021; Haarhaus & Liening, 2020). The RBV postulates that businesses can acquire valuable resources, either resources that are not in their possession but controlled or with ownership costs exceeding the benefits, through the utilisation of inter-organisational integration and strategic partnerships (Kiyabo & Isaga, 2020; Koç et al., 2022). The employment of inter-organisational integration is crucial as the internal strengths and weaknesses of an organisation are more readily manageable compared to external opportunities and threats; therefore, the RBV of organisations primarily focuses on these internal strengths and weaknesses (Shibin et al., 2020). Yet, organisations must prepare themselves for environmental uncertainties to ensure they can adapt and they will likely require different resources and new ways to gain a competitive advantage (Hitt et al., 2021; Nandi et al., 2021).

At this juncture, the matter of resource orchestration gains significance as it involves reconstructing, bundling, and leveraging of internal and external resources along with the realisation of capabilities because when addressing the external environment, achieving successful transformation requires a balance between technological aspects and business practices which is only possible through resource orchestration (Chen & Tian, 2022). As per Haarhaus and Liening (2020), the growing pace of technological advancements poses exceptional challenges for organisations. The reason is that technological uncertainty reflects changes in an organisation's technological resources (Darvishmotevali et al., 2020), but to allow a more suitable development and greater competitiveness, both environmental uncertainty and resource orchestration are considered key to digital transformation (Chen & Tian, 2022; Darvishmotevali et al., 2020). Technological uncertainty occurs due to organisations' 'inability to fully comprehend or predict certain aspects of the technological environment which results from technological unknowns that might emerge or be combined to generate new ideas or solutions, and concurrently, it has the potential to undermine an organization's competitive foundations' (Darvishmotevali et al., 2020). Therefore, digital transformation which refers to artificial intelligence (AI), blockchain, Internet of Things (IoT), and cloud technology, has drawn scholars' attention to investigate transformation preparation, appropriate strategy and implementation along with technology applications that caused the development of the agility concept; agility concept has further developed in the effective integration of technology and strategy (Chen & Tian, 2022).

Organisational Agility

In the current era marked by significant opportunities and formidable challenges, including a globalised economy, disruptive technologies, political disruption driven by income inequality, and the threat of climate change affecting the natural world, the business environment has undergone substantial transformations since the latter part of the twentieth century (Joiner, 2019). This highlights the significance of organisational agility (OA) as a key goal for any organisation seeking to achieve and sustain superior business performance within an unpredictable environment (Walter, 2021). Therefore, OA is now a requirement for organisations worldwide to stay competitive and contribute value in the current business landscape of hypercharge and complexity (Joiner, 2019). OA refers to an organisation's ability to change or adapt in response to environmental alterations which comprehends monitoring and responding to continuous, rapid changes in complicated environments (Darvishmotevali et al., 2020). Therefore, organisations effectively sense uncertain changes both externally and internally and respond to them reactively or proactively, achieved through innovating internal operational processes, engaging customers in exploration and exploitation, and leveraging the capabilities of partners in an organisational business network (Nurjaman et al., 2021).

Moreover, organisations must possess the flexibility to efficiently plan and execute strategic changes, necessitating adaptability, speed, and fostering mindsets that promote inventive thinking and resilience (Darvishmotevali et al., 2020). Therefore, the identifying, seizing, and transforming aspects of dynamic capabilities and RBV undoubtedly function as a strength in the execution of an agile business strategy (Darvishmotevali et al., 2020; Hitt et al., 2021). Nevertheless, although agility is recognised as a vital tool for survival in today's turbulent environment, that stimulates an organisation's performance and boosts competitiveness, it should not be seen as a stand-alone capability, rather, it should be seen as a set of capabilities, with the integration of digital technologies contributing to the overall enhancement of organisational performance (Troise et al., 2022). To accomplish flexibility and deliver customer value through the application of agile principles, effective management encompasses collaboration, empowerment, self-organisation, and continuous improvement (Akkaya et al., 2022; Kuusisto, 2022). Moreover, there are numerous tools and techniques for implementing the agile management process, such as cross-functional teams, feature-driven development, visual management, agile coach, iterative and incremental development and co-location, indicating that agile management primarily involves the utilisation of teams and ecosystems (Akkaya et al., 2022; Kuusisto, 2022).

In this context, individuals collaborate iteratively to adapt to new realities, align with the external world, and deliver value to customers (Akkaya et al., 2022). Additionally, it is observed that organisational agility can improve the resilience of the organisation, characterised as its ability to recover from crises stemming from internal, external, or environmental changes, especially with the adoption of advanced technology that has an impact on heightened organisational agility (Mrugalska & Ahmed, 2021). Furthermore, in today's business environment, advanced technology aligns with globalisation, economic conditions, and the pace of environmental changes, volatility, uncertainty, complexity, and ambiguity emerge as challenges for all organisations to force them to become more dynamic and encourage greater flexibility and agility.

Embracing the VUCA Concept in Industry 4.0

As mentioned previously, the evolution of information technology (IT), gave rise to the fourth industrial revolution, commonly referred to as Industry 4.0, which was driven by the rapid advancement of technologies such as AI, IoT, and Big Data. However, with the emergence of this new type of industry, organisations have found themselves in an unsettled environment, which is related to a world that has become more uncertain and volatile; VUCA (Volatile, Uncertain, Complex, and Ambiguous), that needs successful technology management through the combination and deployment of different innovations, as well as operational, strategic, and business missions (Araújo et al., 2021; Bach & Sulikova, 2021; Hongchai & Weber, 2024). The acronymVUCA describes dynamic shifts in the external environment, directly or indirectly affecting the operations of organisations with its diverse aspects in discovering applicability across various industries (Raja, 2021). It is noteworthy that the concept of VUCA was initially coined at the United States Army War College to capture the features of the world during the latter years of the twentieth century and the initial decades of the twenty-first century (Akkaya et al., 2022; Wolanin, 2022).

VUCA is widely adopted by business intellectuals and managers to signify the true nature of the world, especially for business strategists, the factors driving the current VUCA world could include heightened competition in markets, technological advancements, cost-conscious consumers, environmental challenges, and globalisation (Akkaya et al., 2022). The outcome of these multidimensional changes is the internal restructuring of organisational units, giving rise to the development of competency models and the implementation of diverse decision-making approaches which enables organisations to guide their paths towards achieving goals, fostering innovation, and adapting to the challenges of the VUCA world (Araújo et al., 2021; Wolanin, 2022). This theme is trending in management circles because, despite remarkable advancements in global business, disruptions persist, potentially resulting in business failures that impact stakeholders which need established businesses to encounter a range of threats due to VUCA factors (Raja, 2021). Scholars have emphasised technical and technological ability, alongside efforts made to think in an agile manner as the digitalisation of processes reduces dependence on human labour, with its ability to formulate multiple scenarios for a given situation, oversee a distributed team, and comprehend IT systems in grasping the essence of this concept. Therefore, businesses need to make endeavours to prioritise efficiency-based strategies, aiming to mitigate the widespread adverse impacts on various business functions (Raja, 2021). At this juncture, the significance of leadership becomes evident, as skilled agile leaders own the ability to foster innovation and experimentation, cultivating a culture of creativity while demonstrating the courage to recognise when a particular approach is not effective and can readily shift to more promising alternatives which enables organisations to thrive by maintaining resilience, agility, and innovation (Friedman, 2020).

1.4 Concluding Discussion

In the dynamic structure of ongoing businesses, change is essential for survival and success, but it brings about the significant challenge of uncertainty. Therefore, organisations are frequently coping with evolving uncertainties stemming from various factors, leading to shifts in decision-maker's perspectives and choices. In the context of international business, various types of uncertainty arise from different sources, including environmental factors, and can be classified based on whether they are exogenous or endogenous. Environmental uncertainty in international business, influenced by technological shifts and changes in customer preferences, comprises political, economic, governmental, cultural, and intermittent elements.

At this point, balancing entrepreneurship and managerial thinking becomes critical during high-uncertainty periods, posing challenges for integrating innovative ideas into decisions. However, when it comes to uncertainty in business strategies, the term risk needs to be distinguished from the term uncertainty, as uncertainty has an unquantifiable nature, and the presence of unknowns that hold potential for positive outcomes, but the risk can be measured with probabilities and has a potential for solely negative outcomes (Lima et al., 2022). In light of this, decision-makers need to develop an in-depth understanding of uncertainty management, especially after recent events like the 9/11 terrorist attacks, the Global Financial Crisis, Brexit, and the COVID-19 pandemic underscore the need for adaptable uncertainty measures. As a response to situations with uncertainty, the term resilience signifies an organisation's capacity to absorb disturbances and adapt to new environments (Bartuseviciene et al., 2023).

To achieve and maintain resilience, organisational innovation becomes essential in enabling adjustments to environmental changes and threat mitigation (Aldianto et al., 2021). Therefore, organisations need to adapt their BMs through frequent modifications, which are considered necessary for competitiveness in the dynamic business environment (Granig & Hilgarter, 2020). Furthermore, after the global events mentioned above, at the beginning of the twenty-first century the term 'permacrisis' has emerged to describe the long-lasting state of crisis (Overland & Loginova, 2023). Simply, permacrisis encompasses recurrent and severe catastrophic events such as wars, epidemics, pandemics, climate changes, and regional conflicts (Hosseini, 2023; Vainik et al., 2023). Despite the paradoxical nature of the term permacrisis, which comes from the term 'permanent' that implies enduring without changes and the term 'crisis' that suggests a turning point (Vainik et al., 2023), governments must address emerging challenges alongside long-standing issues, necessitating adaptation and innovation for societal and economic stability (Daglio & Tahlak, 2023).

Permacrisis is characterised by gradual progression, consistently producing adverse effects, and transitioning between phases, ultimately stagnating key areas of social development during uncertain times (Deviatnikova, 2023). Therefore, Giousmpasoglou (2023) argues that permacrisis allows global organisations to transform, emphasising stakeholders' moral responsibility to establish a sustainable working environment for future generations which should be seen as an opportunity. Ultimately, managing uncertainties involves strategies for reducing (risk management) or coping with (strategic management) uncertainty, providing a broader perspective compared to risk management (Goher et al., 2023). The uncertainty management process includes planning and identification, evaluation, and response stages, utilising tools such as literature reviews, SWOT analysis, and professional judgement (Goher et al., 2023).

However, the lack of differentiation among various dimensions of uncertainty in international business literature remains a challenge. Nevertheless, dealing with environmental uncertainty has been vital since the 1960s as effective strategies supporting organisations in adapting, maintaining high performance, and enhancing competitiveness (Darvishmotevali et al., 2020; Haarhaus & Liening, 2020). This necessitates exploring, taking action, learning, and adapting in the face of increasing uncertainty as dynamic capabilities are crucial for organisations (Haarhaus & Liening, 2020). However, technological uncertainty, a significant contributor to environmental uncertainty, requires understanding its factors and preparing for unpredictability (Darvishmotevali et al., 2020) because traditional management approaches are considered limited in handling the current business environment's uncertainty and complexity (Haarhaus & Liening, 2020). In managing uncertain environments strategically, the RBV can be utilised which focus on tangible and intangible assets, operational capabilities, and inter-organisational integration for efficient resource utilisation and sustaining a competitive advantage (Chen & Tian, 2022; Freeman et al., 2021). Secondly, OA is also vital for navigating continuous changes, requiring flexibility, adaptability, and innovative thinking (Darvishmotevali et al., 2020; Nurjaman et al., 2021).

OA involves sensing changes, innovating processes, engaging customers, and leveraging partner capabilities, contributing to resilience, especially with advanced technology adoption (Mrugalska & Ahmed, 2021). Besides, the progression of IT led to the emergence of the fourth industrial revolution, known as Industry 4.0, driven by the swift development of technologies like AI, IoT, and Big Data, has caused a turbulent environment characterised by VUCA (Araújo et al., 2021; Bach & Sulikova, 2021; Hongchai & Weber, 2024). Originating from the United States Army War College, the VUCA concept encapsulates the dynamic shifts in the external environment affecting organisations across industries (Raja, 2021). Business strategists attribute factors like heightened competition, technological advancements, and globalisation to the VUCA world. Organisations respond by restructuring internally, developing competency models, and implementing diverse decision-making approaches to foster innovation and adaptability (Akkaya et al., 2022).

Despite global business advancements, persistent disruptions necessitate agile thinking and technical proficiency to navigate the digital landscape effectively. At this point, leadership plays a pivotal role in fostering innovation, agility, and resilience to thrive in the face of VUCA challenges (Friedman, 2020). In conclusion, strategic management concepts like RBV, OA, and the VUCA framework provide valuable insights and approaches for organisations to enhance adaptability, innovation, and overall resilience in the face of uncertainty, offering a comprehensive framework for survival and thriving in the contemporary business landscape. In Fig. 1.2, a conceptual framework is developed based on all theoretical frameworks that have been emphasised throughout the chapter.

The model begins with uncertainty in business environments, such as environmental uncertainty, encompassing wars, epidemics, pandemics, climate change, etc., leading to permacrisis, which describes the catastrophic events around the globe that cause high levels of uncertainty worldwide. However, technological uncertainty can be considered a pivotal factor in the model because, in the advancement of technology, organisations need to stay competitive in the market while enhancing their values, but this rapid development of technology requires organisations to adapt themselves quickly and enhance their abilities to respond to the changes caused by technological uncertainties, which is one of the main environmental uncertainty. Therefore, in mitigating uncertain environments strategically, the RBV focuses on an organisation's tangible and intangible assets, including its operations capabilities, and integration to gain a competitive edge. Additionally, OA is essential in adapting to continuous changes through being flexible, adaptable, and innovative thinking. OA entails recognising changes, innovating processes, engaging customers, and fostering resilience, particularly through advanced technology adoption.

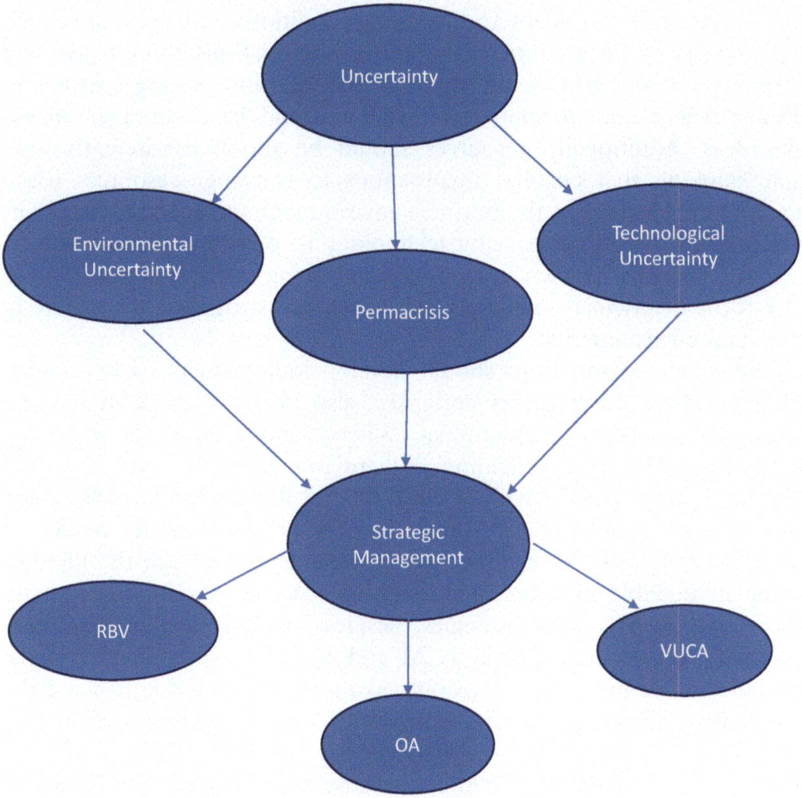

Fig. 1.2 The conceptual framework

1.5 Implications and Future Research

Based on thorough research on uncertain conditions in business environments, some implications have been identified. First of all, as technological uncertainty is one of the most critical ones among all factors, organisations should be open to continuous learning by gathering data, analysing and monitoring the inclinations to be able to adjust strategies accordingly and stay competitive in the market. Furthermore, as mentioned earlier, the decision-making process should be quick in case of uncertainties and organisations should be aware of possible risks and uncertainties to adapt to changing conditions and minimise negative impacts of uncertainties. Therefore, organisations should prioritise flexibility, rather than being strict in the decision-making process to allow efficient implementation of strategies and to encourage innovative ideas. Additionally, resources should be allocated wisely through agile thinking that enables organisations to rearrange resources based on dynamic changes in the business environment and market conditions which might involve enhancing technology to optimise resource utilisation and improve efficiency. Furthermore, being resilient should be the core focus of organisations especially if they are struggling to operate in uncertain environments.

Therefore, organisations should develop long-term plans by considering potential uncertainties and risks, also need to invest in training employees to obtain organisational resilience and mitigate the impact of disruptions. Ultimately, building resilient organisations leads us to the final implication point which is planning and investment in technology. Organisations should prepare themselves for various scenarios in case of potential consequences in uncertain environments through the identification of possible problems and assessing risks, to develop appropriate uncertainty management strategies. Besides, investing in the latest technological advancements, such as AI and IoT, is useful for operational efficiency while improving decision-making processes and enhancing the competitive advantage of an organisation. As for future research, it is suggested that technological aspects need detailed investigation to identify their impacts on organisations because technological advancements are continuous in the era we live in and it is essential to find out how technology affects organisational strategies and operations in uncertain environments.

Finally, in order to build organisational resilience in dynamic business environments, the role of dynamic capabilities should be investigated in uncertain environments for future development and efficient adaptation of organisations into changing market conditions, as well as to minimise risks and increase opportunities. Last but not least, the link between organisational agility and environmental uncertainty should be examined thoroughly to explore how organisations develop and employ agile strategies as its importance is emphasised in the current literature but there is nothing clear about 'how' organisations utilise this strategy.

References

Akkaya, B., Waritay Guah, M., Jermsittiparsert, K., Bulinska-Stangrecka, H., & Kaya Koçyiğit, Y. (2022). Agile management and VUCA 2.0 (VUCA-RR) during industry 4.0. In *Agile management and VUCA-RR*. Emerald Publishing Limited.

Aldianto, L., Anggadwita, G., Permatasari, A., Mirzanti, I. R., & Williamson, I. O. (2021). Toward a business resilience framework for startups. *Sustainability (Basel, Switzerland), 13*(6), 3132.

Araújo, M., Reis, L., & Morais, I. (2021). *Innovation strategies for adaptation of organizations in a VUCA world*. Academic Conferences International Limited, Reading, p. 1245.

Bach, C., & Sulikova, R. (2021). Leadership in the context of a new world: Digital leadership and industry 4.0. *Managing Global Transitions, 19*(3), 209–226.

Bartuseviciene, I., Rakauskiene, O. G., & Valackiene, A. (2023). Assessing the resilience of organizations in the context of uncertainty. *Measuring Business Excellence, 27*(2), 211–226.

Buhalis, D., Efthymiou, L., Uzunboylu, N., & Thrassou, A. (2024). Charting the progress of technology adoption in tourism and hospitality in the era of industry 4.0. *Tourism & Hospitality in the Digital Era: Technology and its (im)Possibilities. Special Issue in Euromed, Journal of Business*. https://doi.org/10.1108/EMJB-11-2023-0310

Chen, H., & Tian, Z. (2022). Environmental uncertainty, resource orchestration and digital transformation: A fuzzy-set QCA approach. *Journal of Business Research, 139*, 184–193.

Daglio, M., & Tahlak, A. (2023). *Global trends in government innovation 2023* (1st ed.). Organization for Economic Cooperation & Development.

Darvishmotevali, M., Altinay, L., & Köseoglu, M. A. (2020). The link between environmental uncertainty, organizational agility, and organizational creativity in the hotel industry. *International Journal of Hospitality Management, 87*, 102499.

de Lima, F. A., Seuring, S., & Sauer, P. C. (2022). A systematic literature review exploring uncertainty management and sustainability outcomes in circular supply chains. *International Journal of Production Research, 60*(19), 6013–6046.

Deviatnikova, K. G. (2023). *Permacrisis, metacrisis, polycrisis: Determining the nature of the phenomena using semantic analysis*. Современное педагогическое образование.

Freeman, R. E., Dmytriyev, S. D., & Phillips, R. A. (2021). Stakeholder theory and the resource-based view of the firm. *Journal of Management, 47*(7), 1757–1770.

Friedman, H. H. (2020). *Organizational agility, visionary leadership in the age of VUCA*. SSRN.

Giousmpasoglou, C. (2023). *People management in Permacrisis: Challenges and opportunities for the global hospitality industry*. Bournemouth University Business School.

Goher, K., Al-Ashaab, A., Sarfraz, S., & Shehab, E. (2023). An uncertainty management framework to support model-based definition and enterprise. *Computers in Industry, 150*, 103944.

Granig, P., & Hilgarter, K. (2020). Organisational resilience: A qualitative study about how organisations handle trends and their effects on business models from experts' views. *International Journal of Innovation Science, 12*(5), 525–544.

Haarhaus, T., & Liening, A. (2020). Building dynamic capabilities to cope with environmental uncertainty: The role of strategic foresight. *Technological Forecasting & Social Change, 155*, 120033.

Henri, J.-F., & Wouters, M. (2020). Interdependence of management control practices for product innovation: The influence of environmental unpredictability. *Accounting, Organizations and Society, 86*, 1–14.

Hitt, M. A., Arregle, J., & Holmes, R. M. (2021). Strategic management theory in a post-pandemic and non-ergodic world. *Journal of Management Studies, 58*(1), 257–262.

Hongchai, D. M., & Weber, C. M. (2024). Leadership for technology management in a Volatile, Uncertain, Complex, And Ambiguous (VUCA) world: A review of the literature and a research agenda. *PICMET (Portland International Center for Management of Engineering and Technology*, p. 1.

Hosseini, M. (2023). Building global health solidarity in a permacrisis: Legal impacts of a pandemic treaty. *Irish Studies in International Affairs*.

Joiner, B. (2019). Leadership agility for organizational agility. *Journal of Creating Value, 5*(2), 139–149.

Kiyabo, K., & Isaga, N. (2020). Entrepreneurial orientation, competitive advantage, and SMEs' performance: Application of firm growth and personal wealth measures. *Journal of Innovation and Entrepreneurship, 9*(1), 1–15.

Koç, E., Delibaş, M. B., & Anadol, Y. (2022). Environmental uncertainties and competitive advantage: A sequential mediation model of supply chain integration and supply chain agility. *Sustainability (Basel, Switzerland), 14*(14), 8928.

Kuusisto, E. (2022). *Approaching VUCA environment with enterprise agility in government organization*.

Mrugalska, B., & Ahmed, J. (2021). Organizational agility in industry 4.0: A systematic literature review. *Sustainability (Basel, Switzerland), 13*(15), 8272.

Nandi, S., Sarkis, J., Hervani, A., & Helms, M. (2021). Do blockchain and circular economy practices improve post COVID-19 supply chains? A resource-based and resource dependence perspective. *Industrial Management + Data Systems, 121*(2), 333–363.

Nurjaman, R., Rahayu, A., Wibowo, L. A., Widjajani, & Mujiarto. (2021). The relationship between strategic agility and resource base view of the firm performance in manufacturing industry: The research framework. *Journal of Physics. Conference Series, 1764*(1), 12148.

Overland, I., & Loginova, J. (2023). The Russian coal industry in an uncertain world: Finally pivoting to Asia? *Energy Research & Social Science, 102*, 103150.

Pratono, A. H. (2022). The strategic innovation under information technological turbulence: The role of organisational resilience in competitive advantage. *Competitiveness Review, 32*(3), 475–491.

Raja, A. S. (2021). Business research in the VUCA world. *USHUS Journal of Business Management, 20*(1), v–xvi.

Settembre-Blundo, D., González-Sánchez, R., Medina-Salgado, S., & García-Muiña, F. E. (2021). Flexibility and resilience in corporate decision making: A new sustainability-based risk management system in uncertain times. *Global Journal of Flexible Systems Management, 22*(Suppl 2), 107–132.

Shibin, K. T., Dubey, R., Gunasekaran, A., Hazen, B., Roubaud, D., Gupta, S., & Foropon, C. (2020). Examining sustainable supply chain management of SMEs using resource based view and institutional theory. *Annals of Operations Research, 290*(1–2), 301–326.

Thrassou, A., Efthymiou, L., Vrontis, D., Weber, Y., Shams, S. M. R., & Tsoukatos, E. (2022). Editorial introduction: Crisis in context. In D. Vrontis, A. Thrassou, Y. Weber, S. M. R. Shams, E. Tsoukatos, & L. Efthymiou (Eds.), *Business under crisis, Volume I: Contextual transformation. Palgrave Studies in Cross-disciplinary Business Research. In Association with EuroMed Academy of Business*. Palgrave Macmillan. https://doi.org/10.1007/978-3-030-76567-5_1.

Troise, C., Corvello, V., Ghobadian, A., & O'Regan, N. (2022). How can SMEs successfully navigate VUCA environment: The role of agility in the digital transformation era. *Technological Forecasting & Social Change, 174*, 121227.

Vainik, E., Constantinescu, M., & Chłopicki, W. (2023). Communication in times of permacrisis. Introduction to the special issue. *Tertium Linguistic Journal, 8*(1), 1–4.

Vrontis, D., Thrassou, A., Efthymiou, L., & Bozat, M. (2024). Delineating business for sustainability: Contextual evolution and elucidation. In D. Vrontis, A. Thrassou, L. Efthymiou, Y. Weber, S. M. R. Shams, & E. Tsoukatos (Eds.), *Business for sustainability, Volume II. Palgrave Studies in Cross-disciplinary Business Research. In Association with EuroMed Academy of Business*. Palgrave Macmillan. https://doi.org/10.1007/978-3-031-37365-7_1

Vrontis, D., Thrassou, A., Efthymiou, L., Weber, Y., Shams, R., & Tsoukatos, E. (2022). Editorial introduction: Business under crisis—Avenues for innovation, entrepreneurship and sustainability. In D. Vrontis, A. Thrassou, Y. Weber, S. M. R. Shams, E. Tsoukatos, & L. Efthymiou (Eds.), *Business under crisis, Volume III: Avenues for innovation, entrepreneurship and sustainability. Palgrave Studies in Cross-disciplinary Business Research. In Association with EuroMed Academy of Business*. Palgrave Macmillan. https://doi.org/10.1007/978-3-030-76583-5_1

Vrontis, D., Thrassou, A., Uzunboylu, N., & Efthymiou, L. (2023). An overview of business for sustainability: Strategic avenues and managerial approaches. In D. Vrontis, A. Thrassou, L. Efthymiou, Y. Weber, S. M. R. Shams, & E. Tsoukatos (Eds.), *Business for sustainability, Volume I. Palgrave Studies in Cross-disciplinary Business Research. In Association with EuroMed Academy of Business*. Palgrave Macmillan. https://doi.org/10.1007/978-3-031-37361-9_1

Walter, A. (2021). Organizational agility: Ill-defined and somewhat confusing? A systematic literature review and conceptualization. *Management Review Quarterly, 71*(2), 343–391.

Wolanin, M. (2022). Competencies of top management, and the needs of 21st century enterprises in a VUCA world. *VUZF Review, 7*(2), 170–182.

CHAPTER 2

How to Evaluate Sustainability Transition Pathway: Corporate Sustainability Maturity Assessment

Joana Ramanauskaitė, Eglė Staniškienė, and Živilė Stankevičiūtė

2.1 Introduction

Corporate sustainability can be defined as a balance among economic profit, preservation of the environment, and social concerns, regarding the needs of the future generations (Jouber, 2023; Sari et al., 2020). Moreover, corporate sustainability has a long-term approach and is

J. Ramanauskaitė (✉) · E. Staniškienė · Ž. Stankevičiūtė
School of Economics and Business, Kaunas University of Technology, Kaunas, Lithuania
e-mail: joana.ramanauskaite@ktu.lt

E. Staniškienė
e-mail: egle.staniskiene@ktu.lt

Ž. Stankevičiūtė
e-mail: zivile.stankeviciute@ktu.lt

D. Vrontis et al. (eds.), *Business in Uncertainty*, Palgrave Studies in Cross-disciplinary Business Research, In Association with EuroMed Academy of Business, https://doi.org/10.1007/978-3-031-65587-6_2

oriented towards meeting stakeholders' needs (Dyllick & Hockerts, 2002), to which Edgeman and Williams (2014) add that the triple bottom line should be met for the organisation, stakeholders and the overall society both long and short-term (Sari et al., 2020). Thus, the incorporation of sustainable development of the organisation, synthesising social value, institutional factors, technological artefacts and regarding contextual conditions can be called corporate sustainability (Baumgartner & Ebner, 2010; Buhalis et al., 2024; del Vecchio et al., 2022; Hansmann et al., 2012; Herrick & Pratt, 2013; Vrontis et al., 2024). Corporate sustainability is defined as a complex synthesis of sustainable development idea being incorporated into the organisation, containing all three pillars of sustainable development: economic, environmental and social, which maintain change in a balanced environment. This definition has been inspired by Baumgartner and Ebner (2010), Hugé et al. (2018), Humanities Education Centre (2009), and Siano et al. (2016). Furthermore, corporate sustainability and sustainable development encompass a time frame, which can be both long and short-termed, aiming at the long-term impact; thus, the journey, which is often referred to as the transition towards sustainability, becomes important (Vrontis et al., 2023).

Sustainability transitions are long-term, complex, fundamental transformations of organisational systems (Markard et al., 2012). They are part of the social construct and can be addressed at different levels of maturation (Ramanauskaitė & Staniškienė, 2020). Describing and measuring maturity is rationalised to be more subjective than objective (Andersen & Jessen, 2003), providing more freedom or analysing; thus, more ways to go astray. Therefore, it is important to set rules for measuring and analysing maturity of sustainable transitions in organisations, because a precise maturity level provides a foundation for achieving success in maturation and process improvement (Paulk et al., 1993). These maturity levels or phases comprise measurement-driven maturity models and most of them are standards or sets of criteria for organisations to evaluate their own management excellence (AlShathry, 2016), addressing hierarchy and systemic patterns in the pathway of developing organisational capabilities (Sari et al., 2020).

Corporate sustainability transitions as well fit in this definition but have a more specific context, i.e., organisations; therefore, in this research, they are viewed as long-term changes that are multidimensional and fundamental transformations of organisational systems towards more sustainable modes of production and consumption. The changes towards sustainability, even though discussed in the scientific literature, have significant grey areas, which create a field for discussion and exploration.

2.2 Literature Review

In this paper, "sustainability transitions" are facilitated into sustainability maturity levels of the organisations as transitions are long-term, complex processes, making it intangible to explore. Maturity in the organisation defines to what extent the processes of organisation provide satisfactory outcomes for the stakeholders as well as its capabilities advancement towards an effective strategy and process management (Terouhid & Ries, 2016). Nonetheless, there is no final stage of maturity in organisations, which makes it practical to describe maturity by a particular degree that measures and characterises maturity of the organisation (Andersen & Jessen, 2003). This could be applied to corporate sustainability as well, where no organisation can be maximum sustainable, having no space for improvement, thus making it pragmatic to view corporate sustainability through its maturity levels. However, the sustainability maturation in an organisation can be perceived through a lens of social issue maturation and described as an organisation being aware and taking ownership over sustainability issues, where the evolvement or maturation could be observed through phases, tasks and results (Hugé et al., 2018; McGrail et al., 2013). The measurement of maturity of the organisations has been discussed in scientific literature, and it is as well being analysed in the context of corporate sustainability maturation in the contemporary works of the field. The following paragraphs investigate corporate sustainability maturation and its phases in more detail.

Since sustainability transitions are long-term changes, a more defined time frame is more beneficial and logical for the scope of the paper. Therefore, corporate sustainability transitions will be addressed through the lens of their maturity. In the process of maturation, the organisations develop skills and become more advanced in managing their activities and processes (Terouhid & Ries, 2016). The incorporation of sustainability issues into the organisation, at the best scenario, should affect all areas of corporate activities, and developing as an organisation would mean developing sustainably. Corporate sustainability maturity is going to be viewed as suggested by Hugé et al. (2018) through the key stages motivated by the social issue maturation process: Phase 1: Emergence, Phase 2: Popularisation, Phase 3: Formalisation into a governance framework and Phase 4: Maturity reflected in normative changes (i.e., taking sustainability as a norm). Most relevant maturity definitions (Ramanauskaitė, 2023):

- "Maturity in organizations ... investigates whether an organization has advanced in becoming capable of managing organizational processes and effectively proceeding towards its strategies" (Terouhid & Ries, 2016, p. 913).
- "Our view is that maturity within the business community is best explained as the sum of action (ability to act and decide), attitude (willingness to be involved), and knowledge (an understanding of the impact of willingness and action)" (Andersen & Jessen, 2003, p. 458).
- "Social issue maturation refers to growing awareness of a particular issue, and to a growing ownership of that issue by an organization, institution and/or community (McGrail et al., 2013)" (Hugé et al., 2018, p. 4279).
- "For a presentation of sustainability in organisation, a four-level maturity grid is used: level 1 stands for a rudimentary level; maturity level 2 marks that an elementary integration of this aspect is focused on compliance with sustainability-related laws; level 3 represents a satisfying consideration and maturity; sophisticated maturity is defined by level 4" (Baumgartner & Ebner, 2010, p. 81).

Most commonly, the process maturation refers to the capability maturity model (CMM) proposed by (Paulk et al., 1993) that describes the maturation of software developing organisations. Their model provides steps and characteristics of five maturity levels that are supposed to lead to continuous process improvement when developing software. Even though referring to the quality management, the continuous process improvement is based more often on gradual, evolutionary steps, sustainable transitions than requiring revolutionary innovation and radical decisions (Geels, 2002; Rotmans & Loorbach, 2009). CMM identifies that a certain culture must be established by going step by step and building a foundation for the next level in an organisation in order to reach excellence and mature (Paulk et al., 1993); however, maturation of sustainability might transpire in discontinuous, cyclical paths, skipping levels while reacting to the changing environment; the linearity of transition is not guaranteed (Hugé et al., 2018). Nevertheless, the phases of sustainable transitions can be described and characterised according to their state of maturity in the internal and overall contexts. Several studies have already used a concept of sustainability related to the issue maturity (Bastas & Liyanage, 2019; Baumgartner & Ebner, 2010; Hugé et al., 2018; Machado et al., 2017; Marques-Mendes & Santos, 2016; Robinson et al., 2006; Sari et al., 2020; Willard, 2005), with the majority of scientific literature referring to the study of Baumgartner and Ebner (2010).

Maturity measurement provides insight to what extent certain processes are characterised, controlled, maintained and improved (Paulk et al., 1993), evaluating whether the requirements of each maturity level have been achieved (Benmoussa et al., 2015). In order to provide a more detailed approach, each maturity level should have achievable performance indicators identified (Sari et al., 2020). Previous studies have used 3 to 6 levels to describe maturation, starting from the level zero, where the issue is ignored or not addressed, to level six, where the issue is the most matured. Even though not all analysed studies were describing sustainability, some insights could be applied to the field. Table 2.1 describes the main aspects of different possible maturity levels.

However, the evaluation of corporate sustainability maturity is rather qualitative than quantitative, making it more subjective and easily biased regarding the content of information that is available on the corporate activities and initiatives. More detailed maturity assessment frameworks are used intrinsically by the organisations to evaluate themselves, while frameworks or models for external evaluation are less detailed, providing rather obscure guidelines for assessing secondary data and interviews/ panel studies. The more levels there are in the maturity framework, the more detailed their descriptions and evaluation guidelines and indicators there must be to visualise the maturity of the organisational issue that is concerned. External corporate sustainability maturity assessment could be encumbered by limited secondary information availability and biased informants, who might want to favour their organisation or have limited view due to their qualifications. In order to minimise the possibility of misinterpreting information and avoid the lack of data that is available, distorting the results, it is optimal to choose less maturity levels that describe corporate sustainability. McGrail et al. (2013) uses several environmental issues, such as climate change or ozone protection, to

Table 2.1 Description of different maturity levels

Level	*Keywords*	*Sources*
0	Pre-compliance. The company feels no obligation beyond profits Observation. Discovery. Trigger event(s) or phenomena Negation No evidence of implementation Laggard	Bastas and Liyanage (2019), Marques-Mendes and Santos (2016), McGrail et al. (2013), Pizzutilo and Venezia (2021), and Willard (2005)
1	Initial. The software process is characterized as ad hoc Compliance. Obey the law and all regulations Start-up stage. Increasing awareness of benefits for business improvement Rudimentary level, possibly beginning consideration of sustainability aspect Emergence. Initial theorisation, discourse development Observance Compliance and conformity Willing to change Informal or ad hoc Communication and networking among different categories of actors is key Aware	Bastas and Liyanage (2019), Baumgartner and Ebner (2010), Hugé et al. (2018), International Standard Organization (2018), Machado et al. (2017), Marques-Mendes and Santos (2016), McGrail et al. (2013), Parker et al. (2017), Paulk et al. (1993), Pizzutilo and Venezia (2021), Robinson et al. (2006), Sari et al. (2020), and Willard (2005)

(continued)

Table 2.1 (continued)

Level	*Keywords*	*Sources*
2	Repeatable. Basic project management processes are established to track cost, schedule and functionality Take-off stage. Developing KM strategy and working definition Focus on compliance with sustainability-related laws but going slightly further Popularisation. Growing awareness. Formation of issue-specific organisations Efficiency Operations' eco-efficiency. Operations efficiency and productivity Want to change Somewhat documented, partly ad hoc Broadening of support base and the planning of future management steps Partially implemented. Sustainability priorities are established	Bastas and Liyanage (2019), Baumgartner and Ebner (2010), Hugé et al. (2018), International Standard Organization (2018), Machado et al. (2017), Marques-Mendes and Santos (2016), McGrail et al. (2013), Parker et al. (2017), Paulk et al. (1993), and Robinson et al. (2006)
3	Defined. Documented, standardized and integrated processes Beyond compliance. The company moves from defence to offence Expansion stage. Increasing the visibility of KM leadership and initiatives Challenge. Intensified societal engagement. Growing research interest Strategic innovation Sustainability management system Ready for change Known and key aspects managed Formal process in place, sustainability priorities are established The managed stage: organisations in which process management is weak Implementer	Bastas and Liyanage (2019), International Standard Organization (2018), Machado et al. (2017), Marques-Mendes and Santos (2016), McGrail et al. (2013), Parker et al. (2017), Paulk et al. (1993), Pizzutilo and Venezia (2021), Robinson et al. (2006), Sari et al. (2020), and Willard (2005)

(continued)

Table 2.1 (continued)

Level	*Keywords*	*Sources*
4	Managed Integrated strategy. A company committed to sustainability and integrates sustainability with key business strategies Progressive stage. Improving the performance of KM activities Satisfying consideration and maturity of a specific sustainability aspect Governance. Policy responses. 'Big business' visionaries show leadership Strategic integration Network and stakeholders' integration Systemic change, management, standardisation Formalization Evidence of continuous improvement Exploiter	Bastas and Liyanage (2019), Baumgartner and Ebner (2010), Hugé et al. (2018), International Standard Organization (2018), Machado et al. (2017), Marques-Mendes and Santos (2016), McGrail et al. (2013), Parker et al. (2017), Paulk et al. (1993), Robinson et al. (2006), and Willard (2005)
5	Optimizing Purpose and passion Sustainability stage Outstanding effort towards sustainability Normative. Socialisation. In-depth, mainstream public understanding and ownership/management of the issue Transformational Sustainable operations' integration. New business model is defined Corporate culture Monitored, reviewed, evaluated, implemented, maintained, planned, all is considered A network of interlinked, innovative sustainability entrepreneurs Fully implemented inclusive of all GRI sustainability indicators The optimised stage: mature organisations in which process management is applied to measure organisational performance and evaluate the process improvement efforts/programmes Pioneer	Bastas and Liyanage (2019), Baumgartner and Ebner (2010), Hugé et al. (2018), International Standard Organization (2018), Machado et al. (2017), Marques-Mendes and Santos (2016), McGrail et al. (2013), Parker et al. (2017), Paulk et al. (1993), Robinson et al. (2006), Sari et al. (2020), and Willard (2005)

visualise social issue maturation. Putting them together allows addressing sustainability transitions in general and how it matures in a smaller environment of an organisation rather than overall. Therefore, social issue maturation framework is selected to assess corporate sustainability maturity in this paper. The process of maturation is understood in line with growing awareness of the issue by the organisations and accordingly increasing the willingness for action and actual sustainability activities. The more mature is the organisation regarding sustainability, the more likely it is to have sustainability under its strategy, take ownership for its actions and impact on the environment. This study takes the approach of Baumgartner and Ebner (2010) and Hugé et al. (2018) and uses four corporate sustainability maturity levels described further on. Each level is characterised by using the characteristics described in the categorisation described previously.

Level 1: rudimentary or **emergence** level where sustainability is only starting to be discussed in the organisation; no rules are set, except for those that are defined by the law. All of the aspects given in the scientific literature maturity level analysis apply that were attributed to Level 1. However, in case there are organisations that do not take any kind of ownership of sustainability-related issues in their activities, their sustainability maturity will be ascribed to Level 1.

Level 2: **popularisation**. At this point of sustainability maturation, an organisation takes a step further towards sustainability, it becomes more popular and more widely debated in the organisation; however, sustainability is only fragmentarily visible in the processes and the documentation of the organisation, or not visible at all; it might be incorporated ad hoc, having random initiatives at all levels of the organisation. Most of level 2 and 3 characteristics of the literature analysis can be attributed to this level as well, since sustainability still relies on egocentric incentives.

Level 3: **formalisation** of sustainability activities reveals the consistency in the organisation's actions to achieve it. In this case, it is well documented; the indicators are attributed to measure the performance and implement improvement strategies. When benchmarking, an organisation can be considered above the industry average in the coverage of sustainability-related issues. Level 4 attributes of literature review can be assigned to this level of formalisation.

Level 4: **optimisation**. However, as complete sustainability cannot be reached, and there is always space for improvement, this level indicates an outstanding effort to achieve corporate sustainability. Level 5 of literature analysis can be used to define this level, where an organisation utilises sustainable business model, builds or takes part in sustainability-related associations, involving all groups of stakeholders. At this stage, sustainability is more a norm than a concept to be debated.

2.3 Research Design

In order to embrace the rigour of scientific research, this research takes inductive embedded multiple-case design that allows researchers to collect rich, descriptive and contextually situated data in order to understand, illustrate and complement the existing literature on corporate sustainability transitions best. Therefore, the case of this study is understood as the organisations of certain maturity level; the unit of analysis of this case study is the sustainability practices of organisations analysed internally (interviews) and externally (corporate websites and sustainability reports).

Methods

Data triangulation is used to define the corporate sustainability maturity levels. The primary and secondary data are used to assess corporate sustainability maturity externally. Given the complexity of external assessment, four levels of corporate sustainability maturity were selected. The assessment will measure at what stage is the analysed organisation, regarding its sustainability. The sources to assess corporate sustainability maturity are corporate websites, sustainability/corporate social responsibility or related public reports and interviews.

The analytical hierarchy process (AHP) (Saaty, 1987, 1990) can be used for prioritising and weighting the criteria for corporate sustainability maturity level assessment (cf. Forman & Gass, 2001). The chosen criteria of the interview, corporate website and sustainability reporting, by which corporate sustainability maturity level is going to be analysed, have different weights; therefore, their priorities are attributed using the literature analysis, and they are compared pairwise, using the AHP (Lin et al., 2008), resulting in normalised weights. The corporate sustainability will be assessed using the following formula (Ramanauskaitė, 2023):

$$x \times \mathrm{IV} + y \times \mathrm{CW} + z \times \mathrm{SR} = \mathrm{CSML} \tag{2.1}$$

where IV is the maturity level from the interview, ranging from 1 to 4; CW—the maturity level from the website, ranging from 1 to 4; SR—the maturity level from sustainability report, ranging from 1 to 4; CSML—the corporate sustainability maturity level, ranging from 1 to 4; the weights named x, y and z are going to be calculated using the AHP.

When comparing pairwise, the relative importance or preference between the two elements is considered (Lin et al., 2008), and the importance is attributed ranging from 1 to 9 (1 is equal importance, 9 is extreme importance). Considering that not all the organisations might report their sustainability initiatives via reports and as it is not mandatory for every organisation, this component is less important than criteria IV and CW. Nonetheless, it is important for the organisations to be as open as possible about their sustainability initiatives, results, and possibly, even failures. Therefore, sustainability reports are not omitted out of the overall assessment of corporate sustainability maturity. The other two components of corporate sustainability maturity levels assess content provided via interviews and in the corporate websites and will be attributed equal priorities (2.1). IV, compared to SR, has a strong importance, meaning that IV is more important in assessing CSML; therefore, it is attributed to priority 5. CW, compared to SR, has a very strong importance, since it is used to store the SR and other information, not only related to the corporate sustainability, which might be important as well in the overall corporate sustainability; therefore, it is attributed to priority 7. Followingly, the resulting weights for the criteria based on pairwise comparisons are provided:

- IV—43.5%
- CW—48.7%
- SR—7.8%

λ max = 3.013; CI = 0.007; CR = 1.3%.

The final result of corporate sustainability maturity level is calculated by using the following formula:

$$0.487 \times CW + 0.435 \times IV + 0.078 \times SR = CSML \tag{2.2}$$

The multi-methods used to assess corporate sustainability maturity are presented in Table 2.2.

Table 2.2 Multi-method corporate sustainability maturity assessment

Dimension	*Abbreviation*	*Description/resources*			
Corporate sustainability maturity level assessment through interviews	IV	The keyword analysis is applied to determine the corporate sustainability maturity level. The answers for each level should encompass these or similar characteristics (keywords), which reveal certain manner or habit			
		Level 1: Emergence • No evidence of implementation • Informal/ inadequate processes in place • Beginning consideration of sustainability aspect • Compliance with the regulations	Level 2: Popularisation • Partially implemented • Efficiency oriented • Sustainability management system might be under development • Elementary integration of sustainability • Randomness • Fragmentation	Level 3: Formalisation • Compliance with additional benefits • Strategic integration • Satisfying consideration of specific sustainability aspects • Network and stakeholders' integration • Evidence of continuous improvement • Documentation • Reporting • Measured performance	Level 4: Optimisation • Outstanding effort towards sustainability • Purpose and passion • Transformational • Sustainability associations • Commitment • Sustainability as a norm • Giving back to the society

Dimension	*Abbreviation*	*Description/resources*
Corporate sustainability maturity level assessment through websites	CW	The websites of organisations were analysed by using an OSEC model proposed by Siano et al. (2016). The score from the model can relate to a certain corporate sustainability maturity level (Ramanauskaitė & Staniškienė, 2020): • Level 1: Emergence, score <49 • Level 2: Popularisation, the score is between 50–69 • Level 3: Formalisation into a governance framework, the score is between 70–79, Level 4: Optimisation, reflected in normative changes, the score is >80
Corporate sustainability maturity level assessment through sustainability reports	SR	Consistency of sustainability reporting The levels from 1 to 4 will be attributed to the corporate sustainability maturity via corporate sustainability report using the logic when an organisation has been reporting: • Consistently for at least 5 years—level 4 • Consistently for up to 5 years—level 3 • Inconsistently—level 2 • None—level 1

As provided in Table 2.2, semi-structured interviews were carried out in organisations that reveal their sustainability intentions. The respondents were asked how their organisations understand their part/role in the context that they are acting in and how responsible do they feel about their impact on the overall context/environment. This question was designed to address corporate sustainability as suggested by the social issue maturation framework (McGrail et al., 2013) and awareness of sustainability as a social issue (Hugé et al., 2018). The respondents were asked to view it through the lens of their organisation and not as individuals. Furthermore, organisations engage with multiple communication channels for communicating their sustainability actions to the stakeholders (Gomez & Chalmeta, 2011) and as the internet has become one of the main contemporary communication channels and has a prominent role in sustainability and CSR communication (Basil & Erlandson, 2008; Gomez & Chalmeta, 2011; Ramanauskaitė & Staniškienė, 2020; Siano et al., 2016), the corporate websites were also included into the assessment tool, using the OSEC model proposed by Siano et al. (2016). Since most information about corporate sustainability practices are provided via interviews and the reports are mostly present in the websites of organisations, only consistency of reporting was selected in this assessment tool. The threshold of five years was selected because sustainability movements and development of network for responsible organisations began around 2005 (Lietuvos Respublikos Vyriausybė, 2003); thus, it is reasonable to expect mature organisations to be committed and report for at least 5 years.

Sample

The organisations that take interest in sustainability were selected for the review from the region of emerging economy. These organisations were selected with an interest to follow up with the interviews with them regarding their transition towards sustainability. A broad approach to one organisation might show whether they are truly interested in sustainability; therefore, the websites of organisations will be revised as well.

Nonprobability purposive sampling is selected to explore the issue of corporate sustainability maturity in this research (Daniel, 2014), where eighteen organisations from transitioning economy of Lithuania were selected for the analysis. Convenient sampling was chosen for selecting organisations that are taking interest and participating in any kind of sustainability-related initiatives.

2.4 Results

The overall corporate sustainability maturity assessment of all analysed organisations is represented in Table 2.3.

None of the analysed organisations can be attributed to the optimisation level of corporate sustainability maturity, addressing all three dimensions of the assessment tool. However, three organisations scored above 3 points in the sum. Three organisations are at the emergence level. The majority of analysed organisations can be assigned to the popularisation level.

Table 2.3 CSML of analysed organisations

	Size	*Sector*	*IV*	*CW*	*SR*	*CSML*	*Level*
OrgN	Large	Bank	4	3	2	3.36	3 (Formalisation)
OrgM	Small	Support Services	4	2	4	3.03	3 (Formalisation)
OrgR	Large	Bank	4	2	4	3.03	3 (Formalisation)
OrgP	Large	Support Services	4	2	3	2.95	3 (Formalisation)
OrgC	Very small	Support Services	4	1	4	2.54	3 (Formalisation)
OrgF	Large	Academic	4	1	2	2.38	2 (Popularisation)
OrgJ	Medium	Support Services	3	2	1	2.36	2 (Popularisation)
OrgK	Small	Support Services	4	1	1	2.31	2 (Popularisation)
OrgB	Small	Support Services	3	1	4	2.10	2 (Popularisation)
OrgE	Large	Gas, Water and Multiutilities	3	1	4	2.10	2 (Popularisation)
OrgD	Large	Academic	2	2	3	2.08	2 (Popularisation)
OrgA	Medium	General Industrials	3	1	3	2.07	2 (Popularisation)
OrgL	Medium	Public Institution	2	2	1	1.92	2 (Popularisation)
OrgO	Medium	Personal Goods	2	2	1	1.92	2 (Popularisation)
OrgI	Very small	Support Services	3	1	1	1.87	2 (Popularisation)
OrgG	Large	General Industrials	2	1	1	1.44	1 (Emergence)
OrgH	Medium	General Industrials	1	1	1	1.00	1 (Emergence)
OrgS	Large	Industrial Transportation	1	1	1	1.00	1 (Emergence)

Adapted from Ramanauskaitė (2023)

2.5 Discussion

The organisations at the *emergence level* attribute only some attention to the sustainability issues. Even though they address that sustainability is an important issue via their interviews, no information can be found on their websites, and they do not provide sustainability reports. Moreover, the sustainability understanding provided by these organisations is shallow, encompassing only one sustainability dimension, not seeing the bigger picture (McGrail et al., 2013), i.e., how their activities interconnect and affect all aspects of sustainability. A couple of examples that illustrate how these organisations see themselves from the perspective of sustainability can be drawn from the interviews. OrgG, even having sustainability in their mission, considering more social initiatives and involving their employees, still does not consider that they "are having any kind of impact on the environment". OrgH focuses mostly on the well-being of employees, the digitalisation and automation of the processes. OrgS is all about profit and complying with the laws and regulations (Willard, 2005). Therefore, the organisations at the emergence level can be described as considering sustainability issues and seeing it as an important aspect of their business, but they have not moved further from complying with the laws and attributing higher importance to the documentation.

Ten out of analysed organisations are ranked at the *popularisation level*. Corporate sustainability at this level is fragmented with only some visible initiatives (International Standard Organization, 2018). Most of the organisations are efficiency-oriented, trying to improve their processes and minimise the losses (Machado et al., 2017). However, they conduct certain, even if random, sustainability initiatives. Interestingly, OrgF is in a transition towards sustainability. Their activities and initiatives started earlier; at the moment, the strategy and processes are revised in accordance with sustainability, consulting with the specialists in the field, putting their values and mission into strategy. Simultaneously, OrgE is a state-owned energy company that currently is participating and pushing forward the energy decentralisation in Lithuania, endorsing users to become energy producers, developing renewable energy parks, etc. Nevertheless, as required by several stakeholders, OrgE has integrated sustainability in their strategy and documentation, though revealing that some aspects, e.g., procurement documentation, are not thorough with sustainability requirements, having them described fragmentarily.

However, sustainability has become a much broader term, expanding throughout the organisation on strategic level at OrgE.

At the same level, there are organisations that, regardless of having long-term practices and involved leaders, have some shortcomings (Marques-Mendes & Santos, 2016; McGrail et al., 2013), such as using plastic packaging for their products. An example could be OrgO that is vested in creating sustainable, greener products, but sustainable solutions are "nice to have, but not for" them, because their business strategy is centred on "reasonable prices". Moreover, OrgO has a very detailed understanding of what they are doing and how; at the moment, they can achieve their level of sustainability and what is unreachable for them. Therefore, it is understandable why they choose not to produce more expensive but more sustainable products and why their communication on the website and via sustainability reports is limited. The stories of organisations at the popularisation level are different. This well illustrates their different choices, pathways and decisions towards sustainability, explaining why this level is called popularisation, having organisations that are implementing different corporate sustainability communication practices via their websites and sustainability reports and expressing various initiatives via interviews, where data seems to be scattered throughout the whole range. However, all of them, except for one, have sustainability more or less integrated into their business strategies.

There are interesting cases at the *formalisation level* as well. This level is not easily described, trying to find unified definitions for all five organisations that are included. Most likely, the corporate purpose and passion, commitment, giving back to the society and having sustainability as a norm could be considered as the conjunctive factors (Baumgartner & Ebner, 2010; Robinson et al., 2006; Willard, 2005). Three organisations at this level show commitment in their reporting initiatives; one has recently started communicating its progress through the sustainability reports; sadly, one has stopped its reports that used to be regular. Four out of the five organisations at the formalisation level are at the top of the sample when communicating about sustainability via their websites. However, one organisation of the formalisation level does not have such a practice to communicate its sustainability throughout the website. All organisations at this level have revealed their transcendental stance towards sustainability.

OrgM is a non-governmental non-profit organisation that acts in the environmental protection area. Their mission is sustainability-related;

thus, it obliges them to address the issues. The majority of OrgM initiatives start when their stakeholders, such as "politicians or enterprises are not doing something they should". Other initiatives of OrgM include educational activities on the environmental issues, shorter work week for their employees, multiple events for employees and other stakeholders that are organised using sustainable ideas (i.e., vegan menu), technical solutions in the office that are as environmentally friendly as possible (i.e., adobe flooring). This organisation, setting a sustainable example, encourages its customers and partners to take this approach, educates them on the matter and provides assistance. However, this organisation does not have sustainability detailed in their strategy or documented in the procedures.

Another example is OrgC that is a public relations organisation with affiliation to a larger company abroad. Even though sustainability was lowered down to them when joining a larger network, these ideas were not new to the company and were easily assimilated to the working model of the organisation. OrgC positions itself as an innovator in promoting sustainability and social responsibility, providing its clients with new social projects that were not yet trending at the time. This company acts as a promoter of sustainability ideas for their clients, not tolerating greenwashing or other misinformation that the companies might want to provide to look more appealing: "we do not tell the public what does not exist; we do not say things we do not believe in. We do not work with clients we do not believe. Or, if crisis situations happen in business, we promote maximum openness, maximum transparency and customer responsibility both to our employees and society; this is the philosophy we spread widely in the field in which we work". Nonetheless, this organisation as well provides extra care for its employees, surpassing what is required of them by the law.

OrgN is the highest-ranking organisation from the selected sample regarding their corporate sustainability maturity. Even though it does not have a perfect sustainability reporting practice and reveal its sustainability via interviews at the same level as their colleagues at the formalisation level, this organisation scores satisfactory via their websites, being the only organisation attributed level 3 through the website analysis, leading it to the top of the corporate maturity levels. Contradictory, there are two banks at the formalisation level, but the one with higher score shows a demeaning stance towards OrgR (nicknaming), where OrgR revealed their sustainability only through their own initiatives. Nonetheless, OrgN reveals a strong commitment to the sustainability issues, "attributing 95% of their impact to their products and services". They as well pay close attention to the growth of the small businesses, greener energy projects, etc.

As indicated by the results, the top two banks in Lithuania scored among the top five organisations from the sample, regarding their sustainability maturity. Moreover, three of the five top sample organisations expressed that they feel that the stakeholders or shareholders from Scandinavia still have an impact on their sustainability practices. There is one large organisation (OrgP) with a high level of sustainability maturity that is interested in implementing technical innovations in its field and business practice. However, not only large organisations can achieve this level. OrgM is a small non-governmental consultancy firm, and OrgC is a very small public relations organisation, where they both are very keen on promoting sustainability ideas, having a high set of sustainability-oriented values among their employees. Nonetheless, the organisations agree, that there are financial benefits in partaking in social, ethical (Chouaibi et al., 2022) and environmental initiatives. All of the formalisation-level organisations show interest in educating broader society regarding sustainability and acting accordingly which is in line with the other research, emphasising the importance of stakeholder engagement (Meza-Ruiz et al., 2017). Research of Nikolaou et al. (2019) proposes that both social and environmental dimensions are crucial for achieving higher sustainability performance. However, this article visualises that the higher maturity of the sample organisations, the more importance is attributed to social aspects.

2.6 Concluding Discussion and Recommendations

The proposed corporate sustainability maturity assessment is a contribution to maturity assessment and the tool proved to be useful evaluating organisations in the context of Lithuania, enabling the evaluator to distinguish differences and similarities. The four selected maturity levels include: emergence where organisation is at the starting point of considering sustainability in its activities and the overall impact to the environment in the broad sense; popularisation where organisation shows increased interest among the stakeholders and some standardisation and setting of rules begin to form but still fragmentarily; formalisation where sustainability is formalised into the strategy and everyday routines and activities of the organisation, building on the values; optimisation where sustainability becomes as a norm, a transcendental perception is incorporated into routines, strategies and activities, building sustainability as a norm among the stakeholders and society. Moreover, this approach allows addressing corporate sustainability maturity externally, as more complex maturity models with larger number of levels requiring internal approach and analysis.

The selected organisations for the sample of the empirical research did not reach the highest maturity level, i.e., optimisation. The top five organisations of the sample revealed the qualities that are attributable to the formalisation level of corporate sustainability maturity. These organisations show passion, purpose and commitment towards sustainability: a wish to give back to the society and educate it regarding sustainability. However, some formal practical implications might be hindering the process of achieving the optimisation level, e.g., the lack of strategic implementation, documentation, measurement of performance. There was no significant distinction between the size or sector of the organisations and their achieved maturity level. However, the two banks that were present in the sample scored among the top three organisations, regarding their corporate sustainability maturity. This indicates that some sectors might be more prone to implement sustainability and communicate it, as they feel their impact on the overall environment. Moreover, a huge impact from the Scandinavian stakeholders is visible as three of five top organisations are in relation to the Nordic countries, expressing the sense of their influence.

As corporate sustainability transitions are individual and unique experience for any organisation, the recommendations stemming from this research would be to thoroughly analyse their context, join networks, communicate with stakeholders to get the sense of direction to prioritise activities. Enabled leaders are also crucial in maturing towards sustainability and incorporating it into the strategy and business logics. However, this study could be strengthened by testing the corporate sustainability maturity assessment tool in different contexts.

References

AlShathry, O. (2016). Business process management: A maturity assessment of Saudi Arabian organizations. *Business Process Management Journal, 22*(3), 507–521. https://doi.org/10.1108/BPMJ-07-2015-0101

Andersen, E. S., & Jessen, S. A. (2003). Project maturity in organisations. *International Journal of Project Management, 21*(6), 457–461. https://doi.org/10.1016/S0263-7863(02)00088-1

Basil, D. Z., & Erlandson, J. (2008). Corporate social responsibility website representations: A longitudinal study of internal and external self-presentations. *Journal of Marketing Communications, 14*(2), 125–137.

Bastas, A., & Liyanage, K. (2019). Setting a framework for organisational sustainable development. *Sustainable Production and Consumption, 20*, 207–229. https://doi.org/10.1016/j.spc.2019.06.005

Baumgartner, R. J., & Ebner, D. (2010). Corporate sustainability strategies: Sustainability profiles and maturity levels. *Sustainable Development, 18*(2), 76–89. https://doi.org/10.1002/sd.447

Benmoussa, R., Abdelkabir, C., Abd, A., & Hassou, M. (2015). Capability/maturity based model for logistics processes assessment. *International Journal of Productivity and Performance Management, 64*(1), 28–51. https://doi.org/10.1108/IJPPM-08-2012-0084

Buhalis, D., Efthymiou, L., Uzunboylu, N., & Thrassou, A. (2024). Charting the progress of technology adoption in tourism and hospitality in the era of industry 4.0. *Tourism & Hospitality in the Digital Era: Technology and its (im)Possibilities. Special Issue in Euromed Journal of Business*. https://doi.org/10.1108/EMJB-11-2023-0310

Chouaibi, S., Chouaibi, J., & Rossi, M. (2022). ESG and corporate financial performance: The mediating role of green innovation: UK common law versus Germany civil law. *EuroMed Journal of Business, 17*(1), 46–71. https://doi.org/10.1108/EMJB-09-2020-0101

Daniel, J. (2014). Choosing between nonprobability sampling and probability sampling. In *Sampling essentials: Practical guidelines for making sampling choices* (pp. 66–80). Sage Publications. https://doi.org/10.4135/9781452272047.n3

del Vecchio, P., Malandugno, C., Passiante, G., & Sakka, G. (2022). Circular economy business model for smart tourism: The case of Ecobnb. *EuroMed Journal of Business, 17*(1), 88–104. https://doi.org/10.1108/EMJB-09-2020-0098

Dyllick, T., & Hockerts, K. (2002). Beyond the business case for corporate sustainability. *Business Strategy and the Environment, 11*(2), 130–141. https://doi.org/10.1002/bse.323

Edgeman, R., & Williams, J. A. (2014). Enterprise self-assessment analytics for sustainability, resilience and robustness. *The TQM Journal, 26*(4), 368–381. https://doi.org/10.1108/TQM-01-2014-0012

Forman, E. H., & Gass, S. I. (2001). The analytic hierarchy process—An exposition. *Operations Research, 49*(4), 469–486. https://doi.org/10.1287/opre.49.4.469.11231

Geels, F. W. (2002). Technological transitions as evolutionary reconfiguration processes: A multi-level perspective and a case-study. *Research Policy, 31*(8–9), 1257–1274. https://doi.org/10.1016/S0048-7333(02)00062-8

Gomez, L. M., & Chalmeta, R. (2011). Corporate responsibility in U.S. corporate websites: A pilot study. *Public Relations Review, 37*(1), 93–95. https://doi.org/10.1016/j.pubrev.2010.12.005

Hansmann, R., Mieg, H. A., & Frischknecht, P. (2012). Principal sustainability components: Empirical analysis of synergies between the three pillars of sustainability. *International Journal of Sustainable Development & World Ecology, 19*(5), 451–459. https://doi.org/10.1080/13504509.2012.696220

Herrick, C. N., & Pratt, J. L. (2013). Communication and the narrative basis of sustainability: Observations from the municipal water sector. *Sustainability (Switzerland), 5*(10), 4428–4443. https://doi.org/10.3390/su5104428

Hugé, J., Mac-Lean, C., & Vargas, L. (2018). Maturation of sustainability in engineering faculties—From emerging issue to strategy? *Journal of Cleaner Production, 172*, 4277–4285. https://doi.org/10.1016/j.jclepro.2017.07.143

Humanities Education Centre. (2009). *No Title*. https://www.globalfootprints.org/sustainability/

International Standard Organization. (2018). *ISO 9004:2018—Managing for the sustained success of an organization—A quality management approach* (Vol. 04). ISO Copyright Office.

Jouber, H. (2023). Environmental sustainability performance and shareholder value: An international fuzzy-set qualitative comparative analysis. *EuroMed Journal of Business*. https://doi.org/10.1108/EMJB-09-2022-0161

Lietuvos Respublikos Vyriausybė. (2003). Nutarimas Nr. 1160 „Dėl nacionalinės darnaus vystymosi strategijos patvirtinimo ir įgyvendinimo". In *Valstybės žinios* (Issues 89-4029, p. 2009). https://e-seimas.lrs.lt/portal/legalAct/lt/TAD/TAIS.217644/WPqyZkDuCy

Lin, K., Lin, C., & Kuo, W. (2008). The adoption and management of interactive digital TV commerce in Taiwan. *International Journal of Management, 25*(2), 287–299. https://espace.curtin.edu.au/bitstream/handle/20.500.11937/35433/118060_Adoption%2520and%2520management%2520Digital%2520TV.pdf?sequence=2&isAllowed=y

Machado, C. G., Pinheiro de Lima, E., Gouvea da Costa, S. E., Angelis, J. J., & Mattioda, R. A. (2017). Framing maturity based on sustainable operations management principles. *International Journal of Production Economics, 190*(December 2016), 3–21. https://doi.org/10.1016/j.ijpe.2017.01.020

Markard, J., Raven, R., & Truffer, B. (2012). Sustainability transitions: An emerging field of research and its prospects. *Research Policy, 41*(6), 955–967. https://doi.org/10.1016/j.respol.2012.02.013

Marques-Mendes, A., & Santos, M. J. (2016). Strategic CSR: An integrative model for analysis. *Social Responsibility Journal, 12*(2), 363–381. https://doi.org/10.1108/SRJ-04-2015-0055

McGrail, S., Halamish, E., Teh-White, K., & Clark, M. (2013). Diagnosing and anticipating social issue maturation: Introducing a new diagnostic framework. *Futures, 46*, 50–61. https://doi.org/10.1016/j.futures.2012.10.001

Meza-Ruiz, I. D., Rocha-Lona, L., del Rocío Soto-Flores, M., Garza-Reyes, J. A., Kumar, V., & Lopez-Torres, G. C. (2017, June). Measuring business sustainability maturity-levels and best practices. *Procedia Manufacturing, 11*, 751–759. https://doi.org/10.1016/j.promfg.2017.07.176

Nikolaou, I. E., Tsalis, T. A., & Evangelinos, K. I. (2019). A framework to measure corporate sustainability performance: A strong sustainability-based view of firm. *Sustainable Production and Consumption, 18*, 1–18. https://doi.org/10.1016/j.spc.2018.10.004

Parker, D. W., Loh, A., Chevers, D., Minto-Coy, I., & Zeppetella, L. (2017). Operations sustainability maturity model: Preliminary findings of financial services in developing and developed countries. *Measuring Business Excellence, 21*(4), 309–336. https://doi.org/10.1108/MBE-08-2016-0044

Paulk, M., Curtis, B., Chrissis, M., & Weber, C. (1993). *Capability maturity model for software, Version 1.1.* Software Engineering Institute, Carnegie Mellon University.

Pizzutilo, F., & Venezia, E. (2021). On the maturity of social responsibility and sustainability integration in higher education institutions: Descriptive criteria and conceptual framework. *The International Journal of Management Education, 19*(3), 100515. https://doi.org/10.1016/j.ijme.2021.100515

Ramanauskaitė, J. (2023). *Antecedents of tensions of corporate sustainability maturity* [Kauno technologijos universitetas]. https://epubl.ktu.edu/object/elaba:157059828/

Ramanauskaitė, J., & Staniškienė, E. (2020, October 1). Revealing corporate sustainability maturity levels through corporate websites. *CISABE'2020: 8th International Scientific Conference Changes in Social and Business Environment, Panevėžys, Lithuania*, 51–59. http://www.edlearning.it/ebook/DX01_CISABE.pdf

Robinson, H. S., Anumba, C. J., Carrillo, P. M., & Al-Ghassani, A. M. (2006). STEPS: A knowledge management maturity roadmap for corporate sustainability. *Business Process Management Journal, 12*(6), 793–808. https://doi.org/10.1108/14637150610710936

Rotmans, J., & Loorbach, D. (2009). Complexity and transition management. *Journal of Industrial Ecology, 13*(2), 184–196. https://doi.org/10.1111/j.1530-9290.2009.00116.x

Saaty, R. W. (1987). The analytic hierarchy process—What it is and how it is used. *Mathematical Modelling, 9*(3–5), 161–176. https://doi.org/10.1016/0270-0255(87)90473-8

Saaty, T. L. (1990). How to make a decision: The analytic hierarchy process. *European Journal of Operational Research, 48*(1), 9–26.

Sari, Y., Hidayatno, A., Suzianti, A., Hartono, M., & Susanto, H. (2020). A corporate sustainability maturity model for readiness assessment: A three-step development strategy. *International Journal of Productivity and Performance Management* (ahead-of-print). https://doi.org/10.1108/IJPPM-10-2019-0481

Siano, A., Conte, F., Amabile, S., Vollero, A., & Piciocchi, P. (2016). Communicating sustainability: An operational model for evaluating corporate websites. *Sustainability, 8*(9), 1–16.

Terouhid, S. A., & Ries, R. (2016). Organizational sustainability excellence of construction firms—A framework. *Journal of Modelling in Management, 11*(4), 911–931. https://doi.org/10.1108/JM2-06-2014-0055

Vrontis, D., Thrassou, A., Efthymiou, L., & Bozat, M. (2024). Delineating business for sustainability: Contextual evolution and elucidation. In D. Vrontis, A. Thrassou, L. Efthymiou, Y. Weber, S. M. R. Shams, & E. Tsoukatos (Eds.), *Business for sustainability, Volume II. Palgrave Studies in Cross-disciplinary Business Research. In Association with EuroMed Academy of Business*. Palgrave Macmillan. https://doi.org/10.1007/978-3-031-37365-7_1

Vrontis, D., Thrassou, A., Uzunboylu, N., Efthymiou, L. (2023). An overview of business for sustainability: Strategic Avenues and Managerial Approaches. In D. Vrontis, A. Thrassou, L. Efthymiou, Y. Weber, S. M. R. Shams, & E. Tsoukatos (Eds.), *Business for sustainability, Volume I. Palgrave Studies in Cross-disciplinary Business Research. In Association with EuroMed Academy of Business*. Palgrave Macmillan. https://doi.org/10.1007/978-3-031-37361-9_1

Willard, B. (2005, June). The next sustainability wave (book excerpt). *Ubiquity, 2005*, 1–1. https://doi.org/10.1145/1071916.1071917

CHAPTER 3

A Meta-Analysis on the Role of Green Marketing in SMEs and Its Payoff

Michela Matarazzo, Stephen Oduro, and Bruno Marsigalia

3.1 Introduction

The world's population continues to grow at an alarming rate, and along with it is the growing level of greenhouse gases in the environment and a hole in the ozone layer unearthed by chlorofluorocarbons (Mukonza & Swarts, 2020). Against this background, the necessity

M. Matarazzo (✉) · B. Marsigalia
Department of Economics and Business Sciences, Marconi University of Rome, Rome, Italy
e-mail: m.matarazzo@unimarconi.it

B. Marsigalia
e-mail: b.marsigalia@unimarconi.it

S. Oduro
Faculty of Economics and Management, Free University of Bozen-Bolzano, Bolzano, Italy
e-mail: stephen.oduro@unibz.it

D. Vrontis et al. (eds.), *Business in Uncertainty*, Palgrave Studies in Cross-disciplinary Business Research, In Association with EuroMed Academy of Business, https://doi.org/10.1007/978-3-031-65587-6_3

to develop sustainable measures in all levels of production, consumption, and general dynamics of livelihood has been highly emphasized by local governments and international organizations (UN) and supra-organizations (EU, AU, etc.), leading to green economy agenda and policy initiatives of governments and international organizations to grow economies and facilitate the well-being of people while at the same time safeguarding the environment.

Green economy policies and initiatives can create green jobs, enhance the well-being and livelihood of the world's poor, promote investment and innovation, and create business opportunities (Gelderman et al., 2021). The current problems bewildering the world demand managers and owners in all forms of businesses to develop and implement strategies that protect and preserve the environment and natural resources (Amoako et al., 2021). To this end, most companies also implement green marketing strategies in their strategic and corporate orientations. The phenomenon of green marketing (GM) developed between the 1960s and early 1970s because of the consequence of production and consumption dynamics on the environment (Konar & Cohen, 2001). Since the late 1980s, GM has received tremendous attention due to the emergence of green consumerism (Mishra & Sharma, 2010).

It has been argued that companies must adopt GM strategies to achieve sustainable competitive advantage (Vrontis et al., 2023a). Research shows that conventional manufacturing firms that change their production philosophies by switching to green philosophies are more profitable and have the upper hand over those that hold to traditional production ideologies (CDP, 2017; Taylor et al., 2013). Thus, it is necessary to examine GM and its implications for business performance, particularly in a resource-constraint context like SMEs.

Green marketing is defined as the "holistic management process responsible for identifying, anticipating and satisfying the needs of customers and society, in a profitable and sustainable way" (Leal-Filho et al., 2009, p. 2). Companies mainly use eco-friendly, ecological marketing messages via advertising to persuade ecologically conscious consumers to increase their sales and profits, corporate image, and competitive advantage, enhancing their comprehensive enterprise performance (Mukonza & Swarts, 2020).

Albeit, the issue is that not all GM claims are considered a true reflection of a firm's environmental conduct and can be seen as "greenwashing," which is "the process of conveying a false impression or providing misleading information about how a company's products are more environmentally sound" (Szabo & Webster, 2020, p. 1). This perceived incongruency between a firm's environmental claim and its actual actions can adversely affect the profitability and reputation of firms (Szabo & Webster, 2020). Apart from the issue of greenwashing, the empirical findings on the relationship between GM and enterprise performance are inconclusive and contradictory, with some studies reporting positive relationships (e.g., Martins, 2021; Roh et al., 2022), some no significant relationship (e.g., Khan et al., 2019; Mwaura, 2021), and others negative relationships (e.g., Amero, 2012; Gelderman et al., 2021). Furthermore, the empirical studies are fragmented across contexts, cultures, countries, and disciplines, making it challenging to understand comprehensively the extent to which GM influences the performance of SMEs and the boundary-spanning conditions (moderators) that facilitate or impede the success of GM strategies by SMEs. Although there is little consensus among scholars about the true nature of the impact of GM on SMEs' performance, to the best of our knowledge, a meta-analysis that examines the GM—firm performance relationships in this research stream to clarify the anecdotal results is non-existent.

To close this gap, we develop a meta-analysis, which is "a quantitative, formal, and epidemiological study design that is used to systematically combine and assess the results of previous scientific studies to derive conclusions about that body of research" (Haidich, 2010, p. 12), to quantify and summarize the disparities and commonalities of the extant literature on the GM-SMEs performance relationships while exploring the contingencies that may account for between-study variance. More specifically, we aim to (1) examine the degree to which GM—green product, green price, green distribution, and green promotion impact diverse firm performance indicators of SMEs across the extant literature and (2) test boundary-spanning conditions, namely contextual moderators, i.e., sector (agriculture, manufacturing vs. service), economic development (developing vs. developed), country global sustainable competitiveness (high GSCI vs. low GSCI), and culture (high vs. low individualism) that may moderate this focal relationship.

In doing so, we contribute to the marketing and sustainability literature in several ways. First, our study provides a pioneering conceptual framework that integrates all the dimensions of GM and their impact on SME performance in a single study with a large sample size (43,675) and a wide window period (1982–2020). Thus, our study offers a consolidative map of the research on the relationship between GM and SMEs' performance. Second, given the inconsistent landscape of the findings in the literature, the study helps clarify the conflicting findings to ascertain whether the positive, negative, or neutral results prevail in the literature, reducing the theoretical confusion on the nexus between GM and SME performance. Third, our examination and exploration of the possible contextual factors that may moderate the focal relationship help explain some of the reasons for the mixed results, thereby opening the "theoretical black box" and advancing theoretical consistency and coherence about the phenomenon. A meta-analysis helps resolve mixed results and is the "best method to reach consensus" (Combs et al., 2011, p. 194). Fourth, our methodological design, the meta-analysis, also offers the methodological rigour of the field since the existing studies are mainly quantitative and qualitative individual studies. From a managerial perspective, this study underlines the impacts of GM on a broad spectrum of SME performance and postulates how practitioners can deploy and exploit actionable strategies and moderators, like suitable marketing mechanisms, to satisfy the needs and wants of consumers while preserving the environment. The following section discusses the study's theoretical background about the extant literature.

3.2 Literature Review

Theoretical Background

The GM-SME performance focal relationship is driven by the RBV of the firm, which considers resources and capabilities that are rare, valuable, inimitable, and organizable as the basis of sustainable competitive advantage (Barney, 2001). Green capabilities involve "the ability of a company to exploit its existing resources and knowledge to renew and develop its green organizational capabilities to react to the dynamic market" (Teece et al., 1997, p.34). Thus, SMEs possessing green resources and capabilities are expected to enhance their firm performance (Matarazzo et al., 2020, 2021). Figure 3.1 demonstrates the meta-analytic conceptual framework of the study graphically. The model shows that the four most frequently investigated GM strategies (i.e., green price, green distribution, and green promotion) synchronously influence firm performance—overall and disaggregate (competitive advantage, innovation performance, environmental performance, social performance, economic performance, profitability, corporate reputation, customer performance). Firm performance highlights organizational effectiveness in terms of its operational, economic, and financial performance (Saraf et al., 2007). In this study, it includes profitability and economic performance.

Financial performance measures the degree to which a firm can achieve its financial and economic goals in a given period (efficiency) and includes performance indicators but are not limited to return on equity (ROE), market share, cash flow from operations, return on assets (ROA), Tobin Q, stock price, return on sales (ROS), return on investment (ROI), profit to revenue ratio, revenue growth, productivity, sales growth, and profitability, among others (Hoffmann, 2017; Soto-Acosta et al., 2018). On the other hand, non-financial performance measures the ability of a firm to achieve its effective and operational goals and includes indicators such as internal process improvement, corporate reputation, employee satisfaction, customer loyalty, environmental performance, social performance, business model innovation, new product development, and innovation performance (Leonidou et al., 2020; Oduro & De Nisco, 2023). In this study, non-financial performance is captured by competitive advantage, innovation performance, environmental performance, social performance, corporate reputation, and customer performance.

Green Marketing and Firm Performance

The origin of GM dates to the wave of environmental and climate concerns of the 1970s that birthed the phenomenon of ecological marketing. Peattie and Charter (2012) state that this was associated with industries with the greatest environmental consequences and the development of novel technologies to mitigate specific environmental menaces. Green marketing (GM, hereafter) is defined as the "holistic management process responsible for identifying, anticipating and satisfying the needs of customers and society, in a profitable and sustainable way" (Leal-Filho et al., 2009, p.2). Likewise, Rahman et al. (2012) elucidated GM as a firm operation that reduces waste by producing and offering environmentally friendly products and services, encouraging the sustainability and environmental health of society and saving energy (Efthymiou et al., 2023; Vrontis et al., 2023b). GM, also referred to as sustainable marketing and eco/ecological marketing (Katrandjiev, 2016), has birthed novel ways of doing business that are profitable and sustainable.

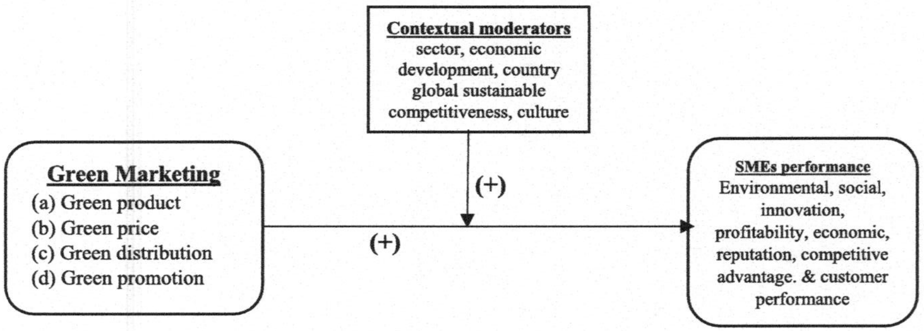

Fig. 3.1 Meta-analytic framework

GM is unarguably important. GM has been promoted for several years for several reasons, such as driving a sustainability agenda, educating consumers concerning ecologically friendly mechanisms, and removing wastefulness. Polonsky (2008) opines that the GM phenomenon grew in relevance because of the fundamental definition of economics, which involves the study of the way people utilize scarce resources to satisfy unlimited needs and wants. Scholars have postulated, in the extant literature, the reasons for firms' increasing adoption of GM. For instance, Keller (1987) highlighted that firms perceive GM as an opportunity to achieve business objectives and goals. Shearer (1990) also affirms that firms believe that they have a moral obligation to be environmentally and socially responsible, whereas cost factors related to the reduction in material usage and waste disposals motivate companies to change their competing behaviours (Azzone & Manzini, 1994).

Several factors drive the adoption of GM by companies, including policies, environmentalism, peer pressure, competitive environment, and legal actions (Li et al., 2018). Leonidou and Leonidou (2011) underscored three critical prongs of GM: Internal green marketing, tactical green marketing, and strategic green marketing. Internal GM refers to the pollination of environmental values and principles across the firm to encompass a broad corporate green culture (Papadas & Avlonitis, 2014). This includes efforts and actions to promote environmental awareness within the company through employee education and training. Tactical GM describes short-run activities that transform the conventional marketing mix of price, place, product, and promotion. It includes product-related actions to decrease environmental footprint (Mukonza & Swarts, 2019). By contrast, strategic GM looks at long-run, top management policies and actions, especially concentrating on firm environmental strategy (Mukonza & Swarts, 2020). Implementing GM strategies demands GM orientation that drives organizational processes, routines, activities, and performance and enhances corporate reputation (Mukonza & Swarts, 2019). GM orientation is a company's comprehensive positioning towards the natural environment (Papadas et al., 2017).

Concerning the impact of GM on SME performance, some studies have demonstrated that investing in green product innovation positively impacts business (Chen et al., 2006). Hasana and Ali (2015) reveal that GM strategies enhance a company's competitive advantage and profitability and promote a greener lifestyle among consumers. The research of Emeizan et al. (2016) postulates that GM strategies increase the sales volume of green cars. Likewise, Wu and Lin (2016) show that organic farms gain corporate image by adopting GM strategies. Thus, we expect that adopting GM can enhance SMEs' performance.

The literature reports four key dimensions of GM, popularly known as the 4Ps-Product, price, distribution, and promotion. We elucidate these factors briefly below.

Green product includes recyclable, reusable, biodegradable, eco-friendly products and packaging that are known to have a low adverse environmental impact (Indicators, 2011, p. 19). Empirical results on the impact of green products on firm performance are mixed, with some showing positive effects on environmental performance and economic performance (Mwaura, 2021; Roh et al., 2022) and others with a negative impact on customer performance (Khan et al., 2019) and corporate reputation (Amero, 2012). *Green pricing* involves both the economic and environmental costs of production and marketing while providing customer value (Pandey et al., 2018). The literature presents contradictory findings on green prices and firm performance. For instance, while Mahmoud et al. (2017) and Al-Murad (2022) found a positive relationship, Amero (2012) found a negative relationship between green price and corporate reputation, economic performance, and customer performance. *Green distribution* deals with the selection of channels that ensure minimal environmental damage and environmental innovation in the value chain in the control and monitoring programmes of the enterprise with the intermediaries and channel partners. Braik (2021) found that green distribution positively influences social, environmental, and economic performance, but Setyawatia et al. (2020) found no significant impact on customer performance and economic performance (Eneizan et al., 2016). Lastly, *green promotion* involves an effective awareness tool by which a firm communicates, informs, and reminds stakeholders about its commitment and achievements towards environmental preservation efforts (Belz & Peattie, 2009) using green marketing messages. Like the other green marketing mix, empirical results on green promotion and firm performance are mixed. Studies (e.g., Braik, 2021; Martins, 2021) observed that green promotion positively influences social, competitive advantage, environmental, profitability, and economic performance, but others (e.g., Eneizan et al., 2019; Memon et al., 2019) found that it is negatively related to profitability and corporate reputation.

This study aims to resolve these mixed effects by ascertaining the degree to which GM and its dimensions affect SMEs' performance.

Despite the mixed results presented in the literature, we expect that GM will have a positive effect on overall SME performance and that green product, green price, green distribution, and green promotion will have a positive effect on SME performance, such that the impact of green product is stronger than green price, green promotion, and green distribution, in that order. Our assumption is based on the fact that it is primarily the products of the firms that consumers tangibly get in touch with to be able to attest whether the firm's products are eco-sustainable or not, hence wielding the greatest influencing factor; however, the price of green products is sometimes high as well as green distribution channels. Moreover, green promotion may not necessarily be accepted or believed by the consumer (remember, perceived greenwashing), so we expect its impact may not be as strong as green products. Moreover, drawing on the contingency theory, which indicates that different contexts or environments mostly have diverse needs, therefore demanding differentiated approaches to operations management (Romero-Silva et al., 2018), we explored sector, economic development, country global sustainable competitiveness (GSCI), and culture as context-dependency moderators.

3.3 Research Design

Building upon the conventional methods of secondary data analysis, we carried out a bibliographic keyword search to select articles that examined the relationship between GM and SMEs performance from 1980 to 2022 (March) in well-known internationally recognized business and management databases: Web of Science, Scopus, EBSCO, Google Scholar, ABI Proquest, and Emerald Insight. We searched the databases by entering the undermentioned keywords in the title, abstract, and keywords field in the databases by using the Boolean operations such as "OR, AND, NOT: GM" (e.g., "ecological marketing," "sustainable marketing," "green marketing," "environmental marketing," "green product," "green price," "green distribution," "green distribution"); SMEs performance (e.g., "SMEs performance," "innovation performance," "customer performance," "environmental performance," "firm performance," "competitive advantage," "financial performance," "marketing performance," "non-financial performance"). To comprehensively capture relevant number of articles, we conducted a reference-by-reference analysis in prior systematic reviews (e.g., Klewitz & Hansen, 2014) and leading journals that frequently publish papers on the theme and in SMEs, including the *Journal of Small Business Management, Journal of Cleaner Production, Journal of Innovation Management, Small Business Economics, Technovation, Technological Forecasting and Social Change, Research Policy, and European Journal of Innovation Management*. Finally, we emailed leading scholars in the field to ask for unpublished papers or working papers, an approach similar to previous meta-analyses (Liu et al., 2023; Oduro et al., 2023).

We included articles using these criteria: (1) English language, full-text online scholarly articles that examined at least one type of GM (e.g., green product, green price, green distribution, green promotion) in association with the performance of SMEs; (2) the study was a quantitative study that provided a correlation coefficient metric or enough statistical information to facilitate the computation of correlation coefficients; and (3) studies without correlation coefficients provided r-variants (F-test, T-test, regression, etc.) that can be converted to r-coefficients.

Our initial search produced a total of 1237 articles. Then, we filtered these papers against different elements such as scholarly articles, year, and English language. Based on this operation, we deleted 456 articles, leaving 781 articles. Next, we also removed the duplicate papers, which amounted to 423 articles, due to merging data from Scopus and Web of Science (WOS). Based on an abstract review, we removed 205 non-quantitatively analysed papers (i.e., qualitative papers), reducing the total to 153. Lastly, we removed 34 studies that did not provide complete information about the correlational coefficients or their r-variants (beta, t-value, etc.).

After the inclusion and exclusion phases, 119 independent scholarly articles were identified, with 47,661 observations and 195 effect sizes. As a next step and based on the procedures of prior meta-analyses (Lipsey & Wilson, 2001), we developed a comprehensive coding scheme to cover various aspects of the study, including the conceptual characteristics, namely GM and its sub-dimensions—green product, green price, green distribution, and green promotion and SME performance with sub-dimensions (e.g., environmental, social, innovation, profitability, economic, reputation, competitive advantage, and customer performance). Moreover, we also coded the contextual moderators of the study, including culture, country development, global sustainable competitiveness index, and sector of operation. Additionally, the coding scheme encompassed critical statistical information of meta-analyses (sample size, means and standard deviations, correlation coefficients, and r-variants of correlation such as p-value, t-value, beta, and f-statistics). Regarding the r-variants like p-values, we followed the recommended procedure of Rosenthal and DiMatteo (2001, p. 72) to convert them into Pearson correlation. For the studies that reported regression coefficients, we applied Peterson and Brown's (2005) formula to convert them to correlation (i.e., $r = 0.98\beta + 0.05\lambda$ with $\lambda = 1$ when $\beta > 0$ and $\lambda = 0$ when $\beta < 0$).

To avoid the problem of overrepresentation of samples, in cases where a study reported two or more correlation coefficients or r-variants for the same association (e.g., profit and ROA), we followed the procedures of previous studies (e.g., Kirca et al., 2005; Roschk et al., 2017) to take the average of those effect sizes to obtain one average effect per study (Kirca et al., 2005). Then, to correct for attenuation that may arise from random sampling error, we adjusted the effect sizes for reliability based on the formula: effect sizes (rxy) were divided by the square root of two variable measurement reliability products $\sqrt{(rxx)} * \sqrt{(ryy)}$ (Hunter & Schmidt, 2004). The articles were coded by one author, after which the remaining two co-authors verified the coded articles with the predefined coding items to ensure coherence and consistency. The cross-examination and assessment yield a 97% inter-rater agreement. All disagreements were handled through cross-evaluation and discussion, confirming the coding scheme's validity (Oduro et al., 2022).

The meta-analysis metric that has been employed is the Pearson correlation coefficient metric. This metric is generally used in business, management, and marketing (Oduro et al., 2023). Another rationale for choosing this metric is that it is easily interpretable and helps researchers compute r-variants when no correlation coefficient is reported (Oduro et al., 2021). The correlation coefficients were either picked directly from the study or calculated through the r-variants (Hunter & Schmidt, 2004). We employed a random-effects model due to merging different studies conducted in various contexts and cultures and with diverse methodological designs (Borenstein et al., 2021). The random effects model has an advantage over the fixed effects model in that it assumes that study-study variance varies for all studies and subgroups that employ diverse methodologies. Moreover, it captures both measurement error and sampling, unlike the fixed effects model that attributes all variances to only sampling error (Borenstein et al., 2021).

Moreover, we tested publication bias, which shows that positive results are easier to publish when compared to negative ones. Against this background, we assessed publication bias by including published (journal articles) and unpublished papers (theses, conference proceedings, working papers) in our analysis. We carried out the publication bias using the conventional method known as the *funnel plot* and Fail-safe N, but we found no publication bias issues. In cases where there is no issue of publication bias, the funnel plot would be symmetric, given that the standard errors vary randomly around the mean effect size estimate (Hedges & Vevea, 1998). On the other hand, the Fail-safe N discloses the number of studies required to reject the study's findings and shows the results' robustness (Borenstein et al., 2021; Oduro et al., 2021).

Finally, we used Q and Higgin (I-square) statistics to assess the heterogeneity of the generalizable effect sizes (study-to-study variance). While the Q measures the homogeneity, Higgin I2 measures the percentage of the variation across studies (Higgins, 2008). We evaluated the moderation effect using the bi-variate psychometric meta-analysis (QB-test), the significance of which was examined via subgroup analysis using QB. The statistical software used for the study is Comprehensive Meta-Analysis (CMA), one of the most widely used statistical software for meta-analysis. The software is easy to use; studies can be removed and added without needing to modify data, and there is a broad range of effect sizes, including correlation, odds ratios, treatment differences, etc. It allows users to choose between fixed and random-effects models and carries out both subgroup and meta-regression analyses. Our results are shown in the next section.

3.4 Presentation and Analysis of Findings/Results

Our first analysis provides the findings of GM's overall or aggregate effect on overall firm performance and the relative effects of the dimensions of GM. First, our results show that the average strength of the aggregate effect sizes is significantly small-moderate (medium) (0.19–0.51), based on the criteria suggested by Cohen (1988), where an effect size of 0.20 is interpreted as small; 0.50 equates to a medium effect, and effect size larger than 0.80 is deemed as large effects (Table 3.1).

In particular, we found that the overall impact of GM on the overall SME performance is positively and significantly moderate ($r = 0.33$)

Table 3.1 Overall effects of GM on SME performance. Bold significance means strong effect sizes

	N	*K*	*rz*	*−CI*	*+CI*	*Z*	*Q*
Aggregate effects							
GM → overall performance	47,661	195	**0.33**	0.29	0.36	16.94	3601
The overall effect of GM by dimensions							
Green product	6480	29	**0.26**	0.17	0.34	5.81	348.67
Green price	4205	18	0.23	0.11	0.35	3.56	285.42
Green distribution	2501	13	0.19	0.04	0.33	2.46	160.56
Green promotion	5834	25	**0.28**	0.19	0.37	5.65	339.36
QB = 15.49; p = 0.001; Fail Safe N = 5769							
Overall effect on performance dimensions							
Non-financial							
Competitive advantage	2311	13	**0.35**	0.22	0.47	4.95	134.35
Corporate reputation	3218	16	**0.36**	0.23	0.47	5.43	217.56
Customer performance	17,505	74	**0.35**	0.30	0.41	11.97	1160.45
Social performance	974	07	0.31	0.05	0.53	2.34	89.11
Environmental performance	3744	17	**0.37**	0.16	0.55	3.30	790.46
Innovation performance	2891	06	**0.47**	0.28	0.62	4.53	155.05
Financial performance							
Profitability	5181	19	0.30	0.17	0.41	4.52	403.24
Economic performance	5233	22	0.22	0.12	0.31	4.35	269.63
QB = 54.63, p = 0.001; Fail Safe N = 11,861							

Note K = effect sizes; N = observations; rz = standardized correlations coefficient; GM = Green Marketing

since the confidence interval does not include zero. The Fail-safe N is very robust, disclosing that 5769 primary studies are required to render this finding non-significant. This implies the GM efforts of SMEs have a significant on their firm performance, financial and non-financial. Concerning the aggregate impact of the sub-dimensions of GM, our results demonstrate that green promotion has the largest effect on SMEs performance ($r = 0.28$), followed by green product ($r = 0.26$), green price ($r = 0.23$), and green distribution ($r = 0.19$), in that order (*QB = 15.49; p = 0.001, meaning the mean difference is significant*). Moreover, vis-à-vis the disaggregate firm performance indicators, our findings show that the impact of GM (all dimensions) on innovation performance is the largest ($r = 0.47$), followed by environmental performance ($r = 0.37$), corporate reputation ($r = 0.36$), competitive advantage ($r = 0.35$), customer performance/marketing performance ($r = 0.35$), social performance ($r = 0.31$), profitability ($r = 0.30$), and economic performance ($r = 0.27$), in that order (***QB = 54.63; p = 0.001***, hence the mean differences are significant). This shows that GM positively affects both the financial performance (profitability and economic performance) and the non-financial performance of SMEs. However, it is observed that the three most influenced performance indicators by SMEs' GM efforts are innovation performance, environmental performance, and firm reputation, in that order.

Study Moderators

The moderator analysis of the contextual factors reveals that sector significantly influences GM performance, such that it is larger in the SMEs involved in agri-business ($r = 0.54$) than those in the service ($r = 0.44$) and manufacturing sector ($r = 0.25$). Moreover, the GSCI of a country (i.e., natural capital, resource efficiency and intensity, intellectual capital, governance efficiency, and social cohesion) also plays a significant moderating role, indicating that SMEs in countries with high GSCI perform better ($r = 0.43$) than those in low GSCI ($r = 0.26$), a finding that highlights that integrated social, environmental, and economic dynamics of a country facilitate sustainable growth and ecological marketing innovations. Also, culture (individualism) has a significant moderating effect on GM performance, such that SMEs operating in low individualistic cultures perform better in GM ($r = 0.34$) than those in a high individualistic culture ($r = 0.23$), which could be partly due to the fact that companies in collectivist cultures are more prone to the adoption of ecological marketing and that people in collectivist cultures tend to care about others and the well-being of the society, thereby assuming responsibility for other members of the society (Table 3.2).

Interestingly, our analysis reveals no significant difference in the performance of SMEs operating in countries with high human development index (HDI) and those with low HDI (*QB = 1.47; p-value = 489*).

Table 3.2 Bivariate moderation analysis of the overall effects of GM on SMEs' performance. Bold significance means strong effect sizes

	N	*K*	*rz*	*−CI*	*+CI*	*Z*	*QB*	*P*
Contextual factors								
Sector							**35.69**	**0.001**
Agriculture	1482	06	**0.54**	0.26	0.74	3.53		
Manufacturing	18,747	85	0.25	0.19	0.30	8.07		
Service	8825	38	**0.44**	0.37	0.50	11.70		
Country development							**1.47**	**0.489**
High HDI	38,896	158	**0.33**	0.29	0.37	15.22		
Low HDI	8043	35	0.32	0.24	0.40	7.04		
Global sustainability index							**24.69**	**0.001**
High GSCI	21,521	76	**0.43**	0.38	0.48	13.64		
Low GSCI	25,418	117	0.26	0.22	0.30	11.73		
Culture-individualism							**5.89**	**0.045**
High IDV	4329	15	0.23	0.10	0.35	3.39		
Low IDV	42,379	177	**0.34**	0.30	0.38	16.51		
Methodological factors								
Performance proxy							**14.98**	**0.001**
Financial measure	9915	39	0.23	0.15	0.30	5.91		
Non-financial	3222	14	**0.45**	0.31	0.57	5.77		
Mixed	34,404	141	0.34	0.30	0.38	14.84		
Sampling technique							**13.68**	**0.001**
Non-probabilistic	9075	38	**0.45**	0.37	0.52	10.30		
Probabilistic	37,222	153	0.30	0.26	0.34	13.84		
Publication status							**1.245**	**0.678**
Published	46,104	175	0.34	0,30	0.37	16.72		
Unpublished	1557	20	0.25	0.09	0.40	2.97		
Study type							**0.051**	**0.878**
Cross-sectional	40,826	169	0.33	0.30	0.36	18.36		
Longitudinal	6835	26	0.31	0.15	0.46	3.61		

Note K = effect sizes; N = observations; rz = standardized correlations coefficient

Vis-à-vis the methodological moderators, only the type of performance measure, such that non-financial indicators like innovation performance, social performance, productivity, and reputation yield larger effects sizes ($r = 0.45$) than financial performance indicators like ROE, ROA, and profitability ($r = 0.23$). This finding also means that the impact of GM on non-financial performance is larger than on financial performance.

3.5 Concluding Discussion and Recommendations

Empirical studies on the GM-SME performance relationships have been gaining increased interest and attention of scientific scholars in the marketing and management literature in recent years due to the growing concerns about the negative ramifications of firms' activities on the environment. While research has been growing steadily, the empirical findings are inconclusive (positive, negative, and insignificant results), creating a theological black box and managerial uncertainty regarding the real impact of GM investment on SME performance. To close this gap, this meta-analytic review makes the first effort to synthesize the findings across the extant literature to establish the extent to which GM influences diverse performance indicators of SMEs.

Our results that GM—green product, green price, green distribution, and green promotion—have a positive and significant impact on overall and disaggregate SMEs' performance—demonstrate that GM investment is worthwhile for SMEs, as it helps them achieve both financial and non-financial performance, thereby increasing their firm competitiveness (Amero, 2012; Setyawatia et al. 2020). It is also interesting to note that GM positively relates to corporate reputation (Braik, 2021; Martins, 2021). These findings demonstrate that although GM campaigns may sometimes suffer from perceived greenwashing, their performance gains far exceed the cost associated with greenwashing, demonstrating that SMEs' ethical and faithful environmental conduct can garner consumers' trust and patronage of its products and services, which in turn, can enhance performance over time.

Another interesting finding regards the positive effect of GM on profitability and economic performance, which shows that even though GM efforts may be capital-intensive, they produce a positive return on investment. This is particularly interesting in a resource-constraint context like SMEs. Thus, consistent with the theoretical proposition of the RBV of the firm, which considers resources and capabilities that are rare, valuable, inimitable, and organizable as the basis of sustainable competitive advantage (Barney, 2001), SMEs possessing green resources and capabilities can enhance their firm performance. Thus, the ability of SMEs to exploit their existing resources and knowledge to develop and renew their green capabilities can improve their competitiveness (Teece et al., 1997).

Based on our findings, we can conclude that the positive view of the literature on the relationship between GM and SMEs' performance prevails over the negative and non-significant relationships. Thus, GM positively influences both the financial and non-financial performance of SMEs.

Based on these conclusions, we contribute to the extant literature by resolving the anecdotal findings and synthesizing the fragmented literature to provide a unifying framework on the GM-SMEs' performance phenomenon. Our large pool of data and broad window period also enhance the accuracy of our prediction of the green behaviour of SMEs. Also, by exploring and identifying some contingent factors on the focal relationship, we are able to account for some of the reasons for the mixed results in the field. As we have shown, the influence of GM on SMEs' performance may be contingent upon the industry of operation, the cultural landscape in which the firm is situated, and the global sustainable competitiveness of the country in which the firm operates. Thus, both sectoral (micro) and institutional contexts (macro) influence the GM performance of SMEs.

For management practice, our results show, in addition to the expected mean effect ($r = 0.33$), that the relative strength of GM on SME performance varies across GM dimensions (e.g., green promotion > green product > green price > green distribution) and performance indicators (innovation performance > environmental performance > corporate reputation). This finding has key implications for SMEs regarding their strategic orientation and resource allocations. Since SMEs have limited resources, for instance, they can devote more resources to green promotion and product development which appear to be the most influential. One conceivable way to accomplish this is by developing genuine biodegradable, reusable, recyclable, and eco-friendly products, packaging and labelling, and promoting them actively by using green marketing and advertising messages in various media like the print media (billboard, flyers), TV, radio, and social media.

Lastly, SME managers will also need to consider the moderating factors like sector, culture, and GSCI of their countries. For instance, those in the agri-business sector can strongly implement GM strategies as well as SMEs in the low individualistic cultures because consumers seek the environment's general well-being, leading them to support companies with green economy orientations. SMEs can also invest more in green promotion in their marketing mix since it greatly impacts SMEs' performance.

For future research, our meta-analysis was based only on bi-variate analysis without examining causal effects. Future studies can employ meta-structural equation modelling to account for mediators. Also, we limited our analysis to a particular context, SMEs, allowing future researchers to include large enterprises for cross-context comparative analysis. Also, our research was limited to the conventional 4Ps, but future studies can include in their framework other emerging marketing mix like green people and green processes.

References

Al-Murad, N. Y. M. (2022). Apply green marketing strategies to improve market performance by competitive advantage as mediating: An analytical study of some small organizations in Iraq. Webology, 19(1), 1266–1281. https://doi.org/10.14704/WEB/V19I1/WEB19085

Amero, P. (2012). The influence of green marketing strategies towards economic sustainability. Retrieved from https://repository.uinjkt.ac.id/dspace/handle/123456789/3105

Amoako, G. K., Doe, J. K., & Dzogbenuku, R. K. (2021). Perceived firm ethicality and brand loyalty: The mediating role of corporate social responsibility and perceived green marketing. *Society and Business Review, 16*(3), 398–419.

Azzone, G., & Manzini, R. (1994). Measuring strategic environmental performance. *Business Strategy and the Environment, 3*(1), 1–14.

Barney, J. B. (2001). Resource-based theories of competitive advantage: A ten-year retrospective on the resource-based view. *Journal of Management, 27*(6), 643–650.

Belz, F.-M., & Peattie, K. (2009). *Sustainability marketing: A global perspective*. Chichester.

Borenstein, M., Hedges, L. V., Higgins, J. P. T., & Rothstein, H. R. (2021). *Introduction to meta-analysis* (2nd ed.). Wiley.

Braik, F. (2021). *Assessing the impact of green marketing practices on organizational sustainable performance in palestinian food industries*. Doctoral dissertation, An-Najah National University.

CDP. (2017). *CDP South Africa climate change: Executive summary*. Adex Innovations. http://piv.nbi.org.za/2017/CDP_Climate_change_2017.pdf

Chen, Y.-S., Lai, S.-B., & Wen, C.-T. (2006). The influence of green innovation performance on corporate advantage in Taiwan. *Journal of Business Ethics, 67*(4), pp. 331-339.

Cohen, J. (1988). *Statistical power analysis for the behavioral sciences* (2nd ed.). Hillsdale, NJ: Lawrence Erlbaum Associates.

Combs, J. G., Ketchen, D. J. Jr., Crook, T. R., & Roth, P. L. (2011). Assessing cumulative evidence within 'macro'research: Why meta-analysis should be preferred over vote counting. *Journal of Management Studies, 48*(1), 178–197.

Efthymiou, L., Kulshrestha, A., & Kulshrestha, S. (2023). A study on sustainability and ESG in the service sector in India: Benefits, challenges, and future implications. *Administrative Sciences, 13*, 165. https://doi.org/10.3390/admsci13070165

Emeizan, B. M., Wahab, K. A., Zainon, S., & Obaid, T. F. (2016). Effects of green marketing strategies on sales volume of green cars. *Singaporean Journal of Business, Economics and Management Studies, 5*(3), 1–14.

Eneizan, B. M., Matar, A., Al-Zawahreh, A., Alkhawaldeh, A. M., & Eneizan, O. (2019). Effects of green marketing strategy on firm financial performance. The moderating role of govern ment policy. *Business and Economic Horizons (BEH), 15*, 304–324.

Gelderman, C. J., Schijns, J., Lambrechts, W., & Vijgen, S. (2021). Green marketing as an environmental practice: The impact on green satisfaction and green loyalty in a business-to-business context. *Business Strategy and the Environment, 30*(4), 2061–2076.

Haidich, A. B. (2010). Meta-analysis in medical research. *Hippokratia, 14*(Suppl 1), 29.

Hasana, Z., & Ali, N. A. (2015). The impact of green marketing strategy on the firm's performance in Malaysia. *Procedia—Social and Behavioural Sciences, 172*, 463–470.

Hedges, L. V., & Vevea, J. L. (1998). Fixed and random-effects models in meta-analysis. *Psychological Methods, 3*(4), 486–504.

Higgins, J. P. (2008). Commentary: Heterogeneity in meta-analysis should be expected and appropriately quantified. *International Journal of Epidemiology, 37*(5), 1158–1160.

Hoffmann, A. L. (2017). Data, technology, and gender: Thinking about (and from) trans lives. In *Spaces for the future* (pp. 3–13). Routledge.

Hunter, J. E., & Schmidt, F. L. (2004). *Methods of meta-analysis: Correcting error and bias in research findings*. Sage.

Indicators, O. E. C. D. (2011). *Towards green growth: Monitoring progress.*

Katrandjiev, H. (2016). Ecological marketing, green marketing, sustainable marketing: Synonyms or an evolution of ideas. *Economic Alternatives, 1*(7), 71–82.

Keller, K. L. (1987). Memory factors in advertising: The effect of advertising retrieval cues on brand evaluations. *Journal of Consumer Research, 14*(3), 316–333.

Khan, E. A., Royhan, P., Rahman, M. A., Rahman, M. M., & Mostafa, A. (2019). The impact of enviropreneurial orientation on small firms' business performance: The mediation of green marketing mix and eco-labeling strategies. *Sustainability, 12*(1), 221.

Kirca, A. H., Jayachandran, S., & Bearden, W. O. (2005). Market orientation: A meta-analytic review and assessment of its antecedents and impact on performance. *Journal of Marketing, 69*(2), 24–41.

Klewitz, J., & Hansen, E. G. (2014). Sustainability-oriented innovation of SMEs: A systematic review. *Journal of Cleaner Production, 65*, 57–75.

Konar, S., & Cohen, M. A. (2001). Does the market value environmental performance? *Review of Economics and Statistics, 83*(2), 281–289.

Leal-Filho, W., Finisterra Do Paco, A., & Raposo, M. L. B. (2009). Identifying the green consumer: A segmentation study. *Marketing, 3*, 4

Leonidou, C. N., & Leonidou, L. C. (2011). Research into environmental marketing/management: A bibliographic analysis. *European Journal of Marketing, 45*(1/2), 68–103.

Leonidou, E., Christofi, M., Vrontis, D., & Thrassou, A. (2020). An integrative framework of stakeholder engagement for innovation management and entrepreneurship development. *Journal of Business Research, 119*, 245–258.

Li, L., Li, D., Goerzen, A., & Shi, W. S. (2018). What and how do SMEs gain by going international? A longitudinal investigation of financial and intellectual resource growth. *Journal of World Business, 53*(6), 817–834.

Lipsey, M. W., & Wilson, D. B. (2001). *Practical meta-analysis*. Sage.

Liu, Z., Geng, R., Tse, Y. K. M., & Han, S. (2023). Mapping the relationship between social media usage and organizational performance: A meta-analysis. *Technological Forecasting and Social Change, 187*, 122253.

Mahmoud, T. O., Ibrahim, S. B., Ali, A. H., & Bleady, A. (2017). The influence of green marketing mix on purchase intention: The mediation role of environmental knowledge. *International Journal of Scientific & Engineering Research, 8*(9), 1040–1048.

Martins, A. (2021). Green marketing and perceived SME profitability: The meditating effect of green purchase behaviour. *Management of Environmental Quality: An International Journal, 33*(2), 281–299. https://doi.org/10.1108/MEQ-04-2021-0074

Matarazzo, M., Penco, L., & Profumo, G. (2020). How is digital transformation changing business models and internationalisation in made in Italy SMEs? *Sinergie-Italian Journal of Management, 38*(3), 89–107.

Matarazzo, M., Penco, L., Profumo, G., & Quaglia, R. (2021). Digital transformation and customer value creation in made in Italy SMEs: A dynamic capabilities perspective. *Journal of Business Research, 123*, 642–656.

Memon, M. A., Cheah, J. H., Ramayah, T., Ting, H., Chuah, F., & Cham, T. H. (2019). Moderation analysis: Issues and guidelines. *Journal of Applied Structural Equation Modeling, 3*(1), 1–11.

Mishra, P., & Sharma, P. (2010). Green marketing in India: Emerging opportunities and challenges. *Journal of Engineering, Science and Management Education, 3*(1), 9–14.

Mukonza, C., & Swarts, I. (2019). Examining the role of green transformational leadership on promoting green organizational behavior. In *Contemporary multicultural orientations and practices for global* leadership (pp. 200–224). IGI Global.

Mukonza, C., & Swarts, I. (2020). The influence of green marketing strategies on business performance and corporate image in the retail sector. *Business Strategy and the Environment, 29*(3), 838–845.

Mwaura, E. N. (2021). *Adoption of ecological marketing mix on consumer purchase decision: A case of the textile and apparel industry in Kenya* (Doctoral dissertation). United States International University-Africa.

Oduro, S., Adhal Nguar, K. D., De Nisco, A., Alharthi, R. H. E., Maccario, G., & Bruno, L. (2022). Corporate social responsibility and SME performance: A meta-analysis. *Marketing Intelligence & Planning, 40*(2), 184–204.

Oduro, S., & De Nisco, A. (2023). From Industry 4.0 adoption to innovation ambidexterity to firm performance: A MASEM analysis. *European Journal of Innovation Management, 25*(2), 567–591.

Oduro, S., De Nisco, A., & Mainolfi, G. (2023). Do digital technologies pay off? A meta-analytic review of the digital technologies/firm performance nexus. *Technovation, 128*, 102836.

Oduro, S., Vincenzo, S., Manfo, C. S. N., & Nguar, K. D. A. (2021). Are we happy together? A meta-analytic review of the impact of open innovation on firm performance. *International Journal of Innovation Management, 25*(09), 2130004.

Pandey, A. K., Tripathi, S., & Singh, P. (2018). Plant essential oils: A substitute for conventional insecticides against Tribolium species (Coleoptera: Tenebrionidae)-achievements and challenges. *Archives of Phytopathology and Plant Protection, 51*(13–14), 696–728.

Papadas, K. K., & Avlonitis, G. J. (2014). The 4 Cs of environmental business: Introducing a new conceptual framework. *Social Business, 4*(4), 345–360.

Papadas, K. K., Avlonitis, G. J., & Carrigan, M. (2017). Green marketing orientation: Conceptualization, scale development and validation. *Journal of Business Research, 80*, 236–246.

Peattie, K., & Charter, M. (2012). Green marketing. In *The marketing book* (pp. 756–786). Routledge.

Peterson, R. A., & Brown, S. P. (2005). On the use of beta coefficients in meta-analysis. *Journal of Applied Psychology, 90*(1), 175.

Polonsky, M. J. (2008). An introduction to green marketing. *Global Environment: Problems and Policies, 2*(1), 1–10.

Rahman, I., Reynolds, D., & Svaren, S. (2012). How "green" are North American hotels? An exploration of low-cost adoption practices. *International Journal of Hospitality Management, 31*(3), 720–727.

Roh, T., Noh, J., Oh, Y., & Park, K. S. (2022). Structural relationships of a firm's green strategies for environmental performance: The roles of green supply chain management and green marketing innovation. *Journal of Cleaner Production, 356*, 131877.

Romero-Silva, R., Santos, J., & Hurtado, M. (2018). A note on defining organizational systems for contingency theory in OM. *Production Planning & Control, 29*(16), 1343–1348.

Roschk, H., Loureiro, S. M. C., & Breitsohl, J. (2017). Calibrating 30 years of experimental research: A meta-analysis of the atmospheric effects of music, scent, and color. *Journal of Retailing, 93*(2), 228–240.

Rosenthal, R., & DiMatteo, M. R. (2001). Meta-analysis: Recent developments in quantitative methods for literature reviews. *Annual Review of Psychology, 52*(1), 59–82.

Saraf, N., Langdon, C. S., & Gosain, S. (2007). Is application capabilities and relational value in interfirm partnerships. *Information Systems Research, 18*(3), 320–339.

Setyawati, H., Suroso, A., Adi, P., & Helmy, I. (2020). Linking green marketing strategy, religiosity, and firm performance: Evidence form Indonesian SMEs. *Management Science Letters, 10*(11), 2617–2624. https://doi.org/10.5267/j.msl.2020.3.031

Shearer, J. W. (1990). Business and the new environmental imperative. *Business Quarterly, 54*(3), 48–55.

Soto-Acosta, P., Popa, S., & Martinez-Conesa, I. (2018). Information technology, knowledge management and environmental dynamism as drivers of innovation ambidexterity: a study in SMEs. *Journal of Knowledge Management, 22*(4), 824–849.

Szabo, S., & Webster, J. (2020). Perceived greenwashing: The effects of green marketing on environmental and product perceptions. *Journal of Business Ethics, 171*(4), 719–739.

Taylor, P., Chuang, S., & Yang, C. (2013). Key success factors when implementing a green-manufacturing system. *Production Planning and Control, 25*(11), 923–937.

Teece, D. J., Pisano, G., & Shuen, A. (1997). Dynamic capabilities and strategic management. *Strategic Management Journal, 18*(7), 509–533.

Vrontis, D., Thrassou, A., Efthymiou, L., Weber, Y., Shams, S. M. R., & Tsoukatos, E. (2023a). *Business for sustainability, Volume I: Strategic avenues and managerial approaches*. Springer Nature.

Vrontis, D., Thrassou, A., Uzunboylu, N., & Efthymiou, L. (2023b). An overview of business for sustainability: Strategic avenues and managerial approaches. In D. Vrontis, A. Thrassou, L. Efthymiou, Y. Weber, S. M. R. Shams, & E. Tsoukatos (Eds.), *Business for Sustainability, Volume I*. Palgrave Studies in Cross-disciplinary Business Research, In Association with EuroMed Academy of Business. Palgrave Macmillan. https://doi.org/10.1007/978-3-031-37361-9_1

Wu, S. I., & Lin, S. R. (2016). The effect of green marketing strategy on business performance: a study of organic farms in Taiwan. *Total Quality Management & Business Excellence, 27*(–1–2), 141–156.

CHAPTER 4

Revolutionizing Waste Management: A Conceptual Framework for Innovative Sustainable Solutions Through Blockchain Technology

Simone Gibellato, Esposito Marialuisa, Veronica Scuotto, and Manlio Del Giudice

4.1 Introduction

Climate change is increasingly affecting the quality of people's lives (Tong & Ebi, 2019). The divergences between rich and poor people have risen in recent years because of the economic crisis (Notteboom

S. Gibellato
University of Turin, Turin, Italy

E. Marialuisa (✉) · M. Del Giudice
Link Campus University, Lazio, Italy
e-mail: marialuisa.lia@unimarconi.it

V. Scuotto
University of Federico II, Naples, Italy

D. Vrontis et al. (eds.), *Business in Uncertainty*, Palgrave Studies in Cross-disciplinary Business Research, In Association with EuroMed Academy of Business, https://doi.org/10.1007/978-3-031-65587-6_4

et al., 2021). In turn, this has requested new innovative solutions to limit and reduce such inequality along with the effects of climate change (George et al., 2021). These new solutions known as eco-innovations (EIs) can mitigate climate change effects (Durán-Romero et al., 2020; Hafeez et al., 2022). EIs use materials efficiently and then recycle and re-manage them (Vence & Pereira, 2019). For example, the European Commission's Waste Package estimated a potential reduction of 443 million tonnes of GHG between 2014 and 2030 thanks to EIs implementation (Durán-Romero et al., 2020). Additionally, researchers show how EIs can allow more and more people to access primary resources such as energy, food, and water (Dogaru, 2020). For instance, in developing countries off-grid energy systems allow the local population to have the availability of energy (Aldieri et al., 2022; Gibellato et al., 2023). EIs improve production systems even though we need more than improving production processes to achieve long-term sustainability (Genovese and Pansera (2021). Alongside EIs, there is the need to develop disruptive innovations that bring radical change at the systemic level to enhance the well-being of all human beings (Seyfang & Smith, 2007).

Disruptive EIs benefit different social classes in different contexts (Fernández et al., 2021). Disruptive EIs cause discontinuous changes or introduce new technologies that do not integrate with current mechanisms, creating new socio-technical systems (Hazarika & Zhang, 2019). In this case, new renewable energy forms and closed-loop systems are examples of disruptive EIs that challenge neoclassical economic systems (Gibellato et al., 2022). Disruptions cause a unique disposition among decision-makers, institutional commitment, technology progress, and user acceptability (De Jesus et al., 2019). From this point of view, the blockchain can promote the birth of disruptive EIs through alternative forms of natural resources management (Swartz, 2017). This technology uses a novel approach using ledgers to reach consensus and exchange money or resources between new markets and stakeholders (Nair et al., 2020). For this reason, it is possible to include new stakeholders in natural resources management because the blockchain simplifies and accelerates information flows and monetary and resource exchanges (Kouhizadeh et al., 2020). Although previous research has analyzed the EIs, the relationship between digital technologies and disruptive EIs is still in its infancy. Projects using the blockchain with a disruptive perspective use this technology to create new socio-technical systems based on new organizational models and business models (Shin & Ibahrine, 2020; Swartz,

2017). In this scenario, the waste sector is assuming more relevance because the blockchain-based system can offer financial support for waste collectors, improving citizens' health and socio-environmental education (França et al., 2020). Therefore, how the blockchain supports the development of disruptive EI in the waste management sector needs to be explored. This paper, thus, shows how the blockchain can stimulate disruptive EIs in the waste sector by implementing new organizational models that involve new stakeholders (as a social cohesion mechanism). After analyzing the management literature, we present a conceptual framework of disruptive EIs to define their characteristics and design the differences with incremental EIs.

In this line, the study contributes to the management literature on blockchain, ecological economics, and innovation management by offering new business models and best practices to develop disruptive EIs.

From the managerial point of view, this research shows how the blockchain can create new innovative processes and best practices for the waste management industry. The analysis is developed as follows: first, it presents a literature review regarding the relationship between disruptive EIs, the blockchain, and the waste management sector. Then, it presents a conceptual framework showing the characteristics of disruptive EIs in the waste management sector. Finally, the analysis describes theoretical and managerial implications, limitations, and future research directions.

4.2 Literature Review

Disruptive EIs and Blockchain

Though deterministic neoclassical models spur gradual changes, they are less helpful for stimulating disruptive changes of socio-technical systems for social transformation (Gowdy & Erickson, 2005). Yet, incremental EIs bring a progressive enhancement to current socio-technical systems, and the birth of new organizational models is unexpected (Chaminade, 2020). Instead, disruptive EIs drive socio-technical transition rather than perpetuate equilibrium states (Berkhout et al., 2004). These disruptive innovations break and generate new norms rather than optimize the current system (Hazarika & Zhang, 2019). For this reason, it is necessary to consider new organizational forms that involve different stakeholders for stimulating disruptive EIs (Gutberlet, 2021; Mutisya & Yarime, 2011).

EIs are considered disruptive when they strengthen social and institutional dimensions (Carrillo-Hermosilla et al., 2010). Multi-stakeholder engagement becomes fundamental for creating disruptive EIs that empower non-institutional and no-entrepreneurial actors (such as citizens) in managing natural resources (Jiménez-Parra et al., 2018). Therefore, disruptive EIs involve all subsystems of co-evolving social, ecological, and institutional systems (Rennings, 2000).

In this scenario, there is the technology of blockchain that emerges. This technology is increasingly used to create disruptive forms of EIs. Many blockchain-related projects are changing global social, economic, and political institutions (Buhalis et al., 2024; Dierksmeier & Seele, 2020). These projects are "radical" because they want to create a new techno-economic system using blockchain technology (Swartz, 2017). These specific projects focus on the decentralization and autonomy of blockchain (Rikken et al., 2019). Therefore, this technology can decentralize, nonhierarchical, autonomous self-governance systems from the bottom (Swartz, 2017). Especially, the blockchain can be used in different sectors to spur new disruptive EIs.

First of all, this technology can be used in the energy sector. The blockchain can strengthen energy systems management by enhancing scalability, data protection, transformation costs, market dynamics, user experience, skills, and multi-stakeholder governance (Ahl et al., 2022). Furthermore, Petri et al. (2020) show that practitioners can use blockchain for peer-to-peer energy management in energy communities. Energy communities use a multi-stakeholder approach that empowers citizens that become prosumers (consumers and producers at the same). Additionally, according to Rösch et al. (2021), the blockchain can be used in off-grid innovative systems for rural development.

Second, the blockchain can enhance water management. The blockchain can support integrative approaches to water sustainability, including water credits and trading (Enescu et al., 2020; Parmentola et al., 2022).

Third, the blockchain can improve carbon trading systems. The blockchain simplifies the blue carbon exchange through peer-to-peer transactions (Hua & Sun, 2019).

Finally, the blockchain can enhance waste management. A blockchain-based system can enable the financial management of garbage collection by involving different stakeholders through incentives or social cryptocurrencies (Ajwani-Ramchandani et al., 2021; França et al., 2020).

Waste Management, Blockchain, and Disruptive EIs

The blockchain is a helpful technology to create new forms of waste management in developing countries, where various stakeholders such as public and private institutions, universities, government, companies, and so on play a primary role (Baralla et al., 2023).

For example, within the São Paulo state, a solid waste management system supported by the blockchain was built in 2017 to propose new forms of waste management (França et al., 2020). The program is an innovative project that involves the low-income population in improving the quality of municipal waste management. Supported by the municipalities' Education Sector and Environment Department and the Health Department, low-income families can exchange recyclable domestic waste (plastic, cardboard, and aluminum) for a green cryptocurrency at market rates. This cryptocurrency can be used in some local registered shops (e.g., bakeries, supermarkets, drugstores, and grocery stores). Weekly, merchants move to the municipal government to exchange the green tokens for money. Municipalities have included only shops that sell garbage to businesses that deal with recycling products in this process.

Furthermore, new forms of waste management have been tested in India. The primary goal of these projects is to improve sanitary waste management and disposal. More specifically, for the disposal of feminine hygiene products, local urban organizations, climate change activists, and NGOs are fighting to advance garbage pickers' human rights and improve local environmental conditions (Ajwani-Ramchandani et al., 2021). Following the Ostrom principles, these projects show that tackling the sanitary waste disposal problem requires a community-led strategy because of its size, scope, and sensitivity. The primary purpose is to use the blockchain to set boundaries around the resources, beneficiaries, and regulations. It is accomplished by establishing closed groups of waste management or by giving out tokens for people and organizations that decide to participate in sanitary waste management.

Finally, alternative forms of waste management have also been implemented in China. In Changzhi, Shanxi Province, companies that own waste management plants use an integrative approach to manage agricultural and rural wastes, including crop residue and rural wastewater, to minimize waste dispersion (Zhang, 2019). Companies collect, move, and dispose of trash with the government's help, turning it into clean energy and agricultural goods, including briquettes, fertilizer, and animal feeding. However, farmers have to be encouraged to participate in the waste recovery process. Due to the lack of incentives, farmers do not take care of waste collection before the implementation of this project. Companies started to reward farmers' garbage collection through cryptocurrencies that can be exchanged for basic needs such as fertilizers or energy. Therefore, the blockchain has been used to connect farmers with companies, helping them to exchange agricultural waste, energy, and by-products (such as fertilizers or feedstock).

Starting from the management literature that connects disruptive EIs with the blockchain in the waste sector, we noticed that there is no understanding of what is the potential of using this technology to propose new organizational models in this sector that spur long-term sustainability (Vrontis et al., 2023a, 2023b). For this reason, to close this gap in the literature, we propose the following research questions:

> R1: Which new stakeholders participate in disruptive EIs within the waste management sector?
> R2: How does the integration of blockchain technology contribute to positive environmental outcomes in the waste management sector?
> R3: What societal implications and advantages can arise from the adoption of blockchain, fostering the birth of disruptive EIs in the waste management sector?

4.3 Research Design: A Theoretical Inductive Exploration

This research adopts an inductive approach (Imenda, 2014) to delve into the transformative potential of blockchain technology within the domain of waste management and disruptive EIs. This study primarily emphasizes an inductive exploration of theoretical constructs, drawing insights from existing management literature, case studies, and conceptual frameworks (Ngulube et al., 2015).

By synthesizing and interpreting existing theoretical perspectives, this study offers a comprehensive understanding of how blockchain can develop disruptive EIs in waste management.

Building a conceptual framework based on an inductive approach, this research focuses on allowing theoretical insights to emerge naturally, avoiding predetermined hypotheses or rigid methodologies associated with deductive approaches (Parker & Roffey, 1997).

Therefore, this study aims to contribute to the existing body of knowledge by proposing a conceptual framework with theoretical linkages. It serves as a foundational exploration, laying the groundwork for future empirical research initiatives and practical applications within the domain. The inductive approach based on previous case studies fosters a nuanced understanding of the theoretical implications of blockchain in waste management, paving the way for a deeper comprehension of its transformative potential (Spanò et al., 2021).

4.4 Presentation and Analysis of Findings: Disruptive Eco-innovation in the Waste Management Sector

Literature Summary

This research shows some projects, supported by the blockchain in the waste management sector, that have unique characteristics compared to incremental EIs, differing in terms of stakeholders involved, environmental impacts, and social implications.

First, the Brazilian projects show that low-income families are directly involved in the waste management sector (França et al., 2020). Furthermore, these projects bring several environmental benefits: encouraging new public policies for recycling solid domestic wastes and reducing solid waste in landfills, land, vacant lots, backyards, and roads (França et al., 2020).

Furthermore, these initiatives yield two primary social advantages: a boost in municipal health indices through the reduction of Dengue, Zika, and Chikungunya infections linked to youth and children who understand the benefits of responsible solid waste management, and an enhancement in economic well-being for marginalized and stakeholder groups who reap the rewards of waste incentives (França et al., 2020). Second, this research shows that different stakeholders have been involved in the Indian context. Indeed, Grassroots entrepreneurs, and NGOs, are directly involved in the management of local medical waste (Ajwani-Ramchandani et al., 2021). Instead, from an environmental point of view, these projects aim to reduce waste, improve resource management, and encourage people to use less environmentally impactful products (Ajwani-Ramchandani et al., 2021). Furthermore, from a social standpoint, Indian initiatives aim to advocate for actions guided by democratic, consensus-based rules that engage various stakeholders in waste management processes, facilitating the adoption and enforcement of new practices.

For this reason, the blockchain simplifies sanitary waste disposal and agreements between local urban bodies, citizen community members, and entrepreneurs to avoid conflicts. Finally, Indian waste management projects aspire to change society. People and cooperatives can sell sanitary waste for money, boosting the income of the most vulnerable groups. It can also encourage new business models to strengthen the relationship among territorial stakeholders and advance gender equality (Ajwani-Ramchandani et al., 2021). Third, farmers in China actively participate in the management of agricultural waste, thanks to the incentives offered by waste recovery companies (Zhang, 2019). From an environmental point of view, this project improves ecosystem conditions and reduces CO_2 emissions through energy recovery, by-product production, and more efficient waste recycling (Zhang, 2019). Moreover, this project exerts a significant social impact. Companies generating waste will no longer need to separate plastics from mixed residential waste, eliminating the need for workers to be exposed to health-hazardous working conditions. For farmers taking on the responsibility of waste separation, female workers in these enterprises no longer have to engage in waste segregation. This advancement enhances health conditions, eliminating the exposure of these workers to toxic wastes (Zhang, 2019).

Conceptual Framework: Disruptive EIs in the Waste Management Sector

The conceptual framework incorporates complex interconnections among institutional, environmental, and social systems as illustrated in Fig. 4.1.

This framework offers a holistic perspective that reveals the transformative capacity of disruptive EIs in the waste sector. It transcends technological progress, exploring the intricate interplay among institutions, the environment, and social structures. As illustrated in Fig. 4.1, these interlinked systems are dynamic and mutually impactful, influencing the course of innovation in waste management. These connections emphasize the importance of holistic, integrated approaches to foster sustainable and effective disruptive EIs in waste management. Hence, this

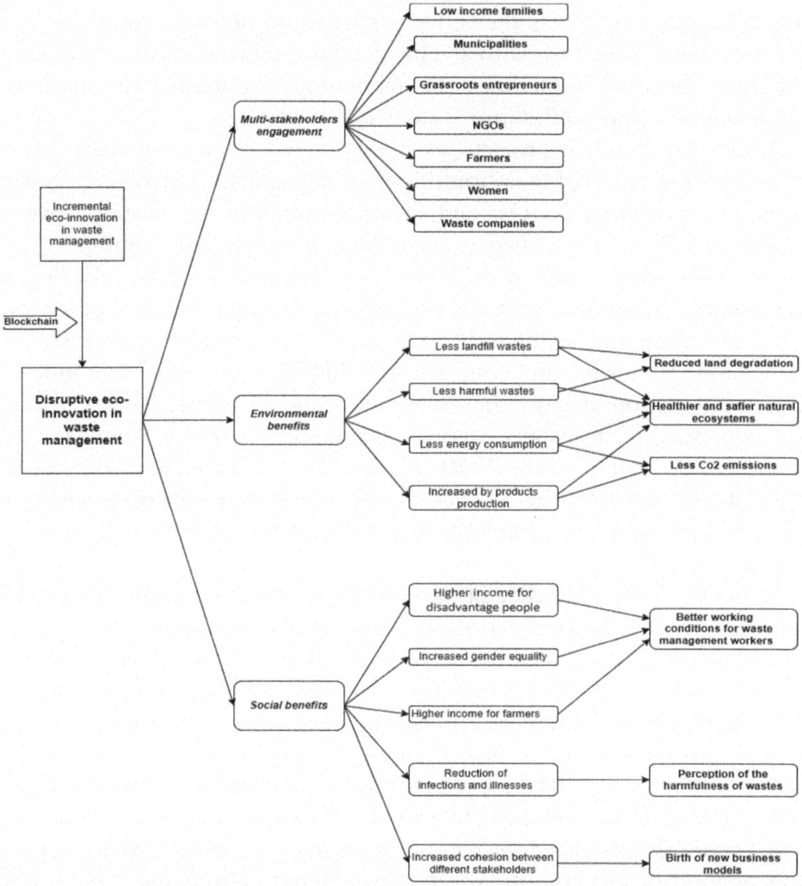

Fig. 4.1 Disruptive eco-innovation in the waste management sector

framework acts as a guiding paradigm, facilitating a nuanced examination of disruptive EIs. It underscores the symbiotic connection among institutions, the environment, and social systems, providing a roadmap for fostering transformative changes in the waste management sector.

From the multi-stakeholder engagement point of view, the Blockchain emerges as a catalyst for inclusivity and transformative change in the waste management sector, particularly by fostering the engagement of diverse stakeholders. Notably, in Brazil, França et al. (2020) showcase how blockchain facilitates the active participation of low-income families in waste management initiatives. This not only addresses socio-economic disparities but also underlines the technology's potential to integrate marginalized communities into sustainable practices.

Additionally, Indian projects, as highlighted by Ajwani-Ramchandani et al. (2021), exemplify a multifaceted engagement involving grassroots entrepreneurs, NGOs, and local communities in waste recovery endeavors. This diversified stakeholder involvement signifies the blockchain's adaptability to different socio-cultural contexts, enabling a collaborative approach toward sustainable waste management practices. The blockchain role extends beyond mere participation; it serves as a cornerstone for instituting a multi-stakeholder waste management model. This model, grounded in the economic value of waste, fosters mutually beneficial relationships among stakeholders (Ajwani-Ramchandani et al., 2021; França et al., 2020; Zhang, 2019). By recognizing waste as a valuable resource, the blockchain encourages active involvement and collaboration, aligning economic incentives with environmental sustainability.

Moreover, the blockchain promotes democratic principles and consensus-driven actions. The inherent transparency and efficiency of blockchain simplify agreements between businesses, community members, and local authorities. This streamlined decision-making process optimizes waste management strategies, mitigating conflicts and promoting the harmonious coexistence of diverse interests (Ajwani-Ramchandani et al., 2021; França et al., 2020). Going beyond conventional waste management paradigms, the blockchain facilitates the expansion of supply chains into previously untapped sectors. For instance, it enables the integration of food producers into waste management ecosystems. This novel approach involves the exchange of garbage and waste for energy sources, by-products, or tokens, creating a symbiotic relationship that contributes to both waste reduction and the sustainability of the supply chain (Zhang, 2019).

In conclusion, the blockchain's ability to empower stakeholders, foster collaboration, and redefine waste as a valuable resource signifies its transformative potential in revolutionizing traditional waste management practices. As this technology continues to evolve, its inclusive and democratic principles hold promise for a more sustainable and harmonized approach to waste management on a global scale. Moreover, the blockchain emerges as a transformative force not only by integrating new stakeholders in waste management but also as a catalyst for significant environmental benefits. By introducing new organizational forms in the waste management sector, projects supported by blockchain actively contribute to heightened awareness among citizens regarding the merits of recycling, ultimately leading to a substantial reduction in household waste directed toward landfills (França et al., 2020). Moreover, the blockchain's impact extends to the optimized management of hazardous wastes, particularly in the realms of medical and organic waste. Ajwani-Ramchandani et al. (2021) and Zhang (2019) highlight this technology's prowess in enhancing the handling, disposal, and reuse of such critical waste categories. This not only ensures the safeguarding of ecosystems but also contributes to improving soil quality, as hazardous wastes find alternative and sustainable disposal pathways beyond traditional landfills. Beyond waste reduction, the blockchain plays a pivotal role in the transformation of waste into valuable resources, such as energy or by-products. This innovative approach not only minimizes the environmental impact associated with waste but also addresses climate concerns. Through waste energy recovery and the creation of products from waste materials, the blockchain becomes a potent tool for reducing CO_2 emissions, thereby positively impacting air quality (Zhang, 2019).

In essence, the blockchain's multifaceted contributions to waste management underscore its role in improving environmental conditions. By fostering awareness, optimizing hazardous waste management, and actively participating in the transformation of waste into valuable resources, this technology stands at the forefront of environmental practices. As waste management continues to evolve, blockchain integration into environmental conservation efforts offers a promising pathway toward a cleaner, healthier planet by making the waste management sector less impactful.

Finally, the application of blockchain technology goes beyond operational enhancements, ushering in systemic changes with profound social benefits. Notably, the heightened awareness of waste's harmful impacts, particularly among vulnerable groups like children, teenagers, and disadvantaged communities, has led to a significant reduction in infections and diseases, including the prevention of outbreaks such as Zika (França et al., 2020). Territorial cohesion, a critical aspect of community development, has been bolstered by blockchain interventions, as evidenced by studies conducted by França et al. (2020) and Zhang (2019). This technology acts as a unifying force, fostering collaboration among diverse stakeholders in waste management practices. Furthermore, blockchain plays a leading role in promoting gender equality. Designs like those explored by Ajwani-Ramchandani et al. (2021) show how blockchain normalizes the management of women's healthcare products. These products go from being a taboo for the female population to a resource for the community, helping to create a more inclusive and equitable society. Additionally, the blockchain has significantly improved working and health conditions for those involved in waste management, as highlighted by Zhang (2019). This technology, promoting transparent and traceable transactions, guarantees safer environments for workers.

Instead, from an economic point of view, blockchain has been used to improve the economic conditions of the various stakeholders interested in the waste management sector. Low-income people and women engaged in waste collection benefit from tokens that can be used to purchase essential goods. Furthermore, cooperatives and local populations find an additional source of income, while farmers participate in an exchange of waste for energy or valuable by-products provided to them by companies (Ajwani-Ramchandani et al., 2021; França et al., 2020; Zhang, 2019). In conclusion, the integration of blockchain into waste management not only revolutionizes operational processes but also emerges as a powerful force for positive social change, promoting health, equality, and economic well-being in diverse communities.

4.5 Concluding Discussion and Recommendations

This paper makes original contributions to the current debate on the role of blockchain in the implementation of disruptive EIs. First, blockchain can change the quality of ecosystems by optimizing waste management bringing economic and social benefits to different stakeholders involved in waste management processes (Ajwani-Ramchandani et al., 2021; França et al., 2020; Zhang, 2019). For this reason, we contribute to the field of EIs by offering a new conceptual framework since no previous research has addressed this topic from a theoretical point of view. Indeed, we show how blockchain can optimize waste resource management according to different aspects, creating a co-evolutionary environment for disruptive EIs in the waste management sector (Ajwani-Ramchandani et al., 2021; França et al., 2020; Zhang, 2019).

Second, this paper also contributes to the field of disruptive innovations. The blockchain can foster new forms of eco-innovation by creating new organizational and sustainable business models (Wang et al., 2022).

Third, this research contributes to the field of ecological economics. Blockchain can optimize the management of natural resources by integrating social, environmental, and economic factors based on principles that go beyond neoclassical economics principles by considering new stakeholders in waste management processes (Upadhyay et al., 2021). Fourth, this paper contributes to the innovation management literature by demonstrating how blockchain can support new organizational forms. Entrepreneurs and citizens can use blockchain to create decentralized organizations without hierarchical structure in the waste management sector (Balaguer Rasillo, 2021; Toufaily et al., 2021).

Finally, our paper contributes to the field of development studies. The blockchain can help to achieve long-term sustainability by supporting the creation of disruptive EIs in developing countries that engage people at the bottom of the pyramid (Bai et al., 2020).

4.6 Managerial Implications

Furthermore, our research also provides some interesting managerial contributions. First, we show that the blockchain can stimulate new organizational forms of waste management in which different stakeholders play an active role (Kouhizadeh et al., 2021). This study aims to show different applications of disruptive EIs in the waste management sector where citizens, entrepreneurs, and governments collaborate to create new business models that include the most disadvantaged stakeholders.

Furthermore, this study carries policy implications since to stimulate disruptive EIs, institutions should intervene to support the implementation of new projects (Christensen et al., 2018). There is not just the need to create laws that allow the use of blockchain in a specific context but it is also necessary for institutions to provide incentives to involve different stakeholders in waste management projects. For this reason, given the specific characteristics of these innovative organizational models, governments have to spur the birth of disruptive EI by creating socio-technical niches that favor the creation of innovative models of waste management (Geels, 2018). Additionally, this research aims to give greater prominence to projects still in the experimental phase but with significant social and environmental impacts. Therefore, we want to stimulate the creation of ad hoc programs within government institutions (such as, for example, the EU and the World Bank) that can simplify the birth of disruptive EI in the waste management sector.

To conclude, through our conceptual framework, we have shown how the blockchain plays a primary role in spurring disruptive eco-innovation in the waste management sector, bringing well-being to the most disadvantaged groups (França et al., 2020; Zhang, 2019). According to our analysis, the blockchain can involve new actors, redistribute revenues, improve hygienic conditions, improve social cohesion between the different actors, improve conditions of natural ecosystems, and improve the sustainability of developing countries (Gillpatrick et al., 2022; Thomason et al., 2018). Nevertheless, our study has several limitations. First, our research has primarily focused on theoretical exploration. Consequently, it is necessary to expand this research by delving into specific case studies. This entails expanding this research through the analysis of qualitative case studies by conducting interviews with diverse stakeholders to comprehensively grasp the impacts of these projects and the intricate involvement of various stakeholders.

Second, future researchers have to extend their analysis to encompass additional sectors such as energy (Gibellato et al., 2022). This analysis is necessary to ascertain that the findings of this study can be extrapolated to different domains, investigating whether blockchain plays a pivotal role in the creation of disruptive EIs across various sectors. Third, this study did not analyze the adverse aspects associated with blockchain utilization. These issues include environmental concerns due to the high energy consumption of blockchain technology, and the institutional limitations in certain countries where blockchain use is restricted (Wang et al., 2021). Fourth, future research in the realm of disruptive EIs supported by blockchain should emphasize the different aspects that have been highlighted. This is essential for validating the theoretical framework. Furthermore, broadening the research scope to be able to compare different sectors would offer valuable insights into the adaptability of blockchain across different contexts. Fifth, to address environmental apprehensions surrounding blockchain, future researchers should conduct comprehensive assessments of the ecological footprint of this technology. Sixth, it will be fundamental to explore the influence of social and cultural factors on the adoption of blockchain in waste management initiatives. A detailed analysis of policies and regulations governing blockchain technology in this context is crucial.

Finally, comparing blockchain technology with other technologies useful for improving the waste management sector will be important to understand whether blockchain is the most suitable technology to support the creation of new organizational and business models in waste management.

References

Ahl, A., Goto, M., Yarime, M., Tanaka, K., & Sagawa, D. (2022). Challenges and opportunities of blockchain energy applications: Interrelatedness among technological, economic, social, environmental, and institutional dimensions. *Renewable and Sustainable Energy Reviews, 166*, 112623.

Ajwani-Ramchandani, R., Figueira, S., de Oliveira, R. T., Jha, S., Ramchandani, A., & Schuricht, L. (2021). Towards a circular economy for packaging waste by using new technologies: The case of large multinationals in emerging economies. *Journal of Cleaner Production, 281*, 125139.

Aldieri, L., Gatto, A., & Vinci, C. P. (2022). Is there any room for renewable energy innovation in developing and transition economies? Data envelopment analysis of energy behaviour and resilience data. *Resources, Conservation and Recycling, 186*, 106587.

Bai, C. A., Cordeiro, J., & Sarkis, J. (2020). Blockchain technology: Business, strategy, the environment, and sustainability. *Business Strategy and the Environment, 29*(1), 321–322.

Balaguer Rasillo, X. (2021). Alternative economies, digital innovation and commoning in grassroots organizations: Analysing degrowth currencies in the Spanish region of Catalonia. *Environmental Policy and Governance, 31*(3), 175–185.

Baralla, G., Pinna, A., Tonelli, R., & Marchesi, M. (2023). Waste management: A comprehensive state of the art about the rise of blockchain technology. *Computers in Industry, 145*, 103812.

Berkhout, F., Smith, A., & Stirling, A. (2004). Socio-technological regimes and transition contexts. In *System innovation and the transition to sustainability: Theory, evidence and policy* (44(106), pp. 48–75). Edward Elgar.

Buhalis, D., Efthymiou, L., Uzunboylu, N., & Thrassou, A. (2024). 'Charting the progress of technology adoption in tourism and hospitality in the era of Industry 4.0'. Tourism & hospitality in the digital era: Technology and its (im)possibilities. *A Special Issue in Euromed Journal of Business*. https://doi.org/10.1108/EMJB-11-2023-0310

Carrillo-Hermosilla, J., Del Río, P., & Könnölä, T. (2010). Diversity of eco-innovations: Reflections from selected case studies. *Journal of Cleaner Production, 18*(10), 1073–1083.

Chaminade, C. (2020). Innovation for what? Unpacking the role of innovation for weak and strong sustainability. *Journal of Sustainability Research, 2*(1), 1–16.

Christensen, C. M., McDonald, R., Altman, E. J., & Palmer, J. E. (2018). Disruptive innovation: An intellectual history and directions for future research. *Journal of Management Studies, 55*(7), 1043–1078.

De Jesus, A., Antunes, P., Santos, R., & Mendonça, S. (2019). Eco-innovation pathways to a circular economy: Envisioning priorities through a Delphi approach. *Journal of Cleaner Production, 228*, 1494–1513.

Dierksmeier, C., & Seele, P. (2020). Blockchain and business ethics. *Business Ethics: A European Review, 29*(2), 348–359.

Dogaru, L. (2020). Eco-innovation and the contribution of companies to the sustainable development. *Procedia Manufacturing, 46*, 294–298.

Durán-Romero, G., López, A. M., Beliaeva, T., Ferasso, M., Garonne, C., & Jones, P. (2020). Bridging the gap between circular economy and climate change mitigation policies through eco innovations and Quintuple Helix Model. *Technological Forecasting and Social Change, 160*, 120246.

Enescu, F. M., Bizon, N., Onu, A., Răboacă, M. S., Thounthong, P., Mazare, A. G., & Şerban, G. (2020). Implementing blockchain technology in irrigation systems that integrate photovoltaic energy generation systems. *Sustainability, 14*(4), 1540.

Fernández, S., Torrecillas, C., & Labra, R. E. (2021). Drivers of eco-innovation in developing countries: The case of Chilean firms. *Technological Forecasting and Social Change, 170*, 120902.

França, A. S. L., Neto, J. A., Gonçalves, R. F., & Almeida, C. M. V. B. (2020), Proposing the use of blockchain to improve the solid waste management in small municipalities. *Journal of Cleaner Production, 244*, 118529.

Geels, F. W. (2018). Disruption and low-carbon system transformation: Progress and new challenges in socio-technical transitions research and the multi-level perspective. *Energy Research & Social Science, 37*, 224–231.

Genovese, A., & Pansera, M. (2021). The circular economy at a crossroads: Technocratic eco-modernism or convivial technology for social revolution? *Capitalism Nature Socialism, 32*(2), 95–113.

George, G., Merrill, R. K., & Schillebeeckx, S. J. (2021). Digital sustainability and entrepreneurship: How digital innovations are helping tackle climate change and sustainable development. *Entrepreneurship Theory and Practice, 45*(5), 999–1027.

Gibellato, S., Ballestra, L. V., Fiano, F., Graziano, D., & Gregori, G. L. (2023). The impact of education on the Energy Trilemma Index: A sustainable innovativeness perspective for resilient energy systems. *Applied Energy, 330*, 120352.

Gibellato, S., Iaia, L., Fiano, F., & Usai, A. (2022). Renewable energy communities and degrowth: Participative governance for energy management. In *2022 IEEE international conference on technology management, operations and decisions (ICTMOD)* (pp. 1–8). IEEE.

Gillpatrick, T., Boğa, S., & Aldanmaz, O. (2022). How can blockchain contribute to developing country economies? A literature review on application areas. *Economics, 10*(1), 105–128.

Gowdy, J., & Erickson, J. D. (2005). The approach of ecological economics. *Cambridge Journal of Economics, 29*(2), 207–222.

Gutberlet, J. (2021). Grassroots waste picker organizations addressing the UN sustainable development goals. *World Development, 138*, 105195.

Hafeez, M., Rehman, S. U., Faisal, C. N., Yang, J., Ullah, S., Kaium, M. A., & Malik, M. Y. (2022). Financial efficiency and its impact on renewable energy demand and CO_2 emissions: Do eco-innovations matter for highly polluted Asian economies? *Sustainability, 14*(17), 10950.

Hazarika, N., & Zhang, X. (2019). Evolving theories of eco-innovation: A systematic review. *Sustainable Production and Consumption, 19*, 64–78.

Hua, W., & Sun, H. (2019). A blockchain-based peer-to-peer trading scheme coupling energy and carbon markets. In *2019 international conference on smart energy systems and technologies* (pp. 1–6). IEEE.

Imenda, S. (2014). Is there a conceptual difference between theoretical and conceptual frameworks? *Journal of Social Sciences, 38*(2), 185–195.

Jiménez-Parra, B., Alonso-Martínez, D., & Godos-Díez, J. L. (2018). The influence of corporate social responsibility on air pollution: Analysis of environmental regulation and eco-innovation effects. *Corporate Social Responsibility and Environmental Management, 25*(6), 1363–1375.

Kouhizadeh, M., Saberi, S., & Sarkis, J. (2021). Blockchain technology and the sustainable supply chain: Theoretically exploring adoption barriers. *International Journal of Production Economics, 231*, 107831.

Kouhizadeh, M., Zhu, Q., & Sarkis, J. (2020). Blockchain and the circular economy: Potential tensions and critical reflections from practice. *Production Planning & Control, 31*(11), 950–966.

Mutisya, E., & Yarime, M. (2011). Understanding the grassroots dynamics of slums in Nairobi: The dilemma of Kibera informal settlements. *International Transaction Journal of Engineering, Management, & Applied Sciences & Technologies, 2*(2), 197–213.

Nair, R., Gupta, S., Soni, M., Shukla, P. K., & Dhiman, G. (2020). An approach to minimize the energy consumption during blockchain transaction. *Materials Today: Proceedings*. https://doi.org/10.1016/j.matpr.2020.10.361

Ngulube, P., Mathipa, E. R., & Gumbo, M. T. (2015). Theoretical and conceptual frameworks in the social and management sciences. In *Addressing research challenges: Making headway in developing researchers* (43–66). Mosala-Masedi Publishers.

Notteboom, T., Pallis, T., & Rodrigue, J. P. (2021). Disruptions and resilience in global container shipping and ports: The COVID-19 pandemic versus the 2008–2009 financial crisis. *Maritime Economics & Logistics, 23*(2), 179–210.

Parker, L. D., & Roffey, B. H. (1997). Methodological themes: Back to the drawing board: Revisiting grounded theory and the everyday accountant's and manager's reality. *Accounting, Auditing & Accountability Journal, 10*(2), 212–247.

Parmentola, A., Petrillo, A., Tutore, I., & De Felice, F. (2022). Is blockchain able to enhance environmental sustainability? A systematic review and research agenda from the perspective of Sustainable Development Goals (SDGs). *Business Strategy and the Environment, 31*(1), 194–217.

Petri, I., Barati, M., Rezgui, Y., & Rana, O. F. (2020). Blockchain for energy sharing and trading in distributed prosumer communities. *Computers in Industry, 123*, 103282.

Rennings, K. (2000). Redefining innovation—Eco-innovation research and the contribution from ecological economics. *Ecological Economics, 32*(2), 319–332.

Rikken, O., Janssen, M., & Kwee, Z. (2019). Governance challenges of blockchain and decentralized autonomous organizations. *Information Polity, 24*(4), 397–417.

Rösch, T., Treffinger, P., & Koch, B. (2021). Regional flexibility markets—Solutions to the European energy distribution grid—A systematic review and research agenda. *Energies, 14*(9), 2403.

Seyfang, G., & Smith, A. (2007). Grassroots innovations for sustainable development: Towards a new research and policy agenda. *Environmental Politics, 16*(4), 584–603.

Shin, D., & Ibahrine, M. (2020). The socio-technical assemblages of blockchain system: How blockchains are framed and how the framing reflects societal contexts. *Digital Policy, Regulation and Governance, 22*(3), 245–263.

Spanò, R., Massaro, M., & Iacuzzi, S. (2021). Blockchain for value creation in the healthcare sector. *Technovation, 120*, 102440.

Swartz, L. (2017). Blockchain dreams: Imagining techno-economic alternatives after Bitcoin. In *Another economy is possible: Culture and economy in a time of crisis* (Chapter 4). Polity Press.

Thomason, J., Ahmad, M., Bronder, P., Hoyt, E., Pocock, S., Bouteloupe, J., et al. (2018). Blockchain—Powering and empowering the poor in developing countries. In *Transforming climate finance and green investment with blockchains* (pp. 137–152). Academic Press.

Tong, S., & Ebi, K. (2019). Preventing and mitigating health risks of climate change. *Environmental Research, 174*, 9–13.

Toufaily, E., Zalan, T., & Dhaou, S. B. (2021). A framework of blockchain technology adoption: An investigation of challenges and expected value. *Information & Management, 58*(3), 103444.

Upadhyay, A., Mukhuty, S., Kumar, V., & Kazancoglu, Y. (2021). Blockchain technology and the circular economy: Implications for sustainability and social responsibility. *Journal of Cleaner Production, 293*, 126130.

Vence, X., & Pereira, Á. (2019). Eco-innovation and circular business models as drivers for a circular economy. *Contaduría y administración, 64*(1), 1–7.

Vrontis, D., Thrassou, A., Efthymiou, L., Weber, Y., Shams, S. M. R., & Tsoukatos, E. (2023a). *Business for sustainability, Volume I: Strategic avenues and managerial approaches*. Springer Nature. https://doi.org/10.1007/978-3-031-37361-9.

Vrontis, D., Thrassou, A., Uzunboylu, N., & Efthymiou, L. (2023b). An overview of business for sustainability: Strategic avenues and managerial approaches. In D. Vrontis, A. Thrassou, L. Efthymiou, Y. Weber, S. M. R. Shams, & E. Tsoukatos (Eds.), *Business for Sustainability, Volume I*. Palgrave Studies in Cross-disciplinary Business Research, In Association with EuroMed Academy of Business. Palgrave Macmillan. https://doi.org/10.1007/978-3-031-37361-9_1

Wang, H., Masi, D., Dhamotharan, L., Day, S., Kumar, A., Li, T., & Singh, G. (2022). Unconventional path dependence: How adopting product take-back and recycling systems contributes to future eco innovations. *Journal of Business Research, 142*, 707–717.

Wang, W., Xu, H.,Alazab, M.,Gadekallu, T. R.,Han, Z., &Su, C. (2021). Blockchain-based reliable and efficient certificate less signature for IIoT devices. *IEEE Transactions on Industrial Informatics, 18*(10), 7059–7067.

Zhang, D. (2019). Application of blockchain technology in incentivizing efficient use of rural wastes: A case study on Yitong system. *Energy Procedia, 158*, 6707–6714.

CHAPTER 5

Managing Intellectual Capital as a Pathway to Improved Performance: Perspectives from Healthcare Organizations

Johana Hajdini, Lea Iaia, Marco Pironti, and Federica Cavallo

5.1 Introduction

The healthcare services are continuously facing pressures to improve performance, to meet the changing needs of populations, to adhere to financial restrictions and allocated budgets, as well as to increase quality

J. Hajdini (✉)
Department of Management and Business Administration, University G. d' Annunzio of Chieti-Pescara, Pescara, Italy
e-mail: johana.hajdini@unich.it

L. Iaia · M. Pironti
Department of Computer Science, University of Turin, Turin, Italy
e-mail: lea.iaia@unito.it

M. Pironti
e-mail: marco.pironti@unito.it

D. Vrontis et al. (eds.), *Business in Uncertainty*, Palgrave Studies in Cross-disciplinary Business Research, In Association with EuroMed Academy of Business, https://doi.org/10.1007/978-3-031-65587-6_5

and efficiency of patient care while keeping costs down (Hewko & Cummings, 2016; van der Geer et al., 2009). The system of healthcare services is a very complex and specific system for the nature itself of the final product it offers: the health of the individual. As such a system, constructed to fulfill the need of "a good health", we should outline that healthcare providers need to ensure "a good performance" of the care provided to customers, that in our context are the patients. Intangible resources are of relevant importance when considering the need to improve performance of healthcare organizations (Carlucci & Schiuma, 2012b). Along with time, several performance indicators have been used to measure healthcare performance: starting from financial indicators focusing at cost per patient care, profit contribution and earnings of a healthcare provider, to quality indicators which for a long time were mostly focused on patient satisfaction as the main indicator of quality of care, and finally institutional indicators developed and controlled from the state apparatus such as mortality rates, bed occupation rates, days of hospitalization, etc.

Despite the large number of indicators developed in the field, the last decades have seen an increased interest to the intangible assets and their influence in the performance of any organization. The intellectual capital (IC) is one of the intangible assets of an organization and its components defined as "*human competencies*, the knowledge embedded in people; *structural capital*, the knowledge embedded in the organization and its systems; and *relational capital*, the knowledge embedded in customers and other relationships external to the organization" (Guthrie et al., 2012, p. 70), can be of interest when assessing performance. Moreover, research has suggested that knowledge-intensive services such as healthcare can experience specific improved performance outcomes if they enhance their IC (Evans et al., 2015).

The topic is yet very fragmented and surrounded with confusion when related to the prioritizing of IC characterized by diverse conceptualizations with a focus on metrics and limited empirical evidence, which calls for a more comprehensive understanding and the synthetizing of extant research from which future investigations can be recommended, instead

F. Cavallo
Department of Economic Sciences, University of Salento, Lecce, Italy
e-mail: federica.cavallo@unisalento.it

of crafting the same old topics. Several researchers have identified the lack of a comprehensive understanding of the IC and the role it plays in the value creation process (Dameri & Ferrando, 2021), and report highly heterogeneous results and contradictory findings when related to performance outcomes (Pflugfelder, 2021). Moreover, considering the impact of the topic not only to the academic communities to bring research forward, but also to the practitioners and the entire society, this study finds motivation.

Following the main interest in understanding how IC relates to healthcare service performance and most specifically, how improvements in IC can derive improvements in performance outcomes, several research questions were developed. Performance is considered as one of the strategic objectives of an organization, and the current investigation aims to understand the most researched mechanisms through which IC can influence the performance of a healthcare organization. Moreover, this investigation will help to understand the evolution of the topic within the domain and address a research agenda for the future. Thus, the following research questions guided the actual study:

> RQ1. How is literature on healthcare performance evolving through the IC lens?
> RQ2. What are the most researched mechanisms and/or components through which IC is researched in terms of healthcare organizations performance?
> RQ3. What are the limits and future trends within the domain?

This study demonstrates how research has evolved in the context of healthcare organizations and how the focus shifted from the consideration of skills and competences to the improved management of organizations.

The chapter is structured as follows. In the next section a literature review is presented, followed by the research design. Then, the results of the investigation are reported, where the two first research questions (RQ1 and RQ2) find answers. Section four presents concluding discussions and recommendations. As final to this, research limitations and future research avenues are provided, answering the third research question (RQ3).

5.2 Literature Review

The term of IC is widely employed in an overarching manner to include human capital, organizational capital (or structural capital) and relational capital. Decomposing its components (Petty & Guthrie, 2000a): organizational capital refers to proprietary software systems, networks and supply chains; human capital refers to human resources within the organization and external to the organization, including customers and suppliers; relational capital refers to all relationships as well as external components like collaborations, stakeholder cooperation, and brand identity. In literature the terms of "intellectual capital" and "intangible assets" are frequently used interchangeably, even though they are quite distinct. An important distinction comes from the work of OECD that places IC as a subset of the entire intangible assets (OECD—Secretariat, 1998). The knowledge and skills of professionals account among the most valuable assets of any knowledge-intensive organization. Healthcare organizations' intellectual capital, one of the key intangibles that contributes to competitive advantage and firm value, is comprised of the value obtained from both internal and external interactions (Petty & Guthrie, 2000a). Different components of IC, as well as various methods and capabilities for exploiting it, may help to explain variations in how well healthcare organizations perform. In the healthcare context, considering the know-how among other resources is the enabler of the system, understanding and managing IC gains increased importance. Yet very few healthcare organizations manage the IC in accordance with their strategic plans. IC is rarely quantified and monitored in meaningful ways that go beyond the use of indicators that are mandatory to measure and report in a country level by legislation. Mostly companies focus on financial and tangible capital, which is commonly measured and reported as considered important for the survival of the organization.

Contrary to the literature on healthcare, the general scholarship on IC acknowledges important attention to financial value and therefore is contingent to financial evaluation methods. This said, in measurement approach a percentage of the organizations' worth is assigned to the different assets that are reported in the balance sheet (Evans et al., 2015), and the remained value is assigned to the intangible assets, making it difficult to understand its real contribution to the organizations' value.

The area of IC is diverse, and it extends from management to financing, leadership, and much more (Kianto et al., 2013). Several authors have focused on the importance of IC management and have provided different definitions. According to Sullivan (1999), management of IC refers to a balancing between company's IC and its vision. Yet, other authors stress the importance of management of IC as a need to monitor, measure and manage organizations' practices in order to be prepared to challenges and opportunities coming from the competitive environment across different business industries (Leliaert et al., 2003; Petty & Guthrie, 2000b). Summing up, IC management is an important managerial practice that should ensure a proper strategic planning of the organization to the execution of activities that exploit intangibles in a way that generates value (Bornemann et al. 1999). It is not surprising though that there exist different approaches to measure IC. They are basically a mix of different aspects of organizations that align with their strategic plans, that use either theoretical underpinnings or rely on heuristics that are susceptible due to constraints related with the time and the context on which they were established. Therefore, it is still debated in literature the possibility to capture IC and to manage it in the organizational context.

The above discussion gets even more complicated when considering the healthcare context. On its own, the healthcare system faces a complexity of performance evaluation as it represents the interests of different and diverging stakeholders. For a long time, the Balanced Scorecard method (BSC) has been widely used to report financial and non-financial indicators. In extant research there is a lack of clarity related to the concept, as well as a lack of methodological rigor (Evans et al., 2015). Moreover, empirical studies rely mostly on measuring than managing IC, thus raising the need to adopt a managerial approach in developing a set of guidelines that help organizations in the prioritization of IC and achievement of improved performance.

So far, the majority of the research on IC in healthcare context has been on the organizational level. Even though more research is needed to improve understanding of the nature and impact of IC at the organizational level, IC is also significant to the development of inter-organizational networks and health system performance. Despite the fact that different data sources and indicators are suggested, only general, high-level suggestions and examples are offered on how organizations utilize or attempt to enhance IC. The concept of transforming data into knowledge and knowledge into products and services to fulfill the market needs or to offer public goods such as healthcare, is ultimately what the difficulties of assessing IC and managing knowledge boil down to.

5.3 Research Design

Considering the main aim of this study and the identified need to develop a more comprehensive understanding of the IC for improved performance in the healthcare context, the decision to use a qualitative approach based on a structured literature review, seems appropriate to the purpose. The interest in literature review is growing due to the importance of synthetizing abundant information consisting of diverse views or lacking a common consensus among researchers (Ferrari, 2015). It responds to the need to summarize data on IC in healthcare performance and to explore the narrative of the articles selected for this review, to report the state of research, the most researched components, the trend in the literature and possible limits to overcome in the future.

The databases of Scopus, EBSCO and Web of Science were searched using a combination of terms such as "performance", "intellectual capital", and "healthcare". The combination of keywords was searched in the title, abstract and keywords. This step provided a total of 146 results considering all the three datasets (respectively 35 results from EBSCO, 85 results from Scopus, and 26 results from Web of Science). Next a set of inclusion and exclusion criteria was applied to the extraction of articles. The inclusion and exclusion criteria were chosen to ensure the quality of the articles to be considered for the sample, as well as to better reflect the aim of this research and answer the research questions. The search in EBSCO and Web of Science was limited to research articles, published in academic peer-reviewed journals, and published in English language, while the search on Scopus was limited to research articles in the business, management and accounting area and English language. In this step from all the results, 69 articles were eligible according to these criteria. From the 69 results, only articles published in ABS ranked journals (1, 2, 3, 4, 4* journals) were considered. This is done to ensure the quality of the articles in the sample as journals included in the ABS ranking prove to be of high rigor and quality. Therefore, the results were further restricted to a total of 39 articles in this step. No restriction to a specific time-period was considered as the aim is to capture the full evolution of the debate from the very beginning, when the concept was initially introduced in healthcare performance research. After the search and the inclusion and exclusion criteria application, to assess the relevance of the 39 articles, full text reading was considered. In this step a check for duplicates was performed. 9 articles were excluded, leaving a total of 30 articles in our final sample, to be considered for further analysis. The small sample of articles is a first insight that an integration of the IC perspective to the management of performance in the healthcare context is still at its early stages, with the focus in measuring, managing and reporting for external parties and lacks a multi-focused approach of integration, which less than a decade ago was also found for other organizations than the ones in the healthcare industry (Dumay et al., 2020). The flow chart of the search strategy is reported in Fig. 5.1.

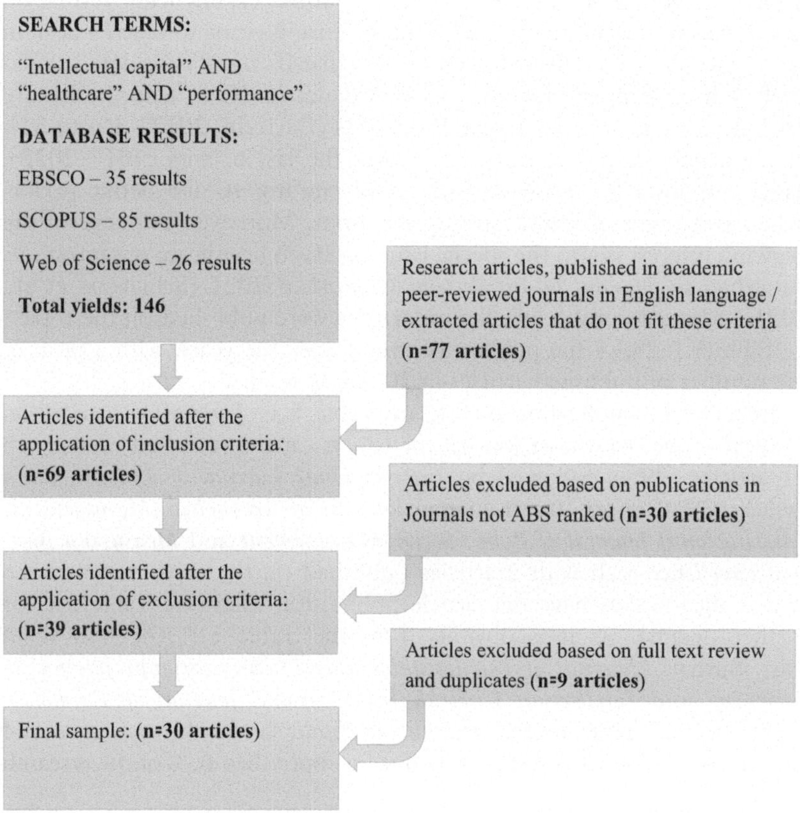

Fig. 5.1 Flow chart of search strategy

5.4 Results

Literature Evolution

From the analysis of articles in the sample, considering the adoption of the eligibility criteria, we find that 28 articles have been published on the topic in an eighteen-year period (2004–2022); this may be attributable to the growing attention on IC for the improvement of healthcare performance in the recent years. It is important to note that even though no time restriction was introduced to the article's selection process, the first studies in the sample account to the year 2004, experiencing several up and downs in the number of publications during years, to reach a peak in year 2020 ($N = 7$). This enforces the idea that IC is still considered a relatively new concept and literature lacks evidence on IC value for healthcare organization, as previous research suggests (Cavicchi, 2017). Up to 51% of the articles have been published over the last 6 years (2017–2022), which supports the growing interest of crafting IC for better performance outcomes of healthcare organizations. Moreover, evidence of the growing interest is also the special issue on IC in healthcare organizations published in *Journal of Intellectual Capital* in 2021 (Schiavone et al., 2021), where a number of relevant articles were published on the topic.

Table 5.1 shows the publication trend over the years, with a peak of the number of published articles in 2020 ($N = 7$).

In terms of publication outlet, see Table 5.1, *Journal of Intellectual Capital* is the main host journal for papers on the reviewed topic, with 11 articles (29%), followed by *International Journal of Learning and Intellectual Capital, International Journal of Technology Management, International Journal of Public Sector Management* and *Measuring Business Excellence* each with 2 articles published on the topic, whereas the remaining journals have one article publication each (see Table 5.1 for further details). As it is obvious from the Table 5.1, the four main host journals (*Journal of Intellectual Capital, International Journal of Learning and Intellectual Capital, International Journal of Technology Management, International Journal of Public Sector Management* and *Measuring Business Excellence*) account for more than 63% of the research publication.

Other important patterns in mapping extant research are the geographical distribution of publications and the authorship characteristics. It gives important insights to understand the most influencing countries on the discipline, as well as helps investigate the geographical outreach

Table 5.1 Publication trend over the years

Publication trend over years	*Year*							
Journals	*2004*	*2007*	*2008*	*2009*	*2011*	*2012*	*2013*	*2015*
Business Horizons		1						
Computers in Industry								
Int. J. of Learning and Intellectual Capital			1					1
Int. J. of Engineering Business Management						1		
Int. J. of Human Resource Management				1				
Int. J. of Public Sector Management								
Int. J. of Technology Management				2				
Irish Journal of Management	1							
Journal of Business Research								
Journal of Cleaner Production								
Journal of Intellectual Capital		1						
Knowledge Management Research and Practice					1			
Measuring Business Excellence						1		
Service Industries Journal							1	
Technological Forecasting and Social Change								
TQM Journal								
Total	1	2	1	3	1	2	1	1

(continued)

Table 5.1 (continued)

Publication trend over years	*Year*						
Journals	*2016*	*2017*	*2019*	*2020*	*2021*	*2022*	*Total*
Business Horizons							1
Computers in Industry				1			1
Int. J. of Learning and Intellectual Capital							2
Int. J. of Engineering Business Management							1
Int. J. of Human Resource Management							1
Int. J. of Public Sector Management				1		1	2
Int. J. of Technology Management							2
Irish Journal of Management							1
Journal of Business Research						1	1
Journal of Cleaner Production		1					1
Journal of Intellectual Capital	1	1		4	4		11
Knowledge Management Research and Practice							1
Measuring Business Excellence			1				2
Service Industries Journal							1
Technological Forecasting and Social Change						1	1
TQM Journal				1			1
Total	**1**	**2**	**1**	**7**	**4**	**3**	**30**

of publication outlets (Boulos, 2005). While regarding the authorship characteristics, they are increasingly important to understand the research teams, and the development of collaborations within the same institution or different institutions.

A total of 69 authors from universities and institutions in 12 countries were identified. When considering the first author geographical location, the sample is dominated by Italy (n = 14 authors), followed by contributions from China (n = 3 authors), India, Finland and Poland (each n = 2 authors), Australia, Canada, Finland, Germany, Greece, Iraq, Poland, UK and USA (n = 1 author each).

Next, when considering the number of authors involved in research, 43% of studies are co-authored by three or more authors and in 53% of cases they are authored by individuals working in the same institution. This calls for future collaborations that can include more than one institution, as the combination of different expertise and resources provides higher impact, and is important not only for networking, but also for the generation of new ideas and perspectives on research, answering to more complex scientific questions, as well as enriching the debate in the domain (Katz & Martin, 1997).

A further investigation is related to the most impactful publications in the domain based on the times that the articles were cited. The citation number was extracted from Google Scholar for all the articles included in the sample. The citations were extracted on 8th February 2023. Therefore, there may be variations in these numbers according to later investigations from the reported time. Analysis based on citations is commonly applied as a measurement tool of manuscript quality, and the citations of a study are important to understand the accumulation of knowledge (Crossan & Apaydin, 2010).

The five most cited articles in the sample are authored by Yang and Lin (2009), (Citations, 425); Tandon et al. (2020), (Citations, 207); Peng et al. (2007), (Citations, 205); Perrott (2007), (Citations, 173); Radaelli et al. (2011), (Citations, 107).

Going through the narratives of these articles, the first article explores the relationship that exists between human resource management and organizational performance in a healthcare setting. Authors investigate the role that IC plays in this relationship and find that "the three components of intellectual capital, namely, human capital, relational capital, and organizational capital, mediate the relationship between HRM practices and organizational performance" (Yang & Lin, 2009, p. 1965). The second most cited article focuses on only one of the IC components, particularly structural capital, and synthetizes research on blockchain technology in a healthcare organization context for the improvement of healthcare processes (Tandon et al., 2020). The next article, investigates "the critical intellectual capital elements and performance indicators regarded as important for performance management practices" (Peng et al., 2007, p. 538). The fourth most cited article crafts the knowledge management concept as a driver of performance, which is often investigated across our sample of articles (Bontis & Serenko, 2009; Kucharska, 2021; Perrott, 2007; Pflugfelder, 2021). The knowledge concept is also present in the next most cited article of the sample that "provides a clear interpretation of how intellectual capital relates to knowledge sharing" (Radaelli et al., 2011, p. 349).

These articles consist in important pillars of the domain and frame the evolution of research, while being considered as starting blocks of future investigations. Overall, considering also other articles in this sample, not only the ones represented in the most cited articles table, comes clear the shift of IC from a concept focused on skills and competences, to a more holistic understanding for improved management and increased performance within healthcare organizations.

Dominant Features of Extant Research

Most articles included in the sample, approximately 73%, are empirical articles. Out of the 22 empirical articles in the sample, the majority (N = 17 articles), adopt a quantitative approach, where the questionnaire dominates as a method to collect data. These results are a clear call for more qualitative research.

Other features to further investigate are related to the theoretical underpinnings used in the sample of articles. An understanding of the theoretical underpinnings most used in the domain gives important insights to future publications for the research design process, from the development of research question to data selection and interpretation (Collins & Stockton, 2018).

Among the most used theoretical perspectives to investigate IC in healthcare domain are the *Knowledge-based view* and *Resource-based view*. The *Resource-based view* considers the firm as a collection of distinctive resources and capabilities and assumes that high performance and competitive advantage may arise from having resources that are unique and that other organizations may be unable to imitate (Miller, 2019; Rugman & Verbeke, 2002). The *Knowledge-based view* can be considered as an extension of the *Resource-based view*, and it assumes knowledge is the most significant resource of any organization (Bollinger & Smith, 2001). Therefore, considering that organizations possess different levels of knowledge, as well as use the knowledge they possess in different ways, this contributes to the differing of performance (Grant, 1996).

Considered altogether, the common line of logic among these two theories is that high performance derives from firm capabilities in managing IC and aligning it to their strategic plans.

Other theories include *Complexity theory, Econometric theory, Economic growth theory, Human capital theory, Intellectual capital theory, Social-exchange theory, Stakeholder theory, Theory of planned behavior, Transformational leadership theory* and *Value creation theory.* Each of them finds relevance in explaining the importance of intangible resources into different contexts of investigation, with the common trait of suggesting that a combination and management of these resources exert important influence on the firm performance and account for firm value.

Most articles adopt existing measures of IC to measure human, structural and/or relational capital. Only one article from the sample extends existing measures: the article of Vishnu and Gupta (2015), that develops an extended and modified version of the Value Added Intellectual Coefficient (VAIC) model. All the other articles in the sample use previously developed and validated measures.

Among the components of IC, human capital is mainly conceptualized in terms of competences and skills, training possibilities and educational capital, as well as motivation and experience. Human capital is also considered in terms of employee satisfaction. While considering structural capital, it is conceptualized in terms of organizational capital, technological capital, resource allocation and culture. For the third component, relational capital is also reported as social capital or customer capital and conceptualized in terms of network, collaboration and support from territorial stakeholders and relations with patients.

Old Topics and New Directions

All the articles in the sample extracted for this investigation were further clustered in broad research themes. This information is important because it helps to understand the most researched themes and the emerging ones, referring to themes that have been less researched in the sample of this systematic literature review, to provide a starting point for future research, or what can be accounted as the new direction of the debate. The overall sample was distributed into 9 clusters, respectively (1) IC for improved performance; (2) IC and knowledge management; (3) IC disclosure; (4) Technologies for healthcare performance; (5) IC and innovation; (6) IC and organizational culture; (7) IC for sustainable healthcare; (8) IC for patient-centered care; and (9) IC and professional incompetence.

These results are not surprising. Of course, due to the search string, a greater number of articles will fall into the first cluster of IC for improved performance. This is in line with extant research supporting the increased importance of intangible resources when there is the need to improve performance, especially in healthcare services (Carlucci & Schiuma, 2012a). Regarding the second cluster, previous research supports that healthcare is a knowledge-based industry and knowledge plays a key role on performance (Ferreira et al., 2010; Inkinen, 2016). The third cluster contains articles on IC disclosure which is increasingly becoming important for the accountability of the firm (Melloni, 2015; Veltri et al., 2011). Next cluster contains articles on technologies for healthcare performance, which is also not surprising due to the rapid technological advancement (Buhalis et al., 2024) and the opportunities it opens to service firms to provide better services for the public and improve customer satisfaction (Bitner et al., 2000). The fifth cluster consists of IC and innovation, with 3 articles included, as it is widely accepted in extant research that the components of IC play an important role in the innovative capabilities of any organization (Edvinsson et al., 2004). Another important concept related to IC and performance of healthcare organizations from the sample of articles is the organizational structure, present in the third cluster named IC and organizational structure, consisting of two articles. It is clear to companies that certain features of the organization structure, such as hierarchy, line of authority, labor division, flexibility, etc., may affect the IC within an organization (Ramezan, 2011). Another rising and interesting topic with the introduction of the Sustainable Development Goals (SDG) is the one on sustainable healthcare in terms of economic, social and environmental sustainability challenging healthcare organizations (Bottero et al., 2015; Efthymiou et al., 2023; Vrontis et al., 2023, 2024). The two last clusters consist of single detached themes and basically are related to patient-centered care and professional incompetence, which can be considered as new emerging topics that can gain further research interest in the future.

Reporting Findings on the Integrative Conceptual Framework

A detailed analysis of the studies aimed to report findings that can be integrated within a group of categories, respectively antecedents-phenomenon-outcomes, adopted by Narayanan, Zane and Kemmerer (2011). This categorization is done purposely to be of help in addressing and understanding the benefits coming from the phenomenon, prioritization of IC in healthcare organizations, which can be a starting point of future investigations, as well as evidence of the practical role of IC when aligning objectives with strategies within organizations. Considering that the main concept of investigation is the prioritization of IC in healthcare organizations, it will consist of the phenomenon in this categorization. The articles in the sample were carefully investigated for the relevance of delivering information on possible antecedents and outcomes of IC prioritization, and this information was integrated within the framework.

The antecedents report all the pre-existing conditions that give rise to the prioritization of IC in healthcare organizations. The existence of such conditions as leadership support, stakeholder collaboration, increased competition, increased healthcare demands, etc., are some of the drivers to actions that prioritize IC within the organization. These actions on their own will result in different outcomes, benefiting the healthcare organization, the different stakeholders, etc., such as improved performance, reduced staff turnover, improved sustainability of organization, among others.

All the antecedents and outcomes have been integrated in the framework (Fig. 5.2).

5.5 Concluding Discussion and Recommendations

The purpose of this chapter was to synthetize and analyze the body of knowledge in IC and healthcare performance. Therefore, a structured review of the literature was carried to investigate papers published in the domain, to answer the three main research questions on evolution of the literature, the most researched components in terms of healthcare organizations' performance and to develop a future research agenda

ANTECEDENTS	PHENOMENON	OUTCOMES
Leadership support	**IC PRIORITIZATION IN HEALTHCARE ORGANIZATIONS**	Improved overall performance
Stakeholder collaboration		Reduced staff turnover
Increased competition		Improved sustainability of healthcare organizations
Increased healthcare demands		Competitive intelligence
Philanthropic motivation		Knowledge development and protection
Employee engagement		Maximization of competitive advantage
Learning culture		Improved social reporting
Rapidly changing and turbulent operating environments		Increased value
Corporate governance requirements		Improved work processes
Introduction of new technologies on a global scale		Increased patient satisfaction
Growing financial pressures		High quality of service
Increased digital innovation		Reduction of medical errors
Establishing a formal reporting procedure		Extended reach and responsiveness of health system
Increased healthcare expenditure		Improved decision making

Fig. 5.2 Integrative framework

based on the identified methodological gaps and unanswered questions. These findings will benefit and bring forward research in the domain. The evidence that emerged from the reviewed studies shows that IC is gaining increased interest in healthcare organizations, especially in the last years with an increased level of publication. Thus, even though the debate on IC and healthcare performance has received growing attention in the last years, it still is in its initial stage. A driver to increased interest can be partly explained by the increased competition, as well as pressure on healthcare organizations from different stakeholders. Moreover, prioritizing different components of IC has been the solution to improve stakeholders' satisfaction (Carlucci et al., 2004; Longo & Mura, 2011). In a knowledge-intensive industry such as the healthcare industry, IC is a core factor of performance and can offer competitive advantage to organizations (Tiwari, 2020). This investigation highlighted several areas requiring further attention, while considering that the debate is very much fragmented and a comprehensive approach when assessing the role of IC in performance outcomes of healthcare organizations is much needed.

Therefore, the findings of this investigation have several implications for theory and practice. From a theoretical perspective, the findings show the evolution of the concept from skill-focused investigations to emerging topics of patient-centered care and sustainable health, as well as innovative technologies, i.e., blockchain technology, as important factors for improved performance. These drivers of increased performance can be further investigated in future research for the development of strategies to optimize the benefits to organizations. Moreover, the findings contribute to theory, providing insights on the gaps in extant research while developing a list of future investigations to fill these gaps through specific methodologies and addressing questions of important potential in developing the domain. From a managerial perspective, the findings of this study offer important insights to managers to improve the performance of healthcare organizations by prioritizing specific components of IC. Going through the contents of the articles in the sample, we notice clear evidence of the use of IC as a source for value creation, to improve satisfaction of the final user, the patient, but also other actors within the complex healthcare system. An outcome-oriented approach can be helpful to understand that IC is a tool for achieving the purpose of improved performance.

From this perspective, the findings theoretically help to understand the determinants of prioritization of IC in healthcare organizations, while practically are useful to provide alignment of firm objectives with strategies, for the achievement of the desired outcomes. We strongly believe that the synthetizing of extant research and the insights provided here will be of help to future investigations and will open new directions of crafting the domain, to bring research forward and bridge the theory–practice gap of IC and performance within the healthcare context.

5.6 Limitations and Future Research Avenues

Limitations of this study concern the limited size of the sample. Considering that this study deals with a small sample of articles, that can be due to the early stages of research within the domain, or the confusion surrounding the prioritizing of IC in healthcare organizations, following a lack of a comprehensive unifying approach, future studies should consider overcoming this pitfall. Another important limitation of this study is linked with the manual screening of the literature, to assess the relevance of the articles in the result list by the insertion of the search query in the selected databases. This process in its own implies a degree of subjectivity to the article selection. Therefore, future studies can use more advanced tools to support and improve the process of article screening (i.e., revtools, etc.). Moreover, future research may discuss how IC has been interpreted and approached in a cross-cultural context. In addition, different empirical contributions can be of relevant interest, such as the reporting of case studies or best practices to bring research forward.

From a careful analysis of the reviewed articles, a list of possible future research ideas is developed. Therefore, future research is addressed on:

a. Case studies on how IC management in healthcare organizations is contributing to a better service provision.
b. Comparative studies of IC management in healthcare between eastern and western cultures.
c. An investigation of enabling factors of knowledge transfer in the healthcare services.
d. Management of knowledge and relational capital in healthcare services: best practices.

e. Evolution from human capital to integration of human, structural and relational capital. How will integration serve to better outcomes?
f. Developing a measurement approach to investigate knowledge transfer.

The above listed research ideas are just a few of the possible investigations within the domain emerging from this literature review. Other research avenues can also be of interest to the entire academic communities as well as to healthcare organizations for the practical implementation of evidence-based decision-making to improve performance outcomes.

References

Bitner, M. J., Brown, S. W., & Meuter, M. L. (2000). Technology infusion in service encounters. *Journal of the Academy of Marketing Science, 28*(1), 138–149.

Bollinger, A. S., & Smith, R. D. (2001). Managing organizational knowledge as a strategic asset. *Journal of Knowledge Management, 5*(1), 8–18.

Bontis, N., & Serenko, A. (2009). Longitudinal knowledge strategising in a long-term healthcare organisation. *International Journal of Technology Management, 47*(1–3), 250–271. https://doi.org/10.1504/ijtm.2009.024125

Bornemann, M., Knapp, A., Schneider, U., & Sixl, K. I. (1999). Holistic measurement of intellectual capital. In *International symposium: Measuring and reporting intellectual capital: Experiences, issues and prospects*. www.oecd.org/dataoecd/16/20/1947871.pdf. Accessed 4 April 2010.

Bottero, M. C., Buffoli, M., Capolongo, S., Cavagliato, E., di Noia, M., Gola, M., Speranza, S., & Volpatti, L. (2015). Healthcare sustainability challenge. *Green Energy and Technology, 218*, 31–114. https://doi.org/10.1007/978-3-319-14036-0

Boulos, M. N. K. (2005). On geography and medical journalology: a study of the geographical distribution of articles published in a leading medical informatics journal between 1999 and 2004. *International Journal of Health Geographics, 4*(1), 7. https://doi.org/10.1186/1476-072X-4-7

Buhalis, D., Efthymiou, L., Uzunboylu, N., & Thrassou, A. (2024). 'Charting the progress of technology adoption in tourism and hospitality in the era of industry 4.0'. Tourism & hospitality in the digital era: Technology and its (im)possibilities. Special Issue in *Euromed, Journal of Business*. https://doi.org/10.1108/EMJB-11-2023-0310

Carlucci, D., Marr, B., & Schiuma, G. (2004). The knowledge value chain: How intellectual capital impacts on business performance. *International Journal of Technology Management, 27*(6–7), 575–590.

Carlucci, D., & Schiuma, G. (2012a). Assessing and managing organizational climate in healthcare organizations: An intellectual capital based perspective. *International Journal of Information Systems in the Service Sector, 4*(4), 49–61. https://doi.org/10.4018/jisss.2012100103

Carlucci, D., & Schiuma, G. (2012b). Evaluating organisational climate through IC lens: The case of a public hospital. *Measuring Business Excellence, 16*(4), 79–90. https://doi.org/10.1108/13683041211276465

Cavicchi, C. (2017). Healthcare sustainability and the role of intellectual capital: Evidence from an Italian Regional Health Service. *Journal of Intellectual Capital, 18*(3), 544–563. https://doi.org/10.1108/JIC-12-2016-0128

Collins, C. S., & Stockton, C. M. (2018). The central role of theory in qualitative research. *International Journal of Qualitative Methods, 17*(1), 1–10. https://doi.org/10.1177/1609406918797475

Crossan, M. M., & Apaydin, M. (2010). A multi-dimensional framework of organizational innovation: A systematic review of the literature. *Journal of Management Studies*. https://doi.org/10.1111/j.1467-6486.2009.00880.x

Dameri, R. P., & Ferrando, P. M. (2021). Implementing integrated reporting to disclose intellectual capital in health organisations: A case study. *Journal of Intellectual Capital, 22*(2), 311–336. https://doi.org/10.1108/JIC-01-2020-0019

Dumay, J., Guthrie, J., & Rooney, J. (2020, January). Being critical about intellectual capital accounting in 2020: An overview. *Critical Perspectives on Accounting, 70*. https://doi.org/10.1016/j.cpa.2020.102185

Edvinsson, L., Dvir, R., Roth, N., & Pasher, E. (2004). Innovations: The new unit of analysis in the knowledge era: The quest and context for innovation efficiency and management of IC. *Journal of Intellectual Capital*.

Efthymiou, L., Kulshrestha, A., & Kulshrestha, S. (2023). A study on sustainability and ESG in the service sector in India: Benefits, challenges, and future implications. *Administrative Sciences, 13*, 165. https://doi.org/10.3390/admsci13070165

Evans, J. M., Brown, A., & Ross Baker, G. (2015). Intellectual capital in the healthcare sector: A systematic review and critique of the literature. *BMC Health Services Research, 15*, 1–14.

Ferrari, R. (2015). Writing narrative style literature reviews. *Medical Writing, 24*(4), 230–235. https://doi.org/10.1179/2047480615z.000000000329

Ferreira, P. P., Pinheiro, P., Rodrigues, R., & Pintom R. (2010). Intellectual capital and knowledge management practices in health systems. In *Proceedings of the international conference on intellectual capital, knowledge management & organizational learning* (pp. 170–177).

van der Geer, E., van Tuijl, H. F. J. M., & Rutte, C. G. (2009). Performance management in healthcare: Performance indicator development, task uncertainty, and types of performance indicators. *Social Science and Medicine, 69*(10), 1523–1530. https://doi.org/10.1016/j.socscimed.2009.08.026

Grant, R. M. (1996). Toward a knowledge-based theory of the firm. *Strategic Management Journal, 17*(S2), 109–122. https://doi.org/10.1002/smj.4250171110

Guthrie, J., Ricceri, F., & Dumay, J. (2012). Reflections and projections: A decade of intellectual capital accounting research. *British Accounting Review, 44*(2), 68–82. https://doi.org/10.1016/j.bar.2012.03.004

Hewko, S. J., & Cummings, G. G. (2016). Performance management in healthcare: A critical analysis. *Leadership in Health Services, 29*(1), 52–68. https://doi.org/10.1108/LHS-12-2014-0081

Inkinen, H. (2016). Review of empirical research on knowledge management practices and firm performance. *Journal of Knowledge Management.*

Katz, J. S., & Martin, B. R. (1997). What is research collaboration? *Research Policy, 26*(1), 1–18. https://doi.org/10.1016/S0048-7333(96)00917-1

Kianto, A., Andreeva, T., & Pavlov, Y. (2013). The impact of intellectual capital management on company competitiveness and financial performance. *Knowledge Management Research & Practice, 11*(2), 112–122. https://doi.org/10.1057/kmrp.2013.9

Kucharska, W. (2021). Leadership, culture, intellectual capital and knowledge processes for organizational innovativeness across industries: The case of Poland. *Journal of Intellectual Capital, 22*(7), 121–141. https://doi.org/10.1108/JIC-02-2021-0047

Leliaert, P. J. C., Candries, W., & Tilmans, R. (2003). Identifying and managing IC: A new classification. *Journal of Intellectual Capital, 4*(2), 202–214.

Longo, M., & Mura, M. (2011). The effect of intellectual capital on employees' satisfaction and retention. *Information & Management, 48*(7), 278–287.

Melloni, G. (2015). Intellectual capital disclosure in integrated reporting: An impression management analysis. *Journal of Intellectual Capital.*

Miller, D. (2019). The resource-based view of the firm. In *Oxford research encyclopedia of business and management.*

Narayanan, V. K., Zane, L. J., & Kemmerer, B. (2011). The cognitive perspective in strategy: An integrative review. *Journal of Management, 37*(1), 305–351. https://doi.org/10.1177/0149206310383986

OECD—Secretariat. (1998). National efforts to measure intangible investment. *International symposium on measuring and reporting intellectual capital: Experience, issues, and prospects* (pp. 1–39).

Peng, T. J., Ann, S. P., & Roos, G. (2007). Intellectual capital and performance indicators: Taiwanese healthcare sector. *Journal of Intellectual Capital, 8*(3), 538–556. https://doi.org/10.1108/14691930710774902

Perrott, B. E. (2007). A strategic risk approach to knowledge management. *Business Horizons, 50*(6), 523–533. https://doi.org/10.1016/j.bushor.2007.08.002

Petty, R., & Guthrie, J. (2000a). Intellectual capital literature review. *Journal of Intellectual Capital, 1*(2), 155–176. https://doi.org/10.1108/14691930010348731

Petty, R., & Guthrie, J. (2000b). Intellectual capital literature review: Measurement, reporting and management. *Journal of Intellectual Capital, 1*(2), 155–176.

Pflugfelder, N. S. (2021). Knowledge management as a driver of performance in ambulatory healthcare—A systematic literature review through an intellectual capital lens. *Journal of Intellectual Capital, 22*(2), 403–432. https://doi.org/10.1108/JIC-02-2020-0068

Radaelli, G., Mura, M., Spiller, N., & Lettieri, E. (2011). Intellectual capital and knowledge sharing: The mediating role of organisational knowledge-sharing climate. *Knowledge Management Research and Practice, 9*(4), 342–352. https://doi.org/10.1057/kmrp.2011.29

Ramezan, M. (2011). Intellectual capital and organizational organic structure in knowledge society: How are these concepts related? *International Journal of Information Management, 31*(1), 88–95.

Rugman, A. M., & Verbeke, A. (2002). Edith Penrose's contribution to the resource-based view of strategic management. *Strategic Management Journal, 23*(8), 769–780.

Schiavone, F., Ferraris, A., Wamba, S. F., & Singh, S. K. (2021). Guest editorial. *Journal of Intellectual Capital, 22*(2), 213–218. https://doi.org/10.1108/JIC-03-2021-304

Sullivan, P. H. (1999). Profiting from intellectual capital. *Journal of Knowledge Management, 3*(2), 132–143.

Tandon, A., Dhir, A., Islam, N., & Mäntymäki, M. (2020). Blockchain in healthcare: A systematic literature review, synthesizing framework and future research agenda. *Computers in Industry, 122*. https://doi.org/10.1016/j.compind.2020.103290

Tiwari, R. (2020). Nexus between intellectual capital and profitability with interaction effects: panel data evidence from the Indian healthcare industry. *Journal of Intellectual Capital*. https://doi.org/10.1108/JIC-05-2020-0137

Veltri, S., Bronzetti, G., & Sicoli, G. (2011). Reporting intellectual capital in health care organizations: Specifics, lessons learned, and future research perspectives. *Journal of Health Care Finance, 38*(2), 80–97.

Vrontis, D., Thrassou, A., Uzunboylu, N., & Efthymiou, L. (2023). An overview of business for sustainability: Strategic avenues and managerial approaches. In D. Vrontis, A. Thrassou, L. Efthymiou, Y. Weber, S. M. R. Shams, & E. Tsoukatos (Eds.), *Business for Sustainability, Volume I. Palgrave Studies in*

Cross-disciplinary Business Research. In Association with EuroMed Academy of Business. Palgrave Macmillan. https://doi.org/10.1007/978-3-031-37361-9_1

Vrontis, D., Thrassou, A., Efthymiou, L., & Bozat, M. (2024). Delineating business for sustainability: contextual evolution and elucidation. In D. Vrontis, A. Thrassou, L. Efthymiou, Y. Weber, S. M. R. Shams, & E. Tsoukatos (Eds.), *Business for sustainability, Volume II. Palgrave studies in cross-disciplinary business research*. In Association with EuroMed Academy of Business. Palgrave Macmillan, Cham. https://doi.org/10.1007/978-3-031-37365-7_1

Vishnu, S., & Gupta, V. K. (2015). Performance of intellectual capital in Indian healthcare sector. *International Journal of Learning and Intellectual Capital, 12*(1), 47–60. https://doi.org/10.1504/IJLIC.2015.067831

Yang, C. C., & Lin, C. Y. Y. (2009). Does intellectual capital mediate the relationship between HRM and organizational performance? Perspective of a healthcare industry in Taiwan. *International Journal of Human Resource Management, 20*(9), 1965–1984. https://doi.org/10.1080/09585190903142415

CHAPTER 6

An Extended Expectation-Confirmation Model and Post-Adoption Behaviour of Augmented-Reality Game Players

Mathupayas Thongmak

6.1 Introduction

According to Statista.com (2019b) and Statista.com (2019a), games are the most downloaded app category in both the Apple App Store and Google Play Store. Augmented Reality (AR) is a technology combining the physical world and virtual objects (Buhalis et al., 2024; Ghazali et al., 2019a, 2019b; Harborth & Pape, 2017; Rauschnabel et al., 2017). Pokémon Go (PG) is one of the Augmented Reality Games (ARGs) and also a Location-Based Game (LBG), which is the most downloaded game app, the best mobile/ handheld game, and the best family game (Ghazali et al., 2019a, 2019b; Hamari et al., 2019; Harborth & Pape, 2017; Hsiao et al., 2019; Liu et al., 2018). It requires players to locate and catch virtual creatures (Pokémon) hidden in real-world locations (Liu et al., 2018;

M. Thongmak (✉)
Thammasat Business School, Thammasat University, Bangkok, Thailand
e-mail: mathupayas@tbs.tu.ac.th

D. Vrontis et al. (eds.), *Business in Uncertainty*, Palgrave Studies in Cross-disciplinary Business Research, In Association with EuroMed Academy of Business, https://doi.org/10.1007/978-3-031-65587-6_6

Rauschnabel & Rossmann, 2017; Rauschnabel et al., 2017). It leads to the release of other ARGs including Harry Potter and Jurassic World Alive (Ghazali et al., 2019a, 2019b; Harborth & Pape, 2017). However, even Pokémon Go faces difficulty in retaining users' interest and its success momentum (Ghazali et al., 2019a, 2019b; Hsiao et al., 2019).

Game marketing has been neglected by academia and researchers for decades. Previous research states that there is not much empirical evidence to support existing theories in gamers' consumption (Rezaei & Ghodsi, 2014). The Theory of Consumption Values (TCV) or Consumption Value Theory (CVT) is a well-known framework to understand the behaviour of hedonic technologies' users (Kaur et al., 2018). The important roles of perceived value on consumer behaviour, competitive advantage, and loyalty have been confirmed by a number of previous studies, but not for games (Luo & Lee, 2018; Rezaei & Ghodsi, 2014). Mobile game research has largely focused on the pre-adoption phase rather than the post-adoption phase Merikivi et al. (2017). Another theory widely used in the field of consumer behaviour is the Expectation-Confirmation Theory (ECT), which is generally applied to interpret consumers' post-purchase behaviour. The ECT theory was later modified to be the Expectation-Confirmation Model (ECM), which incorporates the post-acceptance factors such as perceived usefulness driving IS users' satisfaction and continuance intention (Hsu & Lin, 2019).

Due to the rapid proliferation of mobile devices, game addiction has increasingly become a serious social concern because it significantly decreases the academic performance of college students and lowers their self-esteem (Seok et al., 2018; Toker & Baturay, 2016). Besides, the rate of youth becoming addicted to Internet games is increasing, indicating the need for research relating to game addiction (Seok et al., 2018). Previous research frequently explores the effect of flow on game addiction, for instance, the study of Sun et al. (2015), but not the impact of continuance intention or satisfaction on game addiction. In terms of AR, only a few research has been done on users' acceptance of AR technology or AR applications, particularly in AR gaming applications (Ghazali et al., 2019a, 2019b; Harborth & Pape, 2017; Jung et al., 2015; Thrassou et al., 2022a, 2022b; Vrontis et al., 2023). Coursaris et al. (2016) and Rezaei and Ghodsi (2014) emphasize that the design and implementation of the game feature to trigger or satisfy gamers' motivation and to retain them have been far less investigated.

To bridge these gaps, the objectives of this research are as follows: (1) to enhance the understanding of drivers retaining players' interests and increasing the success momentum of Pokémon Go in Thailand, (2) to expand the consumer research in mobile location-based AR game marketing using well-established theories: TCV and ECT/ ECM, (3) to apply multidimensional constructs to represent perceived value (functional value, emotional value, and conditional value) and loyalty (continuance intention and intention to recommend), and (4) to explore the antecedents e.g. game features and consequences of game satisfaction, both positive and negative ones i.e. loyalty factors, intention to use other Location-Based Services (LBSs), and game addiction.

6.2 Literature Review

Coursaris et al. (2016) proposed a model to predict usage continuance and subsequent purchases in online Free-to-Play (F2P) mobile games. Achievement, social, and immersion motivations resulted in greater enjoyment, which later increased continuance use and purchase intention. Toker and Baturay (2016) studied antecedents and the consequences of game addiction. Socio-economic status, smoking, online gaming, computer gaming, and mother employment status increased game addiction, but gender (female) and mother education level decreased the addiction. Hsiao and Chen (2016) examined the antecedents of in-app purchase intention of mobile games. Mobile games' loyalty, which was affected by perceived values of the game (playfulness, connectedness, access flexibility, and reward), together with the good price had a significant impact on intention to make an in-app purchase. Merhi (2016) empirically tested an integrated model for online game adoption. The results showed that enjoyment, achievement, and social interactions were important factors for intention to play. Wang et al. (2017) explored factors enhancing the continued usage of mobile games. Satisfaction, flow, perceived system quality, perceived peer influences, and perceived usefulness positively impacted the continued usage of smartphone games, whereas perceived cost and confirmation had insignificant influences. Merikivi et al. (2017) investigated the role of enjoyment and its antecedents as a motive for continual mobile game use. Findings indicated the importance of ease of use, novelty, design aesthetic, and challenge on enjoyment. Harborth and Pape (2017) examined Pokémon Go's acceptance factors. Hedonic motivation including fun and pleasure from playing the game strongly influenced the intention to play the game. The effort expectancy also affected behavioural intention. Djamaluddin et al. (2017) investigated consumption values influencing users' intention to purchase Dot 2 virtual goods. Functional value, social value, emotional value, satisfaction with the game, and character identification significantly affected users' purchase intention. Rauschnabel et al. (2017) examined the drivers of gaming continuance and willingness to make in-app purchases in Pokémon Go. Hedonic, emotional, and social benefits and social norms are positively associated with consumer reactions, while physical risks are negatively related to consumer behaviours.

Luo and Lee (2018) investigated the role of perceived values and loyalty in predicting Massive Multiplayer Online gamers' behaviour. Quality value, social value, emotional value, and price value were significant drivers of gamers' repurchase intention, whereas quality value, social value, and emotional value significantly increased WOM. Teng (2018) applied the TCV to examine the relationships among consumption values, expectancy for character growth, and loyalty of online gamers. Hsiao et al. (2019) proposed and tested a research framework based on the theory of perceived values and satisfaction to investigate drivers of the intention to conduct in-game purchases. Flow, design aesthetics, social self-expression, and good price directly impacted players' perceived value, which later strongly affected in-app purchase intention together with satisfaction. E. M. Ghazali et al., (2019a, 2019b) applied Uses and Gratification (U&G) factors to predict intention to continue playing Pokémon Go. Findings revealed that enjoyment is the most vital mediator of the relationships between three U&G constructs (achievement, escapism, challenge, and social interaction) and continuance intention. E. Ghazali et al., (2019a, 2019b) specified the influential factors of Pokémon Go players' continuance intention to play. Gamers' continuance intention was influenced by enjoyment, network externalities, community involvement, and need-to-collect.

6.3 Theoretical Model and Hypotheses Development

Expectation Confirmation Theory and Expectation Confirmation Model

The Expectation-Confirmation Theory (ECT) is a theory extensively used in the marketing domain to explain consumers' satisfaction and their post-purchase behaviour. The theory, modified as Expectation-Confirmation Model (ECM) by integrating the ECT with the Technology Acceptance Model (TAM), is also widely accepted in determining users' satisfaction and IS continuance intention (Huang et al., 2019; Oghuma et al., 2016) (Fig. 6.1).

Expectation: Expected Game Features: Game design in terms of challenge, novelty, and design aesthetics significantly increased players' perceived enjoyment, which was a significant driver of continuance intention of playing mobile games (Merikivi et al., 2017). Achievement,

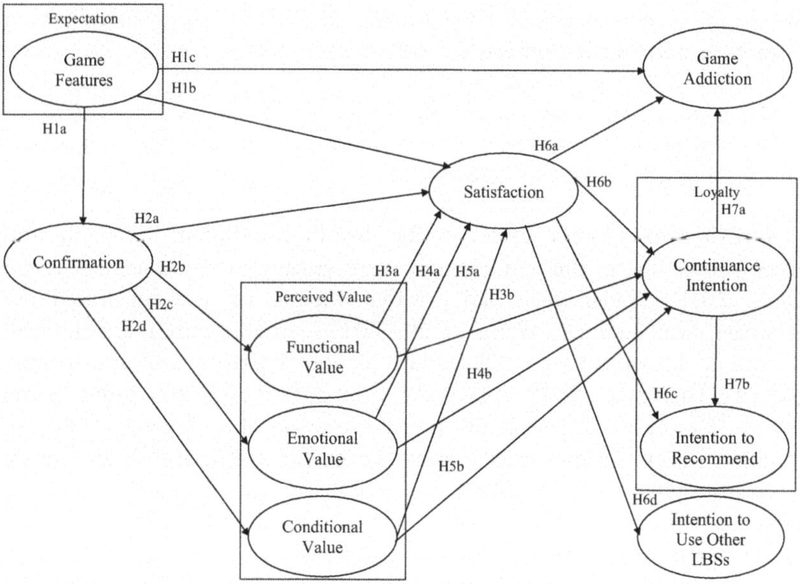

Fig. 6.1 Conceptual model

challenge, and social interaction significantly affected continuance intention to play PG, mediated by perceived enjoyment of the game (Ghazali et al., 2019a, 2019b). Game enjoyment significantly led to game addiction (Chuang et al., 2012). Game users' challenge, attack, entertainment, and fellowship motives directly or indirectly extended gamers' intention to continue playing (Lee, 2015). Based on previous reports, the following hypothesis and sub-hypothesis are formulated.

H1: Expected game features are positively associated with (a) players' confirmation, (b) their satisfaction, and (c) game addiction.

Confirmation: Confirmation was proposed to have positive influences on perceived usefulness and satisfaction of smartphone games (Wang et al., 2017). It positively significantly affected the perceived usefulness and satisfaction of the selection of Communication and Collaboration Technologies (CCT) in an IT project context (Cuellar et al., 2019) and gamification application services (Huang et al., 2019). Expectation confirmation positively impacted the perceived advantage, aesthetic experience, and perceived enjoyment of AR (Chung et al., 2018). Thus, the following hypothesis and sub-hypothesis are offered.

H2: A game player's expectation confirmation is positively associated with (a) his or her satisfaction, (b) perceived functional value, (c) perceived emotional value, and (d) perceived conditional value.

Satisfaction: Players tended to be deeply involved in the game and invest more time in the game if they were satisfied with the game (Hsiao et al., 2019). Satisfaction had positive impacts on the continued use of smartphone games (Wang et al., 2017), in-app purchase intention of mobile location-based AR games for both paying and non-paying groups (Hsiao et al., 2019), players' continuance intention of online social games (Zhu et al., 2014), continuance intention of SNS games (Chuang et al., 2012). Customer satisfaction was the most crucial indicator while exploring their perception of reusing mobile services. It is also one of the most influential factors for mobile services' loyalty (Jung et al., 2015). AR satisfaction also had a significant and positive impact on the intention to recommend AR applications (Jung et al., 2015). Accordingly, the following hypothesis and sub-hypothesis are proposed.

H6: A game player's satisfaction is positively associated with (a) his or her addiction to the game, (b) continuance intention, (c) intention to recommend the game to others, and (d) intention to use other LBSs.

Theory of Consumption Values

In this study, post-acceptance factors of the ECM were represented using perceived value. Perceived value differed from customer satisfaction, but was related to it (Deng et al., 2010). Five values included functional value, emotional value, social value, conditional value, and epistemic value (Deng et al., 2010; Kaur et al., 2018; Klézl et al., 2018; Luo & Lee, 2018; Yoo, 2015). To decrease the complexity of research framework, this study focused on two most-adopted values in past studies: functional value and emotional value and added one more value (conditional value) that was suitable for the mobile location-based AR game context.

Functional Value: The functional value was the perceived utility gained from an alternative's capacity regarding functional, utilitarian, or physical performance (Kaur et al., 2018; Yang & Lin, 2017; Zhu et al., 2010). Functional value positively associated with the perceived value of an innovation service (Zhu et al., 2010). Character competency and price utility as functional values significantly increased players' intention to buy virtual goods in online games (Ho & Wu, 2012). Functional value was similar to the perceived usefulness of TAM or usability (Zhu et al., 2010). The perceived advantage of AR significantly enhanced satisfaction with AR (Chung et al., 2018). Based on the preceding discussion, following hypothesis and sub-hypothesis are offered.

H3: A game player's perceived functional value is positively associated with (a) his or her satisfaction and (b) continuance intention to play Pokémon Go.

Emotional Value: In terms of hedonic products, emotional involvement is required in the consumption process of hedonic products (Yoo, 2015). In terms of Pokémon Go, hedonic motivation positively affected behavioural intention (Harborth & Pape, 2017). Perceived hedonic benefits positively influenced both users' continuance intention and satisfaction (Hsu & Lin, 2019). The emotional value was the perceived utility derived from an alternative's capacity to urge feelings or affective states (Kaur et al., 2018; Luo & Lee, 2018; Rezaei & Ghodsi, 2014; Yang & Lin,

2017). The emotional value was crucial in building a loyal customer community (Spink et al., 2011). The emotional dimension of perceived value is positively related to a user's intention to download mobile games (Spink et al., 2011). Emotional value also referred to the gamers' feeling of game enjoyment. Game items provided a user hedonic value rather than utilitarian value. The perceived emotional value of game items significantly increased users' purchase intention (Yoo, 2015). A user's perceived emotional value from buying decorative goods in the virtual world positively influenced his/ her intention to purchase them (Shang et al., 2010). Therefore, the following hypothesis and sub-hypothesis are offered.

H4: A game player's perceived emotional value is positively associated with (a) his or her satisfaction and (b) continuance intention to play Pokémon Go.

Conditional Value: The conditional value was the perceived utility received from an alternative as the result of the specific situation/ circumstances facing the choice maker (Hwang & Lee, 2013; Kaur et al., 2018; Yang & Lin, 2017). Conditional value significantly positively impacted consumers' intention to use social network mobile. People played a game to have fun while waiting for an appointment, to relieve the boredom, or to consume their spare time (Hwang & Lee, 2013). Conditional value influenced the overall value, which was a significant driver of behavioural intention to use LBSs (Zhang & Mao, 2013). Based on the preceding arguments, the following hypothesis and sub-hypothesis are given.

H5: A game player's perceived conditional value is positively associated with (a) his or her satisfaction and (b) continuance intention to play Pokémon Go.

Impact of Game Continuance Intention

Internet game addiction was influenced by players' internal motivation (Seok et al., 2018). Online gaming as a leisure-time activity could significantly lead to game addiction. Excessive use of the Internet or video game developed an addiction (Toker & Baturay, 2016). A game's success depended on gamers who continued playing (Ghazali et al., 2019a). In terms of games, gamers' continuance intention was more crucial than their initial intention to play. Post-adoption usage determined the success of game providers (Ghazali et al., 2019b). Positive experience increased gamers' loyalty to the game (Yoo, 2015). Consumer loyalty was a sign of other favourable behaviours such as WOM and recommendations (Casaló et al., 2010). Literature research regarding MMORPGs and Massively Multiplayer Online Game (MMOG) measured loyalty intention using repurchase intention and WOM (Luo & Lee, 2018; Rezaei & Ghodsi, 2014). Based on this assertion, the following hypothesis and sub-hypothesis are developed.

H7: A game player's continuance intention is positively associated with (a) his or her addiction to the game and (b) intention to recommend the game to others.

6.4 Research Design and Methods

This study is a sub-project of a project titled POKÉMON GO. A non-probability quota sampling method was applied to collect the data from both studying-aged players and working-aged players, to be more representative of individual populations. Participants in this study were Pokémon Go players in Thailand. After filtering duplicates, 259 valid questionnaires remained, consisting of surveys from 134 full-time students and 125 full-time employees. Total samples were closed to the suggested sample number (100–200) for a chi-squared of SEM fit (Lao, 2014; Wu, 2009).

The survey questionnaire consisted of a section describing the target samples and the definitions of LBSs and the description of Pokémon Go, questions for consumption values, questions for ECT/ ECM, questions for user's demographic information, and questions for expected game features and game addiction. The scale items were adapted from relevant literature: functional value (Chong, 2013; Huang & Liao, 2015; Oghuma et al., 2016; Wang et al., 2013), emotional value (Chong, 2013; Hsu et al., 2015; Turel et al., 2010; Wang et al., 2013), conditional value (Pihlström, 2008; Wang et al., 2013), expected game features (Hull et al., 2013; Olsson et al., 2013), confirmation (Chong, 2013; Ho et al., 2015; Oghuma et al., 2016), satisfaction (Ho et al., 2015; Jung et al., 2015; Oghuma et al., 2016), continuance intention to play (Ho et al., 2015; Oghuma et al., 2016; Pihlström, 2008; Turel et al., 2010), intention to recommend (Jung et al., 2015; Kang & Johnson, 2015; Turel et al.,

2010), intention to use other LBSs (Ho et al., 2015; Oghuma et al., 2016; Yun et al., 2013), and game addiction (Kim et al., 2008; Sun et al., 2015; van Rooij et al., 2012). Each item was evaluated using a five-point Likert scale ranging from 1 – strongly disagreed to 5 – strongly agreed and 1 – not at all important to 5 – extremely important for game features. The items were translated from English to Thai and slightly modified to suit the Pokémon Go context.

6.5 Results

Descriptive Statistics

As shown in Table 6.1, the majority of Pokémon Go players in this study were males (55.6 percent). The mean age of the participants was 25 years old. They were studying or received a bachelor's degree (71.0 percent). The average level in the game of them was 18. They played Pokémon Go approximately 3 hours per day and 5 days per week. Their playing game types were Action/ Adventure/ Arcade (69.1 percent), Role Playing/ Simulation/ Strategy (41.3 percent), Sports/ Racing (26.3 percent), Music (25.1 percent), Trivia/ Word/ Puzzle (22.0 percent), Board/ Card/ Casino (18.9 percent), and Educational (13.5 percent), respectively.

Measurement Model Assessment

As presented in Table 6.2, the results of reliability measures for constructs were ranging from 0.784 to 0.961. All Cronbach's alphas were higher than 0.7 (Nunnally & Bernstein, 1967), indicating good reliability. A Confirmatory Factor Analysis (CFA) was conducted to assess the measurement model before testing a structural model. All of the factor loadings were ranging from 0.706 to 0.991, above the recommended standardized loadings of 0.5 (Kline, 2015) and the average loadings per factor are greater than 0.7 (Hair et al., 2006), demonstrating good convergent validity. Average Variance Extracted (AVE) values for all constructs were greater than the benchmark of 0.5 (Fornell & Larcker, 1981), and all Composite Reliability (CR) values exceeded the threshold value of 0.6 (Bagozzi & Yi, 1988).

According to Table 6.3, all correlations between constructs were less than the square roots of the AVE for the corresponding factors, except

Table 6.1 Sample demographics

Demographic characteristics	*Demographic characteristics*	*All participants* N (%)
Gender	Male	144 (55.6%)
	Female	115 (44.4%)
Average Age		25
Education (Studying/ Received)	Lower than Bachelor Degree	26 (10.0%)
	Bachelor's Degree	184 (71.0%)
	Master's Degree	46 (17.8%)
	Doctoral Degree	3 (1.2%)
Avg. Pokémong Go Game Level		18
Avg. Amount of Playing Pokémon Go (hours/ day)		3
Avg. Amount of Playing Pokémon Go (days/ week)		5
Other Game Types Playing	Action/ Adventure/ Arcade	179 (69.1%)
	Board/ Card/ Casino	49 (18.9%)
	Educational	35 (13.5%)
	Music	65 (25.1%)
	Sports/ Racing	68 (26.3%)
	Role Playing/ Simulation/ Strategy	107 (41.3%)
	Trivia/ Word/ Puzzle	57 (22.0%)

Table 6.2 Validation of final measurement model—reliability and convergent validity

	Mean (SD)	*AVE*	*CR*	*Cronbach's alpha*
GAME_FEA	3.30 (1.00)	0.615	0.864	0.860
CONFIRM	3.46 (0.96)	0.813	0.896	0.886
SATIS	3.84 (0.94)	0.828	0.906	0.906
FUNC	3.19 (0.95)	0.654	0.791	0.784
EMO	3.95 (0.95)	0.858	0.923	0.924
COND	3.13 (1.18)	0.802	0.890	0.884
GAME_ADD	2.23 (1.07)	0.668	0.800	0.792
CON_INT_PLAY	3.50 (1.18)	0.925	0.961	0.961
INT_REC	3.50 (1.05)	0.780	0.876	0.876
INT_LBS	3.33 (1.08)	0.917	0.957	0.955

Note Game Features (GAME_FEA), Confirmation (CONFIRM), Satisfaction (SATIS), Functional Value (FUNC), Emotional Value (EMO), Conditional Value (COND), Game Addiction (GAME_ADD), Continuance Intention (CON_INT_PLAY), Intention to Recommend (INT_REC), and Intention to Use Other LBSs (INT_LBS)

Table 6.3 The correlation coefficient matrix and the square roots of AVE

	1	*2*	*3*	*4*	*5*	*6*	*7*	*8*	*9*	*10*
1) GAME_ FEA	**0.784**									
2) CONFIRM	0.535	**0.902**								
3) SATIS	0.515	0.742	**0.910**							
4) FUNC	0.615	0.666	*0.810*	**0.809**						
5) EMO	0.511	0.581	0.710	0.748	**0.926**					
6) COND	0.337	0.440	0.530	0.486	0.437	**0.896**				
7) GAME_ ADD	0.350	0.222	0.224	0.249	0.220	0.323	**0.817**			
8) CON_ INT_ PLAY	0.513	0.569	0.719	0.723	0.726	0.504	0.252	**0.962**		
9) INT_REC	0.616	0.537	0.720	0.790	0.722	0.511	0.319	0.755	**0.883**	
10) INT_LBS	0.405	0.373	0.436	0.422	0.441	0.339	0.271	0.421	0.458	**0.958**

Note Data in bold denotes square root of the AVE and the elements below the diagonal denotes the correlations between constructs

for the correlation between functional value and satisfaction that was slightly greater than the square root of the AVE. Therefore, it could be deduced that the discriminant validity was not ideal, but the questionnaire was qualified for the validity test (Lao, 2014). The measurement model had goodness-of-fit indices within the acceptable level, as presented in Table 6.4, showing an excellent fit and providing the support to proceed with the structural model test.

Structural Model Assessment

After the measurement model assessment, the data were further analyzed through Structural Equation Modeling (SEM). The results were presented in Table 6.4. The fit indices for SEM were found to be acceptable. All hypotheses except for the relationship between functional value and continuance intention, the relationship between conditional value and continuance intention, the relationship between satisfaction and game addiction, and the relationship between continuance intention and game addiction. Figure 6.2 showed the results of a structural model, its standardized path coefficients, and significances. Nine endogenous variables

Table 6.4 Main indices of the model fit test and testing results

Fit Measure	*Acceptable Fit Criteria (Hair et al., 2006; Parry, 2017; Schermelleh-Engel et al., 2003; Schumacker & Lomax, 2004)*	*Indicators Confirmatory factor analysis*	*Indicators Structural equation modeling*
$X^2/$ df	$X^2/$ df ≤ 3	1.452	1.712
GFI	GFI $\geq$ 0.90	0.927	0.904
AGFI	AGFI $\geq$ 0.85	0.887	0.870
NFI	NFI $\geq$ 0.90	0.949	0.932
NNFI	NNFI $\geq$ 0.95	0.977	0.963
CFI	CFI $\geq$ 0.90	0.983	0.970
RMSEA	RMSEA $\leq$ 0.08	0.042	0.053
SRMR	SRMR $\leq$ 0.08	0.0323	0.0657

Note Goodness of Fit (GFI), Adjusted Goodness of Fit (AGFI), Normed Fit Index (NFI), Non-Normed Fit Index (NNFI), Comparative Fit Index (CFI), Root Mean Square Error of Approximation (RMSEA), and Standardized) Root Mean Square Residual (SRMR)

were examined in the model. The proportion of the variances for confirmation, functional value, emotional value, conditional value, satisfaction, game addiction, continuance intention, intention to recommend, and intention to use other LBSs could be explained by its exogenous variables in the amounts of 31.2%, 47.5%, 36.2%, 20.6%, 93.2%, 13.5%, 64.3%, 70.4%, and 26.4%, respectively.

Discussion of Findings

All supported hypotheses were similar to the findings in past studies described in the Theoretical model and hypotheses development section. The insignificant relationship between satisfaction and continuance intention on game addiction could be explained by the low mean of Pokémon Go players' game addiction, similar to the study of Chuang et al. (2012) stating that users normally did not addicted to SNS games and the addiction affected continuance. The insignificant effect of functional value on gamers' continuance intention could be supported by the negative impact of the perceived functional value of a game item on purchase intention (Yoo, 2015) and the insignificant influence of perceived benefit of SoLoMo services on users' continuance intention (Yang & Lin, 2017). The insignificant relationship between conditional value and continuance intention could be explained by the study of Yang and Lin (2017), which

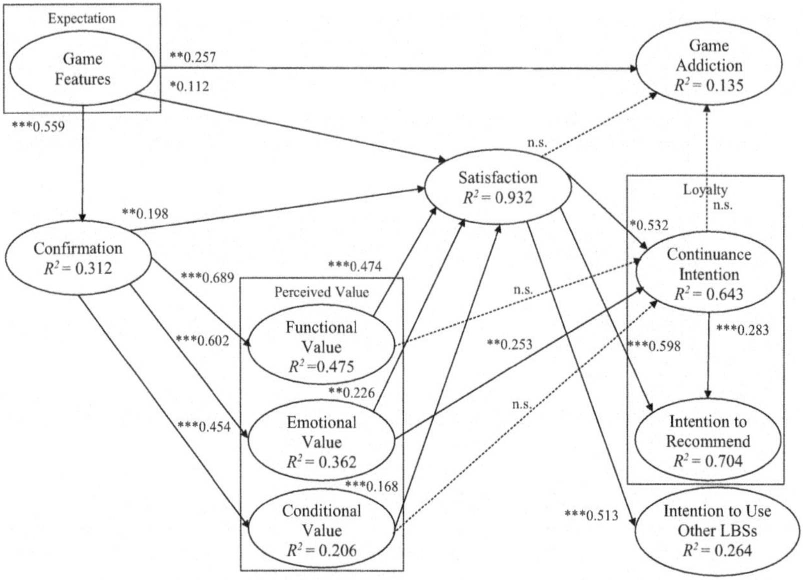

Fig. 6.2 The results of SEM analysis (*Note* ***$p < 0.001$; **$p < 0.01$; *$p < 0.05$)

did not consider the conditional value in the continuance of SoLoMo services because they believed that users might not sort out between the original value and enhanced value. Conditional value could happen from functional and social value enhanced by providing a service at the right time and place (Yang & Lin, 2017).

6.6 Implications and Future Research

Implications

For academic researchers, applying multidimensional constructs is helpful to show insights regarding perceived value and loyalty in the context of a mobile location-based AR game. Utilizing game features to represent expectation also gives a deeper understanding of mobile game researchers. This study also validates the ECT/ ECM and TCV. Expanding the ECM by replacing perceived usefulness with three TCV factors provides a new perspective of the determinants of satisfaction and continuance intention.

The integrative model could explain the substantial variances of the game success in terms of satisfaction, loyalty, and intention to use other LBSs. The significant influence of satisfaction on loyalty (continuance intention and intention to recommend) is supported by an empirical study, enriching the knowledge for marketing researchers in a mobile location-based AR game perspective. Investigating both studying-aged players and working-aged gamers could be an effective representation of PG players. Since LBGs and ARGs have been flourishing, the research framework and method could be imitated and expanded by other researchers to profoundly explore mobile location-based AR games in the future.

Findings from this study could be directly guided Pokémon Go's game providers/ developers and could be carefully applied by mobile location-based AR game practitioners to improve mobile location-based AR games e.g. Let's Hunt Monsters, Jurassic Park Alive, The Walking Dead Our World, Harry Potter Wizards Unite, and Ghostbusters World. First, in terms of game loyalty, players will positively promote this game to others or recommend this game to someone who seeks their advice if they are satisfied by the game or if they have the intention to continue playing the game. They will continue to use this game or have the intention to continue playing this game in the future because of their satisfaction and the perceived enjoyment received from the game. Players' satisfaction not only strongly leads to their loyalty but also their intention to use other LBSs in the future. Second, players are completely satisfied with the game playing experience or pleased with the overall game mainly due to functional value, emotional value, confirmation, conditional value, and game features, respectively. Thus, game marketers should emphasize the game's usefulness, the suitability for gamers' needs, fun or enjoyment received from playing the game, and the additional benefits from the game in some specific situations. For example, a map in this game could help players to identify the current location and guide direction when they get lost. This game could also provide related real-time information such as place information or nearby friends when players are in uncertain circumstances and need more information to facilitate their decision.

Last, confirmation that the game is better than expected or meets players' expectations strongly impacts three consumption values. It is directly affected by the expected game features. Hence, mobile location-based AR game developers should at least provide these features: social features (e.g. contacting friends, providing information about friends, who is in the game, social information features), manipulation and control features (e.g. save features, player management features), narrative and identity features (e.g. avatar creation features, theme and genre features), and reward features (e.g. experience points, bonuses, increasing difficulty or levels), to match players' expectations. Game features are not only the things that gamers hope to see from the game but also satisfy them and increase the chance of their addiction to the game.

Limitations and Future Research

This study exhibits some limitations. First, this work focuses on a particular mobile location-based AR game: Pokémon Go. Future research should replicate this study to other mobile location-based AR games to broaden and generalize findings. Second, this study does not classify players. Players could be categorized as heavy players/ light players or killers / achievers / socializers / explorers (Zichermann & Linder, 2010). Future research should classify players into these categories and compare them to expand the research results. Third, the impact of functional value and conditional value on continuance intention and the influences of satisfaction and continuance intention on game addiction are not supported. Future studies should conduct qualitative research to explore more about the reasons why these associations are not significant, especially for heavy players. Fourth, this study is investigated solely in Thailand. Findings from this study should be compared with other Southeast Asian countries.

References

Bagozzi, R. P., & Yi, Y. (1988). On the evaluation of structural equation models. *Journal of the Academy of Marketing Science, 16*(1), 74–94.

Buhalis, D., Efthymiou, L., Uzunboylu, N. and Thrassou, A. (2024). Charting the progress of technology adoption in tourism and hospitality in the era of industry 4.0. Tourism & hospitality in the digital era: Technology and its (im)possibilities. Special Issue in Euromed, *Journal of Business*. https://doi.org/10.1108/EMJB-11-2023-0310

Casaló, L. V., Flavián, C., & Guinalíu, M. (2010). Determinants of the intention to participate in firm-hosted online travel communities and effects on consumer behavioral intentions. *Tourism Management, 31*(6), 898–911.

Chong, A.Y.-L. (2013). Understanding mobile commerce continuance intentions: An empirical analysis of Chinese consumers. *Journal of Computer Information Systems, 53*(4), 22–30.

Chuang, Y.-H., Lin, C.-S., & Shu, W. (2012). *Continuing use of SNS games for the growth of social network services*. International Conference on Information Resources Management (CONF-IRM).

Chung, N., Lee, H., Kim, J.-Y., & Koo, C. (2018). The role of augmented reality for experience-influenced environments: The case of cultural heritage tourism in Korea. *Journal of Travel Research, 57*(5), 627–643.

Coursaris, C. K., Van Osch, W., & Sese, F. (2016). *Exploring the empirical link between game features, player motivation, and game behavior*. MCIS.

Cuellar, M. J., Tabatabaei, M., & Case, T. (2019). Antecedents of technology selection for project use. *Journal of Computer Information Systems*, 1–15.

Deng, Z., Lu, Y., Wei, K. K., & Zhang, J. (2010). Understanding customer satisfaction and loyalty: An empirical study of mobile instant messages in China. *International Journal of Information Management, 30*(4), 289–300.

Djamaluddin, R., Kindangen, P., & Tielung, M. (2017). Analyzing the effect of consumption values on customer purchase of virtual goods in Dota 2: A case at Feb Unsrat Manado. *Jurnal EMBA: Jurnal Riset Ekonomi, Manajemen, Bisnis dan Akuntansi, 5*(3).

Ferreira, G. C., & Ferreira, J. J. (2017). Absorptive capacity: An analysis in the context of Brazilian family firms. *RAM. Revista De Administração Mackenzie, 18*(1), 174–204.

Fornell, C., & Larcker, D. F. (1981). Evaluating structural equation models with unobservable variables and measurement error. *Journal of Marketing Research*, 39–50.

Ghazali, E., Mutum, D. S., & Woon, M.-Y. (2019a). Exploring player behavior and motivations to continue playing Pokémon GO. *Information Technology & People, 32*(3), 646–667.

Ghazali, E. M., Mutum, D. S., & Woon, M. Y. (2019). Multiple sequential mediation in an extended uses and gratifications model of augmented reality game Pokémon Go. *Internet Research*.

Guo, Z., Xiao, L., Van Toorn, C., Lai, Y., & Seo, C. (2016). Promoting online learners' continuance intention: An integrated flow framework. *Information & Management, 53*(2), 279–295.

Hair, J. F., Black, W. C., Babin, B. J., Anderson, R. E., & Tatham, R. L. (2006). *Multivariate data analysis* (6th ed.). Pearson Prentice Hall.

Hamari, J., Malik, A., Koski, J., & Johri, A. (2019). Uses and gratifications of Pokémon Go: Why do people play mobile location-based augmented reality games? *International Journal of Human-Computer Interaction, 35*(9), 804–819.

Harborth, D., & Pape, S. (2017). *Exploring the hype: Investigating technology acceptance factors of Pokémon Go*. 2017 IEEE International Symposium on Mixed and Augmented Reality (ISMAR).

Ho, C.-H., & Wu, T.-Y. (2012). Factors affecting intent to purchase virtual goods in online games. *International Journal of Electronic Business Management, 10*(3).

Ho, S.-C., Chen, J.-L., & Luo, S.-T. (2015). What users want: The factors that determine the retention of social location-based services. *Pacific Asia Journal of the Association for Information Systems, 7*(1).

Hong, F.-Y., Huang, D.-H., Lin, H.-Y., & Chiu, S.-L. (2014). Analysis of the psychological traits, Facebook usage, and Facebook addiction model of Taiwanese university students. *Telematics and Informatics, 31*(4), 597–606.

Hsiao, K.-L., & Chen, C.-C. (2016). What drives in-app purchase intention for mobile games? An examination of perceived values and loyalty. *Electronic Commerce Research and Applications, 16*, 18–29.

Hsiao, K.-L., Lytras, M. D., & Chen, C.-C. (2019). An in-app purchase framework for location-based AR games: the case of Pokémon Go. *Library Hi Tech.*

Hsu, C.-L., & Lin, J. C.-C. (2019). Understanding continuance intention to use online to offline (O2O) apps. *Electronic Markets*, 1–15.

Hsu, C.-L., Yu, C.-C., & Wu, C.-C. (2014). Exploring the continuance intention of social networking websites: An empirical research. *Information Systems and e-Business Management, 12*(2), 139–163.

Hsu, M.-H., Chang, C.-M., Lin, H.-C., & Lin, Y.-W. (2015). Determinants of continued use of social media: the perspectives of uses and gratifications theory and perceived interactivity. *Information Research, 20*(2).

Huang, C.-K., Chen, C.-D., & Liu, Y.-T. (2019). To stay or not to stay? Discontinuance intention of gamification apps. *Information Technology & People.*

Huang, T.-L., & Liao, S. (2015). A model of acceptance of augmented-reality interactive technology: The moderating role of cognitive innovativeness. *Electronic Commerce Research, 15*(2), 269–295.

Hull, D. C., Williams, G. A., & Griffiths, M. D. (2013). Video game characteristics, happiness and flow as predictors of addiction among video game players: A pilot study. *Journal of Behavioral Addictions, 2*(3), 145–152.

Hwang, K., & Lee, E. (2013). The role of entertainment and external values in consumer's intention to use Social Network Mobile. *International Proceedings of Economics Development and Research, 63*, 33.

Jung, T., Chung, N., & Leue, M. C. (2015). The determinants of recommendations to use augmented reality technologies: The case of a Korean theme park. *Tourism Management, 49*, 75–86.

Kang, J.-Y.M., & Johnson, K. K. (2015). Positive word-of-mouth for mobile location-based service retail apps usage. *International Journal of Mobile Communications, 13*(6), 599–618.

Kaur, P., Dhir, A., Rajala, R., & Dwivedi, Y. (2018). Why people use online social media brand communities: A consumption value theory perspective. *Online Information Review, 42*(2), 205–221.

Kim, E. J., Namkoong, K., Ku, T., & Kim, S. J. (2008). The relationship between online game addiction and aggression, self-control and narcissistic personality traits. *European Psychiatry, 23*(3), 212–218.

Klézl, V., Rebrošová, K., & Vyhlídalová, M. (2018). What Drives Gamers to Buy Virtual Goods? A Comparative Study of European Gamers. *On European Integration 2018*, 729.

Kline, R. B. (2015). *Principles and practice of structural equation modeling*. Guilford Publications.

Lao, K. (2014). Research on mechanism of consumer innovativeness influencing green consumption behavior. *Nankai Business Review International, 5*(2), 211–224.

Lee, Y., Kim, J., Lee, I., & Kim, H. (2002). A cross-cultural study on the value structure of mobile internet usage: Comparison between Korea and Japan. *Journal of Electronic Commerce Research, 3*(4), 227–239.

Lee, Y. J. (2015). A cause-effect analysis of the relationship between game use motives and continuous intention: Mediated effect of the attitude toward the shutdown system. *Indian Journal of Science and Technology, 8*(S8), 371–379.

Li, D., Chau, P. Y., & Van Slyke, C. (2010). A comparative study of individual acceptance of instant messaging in the US and China: A structural equation modeling approach. *Communications of the Association for Information Systems, 26*(1), 5.

Liu, B., Zhou, W., Zhu, T., Gao, L., & Xiang, Y. (2018). Location privacy and its applications: A systematic study. *IEEE Access, 6*, 17606–17624.

Luo, W., & Lee, Y.-C. (2018). Examining the loyalty of MMOG players: A comparative study between casual and core players. *The Journal of Internet Electronic Commerce Research, 18*(5), 139–165.

Ma, S. C., & Kaplanidou, K. (2019). Service quality, perceived value and behavioral intentions among highly and lowly identified baseball consumers across nations. *International Journal of Sports Marketing and Sponsorship*.

Magro, M. (2009). *Second life experience: Preliminary analysis regarding novel experience as a necessary component of customer expectation in second life*. The Southwest Decision Sciences Institute (SWDSI) Annual Meeting.

Merhi, M. I. (2016). Towards a framework for online game adoption. *Computers in Human Behavior, 60*, 253–263.

Merikivi, J., Tuunainen, V., & Nguyen, D. (2017). What makes continued mobile gaming enjoyable? *Computers in Human Behavior, 68*, 411–421.

Naranjo-Zolotov, M., Oliveira, T., & Casteleyn, S. (2019). Citizens' intention to use and recommend e-participation: Drawing upon UTAUT and citizen empowerment. *Information Technology & People, 32*(2), 364–386.

Natarajan, T., Balasubramanian, S. A., & Kasilingam, D. L. (2017). Understanding the intention to use mobile shopping applications and its influence on price sensitivity. *Journal of Retailing and Consumer Services, 37*, 8–22.

Nunnally, J., & Bernstein, I. (1967). *McGraw-Hill series in psychology. Psychometric theory*. McGraw-Hill.

Oghuma, A. P., Libaque-Saenz, C. F., Wong, S. F., & Chang, Y. (2016). An expectation-confirmation model of continuance intention to use mobile instant messaging. *Telematics and Informatics, 33*(1), 34–47.

Oliveira, T., Thomas, M., Baptista, G., & Campos, F. (2016). Mobile payment: Understanding the determinants of customer adoption and intention to recommend the technology. *Computers in Human Behavior, 61*, 404–414.

Olsson, T., Lagerstam, E., Kärkkäinen, T., & Väänänen-Vainio-Mattila, K. (2013). Expected user experience of mobile augmented reality services: A user study in the context of shopping centres. *Personal and Ubiquitous Computing, 17*(2), 287–304.

Omigie, N. O., Zo, H., Rho, J. J., & Ciganek, A. P. (2017). Customer pre-adoption choice behavior for M-PESA mobile financial services: Extending the theory of consumption values. *Industrial Management & Data Systems, 117*(5), 910–926.

Park, B.-W., & Lee, K. C. (2011). An empirical analysis of online gamers' perceptions of game items: Modified theory of consumption values approach. *Cyberpsychology, Behavior, and Social Networking, 14*(7–8), 453–459.

Parry, S. (2017). *Fit Statistics commonly reported for CFA and SEM*. Cornell University.

Pihlström, M. (2008). *Perceived value of mobile service use and its consequences*. Svenska handelshögskolan.

Rauschnabel, P., & Rossmann, A. (2017). Exploring user adoption of augmented reality applications based on Pokémon Go. *Digital Enterprise Computing (DEC 2017).*

Rauschnabel, P. A., Rossmann, A., & tom Dieck, M. C. (2017). An adoption framework for mobile augmented reality games: The case of Pokémon Go. *Computers in Human Behavior, 76*, 276–286.

Rezaei, S., & Ghodsi, S. S. (2014). Does value matters in playing online game? An empirical study among massively multiplayer online role-playing games (MMORPGs). *Computers in Human Behavior, 35*, 252–266.

Rodrigues, L. F., Costa, C. J., & Oliveira, A. (2014). *How gamification can influence the web design and the customer to use the e-banking systems*. Proceedings of the International Conference on Information Systems and Design of Communication.

Rodrigues, L. F., Costa, C. J., & Oliveira, A. (2017). How does the web game design influence the behavior of e-banking users? *Computers in Human Behavior, 74*, 163–174.

Schermelleh-Engel, K., Moosbrugger, H., & Müller, H. (2003). Evaluating the fit of structural equation models: Tests of significance and descriptive goodness-of-fit measures. *Methods of Psychological Research Online, 8*(2), 23–74.

Schumacker, R. E., & Lomax, R. G. (2004). *A beginner's guide to structural equation modeling*. psychology Press.

Seok, H. J., Lee, J. M., Park, C.-Y., & Park, J. Y. (2018). Understanding internet gaming addiction among South Korean adolescents through photovoice. *Children and Youth Services Review, 94*, 35–42.

Shang, R.-A., Chen, Y.-C., & Huang, S.-C. (2010). *Buying decorative virtual goods for the avatars in the virtual world*. 2010 7th International Conference on Service Systems and Service Management.

Spink, P., Rahim, M. M., & Singh, U. B. (2011). *User intentions of downloading games on mobile phones: an empirical evaluation using consumption value model*.

Statista.com. (2019a). *Most popular Apple App Store categories in May 2019, by share of available apps*. https://www.statista.com/statistics/270291/popular-categories-in-the-app-store/

Statista.com. (2019b). *Most popular Google Play app store categories from 1st quarter 2016 to 2nd quarter 2019, by number of downloads (in millions)*. https://www.statista.com/statistics/256772/most-popular-app-categories-in-the-google-play-store/

Sun, Y., Zhao, Y., Jia, S., & Zheng, D. (2015). *Understanding the antecedents of mobile game addiction: the roles of perceived visibility, perceived enjoyment and flow*. Proceedings of the Pacific Asia Conference on Information Systems.

Sundram, V., Shanmugam, J., & Bhatti, M. (2013). *Supply Chain Integration: A Framework of Validation using Structural Equation Modeling*. Available at SSRN 2248408.

Sunny, P. & Ajimon, G. (2016). Determinants of behavioral intention to use mobile wallets—A conceptual model. *Journal of Management (JOM), 5*(5), 52–62.

Tavares, J., & Oliveira, T. (2018). New integrated model approach to understand the factors that drive electronic health record portal adoption: Cross-sectional national survey. *Journal of Medical Internet Research, 20*(11), e11032.

Teng, C.-I. (2018). Look to the future: Enhancing online gamer loyalty from the perspective of the theory of consumption values. *Decision Support Systems, 114*, 49–60.

Thrassou, A., Vrontis, D., Efthymiou, L., & Uzunboylu, N. (2022a). An overview of business advancement through technology: Markets and marketing in transition. In A. Thrassou, D. Vrontis, L. Efthymiou, Y. Weber, S. M. R. Shams, & E. Tsoukatos (Eds.), *Business advancement through technology. Volume I. Palgrave studies in cross-disciplinary business research.*

In Association with EuroMed Academy of Business. Palgrave Macmillan. https://doi.org/10.1007/978-3-031-07769-2_1

Thrassou, A., Vrontis, D., Efthymiou, L., Uzunboylu, N. (2022b). An overview of business advancement through technology: The changing landscape of work and employment. In A. Thrassou, D. Vrontis, L. Efthymiou, Y. Weber, S. M. R. Shams, & E. Tsoukatos (Eds.), *Business advancement through technology. Volume II. Palgrave studies in cross-disciplinary business research. In Association with EuroMed Academy of Business*. Palgrave Macmillan. https://doi.org/10.1007/978-3-031-07765-4_1

Toker, S., & Baturay, M. H. (2016). Antecedents and consequences of game addiction. *Computers in Human Behavior, 55*, 668–679.

Turel, O., Serenko, A., & Bontis, N. (2010). User acceptance of hedonic digital artifacts: A theory of consumption values perspective. *Information & Management, 47*(1), 53–59.

van Rooij, A. J., Schoenmakers, T. M., Van den Eijnden, R. J., Vermulst, A. A., & van de Mheen, D. (2012). Video game addiction test: Validity and psychometric characteristics. *Cyberpsychology, Behavior, and Social Networking, 15*(9), 507–511.

Vrontis, D., Thrassou, A., Uzunboylu, N., & Efthymiou, L. (2023). An overview of business for sustainability: Strategic avenues and managerial approaches. In D. Vrontis, A. Thrassou, L. Efthymiou, Y. Weber, S. M. R. Shams, & E. Tsoukatos (Eds.), *Business for sustainability. Volume I. Palgrave studies in cross-disciplinary business research*. In Association with EuroMed Academy of Business. Palgrave Macmillan. https://doi.org/10.1007/978-3-031-37361-9_1

Wang, H.-Y., Liao, C., & Yang, L.-H. (2013). What affects mobile application use? The roles of consumption values. *International Journal of Marketing Studies, 5*(2), 11.

Wang, X., Zhang, P., & Fang, X. (2017). Factors influencing continued usage of smartphone games. *International Journal of u-and e-Service, Science and Technology, 10*(5), 67–78.

Wu, M. (2009). *Structural equation modeling: Operation and application of AMOS*. Chongqing Univ.

Yang, H.-L., & Lin, R.-X. (2017). Determinants of the intention to continue use of SoLoMo services: Consumption values and the moderating effects of overloads. *Computers in Human Behavior, 73*, 583–595.

Yoo, J. M. (2015). Perceived value of game items and purchase intention. *Indian Journal of Science and Technology, 8*(19), 2–7.

Yun, H., Han, D., & Lee, C. C. (2013). Understanding the use of location-based service applications: Do privacy concerns matter? *Journal of Electronic Commerce Research, 14*(3), 215.

Zhang, J., & Mao, E. (2013). *Management of location-based services innovation: Insights from consumers*. 2013 Suzhou-Silicon Valley-Beijing International Innovation Conference.

Zhu, D. S., Kuo, M. J., & Liou, S. H. (2014). *The study of continuance intention for online social games*. 2014 IIAI 3rd International Conference on Advanced Applied Informatics.

Zhu, G., Sangwan, S., & Lu, T.-J. (2010). A new theoretical framework of technology acceptance and empirical investigation on self-efficacy-based value adoption model. *Nankai Business Review International, 1*(4), 345–372.

Zichermann, G., & Linder, J. (2010). *Game-based marketing: Inspire customer loyalty through rewards, challenges, and contests*. John Wiley & Sons.

CHAPTER 7

The Relationship Between Leadership Style and Organisation's Emotional Climate at Different Life Cycle Stages

Erika Vaiginiene, Živilė Stravinskaitė, and Vaida Balbieriūtė

7.1 Introduction

The aim of this paper is to identify the existing relationships between leadership style and organisation's emotional climate at different life cycle stages. By exploring how leadership styles impact organisations' emotional climate and their life cycles the study identifies the ways in

E. Vaiginiene (✉)
Faculty of Economics and Business Administration, Vilnius University, Vilnius, Lithuania
e-mail: erika.vaiginiene@cr.vu.lt

Ž. Stravinskaitė
Department of Business Economics and Management, Vilnius University, Vilnius, Lithuania

V. Balbieriūtė
Innovation Agency, Vilnius, Lithuania

D. Vrontis et al. (eds.), *Business in Uncertainty*, Palgrave Studies in Cross-disciplinary Business Research, In Association with EuroMed Academy of Business, https://doi.org/10.1007/978-3-031-65587-6_7

which the emotional climate changes throughout the life cycle stages of an organisation and which leadership styles managers should adopt to integrate their organisations and keep them thriving for as long as possible.

Most modern organisations exist for 15–20 years, while others last centuries due to the ability to make the right decisions at the right time of their development stage. In the face of global crises, such as COVID-19, wars, disruptive technologies, and climate change, among others (Buhalis et al., 2024; Thrassou et al., 2022; Vrontis et al., 2023, 2024) change management has become increasingly prevalent. The role of a leader plays a crucial role in the success of an organisation by determining the emotional climate of the organisation. A manager's ability to make the right decisions based on the problems inherent to the life cycle stage can influence the development of that organisation and employee job satisfaction.

Organisational life cycles have been studied for decades (Freeman & Engel, 2007; Jawahar & McLaughlin, 2001; Miller & Friesen, 1984; Richard et al., 2006) with some authors making distinctions based on the size of the organisation, others providing less detailed characteristics or excluding the decline phase. The classification of life cycle stages developed by Adizes (2015a, 2015b) in the 1980s is based on many years of practice and provides the most detailed taxonomy. Therefore, this article draws on the development stages identified in Adizes' methodology.

The emotional climate of an organisation is a less researched topic, with barely any research done in the Lithuanian context; however, it is becoming increasingly popular. In a broader sense, there is some research on the relationship between managerial leadership style and organisational climate (Jenkins, 2019; Sekerka & Fredrikson, 2008) and its impact on performance (Mumford et al., 2002; Goussak et al., 2011), but the relationship between organisational emotional climate, the organisation's life cycle stage, and managerial leadership style has not been studied yet. This study seeks to answer the question of which leadership style is most conducive to creating a favourable emotional climate in an organisation for it to move into the high-performance phase of the development life cycle.

The Organisation of the chapter is the following: in the next section, the analysis presents a review of the literature. Then, the analysis presents the 'Research Design' of the study and its hypothesis. The subsequent section presents the 'Findings' of the study, prior to summarising with a 'Concluding Discussion and Recommendations'.

7.2 Literature Review

Organisational Life Cycle and the Emotional Climate of the Organisation

Organisations develop in stages rather than as a linear process. The concept of a 'life cycle' to describe the span of an organisation was first used by Boulding in 1950 (von Wobesser, 2016). Since then, many authors have studied the topic—Greiner (1997), Adizes (2015a, 2015b), Zakarevičius (2002), Freeman and Engel (2007), Baird and Meshoulam (1988), Jawahar and McLaughlin (2001), Richard et al. (2006), Miller and Friesen (1984), and Lester et al. (2003). Each stage is characterised by certain patterns, and moving from one cycle to the next requires strategic change, new objectives, and changes in structure and working methods.

Freeman and Engel (2007) delineate two cycles: the realisation of business ideas culminating in prototype sales and revenue generation, marked by customer feedback guiding future steps. Richard et al. (2006) distinguishes early stages (formation and growth) from later ones (maturity and decline). Baird and Meshoulam (1988) identify birth, maturity, and decline as fundamental life cycle stages, emphasising their role as building blocks where activities in one stage underpin the next, with no explicit consideration of organisational death. Jawahar and McLaughlin (2001) propose four phases: birth, growth, maturity, and rebirth, focusing on characteristics such as business plan development in the birth phase, growth-seeking behaviours in the growth phase, and the maturity phase's high revenues, efficiency, stability, and proactivity. Greiner (1997), Miller and Friesen (1984), and Lester et al. (2003) collectively suggest five cycles, with Greiner emphasising growth cycles marked by long-term opportunities and crises, Miller and Friesen distinguishing birth, growth, maturity, revival, and decline, and Lester expanding his sequence to include existence, survival, success, renewal, and decline (Baird & Meshoulam, 1988; Freeman & Engel, 2007; Greiner, 1997; Jawahar & McLaughlin, 2001; Miller & Friesen, 1984; Lester et al., 2003; Richard et al., 2006).

Adizes's (1979) methodology distinguishes 10 life cycle stages: premarital, infancy, Go-Go, adolescence, prosperity, stability, aristocracy, early bureaucracy, bureaucracy, and death. Most organisations do not move from one life cycle to the next in the traditional sense (Lester & Parnell, 2002; Miller & Friesen, 1984), so Adizes (1979) suggests five categories that indicate that an organisation ceases to exist without moving on to the next stage: accidental love affair; death of an infant; founder's family trap; and divorce (premature ageing, unrealised entrepreneur) (Table 7.1).

This article draws on Adizes's (2015a, 2015b) stages of the organisational life cycle, which combine different authors' proposed categorisations and analyse leadership challenges at each stage. According to this theory, the life cycle of an organisation is determined by two factors: flexibility and level of control. Based on this, Adizes divides all development stages into two parts: growing and ageing organisations. Each cycle requires specific managerial behaviour and results in an emotional climate for the employees.

Table 7.1 Models of organisational life cycles

Authors	*Stage 1 Beginning*	*Stage 2 Development*	*Stage 3 Maturity*	*Stage 4 Diversification*	*Stage 5 Decline*
Freeman and Engel (2007)	Realising business ideas and generating revenue				—
Richard et al. (2006)	Early (formation and growth)		Late (maturity and decline)		
Baird and Meshoulam (1988)	Birth	Maturity			Decline
Jawahar and McLaughlin (2001)	Birth	Growth	Maturity	Revival	—
Greiner (1997)	Innovation	Orientation	Delegation	Collaboration	—
Miller and Friesen (1984)	Birth	Growth	Maturity	Revival	Decline
Lester et al. (2003)	Existence	Survival	Success	Renewal	Decline
Adizes (1979)	Pre-marital; Infancy	Go-Go Adolescence	Prosperity	Stability	Aristocracy, Early Bureaucracy, Bureaucracy, Death

Source Compiled by the authors

In growing organisations (Pre-marital, Infancy, Go-go, Adolescence, Prosperity), success is driven by risk-taking, prioritising action over perfection, viewing problems as opportunities, and recognising the leader's pivotal role. Employee clarity on their purpose and value creation for customers is vital. In ageing organisations (Stability Cycle, Aristocracy, Early Bureaucracy, Bureaucracy, Death), risk aversion prevails, and exceeding expectations diminishes due to reduced ambition. The focus shifts towards documentation and organisational objectives, often sidelining customer-centricity. Transformation requires systemic change rather than just leadership alteration. Each life cycle of an organisation offers different opportunities and challenges for employees, which is why emotional well-being is an important indicator of where an organisation is in its life cycle.

The emotional climate of an organisation is a long-term characteristic of the internal environment of an organisation that is experienced by its members and influences their behaviour (Taguiri, 1968). It is determined by the values, goals, beliefs, and attitudes of the organisation, the influences of the social environment (Tran, 1998), managers' behaviour (Kelner et al., 1994; Momeni, 2009), and their leadership style. Organisational climate measures how employees feel in their work environment, the interpersonal relationships fostered among team members and the contribution they make to the overall performance. The climate is created by its leader through the values, culture and working environment of the organisation, helping employees feel important and empowered to achieve their goals (Harel et al., 2021).

Theoretical Analysis of the Leadership Style, Emotional Climate, and Organisational Life Cycle

A manager's leadership style significantly influences the emotional climate of an organisation and the manager-employee relationship (Dele et al., 2015), with recent recognition of its importance in the organisational environment (Samul, 2016). This paper explores three leadership styles: transactional, transformational, and 'Laissez-faire' (or liberal) styles, distinguished by their social interaction aspects.

Transactional leadership, characterised by a leader maintaining a certain distance from employees and emphasising high task standards and short deadlines, can create tension within the organisation when the leader lacks popularity. It often discourages employees from making suggestions, objecting, or expressing creativity due to fear. This leadership style unilaterally defines organisational policies, procedures, team dynamics, and incentives, potentially leading to a punitive atmosphere if goals are not met (Van Wugt et al., 2004). Conversely, a transformational leader inspires and motivates by fostering trust, respect, and individualised attention, encouraging creativity, and ensuring psychological security among followers. This approach enhances productivity, job satisfaction, and organisational commitment (Fiaz et al., 2017; Hassi et al., 2022) while promoting active communication and a safe environment for open expression. In contrast, a laissez-faire leader promotes a loose, informal organisational culture, granting employees decision-making freedom. Although this autonomy can foster development and learning, it may lead to role conflicts and reduced commitment due to a lack of feedback and motivation (Bass & Avolio, 1995; Eagly et al., 2003; Gill, 2014).

In growing organisations, leadership styles should align with the organisation's life cycle stages. During the pre-marital phase, motivating and inspiring teamwork and creativity are vital, while the infancy phase requires more control, ambition, and centralised management. The Go-Go phase benefits from a balance between results-focused transactional management and creativity-encouraging transformational leadership. Adolescence involves shared responsibilities and increased decision-making, where adopting a liberal leadership style might be suitable. The prosperity phase thrives on high employee engagement, ambitious targets, and creativity, making transformational leadership effective, whereas a transactional approach could stifle responsibility and creativity. In the stability cycle, as growth slows, a transformational leader focuses on employee well-being and flexible working conditions, while a liberal leader shares responsibilities with the team. In ageing organisations (aristocracy, early bureaucracy, bureaucracy, and death), employees exhibit low engagement, lack creativity, face internal conflicts, and lack control and goal orientation. A liberal leader may exert insufficient power in these phases, reducing engagement and poor outcomes. A transactional leader sets goals but overlooks team members' emotional states, hindering innovation and goal achievement.

In summary, an organisation should choose a leadership style that is appropriate to sustain the organisation in its life cycle phase of development and enhance the productivity and effectiveness of the employees, as this will determine whether the organisation moves to a higher stage of growth, becomes obsolete or returns to prosperity stage.

7.3 Research Design

Based on the literature review, the research assumption is that (a) emotional climate is significantly correlated with organisational life cycle; (b) leadership style has a significant impact on organisational emotional climate; (c) organisational emotional climate and managerial leadership style have an impact on organisational life cycle.

Following this logic, the study proposes and tests eleven hypotheses:

H1. The emotional climate (^{x1}) has a statistically significant correlation with an organisational life cycle.
H2. The leadership style (^{x2}) has a significant impact on the emotional climate of the organisation.
H3. The emotional climate of the organisation (^{x1}) and the leadership style of the leader (^{x2}) have an impact on the organisation's life cycle.
H4. The leadership style of the leader (^{x2}) has an impact on the organisation's life cycle.
H5. There is a positive relationship between a liberal leadership style and a positive emotional climate in a growing organisation.
H6. There is a positive relationship between a liberal leadership style and a positive emotional climate in ageing organisations.
H7. There is a positive relationship between a growing organisation and a positive emotional climate.
H8. There is a positive relationship between a liberal leadership style and a negative emotional climate in a growing organisation.
H9. There is a positive relationship between a liberal leadership style and a negative emotional climate in an ageing organisation.
H10. There is a positive relationship between an ageing organisation and a transactional leadership style.
H11. There is a positive relationship between a growing organisation and a transformational leadership style.

We used a quantitative survey questionnaire to test those hypotheses. The questionnaire was combined of four constructs:

1. Emotional organisational climate (15 questions);
2. Organisation life cycle (11 questions);

3. Leadership style (21 questions);
4. Demographic data (4 questions).

We have chosen to apply a 15-statement construct developed by Elsa Peña-Suárez, José Muñi, Ángela Campillo-Álvarez, Eduardo Fonseca-Pedrero, and Eduardo García-Cueto (2013) and five points Likert scale to measure the emotional climate (see Table 7.2).

We operationalised Adizes's (2015a, 2015b) life cycle model for the identification of the organisation's life cycle stage (11 questions). For this questionnaire, we applied an opinion rating scale, which requires the respondent to give an opinion about a statement by selecting one statement rather than another according to the given characteristics (Dikčius, 2011). So, we divided the organisation's life cycles into two groups of stages: growing and ageing. *Infancy, Go-Go, Adolescence* and *Prosperity* life cycle stages fell into the category of growing organisations. While, *Stability, Aristocracy, Early Bureaucracy, Bureaucracy,* and *Death* life cycle stages fell into the category of ageing organisations. The description for a *growing organisation* was weighted by '1', and *for an ageing organisation*, it was weighted by '2' (Table 7.3).

The leadership style was determined by using a short form of the Multifactor Leadership Questionnaire 6-S (MLQ-6S) developed by Bass and Avolio (1995), consisting of 21 questions. This instrument is a validated tool for the identification of the leadership styles—transformational, transactional, or 'Laissez-faire'.

The emotional climate and leadership style constructs are based on validated constructs, while the construct for the identification of the organisation's life cycle was developed by us. Thus, it was tested during the pilot study, after which it was corrected before starting the main study.

The reliability of the questionnaires was tested by reliability analysis using Cronbach alpha coefficient. Based on the results, Cronbach's alpha value of all constructs is greater than 0.6, which proves its validity and interrelationship of the items.

The Cronbach's alpha coefficient was used to evaluate the compatibility of the scales with the data, which shows whether the questionnaires and individual blocks of questions described in the theoretical part of the work reflect the analysed phenomenon. Question scales are considered consistent with the data if Cronbach's alpha value is greater than 0.6. The value of Cronbach's alpha coefficient of the data obtained from the emotional climate questionnaire used in the study reaches—0.862, and

Table 7.2 Emotional climate of the organization

Nr	*Items*	*I strongly disagree*	*I disagree*	*I agree more than I disagree*	*I agree*	*I strongly agree*
1.	The relationships with my bosses are good	1	2	3	4	5
2.	My bosses encourage me when I have problems so that 1 can solve them	1	2	3	4	5
3.	My suggestions about the work is listening	1	2	3	4	5
4.	Opportunities for training are offered	1	2	3	4	5
5.	If 1 need help because of a heavy workload, 1 am given the necessary means	1	2	3	4	5
6.	The goal of my work are clearly deñned	1	2	3	4	5
7.	The bosses are willing to listen to their employees	1	2	3	4	5
8.	Socially, my work has the prestige it deserves	1	2	3	4	5
9.	In my Job, innovate contributions are appreciated	1	2	3	4	5
10.	Then 1 do something well, my superiors congratulate me	1	2	3	4	5

(continued)

Table 7.2 (continued)

Nr	*Items*	*I strongly disagree*	*I disagree*	*I agree more than I disagree*	*I agree*	*I strongly agree*
11.	My work is adequately denned	1	2	3	4	5
12.	Deadlines are adequately met	1	2	3	4	5
13.	My bosses watch me closely	1	2	3	4	5
14.	My work is inadequately supervised	1	2	3	4	5
15.	Everything is decided from above	1	2	3	4	5

Source Compiled by the authors based on Elsa Peña-Suárez et al. (2013)

the data of the Organisational Life Cycle questionnaire is—0.82. When assessing the consistency of the leadership style questionnaire (21 statements), Cronbach's alpha was found to be equal to 0.877, with individual style subscales ranging from 0.861 to 0.932.

Eight organisations took part in the study. These were public administration, accommodation, transport, tourism and catering companies, and educational institutions. In total, the questionnaire was filled out by 290 respondents. The coverage of each organisation was more than 50% of their workforce of different levels.

To determine the relationship between the variables, Spearman's correlation coefficient *r*- was applied. To calculate the results of the study *t*-test, Kolmogorov–Smirnov and Shapiro–Wilk tests, regression, and moderator analyses were performed.

Kolmogorov–Smirnov and Shapiro–Wilk tests were conducted to assess the normality of the distribution of emotional climate and leadership style data across organisations. The analysis shows that the data of the questionnaire on the emotional climate of the organisation is $p > 0.05$ for all organisations except for organisation 'A', which means that the distribution of data is statistically normal. The *p*-value for organisations 'A' and

Table 7.3 Construct of the organisation's life cycle stages

1.	(a) The most important thing for employees is "why" and "what" to do. (1)
	(b) For employees, it's all about "how" to do it and "who" will do it. (2)
2.	(a) Even a well done job will not be appreciated if it is not properly documented (2)
	(b) Doing the job well is more important than documenting it properly (1)
3.	(a) Staff are evaluated on their personal qualities rather than on the basis of a clearly measured and defined workload (2)
	(b) Employees are clearly aware of the organisation's reward structure and the criteria against which they are assessed for their contribution to the organisation (1)
4.	(a) Staff are willing to take on responsibility, even when it exceeds their authority (1)
	(b) Staff tend to take on less responsibility than their existing mandate (2)
5.	(a) The created inertia contributes to the organisation's performance. (2)
	(b) The organisation requires continuous managerial intervention (1)
6.	(a) Changing an organisation's behaviour requires changing the whole system. (2)
	(b) To change the behaviour of an organisation, you only need to change the leader (1)
7.	(a) Staff expectations exceed results. (1)
	(b) Staff performance exceeds expectations. (2)
8.	(a) An organisation exists to create value for its customers. (1)
	(b) It is very important for an organisation to maximise its profits/achieve its objectives. (2)
9.	(a) Encouraging workers to take higher risk actions (1)
	(b) Employees are more likely to succeed by setting achievable goals that require less risk (2)
10.	(a) Every opportunity can create new problems (2)
	(b) Every problem is seen as an opportunity (1)
11.	(a) staff only take action when they are convinced that it is explicitly authorised (1)
	(b) Employees behave as if everything that is not forbidden is permitted (2)

Source Compiled by the authors based on I. Adizes (2015a, 2015b)

'C' is <0.05, but the coefficient of asymmetry is (−0.306), and the coefficient of skewness is (−0.230), and they do not exceed 1, which means that the data can be considered as close to normal distribution.

According to the Kolmogorov–Smirnov test, the data from the questionnaire on leadership style for all organisations except 'A' and 'B' are $p > 0.05$, which means that the distribution of data is statistically normal. The Shapiro–Wilk test shows that for organisations, 'A', 'B', and 'G' <0.05, but the coefficient of asymmetry is (−0.587) and the coefficient of skewness is (−0.363), and they do not exceed 1, which means that the data can be considered as being close to normal distribution.

7.4 Findings

This article maintains confidentiality by using letters instead of organisation names.

The survey data analysis reveals that the most positive assessment of the emotional climate is made by the employees of organisations 'B' (mean—3.91) and 'C' (mean—3.98). The emotional climate is also rated quite positively in organisations 'F' (mean—3.6) and 'G' (mean—3.62). Employees in organisations with 'E' (mean 3.3) and 'H' (mean 3.4) are less positive about the organisation's emotional climate. The emotional climate of organisations is rated least favourably by employees in 'A' (mean 3.0) and 'D' (mean 2.9) organisations.

In organisations with the most positive emotional climate, the relationship between employees and their manager was found to be very good. In organisation 'B', the mean score for respondents' good relationship with their manager is 4.38, in organisation 'C' it is 4.43. The role of the manager in supporting and encouraging the employees (both averages above 4.2), taking pride in a job well done (both averages above 4.2) and listening to their suggestions (averages of 4.17) is also very positively expressed in these organisations. These organisations also have a very positive perception of innovative contributions.

In the organisation with the most negative emotional climate, the relationship with the manager was rated the lowest by the respondents ('A' organisation with a mean of 3.21, 'D' organisation with a mean of 3.33). These organisations are also less positive about supporting employees, listening to them and their suggestions, not being provided with tools due to excessive workload, and not having well-defined jobs, which means doing a lot of things that do not belong. The 'decision-making from the top' is also very highly rated. The theoretical part discussed that managers who do not involve employees in decision-making create a less motivating environment, do not maintain a good emotional climate in the organisation and undermine creativity.

Although the most favourable assessment of the relationship with the manager was made by the employees of organisation 'E', their emotional climate is less favourable than that of organisations 'B' or 'C'. Compared to the organisations with the highest emotional climate scores, employees in organisation 'E' indicated that they had a very negative perception of work supervision (mean score—2.77) and meeting deadlines (mean score—2.38). It is possible that a good relationship is built with team members but the focus is not on achieving results, which can lead to employees feeling overlooked and free to not complete work tasks on time, thus creating a disintegrating system.

Survey data demonstrates that three organisations are in the growth phase, and five are in the ageing phase. Organisations 'B', 'C', and 'D' are growing organisations, while 'A', 'E', 'F', 'G', and 'H' are ageing organisations. In all the growing organisations, employees care about their work objectives, are concerned about the quality of their work, are willing to take responsibility, and see problems as opportunities. These organisations have a clear reward system in place, which is an important factor for increasing employee job satisfaction and motivation. In growing organisations, employees are rewarded for taking more risks, thus motivating them to take on more ambitious challenges.

In all the ageing organisations, the inertia created was very pronounced, the loss of control was evident, and change required a change in the whole system, not just the manager. Also, in such organisations, employees are more likely to succeed by setting more achievable goals, i.e. they are motivated to stand still and not challenge themselves.

Leadership styles vary among surveyed organisations. Transactional leadership style is more pronounced in the 'A' (mean 4.2), 'C' (mean 4.3), and 'G' (mean 3.75) organisations, but is not as pronounced in the 'G' organisation as in the other two. According to the employees of organisations 'B' and 'F', the most important factors for the managers of these organisations are those that correspond to the transformational style, but this style is much more pronounced in organisation 'B' (mean—4.5) than in organisation 'F' (mean—3.8). Laissez-faire for the three organisations 'E', 'D', and 'H': the style is most strongly expressed in organisation 'E' (mean—4.5), more weakly in organisation 'D' (mean—3.5) and in organisation 'H' (mean—3.7).

These findings suggest that exists relationship between emotional climate, organisational life cycle, and leadership styles (Table 7.4).

The findings show that there is a weak positive and statistically significant relationship ($r = 0.420$, $p. < 0.001$) between emotional climate and organisational life cycle.

Table 7.4 Research results: leadership style, life cycle and emotional climate

Organization	*Prevailing leadership style*	*Organization life cycle*	*Average emotional climate score*
Organization "A"	Transactional	Aging	3,0505
Organization "B"	Transformative	Growing	3,9163
Organization "C"	Transactional	Growing	3,9822
Organization "D"	Liberal	Growing	2,9611
Organization "E"	Liberal	Aging	3,3179
Organisation "F"	Transformative	Aging	3,6577
Organization "G"	Transactional	Aging	3,6200
Organization "H"	Liberal	Aging	3,4489

An independent *t*-test was used to test the difference between the life cycle and the emotional climate in a growing and an ageing organisation. It was found that the mean emotional climate of a growing organisation is (3.7865) and that of an ageing organisation is (3.2276), which means that there is a correlation between a growing organisation and a positively perceived emotional climate (*p*. 0.025). Data analysis demonstrates that there is a significant correlation between leadership style and the emotional climate of the organisation (coefficient—0.682, $p. < 0.001$).

The regression analysis of the relationship between organisational emotional climate and leadership style in a growing and an ageing organisation showed that the data is suitable for analysis because the Adjusted R square coefficient is 0.489, the Durbin Watson coefficient is 1.995 and the VIF is less than 4, which means that the x's are not correlated. In ageing organisations, emotional climate was found to be directly positively related to transformational leadership style and negatively related to transactional leadership style. It can be concluded that the use of transformational leadership style improves the emotional climate in ageing organisations, while the use of transactional leadership style worsens the emotional climate. Liberal leadership is not an influencing factor for emotional climate in the ageing cycle ($p. > 0.05$). According to the Standardised coefficient Betta, it can be concluded that the regressor of transactional (0.826) leadership style is more influential in the model than the one of transformational leadership style (−0.96), with a $p < 0.05$, and thus it can be said that it is statistically more significant.

The regression analysis shows that there is a direct relationship between transactional and transformational leadership styles and the emotional climate of a growing organisation. As the intensity of these leadership styles increases in growing organisations, the emotional climate improves. A negative statistical relationship was also found between liberal leadership style and positive emotional climate in growing organisations, i.e. there is a positive relationship between liberal leadership style and negative emotional climate in growing organisations. Therefore, it can be concluded that the use of a laissez-faire leadership style in subsequent cycles in growing organisations worsens the emotional climate of the organisation. This is because employees feel that the organisation needs to have systems in place to provide the basis for a growing organisation, but that leaders have left everything to their own devices. In ageing organisations, this hypothesis has not been borne out.

No significant correlation is found between an ageing organisation and a transactional leadership style ($r = 0.134$). The absence of a strong relationship may be attributed to the measurement of only the top manager's leadership style, which may not fully represent the organisation's leadership dynamics when the entire team is involved.

Regression analysis shows that emotional climate also has a direct relationship with the organisation's life cycle (unstandardised coefficient 0.305, $p. < 0.01$), when the Adjusted R square coefficient is 0.489, the Durbin Watson coefficient is 0.255, and the VIF is less than 4, which means that x is not correlated with each other.

The analysis revealed a weak positive relationship (r 0.299, $p. = 0.01$) between emotional climate and organisational life cycle. Subsequently, a regression analysis within ageing organisations indicated that liberal leadership does not significantly influence the emotional climate ($p > 0.05$). Conversely, a positive relationship was observed between the adoption of a transformational leadership style and an improved emotional climate in ageing organisations. Additionally, the study found a negative statistical relationship between transactional leadership style and emotional climate in ageing organisations, implying that a more transactional leadership style is associated with a worsened emotional climate.

A moderator analysis examined how the influence of leadership styles (x) on emotional climate (y) varies based on the organisation's life cycle (w). The results indicate that the impact of Laissez-faire leadership on emotional climate depends on the organisation's life cycle. In contrast, the effect of transformational leadership on emotional climate remains consistent ($p > 0.05$) across all life cycles, demonstrating a consistently positive impact. Furthermore, the impact of transactional leadership on emotional climate is influenced by the organisation's life cycle: it positively affects the emotional climate in growing organisations but negatively in ageing ones. The analysis suggests that the connection between a positive emotional climate and the chosen leadership style is more robust in growing organisations (Tables 7.5 and 7.6).

To summarise, eleven hypotheses were formulated, and the results showed that seven of them were fully approved (1, 2, 6, 7, 8, 10, and 11). These include findings that confirm a significant correlation between emotional climate and organisational life cycle, the impact of leadership style on organisational climate, a positive association between a growing organisation and a positive emotional climate, a positive correlation between an ageing organisation and a transactional leadership style, and a positive relationship between a growing organisation and a transformational leadership style. Four hypotheses were rejected—3, 4, 5, and 9. However, hypotheses 3 and 4 were not supported, suggesting no statistically significant relationship between organisational life cycle and leadership style due to variations in leadership styles among different organisations. Hypotheses 5 and 9 show mixed results for a liberal leadership style in ageing and growing organisations: it was found that there is a negative relationship between liberal leadership style and positive climate in a growing organisation and a positive relationship between liberal leadership style and negative climate in a growing organisation.

Table 7.5 The moderating role of the organisational life cycle (w) on the emotional climate (y) for different leadership styles (x)

Leadership style	r.	p.
Liberal	0.0674	0000
Transformational	0.0033	0.1044
Transactional	0.0762	0

Table 7.6 The moderating role of a growing organisation's life cycle (w) on the relationship between leadership styles (x) and emotional climate (y)

Leadership style	r.2	p.
Liberal	0.0098	0.0268
Transformative	0.0060	0.0253
Transactional	0.0889	0.000

7.5 Concluding Discussion and Recommendations

The present study aimed to shed light on the connection between leadership styles, the emotional climate of the organisation and its life cycle. The research findings support several hypotheses, including the correlation between emotional climate and organisational life cycle, the influence of leadership style on the organisation's emotional climate, and the variations in these relationships based on an organisation's growth or ageing phase.

Specifically, this study revealed that a leadership style can have a significant impact on the emotional climate of an organisation, with transformational leadership having an overall positive effect on all stages of organisational development, and in ageing organisations in particular, improving the emotional climate, encouraging employees to think creatively, unleashing their inner potential, and giving them hope.

On the other hand, transactional leadership in ageing organisations creates additional tension and competition at an already difficult stage, thus worsening the emotional climate even further. However, the results also show that the emotional climate can be good in ageing organisations, where employees can feel emotionally well if they are not set ambitious goals and the organisation is not committed to change.

A manager's liberal leadership style is not a factor in the emotional climate as the organisation ages, but its use in growing organisations can worsen the emotional climate in the later stages of organisational growth as the organisation expands, responsibilities increase, and the manager might be seen as not taking enough accountability.

The research validates the importance of leadership styles in shaping an organisation's emotional climate and provides empirical findings needed to expand the body of knowledge in this field (Mumford et al., 2002; Jung et al., 2003). It supports existing theories that propose the impact of transactional, transformational, and laissez-faire leadership on organisational dynamics (Samul, 2016), and particularly that the choice of leadership style can significantly impact an organisation's emotional climate and performance (Harel et al., 2021). Also, a positive emotional climate fosters productivity, job satisfaction and commitment among employees (Hassi et al., 2022), while a negative climate can hinder performance and innovation (Bass & Avolio, 1995; Van Wugt et al., 2004).

The findings of the study suggest that managers should adapt their leadership styles to help improve organisational performance and employee satisfaction. Organisations can benefit from regular assessments of their emotional climate to gauge the impact of leadership styles and determine whether adjustments are needed. Training can help leaders understand how to identify organisations life cycle stage and when to employ different leadership styles for optimal results. Additionally, leaders can use emotional climate assessments as a measure of organisational health. A positive emotional climate is linked to higher employee engagement, motivation, and overall well-being, which are vital for long-term success.

This study is limited to the identification of 3 leadership styles: transactional, transformational and 'Laissez-fire'. The life cycles of organisations are divided into two parts: growing and ageing organisations, according to Adizes' methodology. However, for the more precise identification of the specific life cycle stage and its relationship with the emotional climate and the leadership style in the organisation, data triangulation is required. The more detailed data would be obtained by using a quantitative approach to identify the emotional climate and leadership style of the organisation, while qualitative methods (interviews, case studies and document analysis) should be applied to the identification of the organisation's life cycle stage.

References

Adizes, I. K. (2015a). *Managing corporate life cycles. Volume 2: Analyzing organizational behavior and raising healthy organizations*. Adizes Institute Publications. Kindle Edition.

Adizes, I. K. (2015b). *Change management*. Euroimprint.

Bass, B. M., & Avolio, B. J. (1995). *Sample items from the Multifactor Leadership Questionnaire (MLQ) Form 5X-Short*. Online access: https://www.academia.edu/30400319/Sample_Items_From_the_Multifactor_Leadership_Questionnaire_MLQ_Form_5X_Short

Baird, L., & Meshoulam, I. (1988). Managing two fits of strategic human resource management. *Academy of Management Review* (13), 116–128. Online access: http://cursos.itam.mx/sastre/lecturas/baird88.pdf

Buhalis, D., Efthymiou, L., Uzunboylu, N., & Thrassou, A. (2024). 'Charting the progress of technology adoption in tourism and hospitality in the era of Industry 4.0'. Tourism & hospitality in the digital era: Technology and its (im)possibilities. Special Issue in Euromed, *Journal of Business*. https://doi.org/10.1108/EMJB-11-2023-0310

Dele, O. A., Nanle, M., & Abimbola S. O. (2015). Impact of leadership style on organizational climate in the Nigerian Insurance Industry. *International Journal of Business and Industrial Marketing, 1*(3), 45–52. Online access: http://www.aascit.org/journal/ijbim

Dikčius, V. (2011). *The principles of questionnaire development* (p. 47). Vilnius University, Faculty of Economics, Department of Marketing.

Freeman, J., & Engel, J. S. (2007). Models of innovation: Startups and mature corporations. *California Review Management,* (50), 94–119. Online access: https://negocios.udd.cl/files/2013/08/1.2-Models-of-Innovation-Startups-and-Mature-Companies.pdf

Fiaz M., Su, Q., & Saqib A. (2017). Leadership Styles and employees' motivation: Perspective from an emerging economy. *The Journal of Developing Areas*. Accessed 20201–06–0: https://muse.jhu.edu/article/662834/pdf

Greiner, L. E. (1997). Endogenous growth cycles—Arrow's learning by doing reconsidered. *Journal of Macroeconomics, 18*, 587–604. Online access: https://onlinelibrary.wiley.com/doi/epdf/10.1111/j.1741-6248.1997.00397.x

Goussak, G. W., Webber, J. K., & Ser, E. (2011). Applying the full range leadership model to managing employees in the Las Vegas casino-gaming industry. *The Journal of Gambling Business and Economics, 5*(1), 47–67.

Harel, R., Schwartz, D., & Kaufmann, D. (2021). Organizational culture processes for promoting innovation in small businesses. *EuroMed Journal of Business, 16*(2), 218–240.

Hassi, A., Rohlfer, S., & Jebsen, S. (2022). Empowering leadership and innovative work behavior: The mediating effects of climate for initiative and job autonomy in Moroccan SMEs. *EuroMed Journal of Business, 17*(4), 503–518.

Jawahar, I. M., & Mclaughlin, G. L. (2001). Toward a descriptive stakeholder theory: An organizational life cycle approach. *Academy of Management Review, 26*(3), 397–414. http://web.a.ebscohost.com/ehost/pdfviewer/pdfviewer?vid=4&sid=e0327e36-382f-4e05-8988-c5b0dbd33ac4%40sessionmgr4007

Kelner, S., Rivers, C., & O'Connell, K. (1994). *Managerial style as a behavioural predictor of organisational climate*. McBer.

Lester, D. L., Parnell, J. A., & Carraher, S. (2003). Organizational life cycle: A five stage empirical scale. *The International Journal of Organizational Analysis*, (11), 339–354. http://web.a.ebscohost.com/ehost/detail/detail?vid=0&sid=bef2a25d-7624-4335-be31-061baab3761e%40sdc-v-sessmgr01&bdata=JnNpdGU9ZWhvc3QtbGl2ZQ%3d%3d#AN=12015857&db=bth

Miller, D., & Friesen, P. H. (1984). A longitudinal study of the corporate life cycle. *Management Science*, (30), 1161–1183. http://web.b.ebscohost.com/ehost/pdfviewer/pdfviewer?vid=1&sid=bfd3da08-9ac2-4849-86fa-a816451b7a54%40pdc-v-sessmgr03

Momeni. N. (2009). The relationship between mangers' emotional intelligence and the organisational climate they create. *Public Personnel Management, 38*(2).

Mumford, M. D., Scott, G. M., Gaddis, B., & Strange, J. M. (2002). Leading creative people: Orchestrating expertise and relationships. *Leadership Quarterly, 13*(6), 705–750. Viewed: 2022–05–20. https://doi.org/10.1016/S1048-9843(02)00158-3

Richard, O. C., Ford, D., & Ismail, K. (2006). Exploring the performance effects of visible attribute diversity: The moderating role of span of control and organisational life cycle. *The International Journal of Human Resource Management*. http://web.a.ebscohost.com/ehost/pdfviewer/pdfviewer?vid=4&sid=bef2a25d-7624-4335-be31-061baab3761e%40sdc-v-sessmgr01

Peña-Suárez, E., Muñi, J., Campillo-Álvarez, Á., Fonseca-Pedrero, E., & García-Cueto, E. (2013). Assessing organizational climate: Psychometric properties of the CLIOR Scale. *Psicothema, 25*(1), 137–144. https://doi.org/10.7334/psicothema2012.260

Thrassou, A., Vrontis, D., Efthymiou, L., & Uzunboylu, N. (2022). An overview of business advancement through technology: Markets and marketing in transition. In A. Thrassou, D. Vrontis, L. Efthymiou, Y. Weber, S. M. R. Shams, & E. Tsoukatos (Eds.), *Business advancement through technology volume I*. Palgrave Studies in Cross-disciplinary Business Research, In Association with EuroMed Academy of Business. Palgrave Macmillan, Cham. https://doi.org/10.1007/978-3-031-07769-2_1

Tran, V. (1998). The role of emotional climate in learning organisations. *The Learning Organization*, (5), 99–103. https://doi.org/10.1108/09696479810212060

Taguiri, R. (1968). The concept of organizational climate. In R. Taguiri & G. Litwin (Eds.), *Organizational climate: Explorations of a concept* (pp. 11–32). Harvard University Press.

Von Wobesser, L. H. (2016), Life cycle in organizations: A stationary shop case study. *Journal of Business Case Studies, 12*, 35–40. https://clutejournals.com/index.php/JBCS/article/view/9561

Van Wugt, M. (2004). A comprehensive model of organizational leadership: The leadership action cycle. *International Journal of Organizational Theory and Behavior, 7*(2), 173–208.

Vrontis, D., Thrassou, A., Uzunboylu, N., & Efthymiou, L. (2023). An overview of business for sustainability: Strategic avenues and managerial approaches. In D. Vrontis, A. Thrassou, L. Efthymiou, Y. Weber, S. M. R. Shams, & E.

Tsoukatos (Eds.), *Business for sustainability, Volume I. Palgrave Studies in Cross-disciplinary Business Research, In Association with EuroMed Academy of Business*. Palgrave Macmillan, Cham. https://doi.org/10.1007/978-3-031-37361-9_1

Vrontis, D., Thrassou, A., Efthymiou, L., & Bozat, M. (2024). Delineating business for sustainability: Contextual evolution and elucidation. In: D. Vrontis, A. Thrassou, L. Efthymiou, Y. Weber, S. M. R. Shams, & E. Tsoukatos (Eds.), *Business for sustainability, volume II. Palgrave Studies in Cross-disciplinary Business Research, In Association with EuroMed Academy of Business*. Palgrave Macmillan, Cham. https://doi.org/10.1007/978-3-031-37365-7_1

CHAPTER 8

The Effect of Area of Residence and Income on Generation Z Cohort's Intention to Consume Insects

Irene (Eirini) Kamenidou, Stergios Gkitsas, Spyridon Mamalis, Ifigeneia Mylona, Stavros Pavlidis, and Aikaterini Stavrianea

8.1 Introduction

Entomophagy is considered the food of the future to combat the impending world food shortages and environmental problems due to high consumption of animal protein (Woolf et al., 2019). This solution is presented by researchers due to the good nutritional value of insects (Bukkens, 1997), high feed conversion rate (van Broekhoven et al., 2015), and low environmental footprint (Dobermann et al., 2017; Ros-Baró et al., 2022).

I. (Eirini) Kamenidou (✉) · S. Mamalis · I. Mylona · S. Pavlidis
Department of Management Science and Technology, School of Management Science and Accounting, Democritus University of Thrace, Kavala Campus, Kavala, Greece
e-mail: eikamenidou@mst.duth.gr

D. Vrontis et al. (eds.), *Business in Uncertainty*, Palgrave Studies in Cross-disciplinary Business Research, In Association with EuroMed Academy of Business, https://doi.org/10.1007/978-3-031-65587-6_8

As insect-based proteins appear to be a sustainable alternative to meat protein, a new transformative industry is emerging to capitalize on this promising resource-the insect-based food industry (Dossey et al., 2016). The global edible insect market has been estimated at USD 104.74 million from 2021 to 2022 and is expected to grow at a CAGR of 20.66% during the forecast period to reach USD 323.28 million by 2030 (Marketwatch, 2023).

Entomophagy is not something new and has been demonstrated in ancient times (Evans et al., 2015). Today, entomophagy is part of the human diet in several countries (Bukkens, 1997), resulting to at least 2 billion people consuming insects (Van Huis et al., 2013). However, in Western countries, entomophagy is not practiced by a large portion of the population and acceptance rate is very low (Bodenheimer, 2013; Kamenidou et al., 2023; Orsi et al., 2019).

Demographic trends appear to play a role in individuals' dietary habits and acceptance of insects as food (Brunner & Nuttavuthisit, 2019; Niva & Vainio, 2021). For example, income (e.g., Salonen, 2023), age (e.g., Medoro et al., 2022), and area of residence (e.g., Chen et al., 2022; Marchioni et al., 2022) have been found to impact on food consumption behavior, therefore, including insect consumption too.

With respect to entomophagy, which is the focus of this study, in terms of age, the perspective of generational cohorts on consumer acceptance is of particular interest and especially referring to the younger generational cohorts, as they are the future consumers and workforce of a country

S. Mamalis
e-mail: mamalis@mst.duth.gr

I. Mylona
e-mail: imylona@mst.duth.gr

S. Gkitsas
Department of Sciences and New Technologies, School of Primary Education, Aristotle University of Thessaloniki, Thessaloniki, Greece

A. Stavrianea
Department of Communication and Media Studies, School of Economics and Political Sciences, National and Kapodistrian University of Athens, Athens, Greece
e-mail: aikstavria@media.uoa.gr

(Kamenidou et al., 2020). Generational cohorts include people who were born in a particular place and time and experienced the same life-changing events when they "came of age" thus shaping the behavior of that cohort (Mannheim, 1970).

Members of the Z generational cohort, the youngest cohort of adults, were born between 1995 and 2009 (Williams & Page, 2011). They are aware of sustainability issues, they value convenience, and innovation, and are tech-savvy (Khatri & Dixit, 2016; Kymäläinen et al., 2021; Nagy, 2017; Vrontis et al., 2023a, 2023b). Despite the fact that the members of a given generational cohort have similarities, in the literature, it is pointed out that there are differences between the members inside the same cohort, the so-called intragenerational cohort differences (Radaev, 2021). Intragenerational cohort differences are generally an under-researched topic, especially when compared to intergenerational cohort differences, i.e., differences between varying generational cohorts (Mulvey et al., 2020). Pickard (2019) points out that young people (i.e., Gen Y & Gen Z) are not a homogeneous block and there are intragenerational cohort differences depending on the disparate factors studied. Prior studies have found intragenerational differences within members of the Z cohort in their workplace behaviors and priorities (Benítez-Márquez et al., 2022; Leslie et al., 2021; Schroth, 2019), variability in social media use (Mulvey et al., 2020) and information and communication technology literacy (Soysal et al., 2019). In addition, a handful of studies were found related to intragenerational differences and food consumption (e.g., (Brombach et al., 2014). Area of residence and income intragenerational differences of the Z cohort are understudied as a topic too.

Regarding entomophagy, the literature revealed that, to the best of our knowledge, only a handful of studies addressed insect consumption and generational cohort behavior (Ardoin, 2021; Escalante-Aburto et al., 2022; Fasanelli et al., 2020; Johansson & Gustafsson, 2018; Kamenidou et al., 2023; Rovai et al., 2022; Schubiger et al., 2022; Sogari et al., 2019; Tzompa-Sosa et al., 2023), and to the best of our knowledge none examined intragenerational differences in entomophagy behavior among the Z cohort in general and specifically in relation to income and area of residence.

From the above, it is clear that there is a gap in academia regarding intragenerational cohort differences in the Z cohort with respect to entomophagy. A gap that this research attempts to partially fill.

Subsequently, the main objective of this article is to examine the area of residence and income intragenerational differences of the generation Z cohort in relation to entomophagy (the intention to try certain edible insects and insect-based foods and drinks), which, to the best of our knowledge, has not been previously explored.

Therefore, this study contributes to the previous literature by reducing the gap of knowledge regarding generational cohort behavior toward entomophagy, and in particular, behavior of the generation Z cohort, which is extremely rare in academic entomophagy research.

The remainder of the paper is organized as follows: First, the literature review and research methodology are presented. The results are described, and then follow the discussion, implications, limitations, and directions for further research.

8.2 Literature Review

Since no direct research (to the best of our knowledge) addresses the elements of this study (insect consumption of generation Z and intragenerational differences based on area of residence and income), this literature review presents some papers that are related in one way or another to the research objectives. These papers were selected because they examined the effects of area of residence and/or income on entomophagy. Additionally, papers on generation Z and entomophagy are also presented. It is reiterated that none of the following papers combine generational cohort behavior and entomophagy or intragenerational cohort differences and entomophagy in their study.

Dürr and Ratompoarison (2021), in their study of insect consumption in Madagascar ($N = 216$), did not find differences in the amount of insect consumed according to residence (rural vs. urban) or household income (rich vs. poor families). On the other hand, Hlongwane et al. (2020) reported that insect consumption differs by residential area in South Africa ($N = 622$). The same is true in Brazil, where the urban population refuses to accept insects as food, while some rural residents have them in their daily diet (Bisconsin-Júnior et al., 2022). Tzompa-Sosa et al. (2023) examined among others the acceptance level of mealworm consumption (whole or processed), of five different countries (Belgium, China, Italy, Mexico, and the United States) and found that Belgium, Italy, and the United States had low acceptance rate in contrast to Mexico and China where the acceptance level was high.

Matandirotya et al. (2022) report that low-income families in Africa are more likely to consume insects because they are a cheaper alternative to meat protein. In contrast, the study of Aung et al. (2023) in Myanmar (N = 872) found that higher-income individuals consumed insects more regularly than their lower-income peers, while studies in Kenya and China showed that income did not affect the frequency of edible insect consumption (Kisaka, 2018; Liu et al., 2019).

As to generational cohorts' behavior and entomophagy, Kamenidou et al. (2023) explored behavior and attitudes of Gen Zers (i.e., the generation Z cohort) toward insect consumption. The authors also measured intention to try insects and insect-based food and drinks and found that the Gen Zers are generally unwilling to try them. Schubiger et al. (2022) present what they intend to study in their paper, which is the role of AR (augmented reality) and VR (virtual reality) in persuading Gen Zers to try insect-based food, and which of the two is more effective. Sogari et al. (2019, p. 11) found that "younger respondents (e.g., Generation Z) were more willing to try edible insects based on better awareness about the environmental benefits of using this protein source compared to animal-based products." Mendini and Schubiger (2022) explored how generation Z consumers are willing to eat insect-based foods and found that if entomophagy is effectively explained to them as well as the advantages of consuming alternative foods, insect consumption is probable.

Grounded upon the above analysis, and the inconsistency in the findings, it is likely that from generation Z's perspective, area of residence and family income affect their intention to try edible insects and insect-based foods and drinks. Accordingly, based on the overview of the previous studies, this study hypothesizes the following:

> *H1: There will be significant differences in the generation Z cohort's intention to try edible insects and insect-based foods and drinks based on their area of residence.*
> *H2: There will be significant differences in the generation Z cohort's intention to try edible insects and insect-based foods and drinks based on their income.*

It is noted that there are many studies that refer to barriers of entomophagy which observe that unfamiliarity, neophobia, and disgust are the main barriers (e.g., Erhard et al., 2023; Ordoñez López et al., 2023; Pozharliev et al., 2023), some of which focus on generational cohorts (Kamenidou et al., 2023).

8.3 Methodology

For this investigation, one topic in particular was of interest; being the intention to try insects (whole or processed) as a food from the Greek generation Z cohort. Accordingly, an overview of listed insects and insect-based food for human consumption was initially performed in order to adopt a list to use in the research. For so, this research used the list of insects and insect-based food and drinks of previous research (Hartmann et al., 2015; Kamenidou et al., 2023; Ribeiro et al., 2021; Woolf et al., 2019). The question was stated as "Which of the following listed insects, insect-based food and drinks are you willing to try" (dichotomous choices with answers "yes and "no"). The research took place in October and November 2022 (for a little more than a month). Participants were recruited based on a nonprobability sampling procedure that included criteria, convenience, and snowball sampling (Kamenidou et al., 2023; Stavrianea & Kamenidou, 2022) and only through online channels. In order for the questionnaire to be valid, criteria should be met: 1. adult members of the generation Z cohort, 2. access to the internet, and 3. consent for the use of their answers for analysis (first question of the research instrument; law 4624/2019). In this way, the sample used for data analysis was 742 members of the generation Z cohort, a sample size sufficient for the analysis performed (Lehmann et al., 1998).

The validity of the instrument used in this study was based on the validity of the relevant instruments (using the same items) of previous studies which the authors adopted them from. Reliability of the instrument (dichotomous choices) was assessed with the Kuder-Richardson Formula 20 (KR-20; Thompson, 2002, p. 11) and the internal consistency coefficient indicated acceptable reliability of the instrument (KR-20 = 0.955; 22 items). The SPSS ver. 28 program was used for the analysis which included descriptive statistics and chi-square tests.

8.4 Results

Sample Profile

Male subjects accounted for 56.3% of the sample, while female subjects accounted for 43.7%. Furthermore, younger members of the Z cohort (18–20 years of age) were overrepresented, as were single subjects who had completed secondary school and those who were attending university. In terms of area of residence and net monthly family income (in euros), which is the focus of this paper, the following picture emerges. Regarding area of residence, the majority of the generation Z cohort members live in the city ($N = 535$; 72.1%), while 13.5% ($N = 100$) live in towns and 14.4% live in villages ($N = 107$). As to their net monthly family income, this was ≤600.0€ for most participants ($N = 326$; 43.9%); while 26.0% ($N = 193$) had income ranging from 600.01 to 1000.00€; 16.4% ($N = 122$) from 1000.01 to 2000.00€, and 13.7% ($N = 101$) had a monthly net family income ≥2000.01€. It should be noted that the income of Greek Z cohort members living or studying alone was calculated as the amount they receive from their parents plus any other income they may have (e.g., from a part-time or full-time job).

Intention to Try Insects or Insect-Based Foods or Drinks

No one (0.0%) had previous experience, to their knowledge, with entomophagy, i.e., no member of the generation Z cohort had ever eaten edible insects, at least to their knowledge. Participants of the generation Z cohort were presented with a list of 22 items, which were insects or insect-based foods or drinks and were requested to indicate whether they would be willing to try them. Table 8.1 presents generation Z cohorts' intention to try the presented items according to where they lived (%), i.e., city, town, or village. Results reveal that the participants, regardless of their area of residence, are more willing to try insect or insect-based foods or drinks where the insects are not visible. Though, this percentage is generally very low (<15%).

Table 8.2 presents generation Z cohorts' intention to try the presented items based on their family's net monthly income. The participants regardless of net monthly income are willing to try insect or insect-based foods or drinks where the insects are not visible (except for one case: Cicadas in high-income families). This willingness to try is again very low (<10%).

Table 8.1 Intention to try insects or insect-based foods or drinks based on the generation Z cohort's area of residence (%)

Insect	*City*		*Town*		*Village*		*Total*
	Yes	*No*	*Yes*	*No*	*Yes*	*No*	*%*
Grasshoppers	11.1	61.1	1.8	11.7	1.1	13.3	100.0
Crickets	7.5	64.6	1.6	11.9	0.9	13.5	100.0
Mealworm	8.4	63.7	1.2	12.3	1.1	13.3	100.0
Ants	10.9	61.2	1.9	11.6	1.2	13.2	100.0
Cockroaches	6.9	65.2	1.3	12.1	1.1	13.3	100.0
Scarab	6.7	65.4	1.1	12.4	0.7	13.7	100.0
Spiders and scorpions	8.6	63.5	1.9	11.6	0.9	13.5	100.0
Worms	7.7	64.4	1.5	12.0	1.3	13.1	100.0
Caterpillars	7.5	64.6	1.2	12.3	0.9	13.5	100.0
Cicadas	9.3	62.8	1.6	11.9	1.1	13.3	100.0
Fried/grilled/toasted whole insect	14.3	57.8	2.8	10.6	2.3	12.1	100.0
Sugar/chocolate covered insect	11.1	61.1	2.4	11.1	1.2	13.2	100.0
Ground insects in sauces/chutneys	12.3	59.8	2.8	10.6	2.0	12.4	100.0
Ground insects in burger/meatball/nuggets	12.0	60.1	3.2	10.2	1.8	12.7	100.0
Bakery products containing insect flour	14.4	57.7	3.2	10.2	2.8	11.6	100.0
Rice/pasta enriched with insect flour	14.3	57.8	3.0	10.5	2.3	12.1	100.0
Protein bars containing insect protein isolate	13.5	58.6	3.0	10.5	2.4	12.0	100.0
Deep-fried silkworms	8.1	64.0	2.4	11.1	1.1	13.3	100.0
Deep-fried crickets	10.2	61.9	2.8	10.6	0.9	13.5	100.0
Cookies based on cricket flour	14.7	57.4	2.6	10.8	1.9	12.5	100.0
Chocolate chip cookies based on cricket flour	12.9	59.2	2.7	10.8	2.3	12.1	100.0
A drink containing silkworm protein	11.6	60.5	3.4	10.1	1.5	12.9	100.0

Intragenerational Differences Toward Intention to Try Edible Insects and Insect-Based Food and Drinks Based on Area of Residence and Family Net Monthly Income

Table 8.3 offers the outcome of the chi-square tests exploring intragenerational differences in intention to try edible insects and insect-based foods and drinks based on area of residence (H1) and family net monthly income (H2). It is noted that 44 chi-square tests were examined (22 for area of residence and 22 for income), and only eight produced statistically significant differences, which are the only ones presented. The results of the chi-square tests indicate that, in some cases, there is a significant relationship between consumers' area of residence, their net family income,

Table 8.2 Intention to try insects or insect-based foods or drinks based on the generation Z cohort's net monthly family income (%)

	<600.00€		*600.01–1000.00*		*1000.01–2000.00*		*>2000.00*		*Total*
	Yes	*No*	*Yes*	*No*	*Yes*	*No*	*Yes*	*No*	*%*
Grasshoppers	6.1	37.9	3.0	23.0	2.3	14.2	2.6	11.1	100.0
Crickets	3.9	40.0	2.2	23.9	1.6	14.8	2.4	11.2	100.0
Mealworm	4.6	39.4	1.8	24.3	1.5	15.0	2.8	10.8	100.0
Ants	6.5	37.5	3.0	23.0	2.2	14.3	2.4	11.2	100.0
Cockroaches	4.2	39.8	1.8	24.3	1.6	14.8	1.8	11.9	100.0
Scarab	4.3	39.6	1.3	24.7	0.9	15.5	1.9	11.7	100.0
Spiders and scorpions	4.9	39.6	1.8	24.6	1.1	14.2	2.5	11.3	100.0
Worms	5.1	38.8	1.8	24.3	1.5	15.0	2.2	11.5	100.0
Caterpillars	4.3	39.6	1.2	24.8	1.3	15.1	2.8	10.8	100.0
Cicadas	5.0	38.9	2.0	24.0	1.9	14.6	3.1	10.5	100.0
Fried/grilled/toasted whole insect	8.6	35.3	4.7	21.3	3.6	12.8	2.4	11.2	100.0
Sugar/chocolate covered insect	7.3	36.7	2.8	23.2	2.8	13.6	1.8	11.9	100.0
Ground insects in sauces/chutneys	8.2	35.7	4.3	21.7	1.9	14.6	2.7	10.9	100.0
Ground insects in burger/meatball/nuggets	7.8	36.1	3.8	22.2	2.8	13.6	2.6	11.1	100.0
Bakery products containing insect flour	9.0	34.9	5.7	20.4	2.8	13.6	3.0	10.6	100.0
Rice/pasta enriched with insect flour	9.8	34.1	4.0	22.0	3.6	12.8	2.0	11.6	100.0
Protein bars containing insect protein isolate	9.8	34.1	4.3	21.7	3.0	13.5	1.8	11.9	100.0
Deep-fried silkworms	6.6	37.3	2.0	24.0	1.5	15.0	1.5	12.1	100.0

(continued)

Table 8.2 (continued)

	<600.00€		600.01–1000.00		1000.01–2000.00		>2000.00		Total
	Yes	*No*	*Yes*	*No*	*Yes*	*No*	*Yes*	*No*	%
Deep-fried crickets	7.0	36.9	2.8	23.2	2.2	14.3	2.0	11.6	100.0
Cookies based on cricket flour	8.8	35.2	4.0	22.0	3.1	13.3	3.2	10.4	100.0
Chocolate chip cookies based on cricket flour	8.9	35.0	4.0	22.0	2.3	14.2	2.7	10.9	100.0
A drink containing silkworm protein	7.8	36.1	3.2	22.8	2.7	13.7	2.7	10.9	100.0

and their intention to try some of the listed edible insects and insect-based foods and drinks.

Based on Table 8.3, the following can be deduced. Chi-square tests revealed statistically significant differences as regards area of residence and intention to try deep-fried crickets as well as a drink containing silkworm

Table 8.3 Intragenerational differences towards intention to try edible insects and insect-based food and drinks based on area of residence and family net monthly income

Insect	*Variable*	*X2*	*df*	p
1. Deep-fried crickets	Area of residence	9.023	2	0.012*
2. A drink containing silkworm protein	Area of residence	8.340	2	0.015*
3. Crickets	Income	7.853	3	0.049*
4. Mealworm	Income	14.388	3	0.002**
5. Scarab	Income	8.397	3	0.038*
6. Spiders and scorpions	Income	9.638	3	0.022*
7. Caterpillars	Income	20.090	3	0.000**
8. Cicadas	Income	14.534	3	0.002**

*Significant at 0.05; **Significant at 0.01

protein ($\chi_2{}^2 = 9.023$, $p = 0.012$ and $\chi_2{}^2 = 8.340$, $p = 0.015$ respectively). Additionally, observation of the two-way tables revealed that as to the total sample, the highest percentage of the "yes" responses hail from people residing in cities in both cases (73.1% and 70.5% respectively). On the other hand, observation per category of area of residence, the highest percentage of "yes" originates from those residing in towns. Specifically, from the 100% of the participants residing in towns, 21.0% answered "yes" they were willing to try deep-fried crickets (being the highest compared to the other area of residence classes). Lastly, from the 100% of the participants residing in towns, 25.0% answered "yes" they were willing to try a drink containing silkworm protein (being the highest compared to the other area of residence classes).

Referring to net family's monthly income and willing to try the listed items, the following was observed. Firstly, chi-square tests revealed statistically significant differences between family income and intention to try crickets, mealworms, and scarabs ($\chi_3{}^2 = 7.853$, $p = 0.049$, $\chi_3{}^2 = 14.388$, $p = 0.002$ and $\chi_3{}^2 = 8.397$, $p = 0.038$ respectively). Additionally, observation of the two-way tables of the chi-square test revealed that as to the total sample, the highest percentage of the "yes" responses come from low-income families (38.7% < 600.00; 43.0% < 600.00 and 50.8% < 600.00 respectively). On the other hand, observation per category of family income, the highest percentage of "yes" answers derive from those of high-income families. Specifically, from the 100% of the sample with income >2000.00, 17.8%, 20.8%, and 13.9% answered "yes," for crickets, mealworms, and scarabs, respectively (being the highest compared to the other income classes).

Also, chi-square tests revealed statistically significant differences between family income and intention to try spiders and scorpions, caterpillars, and cicadas, ($\chi_3{}^2 = 9.636$, $p = 0.022$, $\chi_3{}^2 = 20.090$, $p = 0.000$, and $\chi_3{}^2 = 14.534$, $p = 0.002$, respectively). A closer inspection of the two-way tables revealed that as to the total sample, the highest percentage of "yes" responses originates from low-income families (42.4% < 600.00; 44.4% < 600.00 and 41.6% < 600.00 respectively). However, through an in-depth observation per category of family income, it is revealed that the highest percentage of "yes" answers are obtained from those of high-income families. Specifically, from the 100% of the participants with income >2000.00, 17.8%, 20.8%, and 22.8% answered "yes," for spiders and scorpions, caterpillars, and cicadas respectively (being the highest compared to the other income classes).

8.5 Discussion

To our knowledge, there is no research on the intragenerational differences of the Z cohort's area of residence and family income, and intention to try edible insects and insect-based foods and drinks. Therefore, all comparisons are made with extreme caution. Referring to the intention to try 22 listed items, participants regardless of their area of residence or family's net monthly income, are "willing to try" insect or insect-based foods or drinks where the insects are not visible (excluding one case: Cicadas in high-income families). Though, this willingness to try is very low: <15% regarding area of residence and <10% based on net family monthly income. Also, the results of the chi-square tests indicate that in some cases there is a significant relationship between generation Z cohort's residence as well as net family income and their intention to try some of the listed edible insects and insect-based foods and drinks. This result is not consistent with the results of the studies of Dürr and Ratompoarison (2021), Kisaka (2018), and Liu et al. (2019). On the other hand, Bisconsin-Júnior et al. (2022) reached similar conclusions to the present study, finding significant differences in insect consumption according to residential area. The findings are also partial in line with the ones of Kamenidou et al. (2023) who found that the generation Z cohort would try the foods and drinks that the insects are not visible, though they did not include in their study area of residence, income, nor did they examine intragenerational differences. The results of this study revealed that in all cases regarding the area of residence and intention to try the selected items the highest percentage of the "yes" responses came from people residing in cities, while per area of residence per category, originates from those residing in towns.

Regarding the generation Z cohort's family net monthly income, the highest percentage of the "yes" responses derive from low-income families, which corresponds with the fact that the lowest-income people and city dwellers make up by far the largest percentage of the sample. Taking into account that meat is becoming more expensive, lower-income families may be more inclined to turn to cheaper alternatives, which is already the case in Africa as mentioned in the study of Matandirotya et al. (2022). Results per income category reveal that the highest percentage of "yes" in all cases that produced statistically significant differences, arises from the highest income ones. One explanation for this could be that high-income Z cohort members are enticed by this type of food as a potentially exotic identification of insect-based foods. This result is in line with the findings of Aung et al. (2023) who found that higher-income individuals consumed insects more regularly, but contrasts with other studies that found no relationship between income and insect consumption (Kisaka, 2018; Liu et al., 2019). Though, as mentioned above, none of them focused on generational cohorts, the generation Z cohort, or intragenerational differences. Also, they did not refer to the specific items, so every comparison is made with caution.

The result of this study arises the issue of sustainability awareness and information regarding insects as future food. Previous research proves that there is a connection between environmental conscious behavior and intention to consume insects (Hartmann et al., 2018). Additionally, as previous research points out (e.g., (Batat & Peter, 2020) consumers need to be educated about the benefits of entomophagy. Therefore, communication marketing is needed to raise awareness and provide information, mainly through contemporary communication channels, since generation Z is technologically savvy (Jain & Raman, 2023; Thrassou et al, 2022).

8.6 Implications

In terms of theoretical implications and contributions, our study adds to previous academic work as it is one of the few studies that address intragenerational cohort differences regarding food. Moreover, to the best of our knowledge, it is the only one to address the generation Z intragenerational cohort differences referring to area of residence and income differences toward intention to try insects, insect-based foods, and drinks. From a practical perspective, the results clearly reveal that the generation Z cohort is not willing to try the listed items in the short run. Though, there were also a small percentage (<15%) that are willing to engage in indirect entomophagy (in the sense that the insects are not visible). It is also evident that the generation Z participants that reside in cities and have low income are more willing to try insect-based food and drinks. Therefore, the present research provides insight into the primary determinant intention to try novel foods and drinks. This could prompt marketers to develop strategies and campaigns to reduce neophobia and disgust and increase willingness to try, since these two elements have been detected as major barriers to insect consumption (Erhard et al., 2023; Ordoñez López et al., 2023; Pozharliev et al., 2023).

Tailored communication messages can reduce the barriers to insect consumption (Schubiger et al., 2022). The fact that insects are a sustainable source of protein and therefore, constitute a way to deal with global warming and deforestation can be a communication pathway for addressing members of the generation Z cohort who are more sensitive regarding sustainability issues (Guiné et al., 2021). Peer influence is extremely important in younger ages (Marquis, 2023), especially when it comes to acquiring information and knowledge on issues that can form their personal value system or alter attitudes and behavior. Thus, marketers and policy makers can use influencer marketing as a tool for insect consumption adoption. Numerous research supports that influencer marketing can act as an important tool that can have an effect on consumers' purchase intentions (Schouten et al., 2021; Vrontis et al., 2021). Influencer marketing offers third-party credibility and affects the willingness of generation Z and Y members to taste food (Schubiger et al., 2022; Widyanto & Agusti, 2020). Moreover, marketers and policy makers can utilize the positive experience that generation Z members may have from tasting insects, which they will communicate to others through social media as an accomplishment and, also as a form of expressing themselves and get empowered. The sharing of this positive experience with others should be reinforced by messages that recognize insect consumption as sustainable behavior, being in the core of marketers and policy makers communication. Therefore, this behavior should be acknowledged as ethical and thus, more appealing to young adults regardless of income group who will find additional drivers, rather than price in order to adapt insect consumption.

Digital media are closely linked to the lifestyles of generation Z members and various social media platforms are their most preferred vehicles for communication, entertainment, and acquiring information (Buhalis et al., 2024; Papathanassopoulos & Miconi, 2023). Thus, marketers and policy makers can inform generation Z members about insect consumption and the benefits of such behavior, with the use of digital media (Instagram, youtube, tiktok, etc.) in a way though, that is interesting, relevant, and engaging to young adults. The evolution of technology brings to light new tools such as Artificial Intelligence (AI), AR, and VR that also can be employed by marketers and policy makers, since they can offer generation Z members innovative, engaging, and impactful experiences that can reinforce their intention to consume insects

(Schubiger et al., 2022; Xu et al., 2021). In addition, better communication can also lead to increased awareness among residents of rural or semi-rural areas who, according to the results of the research, are more reluctant to try this type of food.

8.7 Limitations and Directions for Further Research

This study is not free of limitations, although considerable effort has been made to minimize them as much as possible. The issue of entomophagy in Western society is a topic of growing interest, whereas research is ongoing but still in its infancy, particularly with respect to generational cohorts' behavior. Therefore, the fact that this study is exploratory in nature (to our knowledge, no study on this topic has been found) is already a limitation. Another limitation derives from data collection (online-nonprobability) as well as the sample selected (one cohort- one country). Because of these limitations and in view of the results, no generalizations can be made from the sample to the population. Lastly, another limitation concerns what would motivate the generation Z cohort to try these selected edible insects and insect-based foods and drinks which were not studied in this research. These limitations provide guidance for further investigation and validation of the results of this study. Despite the above limitations, this study provides insight into the generation Z perspective and more specifically intragenerational cohort differences in their intention to engage in entomophagy based on their area of residence and income, a topic that has been neglected in academia.

References

Ardoin, R. P. (2021). *Evaluating US consumers' perception of foods made with cricket powder* (Unpublished Doctoral Dissertation). Louisiana State University and Agricultural & Mechanical College.

Aung, M. T. T., Dürr, J., Borgemeister, C., & Börner, J. (2023). Factors affecting consumption of edible insects as food: Entomophagy in Myanmar. *Journal of Insects as Food and Feed*, 1–20. https://doi.org/10.3920/JIFF2022.0151

Batat, W., & Peter, P. (2020). The healthy and sustainable bugs appetite: Factors affecting entomophagy acceptance and adoption in Western food cultures. *Journal of Consumer Marketing*, *37*(3), 291–303. https://doi.org/10.1108/JCM-10-2018-2906

Benítez-Márquez, M. D., Sánchez-Teba, E. M., Bermúdez-González, G., & Núñez-Rydman, E. S. (2022). Generation Z within the workforce and in the workplace: A bibliometric analysis. *Frontiers in Psychology, 12*, 736820. https://doi.org/10.3389/fpsyg.2021.736820

Bisconsin-Júnior, A., Rodrigues, H., Behrens, J. H., da Silva, M. A. A. P., & Mariutti, L. R. B. (2022). "Food made with edible insects": Exploring the social representation of entomophagy where it is unfamiliar. *Appetite, 173*, 106001. https://doi.org/10.1016/j.appet.2022.106001

Bodenheimer, F. S. (2013). *Insects as human food: A chapter of the ecology of man*. Springer.

Brombach, C., Haefeli, D., & Bartsch, S. (2014). What have we kept and what have we changed? A three generation study on nutrition and food handling. *Ernahrungs Umschau, 61*(11), 171–177. https://doi.org/10.4455/eu.2014.029

Brunner, T. A., & Nuttavuthisit, K. (2019). A consumer-oriented segmentation study on edible insects in Switzerland and Thailand. *British Food Journal, 122*(2), 482–488. https://doi.org/10.1108/BFJ-08-2018-0526

Buhalis, D., Efthymiou, L., Uzunboylu, N., & Thrassou, A. (2024) 'Charting the progress of technology adoption in tourism and hospitality in the era of industry 4.0'. Tourism & Hospitality in the Digital Era: Technology and its (im)Possibilities. Special Issue in *Euromed Journal of Business*. https://doi.org/10.1108/EMJB-11-2023-0310.

Bukkens, S. G. F. (1997). The nutritional value of edible insects. *Ecology of Food and Nutrition, 36*(2–4), 287–319. https://doi.org/10.1080/03670244.1997.9991521

Chen, G., Tan, W., Ran, N., Zhang, J., & Yan, B. (2022). Do urban tourists prefer vegetarianism? An urban-rural comparison of vegetarian consumption in China. *Frontiers in Nutrition, 9*, 996158. https://doi.org/10.3389/fnut.2022.996158

Dobermann, D., Swift, J. A., & Field, L. M. (2017). Opportunities and hurdles of edible insects for food and feed. *Nutrition Bulletin, 42*(4), 293–308. https://doi.org/10.1111/nbu.12291

Dossey, A. T., Tatum, J. T., & McGill, W. L. (2016). Modern insect-based food industry: Current status, insect processing technology, and recommendations moving forward. In *Insects as Sustainable Food Ingredients* (pp. 113–152). Elsevier. https://doi.org/10.1016/B978-0-12-802856-8.00005-3

Dürr, J., & Ratompoarison, C. (2021). Nature's "Free Lunch": The contribution of edible insects to food and nutrition security in the central highlands of Madagascar. *Foods, 10*(12), 2978. https://doi.org/10.3390/foods10122978

Erhard, A. L., Águas Silva, M., Damsbo-Svendsen, M.,Menadeva Karpantschof, B. -E., Sørensen, H., & Bom Frøst, M. (2023). Acceptance of insect foods among Danish children: Effects of information provision, food neophobia, disgust sensitivity, and species on willingness to try. *Food Quality and Preference, 104*, 104713. https://doi.org/10.1016/j.foodqual.2022.104713

Escalante-Aburto, A., Rodríguez-Sifuentes, L., Ozuna, C., Mariscal-Moreno, R. M., Mulík, S., Guiné, R., & Chuck-Hernández, C. (2022). Consumer perception of insects as food: Mexico as an example of the importance of studying socio-economic and geographical differences for decision-making in food development. *International Journal of Food Science & Technology, 57*(10), 6306–6316. https://doi.org/10.1111/ijfs.15995

Evans, J., Alemu, M. H., Flore, R., Frøst, M. B., Halloran, A., Jensen, A. B., Maciel-Vergara, G., Meyer-Rochow, V. B., Münke-Svendsen, C., Olsen, S. B., Payne, C., Roos, N., Rozin, P., Tan, H. S. G., van Huis, A., Vantomme, P., & Eilenberg, J. (2015). 'Entomophagy': An evolving terminology in need of review. *Journal of Insects as Food and Feed, 1*(4), 293–305. https://doi.org/10.3920/JIFF2015.0074

Fasanelli, R., Galli, I., Riverso, R., & Piscitelli, A. (2020). Social Representations of insects as food: an explorative-comparative study among millennials and x-generation consumers. *Insects, 11*(10), 656. https://doi.org/10.3390/insects11100656

Guiné, R. P. F., Correia, P., Coelho, C., & Costa, C. A. (2021). The role of edible insects to mitigate challenges for sustainability. *Open Agriculture, 6*(1), 24–36. https://doi.org/10.1515/opag-2020-0206

Hartmann, C., Ruby, M. B., Schmidt, P., & Siegrist, M. (2018). Brave, health-conscious, and environmentally friendly: Positive impressions of insect food product consumers. *Food Quality and Preference, 68*, 64–71. https://doi.org/10.1016/j.foodqual.2018.02.001

Hartmann, C., Shi, J., Giusto, A., & Siegrist, M. (2015). The psychology of eating insects: A cross-cultural comparison between Germany and China. *Food Quality and Preference, 44*, 148–156. https://doi.org/10.1016/j.foodqual.2015.04.013

Hlongwane, Z. T., Slotow, R., & Munyai, T. C. (2020). Indigenous Knowledge about Consumption of Edible Insects in South Africa. *Insects, 12*(1), 22. https://doi.org/10.3390/insects12010022

Jain, N., & Raman, T. V. (2023). The interplay of perceived risk, perceive benefit and generation cohort in digital finance adoption. *EuroMed Journal of Business, 18*(3), 359–379. https://doi.org/10.1108/EMJB-09-2021-0132

Johansson, H., & Gustafsson, J. (2018). *How do edible insects fly among Swedish consumers?: Exploring consumers' evaluation of edible insects as a meat substitute.*

Kamenidou, I. (Eirini), Mamalis, S., Gkitsas, S., Mylona, I., & Stavrianea, A. (2023). Is generation Z ready to engage in entomophagy? A segmentation analysis study. *Nutrients, 15*(3), 525.

Kamenidou, I., Stavrianea, A., & Bara, E.-Z. (2020). Generational differences toward organic food behavior: Insights from five generational cohorts. *Sustainability, 12*(6), 2299. https://doi.org/10.3390/su12062299

Khatri, K., & Dixit, N. (2016). Managing aspiration of generation "Y" and Generation "Z" at work place. *Khoj Journal of Indian Management Research & Practices.*

Kisaka, C. N. (2018). *Evaluation of consumers acceptance and pricing of edible winged termites (Macrotermes subhylanus) in Kimilili Sub-County, Kenya.*

Kymäläinen, T., Seisto, A., & Malila, R. (2021). Generation Z food waste, diet and consumption habits: A Finnish social design study with future consumers. *Sustainability, 13*(4), 2124. https://doi.org/10.3390/su13042124

Lehmann, D. R., Gupta, S., & Steckel, J. H. (1998). *Marketing research.* Addison-Wesley.

Leslie, B., Anderson, C., Bickham, C., Horman, J., Overly, A., Gentry, C., Callahan, C., & King, J. (2021). Generation Z perceptions of a positive workplace environment. *Employee Responsibilities and Rights Journal, 33*(3), 171–187. https://doi.org/10.1007/s10672-021-09366-2

Liu, A.-J., Li, J., & Gómez, M. I. (2019). Factors influencing consumption of edible insects for Chinese consumers. *Insects, 11*(1), 10. https://doi.org/10.3390/insects11010010

Mannheim, K. (1970). The problem of generations. *Psychoanalytic Review, 57*(3), 378–404.

Marchioni, D. M., Cacau, L. T., De Carli, E., de Carvalho, A. M., & Rulli, M. C. (2022). Low adherence to the EAT-lancet sustainable reference diet in the Brazilian population: Findings from the National Dietary survey 2017–2018. *Nutrients, 14*(6), 1187. https://doi.org/10.3390/nu14061187

Marketwatch. (2023). *Global edible insects market [2023–2030]|Discover the market upcoming performance with detailed statistical report.* MarketWatch. https://www.marketwatch.com/press-release/global-edible-insects-market-2023-2030-discover-the-market-upcoming-performance-with-detailed-statistical-report-2023-04-24

Marquis, D. (2023). Targeting adolescents as agents of change for an entomophageous future. *British Educational Research Journal*, berj.3891. https://doi.org/10.1002/berj.3891

Matandirotya, N. R., Filho, W. L., Mahed, G., Maseko, B., & Murandu, C. V. (2022). Edible insects consumption in Africa towards environmental health and sustainable food systems: A bibliometric study. *International Journal of Environmental Research and Public Health, 19*(22), 14823. https://doi.org/10.3390/ijerph192214823

Medoro, C., Cianciabella, M., Magli, M., Daniele, G. M., Lippi, N., Gatti, E., Volpe, R., Longo, V., Nazzaro, F., Mattoni, S., Tenaglia, F., & Predieri, S.

(2022). Food involvement, food choices, and bioactive compounds consumption correlation during COVID-19 pandemic: How food engagement influences consumers' food habits. *Nutrients, 14*(7), 1490. https://doi.org/10.3390/nu14071490

Mendini, M., & Schubiger, M. D. (2022). Willingness to eat insect-based food among Generation Z consumers: The role of correct information and communication. *AMA Summer Academic Conference*. AMA Summer Academic conference, Chicago, Illinois.

Mulvey, M. S., Lever, M. W., & Elliot, S. (2020). A cross-national comparison of Intragenerational variability in Social Media sharing. *Journal of Travel Research, 59*(7), 1204–1220. https://doi.org/10.1177/0047287519878511

Nagy, S. (2017). The impact of country of origin in mobile phone choice of generation Y and Z. *Journal of Management and Training for Industries, 4*(2), 16–29.

Niva, M., & Vainio, A. (2021). Towards more environmentally sustainable diets? Changes in the consumption of beef and plant- and insect-based protein products in consumer groups in Finland. *Meat Science, 182*, 108635. https://doi.org/10.1016/j.meatsci.2021.108635

Ordoñez López, M. F., Ghnimi, S., & Liu, C. (2023). Willingness to consume insect-based food in France: Determinants and consumer perspectives. *LWT, 185*, 115179. https://doi.org/10.1016/j.lwt.2023.115179

Orsi, L., Voege, L. L., & Stranieri, S. (2019). Eating edible insects as sustainable food? Exploring the determinants of consumer acceptance in Germany. *Food Research International, 125*, 108573. https://doi.org/10.1016/j.foodres.2019.108573

Papathanassopoulos, S., & Miconi, A. (Eds.). (2023). *The media systems in Europe: Continuities and discontinuities*. Springer International Publishing. https://doi.org/10.1007/978-3-031-32216-7

Pickard, S. (2019). *Politics, protest and young people: Political participation and dissent in 21st century Britain*. Palgrave Macmillan.

Pozharliev, R., De Angelis, M., Rossi, D., Bagozzi, R., & Amatulli, C. (2023). I might try it: Marketing actions to reduce consumer disgust toward insect-based food. *Journal of Retailing, 99*(1), 149–167. https://doi.org/10.1016/j.jretai.2022.12.003

Radaev, V. V. (2021). Historical and empirical evidence for the schism in the millennial generation (part 1). *Sociological Research, 59*(1–3), 1–31. https://doi.org/10.1080/10610154.2022.2111188

Ribeiro, J. C., Soares, A., de Moura, A. P., & Cunha, L. M. (2021). Evaluation of consumers' acceptance of bread supplemented with insect protein. In M. M. Cortez Vieira, L. Pastrana, & J. Aguilera (Eds.), *Sustainable innovation in food product design* (pp. 153–170). Springer International Publishing. https://doi.org/10.1007/978-3-030-61817-9_8

Ros-Baró, M., Casas-Agustench, P., Díaz-Rizzolo, D. A., Batlle-Bayer, L., Adrià-Acosta, F., Aguilar-Martínez, A., Medina, F.-X., Pujolà, M., & Bach-Faig, A. (2022). Edible insect consumption for human and planetary health: A systematic review. *International Journal of Environmental Research and Public Health, 19*(18), 11653. https://doi.org/10.3390/ijerph191811653

Rovai, D., Amin, S., Lesniauskas, R., Wilke, K., Garza, J., & Lammert, A. (2022). Are early adopters willing to accept frozen, ready-to-cook mealworms as a food source? *Journal of Sensory Studies, 37*(5). https://doi.org/10.1111/joss.12774

Salonen, A. S. (2023). 'If I could afford an avocado every day': Income differences and ethical food consumption in a world of abundance. *Journal of Consumer Culture, 23*(1), 27–44. https://doi.org/10.1177/14695405211051033

Schouten, A. P., Janssen, L., & Verspaget, M. (2021). Celebrity vs. Influencer endorsements in advertising: The role of identification, credibility, and Product-Endorser fit. In *Leveraged marketing communications* (pp. 208–231). Routledge.

Schroth, H. (2019). Are you ready for gen Z in the workplace? *California Management Review, 61*(3), 5–18. https://doi.org/10.1177/0008125619841006

Schubiger, D. M., Mendini, M., & Peter, P. C. (2022). Enablers of entomophagy willingness to try for Generation Z consumers. *ISPIM Conference Proceedings*, 1–9. https://www.proquest.com/docview/2694497044/abstract/ACB6FECD27754ED7PQ/1

Sogari, G., Bogueva, D., & Marinova, D. (2019). Australian consumers' response to insects as food. *Agriculture, 9*(5), 108. https://doi.org/10.3390/agriculture9050108

Soysal, F., Calli, B. A., & Coşkun, E. (2019). Intra and intergenerational digital divide through ICT literacy, information acquisition skills, and internet utilization purposes: An analysis of Gen Z. *TEM Journal, 8*(1), 264–274.

Stavrianea, A., & Kamenidou, I. (Eirini). (2022). Memorable tourism experiences, destination image, satisfaction, and loyalty: An empirical study of Santorini Island. *EuroMed Journal of Business, 17*(1), 1–20. https://doi.org/10.1108/EMJB-10-2020-0106

Thompson, B. (Ed.). (2002). *Score reliability: Contemporary thinking on reliability issues*. Sage Publications.

Thrassou, A., Uzunboylu, N., Efthymiou, L., Vrontis, D., Weber, Y., Riad Shams, S. M., & Tsoukatos, E. (2022). Editorial introduction: Business under crises: Organizational adaptations. In D. Vrontis, A. Thrassou, Y. Weber, S. M. R. Shams, E. Tsoukatos, & L. Efthymiou (Eds.), *Business under crisis, Volume*

II: Organisational adaptations. Palgrave Studies in Cross-disciplinary Business Research, In Association with EuroMed Academy of Business. Palgrave Macmillan, Cham. https://doi.org/10.1007/978-3-030-76575-0_1

Tzompa-Sosa, D. A., Moruzzo, R., Mancini, S., Schouteten, J. J., Liu, A., Li, J., & Sogari, G. (2023). Consumers' acceptance toward whole and processed mealworms: A cross-country study in Belgium, China, Italy, Mexico, and the US. *PLoS ONE, 18*(1), e0279530. https://doi.org/10.1371/journal.pone.0279530

van Broekhoven, S., Oonincx, D. G. A. B., van Huis, A., & van Loon, J. J. A. (2015). Growth performance and feed conversion efficiency of three edible mealworm species (Coleoptera: Tenebrionidae) on diets composed of organic by-products. *Journal of Insect Physiology, 73*, 1–10. https://doi.org/10.1016/j.jinsphys.2014.12.005

Van Huis, A., Van Itterbeeck, J., Klunder, H., Mertens, E., Halloran, A., Muir, G., & Vantomme, P. (2013). *Edible insects: Future prospects for food and feed security* (Issue 171). Food and agriculture organization of the United Nations.

Vrontis, D., Makrides, A., Christofi, M., & Thrassou, A. (2021). Social media influencer marketing: A systematic review, integrative framework and future research agenda. *International Journal of Consumer Studies, 45*(4), 617–644. https://doi.org/10.1111/ijcs.12647

Vrontis, D., Thrassou, A., Efthymiou, L., Weber, Y., Shams, S. M. R., & Tsoukatos, E. (2023a). *Business for sustainability, Volume I: Strategic avenues and managerial approaches*, Springer Nature. In Association with EuroMed Academy of Business. Palgrave Macmillan, Cham.

Vrontis, D., Thrassou, A., Uzunboylu, N., Efthymiou, L. (2023b). An overview of business for sustainability: Strategic avenues and managerial approaches. In D. Vrontis, A. Thrassou, L. Efthymiou, Y. Weber, S. M. R. Shams, & E. Tsoukatos (Eds.), *Business for sustainability, volume* I. Palgrave Studies in Cross-disciplinary Business Research, In Association with EuroMed Academy of Business. Palgrave Macmillan, Cham. https://doi.org/10.1007/978-3-031-37361-9_1

Widyanto, H. A., & Agusti, C. R. (2020). Beauty influencer in the digital age: How does it influence purchase intention of generation Z? *Jurnal Manajemen Dan Pemasaran Jasa, 13*(1), 1–16.

Williams, K., & Page, R. (2011). Marketing to the generations. *Journal of Behavioral Studies in Business, 3*, 1–17.

Woolf, E., Zhu, Y., Emory, K., Zhao, J., & Liu, C. (2019). Willingness to consume insect-containing foods: A survey in the United States. *LWT, 102*, 100–105. https://doi.org/10.1016/j.lwt.2018.12.010

Xu, C., Siegrist, M., & Hartmann, C. (2021). The application of virtual reality in food consumer behavior research: A systematic review. *Trends in Food Science & Technology, 116*, 533–544. https://doi.org/10.1016/j.tifs.2021.07.015

CHAPTER 9

Creating an Innovative Vocational E-learning Model that Harnesses the Potential of Digital Cultural Heritage

Yianna Orphanidou, Leonidas Efthymiou, and Paraskevi Dekoulou

9.1 Introduction

Vocational education, like many other sectors in our economy and society, has found remarkable ways to change and adapt during recent crises and critical events. This has allowed the sector to keep offering educational opportunities and learning experiences that both learners and instructors pursue. Since instruction frequently revolves around in-person experiences with tangible materials, instructors who teach with cultural heritage materials in particular had difficulty adjusting to remote learning. The

Y. Orphanidou · L. Efthymiou (✉)
Department of Management, School of Business,
University of Nicosia, Nicosia, Cyprus
e-mail: efthymiou.l@unic.ac.cy

Y. Orphanidou
e-mail: orphanidou.y@unic.ac.cy

D. Vrontis et al. (eds.), *Business in Uncertainty*, Palgrave Studies in Cross-disciplinary Business Research, In Association with EuroMed Academy of Business, https://doi.org/10.1007/978-3-031-65587-6_9

transition to remote learning for many instructors highlighted how important teaching with physical collections is to their pedagogy, emphasizing the value of place-based learning and the significance of students' interactions with cultural heritage materials. At the same time, many educators, at different levels of education, devised creative ways to integrate digital cultural heritage resources into their curricula and experimented with alternative ways to modify their courses to support primary source literacy and learning (e.g., Lee, 2023; Li & Kang, 2023).

Learning through cultural heritage cultivates respect and appreciation for cultural diversity, facilitates intercultural dialogue, and contributes to more resilient and inclusive societies (Quintela & Palotás, 2023). This research study focuses on the utilization of digital cultural heritage content for the development of skills and competencies essential for personal and professional development of vocational students. The development of a new conceptual learning model utilizing tangible and intangible cultural heritage is introduced, along with the influence of digital cultural heritage in education. This innovative learning model is based on a combination of tangible and intangible heritage, which enables the protection and perpetuation of cultural heritage through digital cultural heritage. The principle of "learning by doing" is applied as a means of facilitating the active involvement of learners in the learning process (Efthymiou et al., 2021). It also provides the opportunity to learn through concrete experiences and application of what has been learned in a real-life situation.

The proposed learning model takes into account the different needs of learners while adapting to their age, level of knowledge, and abilities. This innovative e-learning model has been developed under the Erasmus+project, titled "DIGICULT Cultural Heritage: a source of resilience and sustainable learning through digital education." The ongoing process of assimilation of experience to knowledge, known as Kolb's learning cycle, involves an interaction between action, reflection, experience, and abstraction (Kolb & Kolb, 2012). The four stages of Kolb's learning cycle are concrete experience that reflective observation,

P. Dekoulou
Department of Journalism and Mass Communications, Aristotle University of Thessaloniki, Thessaloniki, Greece
e-mail: dekoulou@jour.auth.gr

abstract conceptualization, and active experimentation and the foundations of experiential learning. In general, concrete experience is the time when learners engage in the experience in order to learn. Learners review their experiences through reflective observation. Departing from Kolb's learning cycle from Experiential Learning Theory, the paper proposes an e-learning innovative model, while adopting a pedagogical approach of implementing experiential learning in a digital learning environment for vocational education and training of young learners. The entire effort is part of a broader effort for sustainable education.

The current paper aims at strengthening the digital and technological skills of vocational learners with a specific focus on cultural heritage; to improve learners' awareness about the impact and use of digital technology. The results of the paper revealed the importance in increasing vocational learners' resilience by promoting and implementing competencies for the digital transformation (Buhalis et al., 2024; Kulshrestha et al., 2024; Zarifis et al., 2023) and the need to maximize digital possibilities, which allow for learning and engagement with cultural heritage in ways that are not possible physically.

The organization of the paper is the following: the next section provides readers with a review of the literature. The third section, titled "Research Design and Methodology," explains the research processes and methods employed during the course of the study. Then, section four presents the findings of the study, prior to proposing an Innovative e-learning vocational model in section five. At the end, the paper is summarized with a conclusion.

9.2 Literature Review

Digital skills are driving competitiveness in today's economy. Digitally supported education and training can help to strengthen individual skills and competencies. The Institute for Prospective Technological Studies (IPTS), one of the Joint Research Centres of the European Commission, has compiled a thorough review of national approaches to digital education legislation around the world (Conrads et al., 2017). The European Parliament and the Council of the European Union identified digital competence as one of eight key competencies necessary for lifelong (and sustainable) learning in 2006, recognizing the pervasive importance of digital skills at the time. Since then, the EU has developed numerous Digital Competence Frameworks (Dig Comp, DigCompEdu,

DigCompOrg) to assist with the development of digital skills in all citizens, educators, educational organizations, and consumers (DigCompConsumers). Four proficiency levels in five domains were developed (a) information and data literacy, (b) communication and cooperation (c) creation of digital material, (d) safety, and (e) problem solving, letting people to evaluate their own digital skills and allow comparisons between Member States (Vaikutytė-Paškauskė et al., 2018).

Competencies and Skills

The twenty-first century does not focus on cognitive skills but on human, digital, and soft skills. It includes competencies that machines and artificial intelligence do not have or do not excel at, but humans do (EPSC, 2017; Park, 2019). Learners with these skills will be in high demand because they can shape and advance digital transformation (Epaminonda et al., 2022), as well as contribute to the general advancement of society and innovation. Furthermore, the ability to manage change, specifically resilience, adaptability, leadership, and flexibility, are valuable long-term skills to develop in order to be prepared for future developments (Hooft Graafland, 2018).

In 2021, the European Union member states reported the lowest shares of early leavers from education and training. In contrast, the highest shares were recorded in Italy (13%), and Cyprus (10%). The EU Member States have set themselves a target to reduce the rates of early school leavers to below 9% at the EU level by 2030. Sixteen Member States have already met the EU-level target for 2030 for this indicator, including Lithuania (Eurostat 2022). This research study explores the current vocational education system in Lithuania as well as in Cyprus and Italy, in an attempt to understand if there is a need to change the existing vocational education model. The research study supports that a more engaging education model will lead to a decrease of the current dropouts and align with the EU 2030 target.

EU Digital Strategies

The term "digital native" is increasingly being used in public discourse to describe generations of young people who have grown up surrounded by digital technologies. The term implies that young people intuitively understand how to use technology and thus do not require digital education or training. All EU digital strategies in the past decade, Digital Agenda for Europe (2010), Digital Single Market for Europe (2015), and a Europe fit for the digital age (2020) aimed at having every European digital. Research on young people's use of Internet and technology in the Council of Europe Member States is quite limited, but the Eurostat data provides us with some insights into the situation in the European Union. In 2021, 95% of Young Europeans aged 16–29 years reported using Internet every day. However, the share of young people with basic or above-basic digital skills ranges from 93 to 46% with the EU average standing at 71%. According to Eurostat 2021, 76% of all young people have performed basic computer tasks such as copying or moving a file or folder (see Fig. 9.1).

The use of digital technology has increased dramatically over the previous two decades. It has increased human exposure to prolonged screen time, which is becoming increasingly problematic. Digital technology is defined as the use of electronic equipment to store, generate, or analyze data, as well as to promote communication and virtual interactions on social media platforms via Internet (Vizcaino et al., 2020). Computers, laptops, smartphones, tablets, and other similar devices are all considered electronic gadgets that are utilized for interpersonal connection, virtual communication, and virtual engagement. Social media has swiftly changed the way young learners communicate with one another, igniting considerable scientific and public discussion over its possible impact on young learner's socio-emotional well-being and mental health.

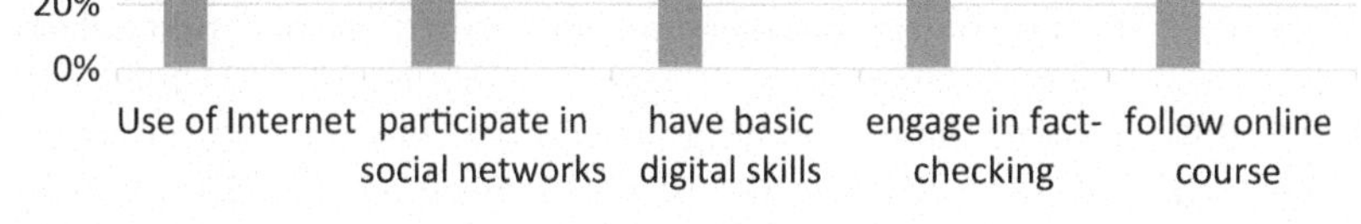

Fig. 9.1 Young Europeans and the Internet

The necessity to bridge this knowledge gap has become increasingly obvious in the light of COVID-19 pandemic (Hamilton et al., 2022). The pandemic has forced people to rely on digital networks to preserve socio-emotional connections (Epaminonda et al., 2021; Kanekar & Sharma, 2020). Most existing jobs will be obsolete due to technological advancements, and employees will require re-skilling and upskilling in order to expand their competencies and remain employed (Thrassou et al., 2022). The use of technology and digital means in the education system has become increasingly important and necessary in order to meet the changing needs of students and provide them with high-quality education that is accessible, flexible, and sustainable (Doukanari et al., 2021; Efthymiou & Zarifis, 2021).

Cultural Heritage

Cultural heritage refers to the behaviors, beliefs, habits, and artifacts that are passed down from generation to generation, forming a community's or society's identity. History, architecture, art, music, literature, and language are all included, as are traditional knowledge, rituals, and festivals (Unesco, 2011). Cultural heritage not only provides individuals and communities with a sense of pride and identity, but it also plays an important role in promoting intercultural discourse, protecting biodiversity, and developing social cohesion. As a result, it is critical to maintaining and conserving cultural heritage for future generations in order to ensure its sustainability and relevance in an ever-changing world (Efthymiou et al., 2023; Vrontis et al., 2023). It is currently gaining public and scholarly interest around the world, and its conceptual reach is expanding. Most social scientists emphasize its functions in promoting ethnic, national, and elite interests, but others highlight its creative and counter-hegemonic aspects. Since the globe has entered the age of globalization, cultural heritage has declined. Young people are increasingly unaware of their cultural identity (Tan et al., 2018). Education for Sustainable Development (ESD) toward achieving Sustainable Development Goals (SDGs) will further strengthen the partnership with other sectors, particularly Culture and Science, integrating the implementation of ESD for 2030 (ESD 2030). One of the overarching goals of ESD is to empower young people, who will not only face the issues of unsustainable development in the present, but will also be decision-makers in the future. This paper seeks to investigate the level of youth awareness, attitudes, and practices regarding the tangible and intangible cultural heritage.

The literature review revealed a need for change in the learning methodology of the young learners. Despite the fact that young learners are increasingly recognized as the fundamental stakeholders in the educational system, the vast majority of educational research continues to focus entirely on learner's viewpoints, positioning learners as passive information providers (Geurts et al., 2023). Young learners are more likely to be digital natives, meaning they grew up with technology and are more comfortable using it. Digital skills have implications for the future of the European workforce. In an increasingly digital economy, those with strong digital skills will have a competitive advantage in the job market. This means that youth who lack these skills will be at a disadvantage when competing for jobs. The introduction of the new innovative e-learning model that connects cultural heritage with digital skills is a new learning methodology that reflects the needs of digital native learners with the aim of developing disciplinary and life skills, improving learners' key competencies as summarized in the recommendations of the European Commission and the European Council (2020). This e-learning pathway can motivate learners and young people at risk of leaving school, since it transforms their knowledge and passion for digital tools (such as video games or social media). At the same time, it facilitates a transformation of their increasing environmental sensitivity into skills useful for their professional future, as part of long-term sustainable education.

9.3 Research Design and Methodology

This research study was conducted in three European countries Cyprus, Italy, and Lithuania during the period of 2021–2022 and required an approach that combined both primary and secondary research techniques. Initially, extensive secondary research was carried out through the in-depth study of vocational education curricula, national reports, European data from Eurostat, publications by the European Commission, the OECD, Partnership for 21st Century Skills, and UNESCO studies and with the aim of obtaining adequate information on the local vocational educational systems, the extent to which vocational education curricula have incorporated cultural heritage subjects Concerning primary research, after evaluating the available options on the basis of their respective strengths and weaknesses, it was concluded that the present study required a mixed research method combining both qualitative and qualitative data in order to get a deeper understanding of the digital and cultural heritage competence of the young learners.

Based on the project's purpose, the quantitative approach was selected, given the need for measuring attitudes, opinions, and characteristics of a large sample (Cooper & Schindler, 2008; Hyde, 2000). Concerning research strategy, the survey strategy was employed, as the present study demanded the collection of a large amount of quantitative data from a sizeable sample (Saunders et al, 2009; Zikmund, 2000). The research population is composed of youth in private and public vocational schools in Cyprus, Italy, and Lithuania, as well as vocational learners at tertiary education and youngsters that have dropped formal education and are more vulnerable in the labor market. Data was collected with the use of an online structured self-administered questionnaire, composed of 14 questions covering areas such as demographics, familiarity with digital means, and level of competence in relation to cultural heritage. With the use of convenience sampling, 820 questionnaires were collected. In order to avoid biased answers and to cope with respondents' cautions and hesitancy to participate in the present survey, answerers were reassured in advance that information generated from completed questionnaires would be anonymous and absolutely confidential, and would be utilized only for the academic purposes of the present inquiry. Moreover, the research topic as well as the research aim were minutely articulated and explained to the research population's members so that they could realize the critical significance of their contribution.

In order to get a more holistic view of stakeholders' opinions, qualitative research was also required. Among the various available types of qualitative data collection methods, the one selected for the implementation of this study was an interview. The interview method was used to facilitate the exchange of information between the researcher and the respondents, since the research question required detailed analysis on the part of the interviewees, and thus demanded a method capable of providing in-depth and exhaustive information. Interview was therefore deemed the most suitable method since it offered the interviewees plenty of freedom to articulate their thoughts and present their opinions based on arguments. Particularly, the face-to-face interviews helped produce a more thorough examination of the topic, as it helped forge and reinforce personal contact between interlocutors, assisted in the probing for more detailed responses, and gave interviewer the opportunity to interpret the interviewee's "visual prompts". In qualitative research, purposeful sampling was applied, since this technique is commonly used in qualitative research and allows optimum use of limited resources (Patton, 2002). This entails locating and selecting individuals or groups of individuals who are particularly knowledgeable about or experienced with a phenomenon of interest (Cresswell & Plano Clark, 2011). Twenty-one (21) semi-structured interviews were conducted with educators, policy makers, and representatives from cultural identities from the three selected countries.

Data was analyzed through conversation analysis and qualitative content analysis. Using this mixed method allowed the researchers to fully explore the status of the competence of youth in digital cultural heritage and the readiness of the current education and cultural providers to deliver digitalized cultural heritage, focusing on enhancing the skills and competence of the young Europeans to enhance their employability and entrepreneurial capability.

9.4 Data Analysis and Results

The questionnaire sample consisted of 239 questionnaires from Cyprus, 458 questionnaires from Italy, and 123 Questionnaires from Lithuania. The gender representation of the sample was 50.3% female and 48.1% male. The sample that participated was equally distributed between the genders with a slight predominance of the female gender. Most of the responders resided in their country of origin with insignificant percentages attributed to other origins. The largest percentage of respondents belonged to the 14–16 age group (58.8% of the sample) followed by the 17–19 age group (41.1%) and lower percentages are to be found in the 20–25 and 26–30 age groups. 87% of the sample had primary to secondary education with 2.4% representing dropouts and 7.3% having a University education. Only 3% of people had pursued but never completed a University education.

Competencies and Digital Means

The first part of the questions aimed to identify the competencies that young participants valued as most important. The participants in the survey had to select from a list of thirteen competencies that had been identified as the most important ones from OECD, the European Commission and the Partnership for 21st Century Skills (P21, 2011).

The data analysis revealed that *foreign languages, creativity, and critical thinking* were valued as the top three important competencies for enhancing employability with pr*oblem solving* and leadership to follow at 57.9%. All thirteen competencies had a significant percentage of 30% and above that indicates equal importance. The replies of the young participants reveal the high level of awareness of the competencies they need to possess to enhance their employability (see Table 9.1).

As the research focuses on the digital native's skills, it was important to identify what type of digital devices young people utilize more often. Smartphones are by far the most commonly used digital device among young people with 98.9% of the sample selecting it as first choice. Second in line are Laptops and PCs at 44.9% and tablets at 28.3%. The Mascheroni and Cuman (2014) study supports that in European countries young people are going online by using multiple devices. Young people have shown preferences for using Internet for gaming, chatting, and social networking purposes (Durkee et al., 2012). Overall, young people today use a wide range of digital devices for a variety of

Table 9.1 Competences importance in enhancing employability

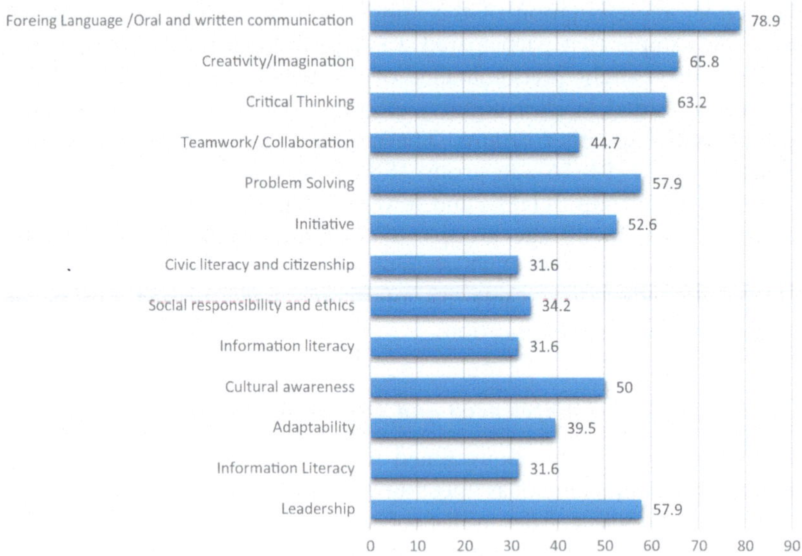

purposes, and the types of devices they use can vary depending on many socioeconomic and cultural characteristics (Table 9.2).

Due to the need for a larger screen and more powerful processing, young people frequently utilize laptops and tablets for studying, gaming, and other activities. Wearable tech, Smartwatches, and other wearable devices are becoming more popular among young people for communication, fitness tracking, and other uses. While older teens (aged 17–19) favor laptops and desktops, younger participants (aged 14–16) appeared to be more likely to utilize tablets or smartphones.

With the advancement of technology and the internet, and the introduction of social media such as Facebook and Instagram affecting the way we live, work, and, more importantly, learn has changed dramatically. Teachers and professors are increasingly incorporating social media into their classes, whether they are online or in person, to engage students and advance their knowledge. In summary, social media is affecting and molding how young learners study and interact today and many educational institutions and organizations have developed online courses and e-learning platforms that provide educational content in a variety of formats such as video lectures, online quizzes, and interactive activities. The data analysis showed that among users between the ages of 14 and 19 who utilize digital methods to get learning and general information, 73.5% of the overall sample ranked YouTube as their top option (see Table 9.2). It is extremely intriguing that e-books and PowerPoint presentations, which are widely used in formal education, are not a preferred

Table 9.2 Use of digital means for learning and information purposes

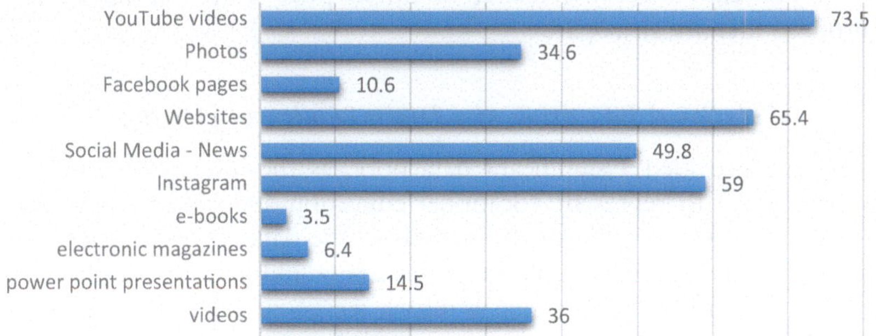

Table 9.3 Identify the following examples in relation to cultural heritage—1 least relevant—5 most relevant

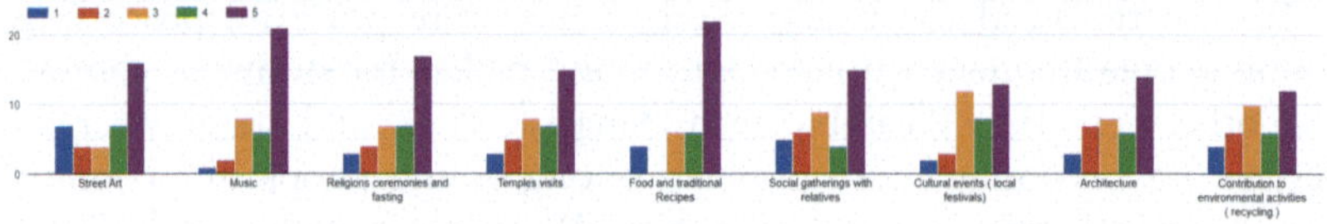

digital medium for people between the ages of 14 and 30. A significant result of this research was the requirement to redesign the pedagogical frameworks for online learning in vocational education.

Cultural Heritage

UNESCO (2011), classifies cultural heritage into three types: tangible, intangible, and natural. Intangible cultural legacy differs from other types of cultural heritage in that it cannot be seen or touched; examples are language, customs, lifestyle, music, art, and dance (Nazri & Aziz, 2011).

An evaluation of the literature suggests that cultural heritage is an important component of our cognitive knowledge and should be taught in schools. Among the aims of this study was to determine how knowledgeable the young participants were about tangible and intangible heritage. We can see from Table 9.3 that there is a lack of awareness of both tangible and intangible cultural heritage, because participants struggled to identify all nine of the assessed cases as cultural heritage. The study's findings confirm the importance of emphasizing cultural heritage in the curriculum because failing to do so puts pride and respect for European identity at jeopardy.

Vocational Education and Digital Cultural Heritage

Interviews provided a significant data pool, as the interviewees purposively selected to represent vocational education and cultural providers in the three countries. From the analysis of the data collected, there is a consensus as far as the way cultural heritage is taught in primary education that involves mostly courses such as music, art, geography, and religion; at secondary education, there is emphasis on languages, history, economics, and civic education. There is a significant gap in how education systems define cultural heritage. From one country and language to another, the terms "culture," "cultural heritage," and "education" were not defined in the same way. There was agreement that "Cultural legacy," which includes both tangible and intangible elements, has an impact on both the past and the present.

From the interview scripts content analysis, there was a strong agreement that heritage and vocational education should be seen as tools for sustainable development, rather than just a reaction to the market-based economy. "Cultural heritage is not a "duty" or an encounter with heritage, but a tool that in the right hands can give good results".

Education is still too knowledge-oriented on a day-to-day basis, lacking flexibility. It is in crucial need of rethinking its main goals and methods, including digital cultural heritage matters. The use of digital cultural heritage education may enhance the development of soft skills and competencies necessary to create resilient European youth.

We can also increase learners' resilience in the cultural sector, by holding various thematic workshops in open spaces (e.g., museums, archaeological parks, nature parks, national parks). Workshops will affect the acquisition of knowledge and skills, or their consolidation, and thus learners will be more resilient. Cultural heritage education thus enhances people's ability to become not only fulfilled citizens, able to live in society but also responsible citizens regarding the protection of cultural heritage. The use of digital cultural heritage education may help to improve the soft skills and competencies required to generate resilient European youth. "Learning about belonging to our society and community access is a must as well as for our cultural identity in order to promote social engagement and active participation in society."

Cultural heritage education improves people's potential to become not just fulfilled citizens capable of living in society, but also responsible citizens in terms of cultural heritage protection. From the interviewees analysis, the authors gathered very strong statements that support the need of the utilization of cultural heritage in education curriculums. The respondents' repetitive feedback on the benefits of using cultural heritage in vocational education provides a strong basis for the need of a new vocational pedagogical model.

9.5 Innovative E-learning Vocational Model

The suggested "Digicult model" (see Fig. 9.2) emphasizes the use of cultural assets to improve skills and competencies in the digital age. Learners develop information, intellectual abilities, and a broader variety of competencies on themes such as cultural heritage maintenance and societal well-being by actively experiencing or analyzing cultural heritage. This type of knowledge leads to long-term economic growth initiatives, including chances for respectable work. The suggested model ensures inclusiveness of young learners aged 14–30, while taking into consideration various educational backgrounds, and motivates them to engage in Lifelong learning.

Moreover, the competencies revealed by the analysis of the questionnaires and the interviews emphasized the need of enhancing foreign languages, written and oral communication, creativity/imagination, critical thinking, problem solving, and the ability to work in a team. The diversity of the audience revealed the need for an innovative curriculum that will take into consideration the individual learning needs as well as creating an environment of inclusivity. The research revealed that

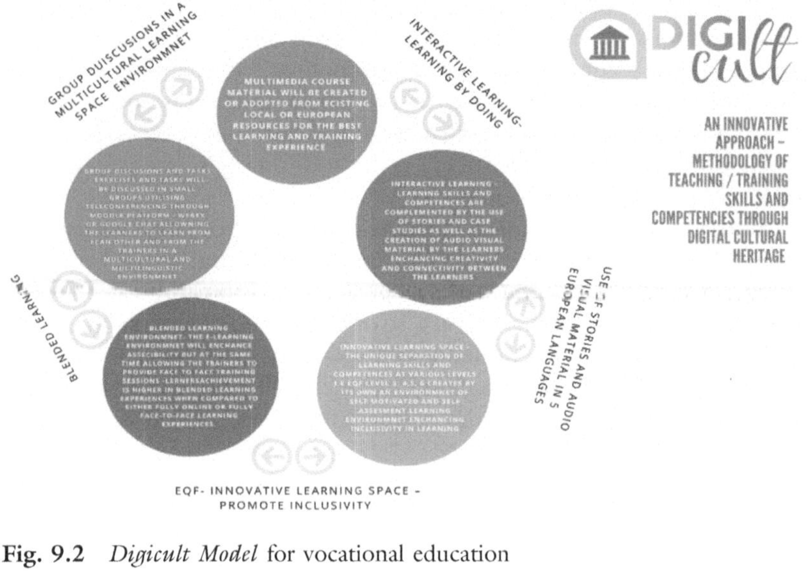

Fig. 9.2 *Digicult Model* for vocational education

an e-learning pathway is not necessarily 100% digitally delivered as the young learners' digital skills varied from country to country. The need for designing a blended mode of delivery has better results in a vocational learning environment. The model focuses on enhancing skills and competencies in a digital era by utilizing cultural heritage. By directly experiencing or analyzing cultural heritage, learners gain knowledge, intellectual skills, and a wider range of competencies on issues such as cultural heritage maintenance or societal well-being. This kind of knowledge leads to sustainable economic growth actions, including opportunities for employment.

9.6 Conclusion

In the public discourse, the term "digital native" is frequently associated with generations of young people who have grown up with digital technologies. The notion implies that young people intuitively understand how to utilize technology and hence do not require digital education or training. All EU digital plans during the last decade, including the Digital Agenda for Europe (2010), the Digital Single Market for Europe (2015), and a Europe fit for the digital age (2020), have attempted to make every European digital native. However, research on young people's usage of the Internet and technology in Council of Europe member countries is limited. Eurostat data provides some insight into the situation in the European Union. In 2021, 95% of Europeans aged 16 to 29 reported using the Internet every day. However, the proportion of young people with basic or above basic digital skills spans from 93 to 46%, compared to the EU average of 71%. 76% of all young people said they had done basic computer tasks like copying or moving a file or folder. Eurostat (Eurostat, 2021) Digital resources can offer valuable learning opportunities and life-changing experiences for students in a range of academic fields, especially those in vocational subjects like hospitality and tourism.

Such educational opportunities offer substantial historical and/or cultural background for a discipline, allowing students to get more deeply involved in their studies or even to recognize themselves for the first time as scholars. They can also be located within the broader context of Sustainable Education and Sustainable Learning. Within this framework, the current research paper developed a new innovative approach and methodology for designing vocational courses. This has been achieved by utilizing digital cultural heritage, and focusing on skills and competencies such as critical thinking, creativity, and innovation through the learning of Cultural heritage (tangible and intangible). According to the e-learning vocational education paradigm, new digital tools and content are required to engage young learners and develop critical core competencies that will increase their employability and productivity. The use of the model in vocational education, which places more emphasis on interactive outputs than on content, can support the design of interactive labs that cover both the acquisition of new digital skills and the development of knowledge and abilities that will unite young people in Europe through a digital cultural environment.

Acknowledgements This paper was supported by the research conducted under the project titled DIGICULT under the 2021-1-IT01-KA220-VOCATIONAL-000034836 Erasmus+ KA220—VOCATIONAL—Cooperation partnerships in vocational education and training.

References

Buhalis, D., Efthymiou, L., Uzunboylu, N., & Thrassou, A. (2024). 'Charting the progress of technology adoption in tourism and hospitality in the era of industry 4.0'. Tourism & Hospitality in the Digital Era: Technology and its (im)Possibilities. Special Issue in *Euromed Journal of Business*. https://doi.org/10.1108/EMJB-11-2023-0310

Conrads, J., Rasmussen, M., Winters, N., Geniet, A., & Langer, L. (2017). Digital education policies in Europeand beyond: Key design principles for more effective policies [JRC Science for Policy Report]. *EuropeanCommission*. https://doi.org/10.2760/462941

Cooper, D. R., & Schindler, P. S. (2008). *Business research methods* (10th ed.). McGraw-Hill.

Council of the European Union. (2020). *Recommendation for a council recommendation on the 2020 national reform programme of cyprus and delivering a council opinion on the 2020 convergence programme of Cyprus.* Available at: https://data.consilium.europa.eu/doc/document/ST-8432-2020-INIT/en/pdf, Accessed 20 August 2022.

Cresswell, J. W., & Plano Clark, V. L. (2011). *Designing and conducting mixed method research* (2nd Sage), Thousand Oaks, CA.

Cultural Heritage ,UNESCO UIS, http://uis.unesco.org/en/glossary-term/cultural-heritage, Accessed 26 August 2022.

Doukanari, E., Ktoridou, D., Efthymiou, L., & Epaminonda, E. (2021). The quest for sustainable teaching Praxis: Opportunities and challenges of multidisciplinary and multicultural teamwork. *Sustainability, 13*, 7210. https://doi.org/10.3390/su13137210

Durkee, T., et al. (2012). Prevalence of pathological internet use among adolescents in Europe:Demographic and social factors. *Addiction, 107*(12), 2210–2222. https://doi.org/10.1111/j.1360-0443.2012.03946.x

Efthymiou, L., Kulshrestha, A., & Kulshrestha, S. (2023). A study on sustainability and ESG in the service sector in India: Benefits, challenges, and future implications. *Administrative Sciences, 13*, 165. https://doi.org/10.3390/admsci13070165

Efthymiou, L., & Zarifis, A. (2021). Modeling students' voice for enhanced quality in online management education. *The International Journal of Management Education, 19*(2), 100464, ISSN 1472-8117. https://doi.org/10.1016/j.ijme.2021.100464

Efthymiou, L., Ktoridou, D., & Epaminonda, E. (2021). *A model for experiential learning by replicating a workplace environment in virtual classes*. Proceedings IEEE Global Engineering Education Conference (EDUCON), Vienna, Austria, pp. 1749–1753. https://doi.org/10.1109/EDUCON46332.2021.9453966

Epaminonda, E., Efthymiou, L., & Doukanari, E. (2022). *Linking digital transformation to learning strategies and pedagogy* (pp. 2088–2092). Proceedings IEEE Global Engineering Education Conference (EDUCON), Tunis, Tunisia, 2022. https://doi.org/10.1109/EDUCON52537.2022.9766614

Epaminonda, E., Efthymiou, L., & Ktoridou, D. (2021). COVID-19 contingency plans: The impact on students' future choices. 2021 IEEE Global Engineering Education Conference (EDUCON), Vienna, Austria, 2021, pp. 1737–1742. https://doi.org/10.1109/EDUCON46332.2021.9454061

EPSC. (2017). *10 trends transforming education as we know it*. European Political Strategy Centre. https://ec.europa.eu/epsc/publications/other-publications/10-trends-transforming-education-weknow-it_en, Accessed 28 August 2022.

European Commission. (2014). *Towards an integrated approach to cultural heritage for Europe—Communication from the Commission to the European Parliament, the Council, the European Economic and Social Committee and the Committee of the Regions*. https://eurlex.europa.eu/legalcontent/EN/TXT/PDF/?uri=CELEX:52014DC0477&from=en, Accessed 11 August 2022.

Geurts, E. M. A., Reijs, R. P., Leenders, H. H. M., et al. (2023). Co-creation and decision-making with students about teaching and learning: A systematic literature review. *Journal of Educational Change*. https://doi.org/10.1007/s10833-023-09481-x

Hooft Graafland, J. (2018). *New technologies and 21st century children: Recent trends and outcomes* (OECD Education Working Paper No. 179). https://doi.org/10.1787/e071a505-en

Hyde, K. F. (2000). Recognising deductive processes in qualitative research. *Qualitative Market Research: An International Journal, 3*(2), 82–90.

Hamilton, J. L., Nesi, J., & Choukas-Bradley, S. (2022). Reexamining social media and socioemotional well-being among adolescents through the lens of the COVID-19 pandemic: A theoretical review and directions for future research. *Perspectives on Psychological Science, 17*(3), 662–679. https://doi.org/10.1177/17456916211014189

Intangible Cultural Heritage of Cyprus, http://www.unesco.org.cy/Programmes-Intangible_Cultural_Heritage_of_Cyprus,EN-PROGRAMMES-04-02-03,EN, Accessed 27 April 2022.

Kanekar, A., & Sharma, M. (2020). COVID-19 and mental well-being: Guidance on the application of behavioral and positive well-being strategies. *Healthcare, 8*(3), 336. https://doi.org/10.3390/healthcare8030336

Kolb, A. Y., & Kolb, D. A. (2012). Experiential learning theory. In N. M. Seel (Ed.), *Encyclopedia of the sciences of learning* (pp. 1215–1219). Springer.

Kulshrestha, A., Kulshrestha, S., Efthymiou, L., Ktoridou, D. (2024). Digital transformation in the Indian service sector: Benefits, challenges and future implications. In A. Zarifis, D. Ktoridou, L. Efthymiou, & X. Cheng (Eds.), *Business digital transformation*. Palgrave Macmillan. https://doi.org/10.1007/978-3-031-33665-2_8

Lee, T. S. C. (2023). Designing art museum E-learning resources for children: Content analysis from education perspectives. *Interactive Learning Environments*. https://doi.org/10.1080/10494820.2022.2162549

Li, X. Z., & Kang, X. (2023). Intangible cultural heritage based augmented reality mobile learning: Application development and heuristics evaluation. Joint International Conference on Digital Arts, Media and Technology with ECTI Northern Section Conference on Electrical, Electronics, Computer and Telecommunications Engineering (ECTI DAMT & NCON), Phuket, Thailand, pp. 26–30, https://doi.org/10.1109/ECTIDAMTNCON57770.2023.10139422

Mascheroni, G., & Cuman, A. (2014). *Net children go mobile: Final report*.

Ministry of Education and Culture, Cyprus pedagogical institute. http://www.moec.gov.cy/ysea/index.html, Accessed 29 April 2022.

Nazri, A. M., & Aziz, H. A. (2011). Program pemuliharaan Taiping Bandar Warisan oleh Majlis Perbandaran Taiping. In H. Abdul Aziz (Ed.), *Pemuliharaan dan pemeliharaan warisan di Malaysia* (pp. 70–118). Universiti Sains Malaysia.

Overview of the Cultural Heritage of Cyprus. http://www.mfa.gov.cy/mfa/Embassies/embassy_berlin.nsf/All/8E0622E689DD1260C2257FBF002F5F31, Accessed 28 April 2022.

P21 (Partnership for 21st Century Skills). (2011). *Framework for 21st century learning*. www.p21.org/our-work/p21-framework, Accessed 26 April 2022.

Park, C.-Y. (2019). *Lifelong learning and education policies to capture digital gains: The future of work and education for the digital age* [G20 insights]. Think20 Japan. https://www.g20-insights.org/policy_briefs/lifelong-learning-and-education-policies-to-capture-digital-gains/, Accessed 28 April 2022.

Patton, M. Q. (2002). *Qualitative research and evaluation methods* (3rd Sage). Sage Publications.

Quintela, J. A., & Palotás, G. (2023). E-Learning platforms in heritage education: A strategy to preserve traditional craftsmanship. In L. Bassa (Ed.), *Combining modern communication methods with heritage education* (pp. 101–114). IGI Global. https://doi.org/10.4018/978-1-6684-6217-1.ch007

Saunders, M., Lewis, P., & Thornhill, A. (2009). *Research methods for business students* (5th ed.). Financial Times/Prentice-Hall.

Tan, S.-K., Tan, S.-H., Kok, Y.-S., Choon, S.-W. (2018). Sense of place and sustainability of intangible cultural heritage—The case of George Town and Melaka. *Tourism Management, 67*, 376–387. ISSN 0261-5177. https://doi.org/10.1016/j.tourman.2018.02.012

Thrassou, A., Vrontis, D., Efthymiou, L., & Uzunboylu, N. (2022). An overview of business advancement through technology: The changing landscape of work and employment. In A. Thrassou, D. Vrontis, L. Efthymiou, Y. Weber, S. M. R. Shams, & E. Tsoukatos (Eds.), *Business advancement through technology volume II. Palgrave studies in cross-disciplinary business research, in association with EuroMed Academy of Business*. Palgrave Macmillan, Cham. https://doi.org/10.1007/978-3-031-07765-4_1.

UNESCO. (2011). *Preparing world heritage nomination* (2nd ed.).

Vaikutytė-Paškauskė, J., Vaičiukynaitė, J., & Pocius, D. (2018). *Research for CULT Committee -Digital skills in the 21st century*. IPOL, European Parliament. http://www.europarl.europa.eu/thinktank/en/document.html?reference=IPOL_STU(2018)617495, Accessed 28 April 2022.

Vizcaino, M., Buman, M., DesRoches, T., & Wharton, C. (2020). From TVs to tablets: The relation between device-specific screen time and health-related behaviors and characteristics. *BMC Public Health, 20*(1), 1–10. https://doi.org/10.1186/s12889-020-09410-0

Vrontis, D., Thrassou, A., Uzunboylu, N., Efthymiou, L. (2023). An overview of business for sustainability: Strategic avenues and managerial approaches. In D. Vrontis, A. Thrassou, L. Efthymiou, Y. Weber, S. M. R. Shams, & E. Tsoukatos (Eds.), *Business for sustainability, volume I. Palgrave studies in cross-disciplinary business research, in association with EuroMed Academy of Business*. Palgrave Macmillan, Cham. https://doi.org/10.1007/978-3-031-37361-9_1

Zarifis, A., Efthymiou, L., & Cheng, X. (2023). Sustainable digital transformation in finance, tourism, transport, entertainment and social innovation. In A. Zarifis, D. Ktoridou, L. Efthymiou, & X. Cheng (Ed.), *Business digital transformation: Selected cases from industry leaders* (pp. 1–16). Palgrave Macmillan. https://doi.org/10.1007/978-3-031-33665-2_1

Zikmund, W. G. (2000). *Business research methods* (6th ed.). The Dryden Pre.

CHAPTER 10

Generational Cohort's Wine Choice: Is Terroir a Significant Factor?

Spyridon Mamalis, Irene (Eirini) Kamenidou, Aikaterini Karampatea, Elisavet Bouloumpasi, and Adriana Skendi

10.1 Introduction

Wineries have been experiencing significant changes in the last decades since they function in an extremely competitive and unpredictable environment due to new laws, new competitors in the marketplace, and changes in consumer behaviour and decision making (Maizza et al., 2014;

S. Mamalis · I. (Eirini) Kamenidou (✉) · A. Skendi
Department of Management Science and Technology, Democritus University of Thrace, Kavala, Greece
e-mail: eikamenidou@mst.duth.gr

S. Mamalis
e-mail: mamalis@mst.duth.gr

A. Skendi
e-mail: antrsken@abo.duth.gr

D. Vrontis et al. (eds.), *Business in Uncertainty*, Palgrave Studies in Cross-disciplinary Business Research, In Association with EuroMed Academy of Business, https://doi.org/10.1007/978-3-031-65587-6_10

Vrontis, Thrassou, Efthymiou et al., 2022; Vrontis, Thrassou, Weber et al., 2022; Thrassou et al., 2007, 2022). Regarding consumer decision making, researchers (Bruwer et al., 2011; Troiano et al., 2016; Vrontis et al., 2011) indicate that wine choice is a complex, high-risk, and challenging process given that wine is an "experience" good, in the sense that its quality is assessed after consumption. Therefore, different elements and cues of a wine depending on consumers subjective importance influence wine choice.

For example, consumers consider that wines from a specific variety or specific country or place are of higher quality than others of a different country, region, or place of origin (Hollebeek et al., 2007; Sáenz-Navajas et al., 2023; Souza Gonzaga et al., 2022), with origin linking to the exclusive attributes of wine terroir (Balestrini & Gamble, 2006). Additionally, previous research proves that other extrinsic cues such as wine cultural identity, price, grape variety, and production method (among others), known as human factors, are also considered important and impact on consumers' wine choice (Bandyopadhyay et al., 2023; Migliore et al., 2020; Reinares-Lara et al., 2023; Vrontis & Paliwoda, 2008). As researchers point out, every wine production region comprises environmental–natural and human-related factors that signify the concept of terroir (Capitello et al., 2021; Malorgio et al., 2008). The above combined with the fact that the wine market has numerous brands which intensifies the already fierce competition (Vrontis et al., 2011) resulted in forcing wineries to improve their marketing tactics. This intense competition made them align with consumers' desires (Giacomarra et al., 2020; Vrontis et al., 2016) and also differentiate their products from their competitors (Charters, 2010). These strategies include reinforcing the connection between territory and wine (Giacomarra et al., 2020), and communicating this association to the consumers (Charters et al., 2017; Riviezzo et al., 2017; Warman & Lewis, 2019).

Accordingly, consumers who are knowledgeable about wines express high level of involvement and associate the wines' quality with the area produced (Famularo et al., 2010; Riviezzo et al., 2014). Therefore, having insight of consumers wine knowledge and the wine's elements

A. Karampatea · E. Bouloumpasi · A. Skendi
Department of Agricultural Biotechnology and Oenology, Democritus University of Thrace, Drama, Greece

they consider important (thus affecting their decision to choose a wine), is compelling for wine makers in order to determine the consumer-market they should target and implement effective marketing strategies (Lai, 2019).

Demographic characteristics affect wine choice, with age considered among the strongest determinants (Alonso et al., 2007; Barber et al., 2006; Brata et al., 2022; Lutskova et al., 2020). Generational cohorts instead of age are continuously gaining interest in consumer behaviour studies, since cohorts incorporate behavioural characteristics (Kamenidou et al., 2020). Wine consumption and generational cohort studies are constantly increasing (Lerro et al., 2019), with some focusing on wine choice behaviour (e.g., Balenović et al., 2021; Bruwer et al., 2019). Thach et al. (2021) point out that researchers should study generational cohorts and the differences between cohorts in a country, since, when one generation predominance, the values that the specific cohort holds will prevail in that country's culture.

Generational cohorts and wine selection is a considerably understudied topic in academia, being a gap that leaves space for further investigation. Other gaps identified are generational cohort subjective knowledge of wines and cohorts wine choice in connection to wine terroir. Finally, the differences between cohorts in wine selection are also a gap in the literature to date due to the lack of studies. Therefore, since there is a paucity of research examining wine choice, wine elements considered important, and generational cohorts, this study explores the wine attributes considered important by generational cohorts and if terroir elements are among them. It additionally has the following objectives (OB) referring to the wine consumers of different generational cohorts:

- OB1: to report cohorts' frequency of wine consumption.
- OB2: to explore subjective wine knowledge of different cohorts.
- OB3: to examine which elements of a wine generational cohorts consider important.
- OB4: to study existing generational cohort differences in wine characteristics considered important.

In order to fulfil the above aim and objectives, it draws data from Greece and specifically from four generational cohorts (Generation X, Y, Z, and Baby Boomers).

This paper makes a theoretical contribution to academia by reducing the abovementioned gaps through the objectives studied. It also provides insight about the Greek consumers of different cohorts regarding their wine behaviour and terroir characteristics considered important by them, an issue that is understudied. Furthermore, exploring existing generational cohort differences regarding wine-related attributes that are considered important (including terroir characteristics) is an issue that up to our knowledge has been extremely understudied (e.g., Koksal, 2019). Additionally, on practical basis, it provides information of the terroir characteristics that are or are not of interest by generational cohorts in order to implement the appropriate marketing strategies.

This paper is organized as follows. The next section offers the literature review related to terroir, subjective knowledge, perceived important factors of wine choice by generational cohorts and cohort differences. Following, the methodology and results of data analysis are presented. Consecutively, the discussion and marketing implications are offered. This paper closes with the conclusion, limitations, and directions for future research.

10.2 Literature Review

There are many definitions of wine terroir (e.g., Vaudour, 2002), which are classified under two broad categories. The first category is the "strict" definition of wine terroir which encompasses the physical and natural environment of the vitivini production. The second category includes the above characteristics of terroir adding the human factor (in the broader sense, including historical and sociocultural factors). Examples of academic works that are in line with the wine terroir definition and include the human element are Patterson and Buechsenstein (2018), Vaudour (2002, 2003), Capitello et al. (2021), Charters et al. (2017), and Castelló (2021).

Van Leeuwen et al. (2010) emphasized that wine terroir is not a simple construct, and many factors shape it which also interreact with each other. That being said, a number of researchers focused on wine terroir, analyzing one specific or more facets of terroir incorporated in its definition (Moran, 2001; Patterson & Buechsenstein, 2018; Vaudour, 2002). Wine terroir research is a continuing issue of interest and uprising in studies since it defines quality by consumers (e.g., Hollebeek et al., 2007). There is a large number of studies that address wine terroir as a concept as well as wine terroir from the winery's point of view (Bramley & Gardiner, 2021; Smith Maguire & Charters, 2021; Van Leeuwen & Seguin, 2006).

Several studies connect wine terroir and wine tourism (e.g., Scorrano et al., 2018) as well as terroir's role in profitability for winegrowers (e.g., De Salvo et al., 2017). As to studies on wine terroir from the consumer perspective, it is mostly studied under wine geographical identification schemes: (e.g., Espejel & Fandos, 2009; Ribeiro & Santos, 2007) or a single or a handful of the elements of wine terroir (e.g., Bramley & Gardiner, 2021; Capitello et al., 2021; Karapetsas et al., 2023; Riviezzo et al., 2017). Likewise, there are a handful of studies that focus on wine terroir and generational cohorts' behaviour (Capitello et al., 2021; Wiedmann et al., 2014).

Moreover, studies referring to generational cohorts and subjective wine knowledge are also an understudied topic, with the majority of studies focusing on Generation Y and the Baby Boomers, while several explore generational cohort differences (Barber et al., 2009; Bauman et al., 2019; Chrysochou et al., 2012). General findings report that the younger generations have lower subjective knowledge of wines compared to the older generations (e.g., Barber et al., 2009; Dodd et al., 2005; Stergiou, 2019; Teagle et al., 2010). For example, Stergiou (2019) investigated (among other issues) wine knowledge of the Greek Generation Z cohort (n = 156). He found that Generation Z participants had little/basic knowledge of wine or "no prior knowledge". The same conclusion was reached in the study by Mamalis et al. (2023), which investigated Greek wine consumers' subjective knowledge and knowledge of terroir and its elements (n = 366, Greece) and found low subjective knowledge and knowledge of both wine terroir as well as its elements. Though they did not refer to generational cohorts. On the opposite side, Teagle et al. (2010) in their study (n = 3000, Australia), found that subjective wine knowledge was found to be higher for Millennials than older generations.

In terms of wine consumption behaviour and generational cohorts, Bruwer et al. (2011) investigated Australian (n = 150) Baby Boomers, Millennials, and Generation X visitors at ten wineries and found that Millennials drink significantly less wine in comparison to the older generations. This contrasted with the findings of Fountain and Lamb (2011) who explored wine consumption behaviour of Generation Y and Generation X individuals in New Zealand and found that Generation Y consumers are "drinking wine more frequently, and in more everyday contexts than their older counterparts were at a similar age, although they are less likely to consume wine on special occasions" (Fountain & Lamb, 2011, p. 107). Seyedimany and Koksal (2022) studied 708 wine customers of three generational cohorts (Baby Boomers, Generation X, and Generation Y) and found that Baby Boomers drink wine more on special occasions compared to the other cohorts, while Generation X drinks more on a weekly basis. Lerro et al. (2020) examined sparkling wine consumption behaviour and cohort differences (n = 1,096; USA; Baby Boomers: 39%; Generation X: 31.0%; Millennials 30%) and found that Baby Boomers drink less frequently sparkling wine, as compared to the other cohorts.

Regarding wine choice and generational cohorts, the vast majority of identified papers refer to wine attributes as drivers of wine choice, without measuring perceived importance, with the bulk of studies focusing on the Generation Y cohort while very few refer to cohort differences (e.g., Capitello et al., 2016; Chrysochou et al., 2012; Lerro et al., 2020; MacDonald et al., 2013). Capitello et al. (2021) analyzed "the role of a carbon reduction claim in consumer choice when it is labelled in conjunction with terroir cues on a bottle of wine" for Generation Y consumers (n = 982; Italy) with a Discrete Choice Experiment. Their results "shows seven consumer segments characterized by different motivations and relationships between the environmental claim and the terroir indications". Lerro et al. (2020) found that Millennials consider the recommendation of the waiter/staff more important than Generation X and Baby Boomers and the type of social occasion at which the wine is consumed compared to Generation X. Lastly, Baby Boomers are the only one considering the brand among the factors affecting sparkling wine choice. Troiano et al. (2016) examined consumers preference for five extrinsic characteristics of wine (area of origin, landscape features, production method) in north-eastern Italy and found that for all participants, the origin designation labelling was the most significant element (though, they did not examine generational cohorts). MacDonald et al. (2013) investigated (among others) importance of the wine choice factors (n = 1229, Australia; Traditionalists: n = 270; Baby Boomers: n = 503; Generation X: n = 270; Millennials: n = 157). They found that the factor "taste" was the most significant element across all cohorts. Price, brand, region, aroma, and grape variety were also important. Chrysochou et al. (2012, p. 516) found in their study exploring differences in wine preferences of Generation Y and older cohorts (n = 260; USA) that "Generation Y preferences for wine are driven by marketing added-value activities such as promotions and labelling, whereas limited importance is given to information about wine, reflecting lack of subjective knowledge, experience and involvement about wine".

The study of Koksal (2019) is to our knowledge directly related to the present study. Koksal (2019) studied 444 Lebanese wine consumers from four different generational cohorts (Baby Boomers, Generation X, Millennials, and Generation Z) and the wine attributes they consider important. They also investigated whether there were statistically significant differences between the cohorts. Koksal (2019) found that there were no statistically significant differences among the generation groups in terms of quality, country of origin, taste, and alcohol content, but there were as regards price, label and packaging, and grape variety. Specifically, Koksal (2019, p. 467) found that "Millennials rated price as the most important wine attribute, followed by Generation Z, Generation X and Baby Boomers. The grape variety was assessed as the most important attribute by Baby Boomers, followed by Generation Z and Generation X. Grape variety was not rated important by Millennials. Label and packaging were found to be a very important attribute by Generation X, Millennials, Generation Z and Baby Boomers, respectively".

As regards Greece and wine terroir, research focuses on the core facets of wine terroir, i.e., soil, climate, and varieties (Karapetsas et al., 2023; Stavridou et al., 2016), wine tourism and terroir (e.g., Sigala & Dimopoulou, 2017), robots used in wines terroirs (Tziolas et al., 2023), cultural identity in the frame of terroir and wine (Sigala, 2019) and consumer behaviour and wines with geographical indications and/or toponymy (Dimara & Skuras, 2003; Skuras & Vakrou, 2002).

10.3 Research Method

A questionnaire was developed as the research tool for this study, of which three questions were dealt with in this paper (excluding participants profiles). The first recorded wine consumption behaviour (frequency) with the presentation of six answers (ranging from special occasions to more than once per day). The second question referred to subjective wine knowledge, rated on a 5-point Likert-type scale (1 = No knowledge at all up to 5 = expert knowledge) adopted from the work of Mamalis et al. (2023). The third question referred to the elements- characteristics that wine consumers consider important. This question was stated as "Please state how important are each of the following elements-characteristics of a wine". The answers were presented on a 7-point Likert-type scale (1 = completely unimportant up to 7 = completely important). This question was developed from the relevant literature on wine attributes and wine terroir and included 44 items adopted from previous research (e.g., Capitello et al., 2021; Castelló, 2021; Charters et al., 2017; Moran, 2001; Patterson & Buechsenstein, 2018; Vaudour, 2002). Following the questionnaire development, small-scale qualitative research was undertaken in forms of personal interviews to validate the items in the questionnaire. Next, a pilot test study was implemented with face-to-face interviews (convenient sample), recording comments made by the participants about comprehension or other issues of the research tool. The final version of the questionnaire was distributed online. The questionnaire was addressed to wine consumers from different generational cohorts (Generation Z, Generation Y, Generation X, Baby Boomers), thus being 18–76 years of age (18 years old may drink wine according to the Greek law, since they are considered as adults). Over a three-week period, 366 usable questionnaires are collected for data analysis.

10.4 Results

Participants Profile

Regarding gender distribution, males were overrepresented, accounting for 59.0% (n = 216) of the sample, while 150 females participated (41.0%). The mean age was 42.9 years (Std = 14.9) and was distributed across four generational cohorts (Generation Z: 25.1%; Generation Y: 27.3%; Generation X: 30.6%; and Baby Boomers: 16.9%). Also, 41.8% were single (n = 153), 50.5% married (n = 185) and 7.7% divorced or widowed (n = 28). Moreover, 63.9% (n = 234) lived in urban areas and 36.1% (n = 132) in rural or semi-rural areas. Concerning education, 44.4% (n = 158) had secondary education (including university students), 10.4% (n = 39) had postsecondary education and 46.2% (n = 169) had at least a university degree. As to profession, 58.7% (n = 215) were on a monthly salary (federal/private employee, on pension, one-year unemployment fund), 16.4% were businesspeople (n = 60), 2.2% (n = 8) were labourers, and 22.7% (n = 83) were dependent on others. With reference to net monthly family income in euros, 35.2% (n = 129) had an income up to 1000.00€, 38.0% (n = 139) 100,001–200,000€, and 26.8% (n = 98) more than 200,000€.

Wine Consumption Behaviour

Concerning wine consumption per cohort as well as per total sample (OB1), most consumers are not heavy users of the product (Table 10.1), with 15.0% drinking wine on special occasions and 42.0% drinking wine 1–3 times per month. On the other hand, 43.0% drink wine at least once per week. In Table 10.1, Gen Z, Gen Y, Gen X, BB, and TS represent the generational cohorts Z, Y, X, Baby Boomers, and the total sample, respectively. The cohort that most frequently (overall) engages in wine consumption is Generation X. Only 13.4% of the cohort (the smallest compared to the other cohorts) drink wine on special occasions, while it has the highest percentage (48.2%) of drinking wine 1–3 times per month, and drinking wine at least once per day (8.1%). Though, on a weekly basis, the cohort that drinks wine the most is the Y cohort, whereas 50.0% drink wine at least once a week.

In terms of subjective or self-assessed level of wine knowledge (OB2), most consumers consider that they have very limited (31.4%; N = 115) or limited knowledge (38.0%; N = 139). In addition, 7.1% (N = 21) consider that they do not have any at all knowledge about wines, and 23.5% (N = 86) considered that they have advanced or expertise knowledge.

Table 10.1 Participants frequency of wine consumption (%)

Frequency of wine consumption	*Gen Z (%)*	*Gen Y (%)*	*Gen X (%)*	*BB (%)*	*TS (%)*
Never	0.0	0.0	0.0	0.0	0.0
Only on special occasions (e.g. Christmas, Easter, etc.)	14.1	15.0	13.4	19.4	15.0
1–3 times a month	42.4	35.0	48.2	41.9	42.1
1–3 times a week	38.0	34.0	22.3	25.8	30.1
4–6 times a week	3.3	12.0	8.0	9.7	8.2
Daily	2.2	4.0	7.1	3.2	4.3
More than once a day	0.0	0.0	1.0	0.0	0.3

Wine Characteristics Considered Important by Cohorts

Forty-four wine-related items/variables were presented to participants and were requested to express how important each one was for them (OB3). Answers were presented on a 7-point Likert-type scale (1 = completely unimportant up to 7 = completely important). Mean scores (MS) were calculated, revealing that answers fitted in the range of 3.51–6.02 of the Likert-type scale. Six items were rated with MS > 5.00 and five were rated with MS < 4.00, while the rest 33 were rated with 4.00 < MS < 4.99. The highest-rated item was "taste" (MS = 6.02), followed by "smell" (MS = 5.58), "price" (MS = 5.39), "aroma" (MS = 5.35), "authenticity" (MS = 5.13), and "clarity and color of wine" (MS = 5.11). In contrast, the least interested items were "landscape architecture" (MS = 3.51), "production ritual" (MS = 3.74), "private label" (MS = 3.94), "historical aspects" (MS = 3.95), and "producer history" (MS = 3.98). Referring to terroir only "authenticity" (MS = 5.13) was rated with a MS > 5.00, considered thus as "somewhat important".

Factor Analysis

All items were subjected to factor analysis to reduce them to a manageable set of variables and proceed to further data analysis. Through factor analysis (Principal Component Analysis with varimax rotation), ten items were dropped due to multiple loading or loading <0.4 on a factor. In this matter, 34 items-elements were accredited to four dimensions which were extracted (KMO = 0.962; BTS = 11,478.987; df = 528; sign = 0.000). These four dimensions accounted for 70.8% of total variance (TV).

The first factor describes 28.3% of TV, is named "Core terroir", and incorporates 14 items that are referred to (according to literature) as different facets of wine terroir (physical-natural terroir and sociocultural terroir). Examples of items included in this factor are "landscape architecture", "climate", and "cultural identity". The loadings of the items on the factor range from 0.561 to 0.848, and its Mean Factor Score (MFS) is MFS = 4.19 (Std = 1.49). The second factor accounts for 14.7% of TV and is named "Product outcome" because it includes items that refer to the wine itself (i.e., the product outcome). It incorporates six items such as "aroma", and "taste", with loadings ranging from 0.612 to 0.865, and MFS = 5.33 (Std = 1.30). The third factor describes 14.2% of TV and is named "Human terroir and gastronomy" as it includes items that refer to the production process and gastronomy of the wine. It incorporates eight items such as "method and means of storage (e.g., in wooden or metal barrels, cellar temperature, etc.)" and "connection with gastronomy". The loadings on this factor range from 0.514 to 0.609, and its MFS = 4.73 (Std = 1.40). Lastly, the fourth factor accounts for 13.6% of TV and is named "Communication terroir" since it includes items that refer to the means that the wine and its terroir are communicated. It incorporates six items such as "name of producer-winery" and "label design connected to the area". The loadings on this factor range from 0.554 to 0.779, and its MFS = 4.42 (Std = 1.43).

Cohort Behaviour Analysis

Table 10.2 presents how each cohort rates the dimensions of wine attributes in terms of importance (extracted from factor analysis; also OB2) in MS, Std, and MFS for each dimension. Regarding the "Core terroir" dimension, among the four cohorts the Generation Y cohort has ranked it as most important, while for the "Product outcome" dimension, the Generation X cohort has ranked it higher. Lastly, the Baby Boomers ranked both the "Human terroir and gastronomy" and the "Communication terroir" dimension higher compared to the other cohorts. Also, it reveals that among the four extracted dimensions, the "Product outcome" is the most significant for cohorts, followed by the "Human terroir and gastronomy" factor. The least significant factor for all cohorts is the "Core terroir" factor.

Generational Cohort Differences

Table 10.3 presents the results of the ANOVA test which explores generational cohort differences based on the wine attributes (dimensions) considered important (OB4). From Table 10.3, it is apparent that the four generational cohorts did not show differences regarding the importance of wine characteristics. This indicates that the cohorts perceive that the dimensions "Core terroir", "Product outcome", "Human terroir and gastronomy", and "Communication terroir", to be similar in their minds in terms of importance.

Table 10.2 Mean score per cohort per dimension

Cohort	*Core terroir*		*Product outcome*		*Human terroir and gastronomy*		*Communication terroir*	
	MS	*Std.*	*MS*	*Std.*	*MS*	*Std.*	*MS*	*Std.*
Generation Z	4.16	1.35	5.34	1.30	4.72	1.22	4.45	1.30
Generation Y	4.30	1.58	5.21	1.30	4.68	1.51	4.37	1.52
Generation X	4.11	1.53	5.42	1.19	4.72	1.43	4.43	1.39
Baby Boomers	4.20	1.51	5.35	1.51	4.86	1.41	4.47	1.55
MFS/ dimension	4.19	1.49	5.33	1.30	4.73	1.40	4.42	1.43

Table 10.3 ANOVA results regarding wine selection dimensions and cohorts

Dimensions		*Sum of squares*	*df*	*Mean square*	*F*	*Sig.*
Core terroir	Between groups	2.126	3	0.709	0.317	0.813
	Within groups	808.301	362	2.233		
	Total	810.427	365			
Product outcome	Between groups	2.520	3	0.840	0.492	0.688
	Within groups	617.917	362	1.707		
	Total	620.437	365			
Human terroir and gastronomy	Between groups	1.279	3	0.426	0.217	0.885
	Within groups	712.369	362	1.968		
	Total	713.647	365			
Communication terroir	Between groups	0.469	3	0.156	0.076	0.973
	Within groups	741.111	362	2.047		
	Total	741.580	365			

10.5 Discussion

From the results of this study, it appears that Greek wine consumers are not "heavy users" of the product, but moderate ones. Also, Generation X is the cohort that consumes wine most frequently (overall), while Generation Y drinks wine more frequently per week, as compared to the other cohorts. One reason could be the consumption of ouzo, which is a traditional drink. These results are partially in line with other researchers such as Bruwer et al. (2011), Fountain and Lamb (2011) and Seyedimany and Koksal (2022).

Another major result is that cohorts' subjective wine knowledge is very limited or limited, raising the topic of educating consumers about wine and its attributes. This result is in line with the results of Stergiou (2019) and Mamalis et al. (2023).

Of the four dimensions of wine attributes considered important, three have MFS < 5.00 and >4.00, being in the "indifferent" zone. Only one dimension has MFS > 5.00, i.e., the dimension "Product outcome", with MFS = 5.33 (and <6.00), being the highest of the four, meaning that cohorts consider "somewhat important" mainly the features of the product rather the terroir features that are the cause of the product outcome. Additionally, the dimension "Human terroir and gastronomy" even though it is in the indifferent zone, it has MFS = 4.73, meaning that for the cohorts this dimension has a tendency to be "somewhat important" since it MS is somewhat near 5.00.

The results of this study cannot be directly compared to other studies since different variables and approaches were utilized. However, indirectly they somewhat are in line with the results of Koksal (2019). Though this comparison is made with extreme caution since Koksal (2019) found that "there are some differences among the generational cohorts with regard to price, label and packaging and grape variety". The wine attributes that Koksal (2019) detected as important by his study, do not fall in a single dimension of our study, but in two, namely "core terroir" and "human terroir". Moreover, in our study, price was ranked third and as "somewhat important" (MS = 5.39). As to the other elements, namely, label and packaging and grape variety, our study found that cohorts rated them with MS < 5.00, thus in the indifferent zone. On the other hand, Koksal (2019, p. 467) in his study found that "Millennials rated price as the most important wine attribute, followed by Generation Z, Generation X, and Baby Boomers. The grape variety was assessed as the most important attribute by Baby Boomers, followed by Generation Z and Generation X. Grape variety was not rated as important by Millennials. Label and packaging were found to be a very important attribute by Generation X, Millennials, Generation Z, and Baby Boomers, respectively".

10.6 Implications

This study reveals the necessity of cohorts' education regarding wine and wine terroir attributes through different means of education, depending on the cohort. As Marquis (2023) points out young ages (therefore cohorts too) rely heavily on peer influence notably when it comes to gaining information on topics that can form their personal value system or changing attitudes and behaviour. Thus, marketers and policy makers can use influencer marketing as a tool for wine terroir and wine-related elements education and thus effect wine consumers choice. Influencers and Instagram could promote wine attributes and wineries pointing out their specific terroir and the taste particularity that it has as a final product. Extant studies support that influencer marketing can act as an important tool that can effect purchase intentions (Schouten et al., 2021; Vrontis et al., 2021). Wineries can also develop a YouTube channel informing potential customers about what wine terroir is and its significance in wine production and products' outcome. Internet and social media would target mainly the younger generations, while television through cooking shows analyzing the specific wine would be appropriate for the older ones.

10.7 Conclusion, Limitations, and Directions for Future Research

The present empirical study contributes to the extant literature on cohort differences and wine and wine terroir attributes considered important in wine choice and sheds light on their behaviour. As Tait et al. (2019) state, the wine industry benefits from gaining insight in wine attribute preferences of generational cohorts. Nevertheless, this study exhibits limitations that are unavoidable. First of all, due to economic and time constraints an online collection method was utilized, restricting those that did not have access to the internet the ability to participate in the research, even though they are wine consumers. Also, a one-country study is implemented, and it would be of interest if other countries cohorts' behaviour could be compared to the Greek ones.

However, it should be noted that this study is an exploratory study, being an additional limitation of the present findings. For so, with its results, we can get a "first picture" of the cohorts' behaviour and their wine knowledge and wine terroir important by them attributes. Although the sample is considered small, it is adequate for the research objectives and data analysis but the results are limited to the sample used and cannot be generalized. These limitations may be important for future research.

Acknowledgements-Funding This research was co-financed by the European Regional Development Fund of the European Union and Greek national funds through the Operational Program Competitiveness, Entrepreneurship, and Innovation, under the call RESEARCH—CREATE—INNOVATE (project code: T2EΔK-02974 Drama terroir).

Ethical Approval "There are no ethical issues involved in the processing of the questionnaire data used in the study. The necessary consents have been obtained by the persons involved, and the anonymity of the participants has been secured. All procedures performed in studies involving human participants were in accordance with the ethical standards of the International Hellenic University research committee and with the 1964 Helsinki declaration and its later amendments or comparable ethical standards".

References

Alonso, A. D., Fraser, R. A., & Cohen, D. A. (2007). Does age matter? How age influences the winery experience. *International Journal of Culture, Tourism and Hospitality Research, 1*(2), 131–139. https://doi.org/10.1108/17506180710751678

Balenović, I., Ignjatijević, S., Stojanović, G., Vapa Tankosić, J., Lekić, N., Milutinović, O., Gajić, A., Ivaniš, M., Bošković, J., Prodanović, R., Puvača, N., & Duđak, L. (2021). Factors influencing wine purchasing by Generation Y and older cohorts on the Serbian wine market. *Agriculture, 11*(11), 1054. https://doi.org/10.3390/agriculture11111054

Balestrini, P., & Gamble, P. (2006). Country-of-origin effects on Chinese wine consumers. *British Food Journal, 108*(5), 396–412. https://doi.org/10.1108/00070700610661367

Bandyopadhyay, A., Hall, J., Wong, H. Y., Lockshin, L., Zhang, Y., & Thaichon, P. (2023). "Regions" as brands: An empirical validation of consumer-based brand equity framework and demonstration of cross-over effect. *Asia Pacific*

Journal of Marketing and Logistics. https://doi.org/10.1108/APJML-03-2023-0196

Barber, N., Almanza, B. A., & Donovan, J. R. (2006). Motivational factors of gender, income and age on selecting a bottle of wine. *International Journal of Wine Marketing, 18*(3), 218–232. https://doi.org/10.1108/09547540610704774

Barber, N., Taylor, D. C., & Dodd, T. (2009). The importance of wine bottle closures in retail purchase decisions of consumers. *Journal of Hospitality Marketing & Management, 18*(6), 597–614. https://doi.org/10.1080/19368620903025014

Bauman, M. J., Velikova, N., Dodd, T., & Blankenship, T. (2019). Generational differences in risk perception and situational uses of wine information sources. *International Journal of Wine Business Research, 32*(2), 247–265. https://doi.org/10.1108/IJWBR-03-2019-0022

Bramley, R. G. V., & Gardiner, P. S. (2021). Underpinning terroir with data: A quantitative analysis of biophysical variation in the Margaret River region of Western Australia. *Australian Journal of Grape and Wine Research, 27*(4), 420–430. https://doi.org/10.1111/ajgw.12491

Brata, A. M., Chiciudean, D. I., Brata, V. D., Popa, D., Chiciudean, G. O., & Muresan, I. C. (2022). Determinants of choice and wine consumption behaviour: A comparative analysis between two counties of Romania. *Foods, 11*(8), 1110. https://doi.org/10.3390/foods11081110

Bruwer, J., Cohen, J., & Kelley, K. (2019). Wine involvement interaction with dining group dynamics, group composition and consumption behavioural aspects in USA restaurants. *International Journal of Wine Business Research, 31*(1), 12–28. https://doi.org/10.1108/IJWBR-06-2018-0027

Bruwer, J., Saliba, A., & Miller, B. (2011). Consumer behaviour and sensory preference differences: Implications for wine product marketing. *Journal of Consumer Marketing, 28*(1), 5–18. https://doi.org/10.1108/07363761111101903

Capitello, R., Agnoli, L., Charters, S., & Begalli, D. (2021). Labelling environmental and terroir attributes: Young Italian consumers' wine preferences. *Journal of Cleaner Production, 304*, 126991. https://doi.org/10.1016/j.jclepro.2021.126991

Castelló, E. (2021). The will for terroir: A communicative approach. *Journal of Rural Studies, 86*, 386–397. https://doi.org/10.1016/j.jrurstud.2021.06.007

Charters, S. (2010). *Marketing terroir: A conceptual approach*, 8–10.

Charters, S., Spielmann, N., & Babin, B. J. (2017). The nature and value of terroir products. *European Journal of Marketing, 51*(4), 748–771. https://doi.org/10.1108/EJM-06-2015-0330

Chrysochou, P., Krystallis, A., Mocanu, A., & Leigh Lewis, R. (2012). Generation Y preferences for wine: An exploratory study of the US market applying the best-worst scaling. *British Food Journal, 114*(4), 516–528. https://doi.org/10.1108/00070701211219531

De Salvo, M., Begalli, D., Capitello, R., Agnoli, L., & Tabouratzi, E. (2017). Determinants of winegrowers' profitability: Evidence from an Eastern Europe wine region. *EuroMed Journal of Business, 12*(3), 300–315. https://doi.org/10.1108/EMJB-12-2016-0043

Dimara, E., & Skuras, D. (2003). Consumer evaluations of product certification, geographic association and traceability in Greece. *European Journal of Marketing, 37*(5–6), 690–705. https://doi.org/10.1108/03090560310465099

Dodd, T. H., Laverie, D. A., Wilcox, J. F., & Duhan, D. F. (2005). Differential effects of experience, subjective knowledge, and objective knowledge on sources of information used in consumer wine purchasing. *Journal of Hospitality & Tourism Research, 29*(1), 3–19. https://doi.org/10.1177/1096348004267518

Espejel, J., & Fandos, C. (2009). Wine marketing strategies in Spain: A structural equation approach to consumer response to protected designations of origin (PDOs). *International Journal of Wine Business Research, 21*(3), 267–288. https://doi.org/10.1108/17511060910985980

Famularo, B., Bruwer, J., & Li, E. (2010). Region of origin as choice factor: Wine knowledge and wine tourism involvement influence. *International Journal of Wine Business Research, 22*(4), 362–385. https://doi.org/10.1108/17511061011092410

Fountain, J., & Lamb, C. (2011). Generation Y as young wine consumers in New Zealand: How do they differ from Generation X? *International Journal of Wine Business Research, 23*(2), 107–124. https://doi.org/10.1108/17511061111142981

Giacomarra, M., Galati, A., Crescimanno, M., & Vrontis, D. (2020). Geographical cues: Evidences from New and Old World countries' wine consumers. *British Food Journal, 122*(4), 1252–1267. https://doi.org/10.1108/BFJ-08-2019-0580

Hollebeek, L. D., Jaeger, S. R., Brodie, R. J., & Balemi, A. (2007). The influence of involvement on purchase intention for new world wine. *Food Quality and Preference, 18*(8), 1033–1049. https://doi.org/10.1016/j.foodqual.2007.04.007

Kamenidou, I., Stavrianea, A., & Bara, E.-Z. (2020). Generational differences toward organic food behavior: Insights from five generational cohorts. *Sustainability, 12*(6), 2299. https://doi.org/10.3390/su12062299

Karapetsas, N., Alexandridis, T. K., Bilas, G., Theocharis, S., & Koundouras, S. (2023). Delineating natural terroir units in wine regions using geoinformatics. *Agriculture, 13*(3), 629. https://doi.org/10.3390/agriculture13030629

Koksal, M. H. (2019). Differences among baby boomers, Generation X, millennials, and Generation Z wine consumers in Lebanon: Some perspectives. *International Journal of Wine Business Research, 31*(3), 456–472. https://doi.org/10.1108/IJWBR-09-2018-0047

Lai, M. B. (2019). Consumer behavior toward wine products. *Case Studies in the Wine Industry*, 33–46. https://doi.org/10.1016/B978-0-08-100944-4.00003-3

Lerro, M., Vecchio, R., Nazzaro, C., & Pomarici, E. (2019). The growing (good) bubbles: Insights into US consumers of sparkling wine. *British Food Journal, 122*(8), 2371–2384. https://doi.org/10.1108/BFJ-02-2019-0139

Lerro, M., Vecchio, R., Nazzaro, C., & Pomarici, E. (2020). The growing (good) bubbles: Insights into US consumers of sparkling wine. *British Food Journal, 122*(8), 2371–2384. https://doi.org/10.1108/BFJ-02-2019-0139

Lutskova, V., Martirosyan, I., & Krupytska, L. (2020). Analysis of consumer preferences when choosing wine. *Ukrainian Journal of Food Science, 8*(1).

MacDonald, J. B., Saliba, A. J., & Bruwer, J. (2013). Wine choice and drivers of consumption explored in relation to generational cohorts and methodology. *Journal of Retailing and Consumer Services, 20*(3), 349–357. https://doi.org/10.1016/j.jretconser.2013.01.013

Maizza, A., Fait, M., Scorrano, P., Vrontis, D., & Thrassou, A. (2014). *Attributes driving the wine choice process*. In 7th Annual Conference of the EuroMed Academy of Business.

Malorgio, G., Hertzberg, A., Grazia, C., Malorgio, G., Hertzberg, A., & Grazia, C. (2008). *Italian wine consumer behaviour and wineries responsive capacity.* https://doi.org/10.22004/AG.ECON.44419

Mamalis, S., Kamenidou, I., Karampatea, A., Bouloumpasi, E., & Skendi, A. (2023). *Do wine consumers know the meaning of wine terroir? Preliminary results from ongoing research in Greece.* In 11th International Conference on Contemporary Marketing Issues, Corfu, Greece, 12–14 July 2023, pp. 92–98.

Marquis, D. (2023). Targeting adolescents as agents of change for an entomophageous future. *British Educational Research Journal, 49*(6), 1161–1186. https://doi.org/10.1002/berj.3891

Migliore, G., Thrassou, A., Crescimanno, M., Schifani, G., & Galati, A. (2020). Factors affecting consumer preferences for "natural wine": An exploratory study in the Italian market. *British Food Journal, 122*(8), 2463–2479. https://doi.org/10.1108/BFJ-07-2019-0474

Moran, W. (2001). Terroir–the human factor. *Australian and New Zealand Wine Industry Journal, 16*(2), 32–51.

Patterson, T., & Buechsenstein, J. (2018). *Wine and place: A terroir reader*. University of California Press.

Reinares-Lara, E., Pelegrín-Borondo, J., Olarte-Pascual, C., & Oruezabala, G. (2023). The role of cultural identity in acceptance of wine innovations in wine regions. *British Food Journal, 125*(3), 869–885. https://doi.org/10.1108/BFJ-07-2021-0802

Ribeiro, J. C., & Santos, J. F. (2007). *Consumer perception of Portuguese quality wine and the region-of-origin effect*. In 47th Congress of the European Regional Science Association, Paris.

Riviezzo, A., Garofano, A., Granata, J., & Kakavand, S. (2014, June). Terroir and wine differentiation. A cross-case analysis on French and Italian wine producers' perceptions. In *VIII International Conference of the Academy of Wine Business Research* (pp. 27–30), Geisenheim University, Geisenheim, Germany. http://www.academyofwinebusiness.com/wp-content/uploads/2014/07/CoO3_Garofano_Antonella.pdf

Riviezzo, A., Garofano, A., Granata, J., & Kakavand, S. (2017). Using terroir to exploit local identity and cultural heritage in marketing strategies: An exploratory study among Italian and French wine producers. *Place Branding and Public Diplomacy, 13*(2), 136–149. https://doi.org/10.1057/s41254-016-0036-4

Sáenz-Navajas, M.-P., Iosifidis, A., Gonzalez-Hernandez, M., Fernández-Zurbano, P., & Valentin, D. (2023). Identification of sensory and voltammetric markers of regional typicality: Tempranillo Rioja wines as a case study. *Beverages, 9*(4), 85. https://doi.org/10.3390/beverages9040085

Schouten, A. P., Janssen, L., & Verspaget, M. (2021). Celebrity vs. Influencer endorsements in advertising: The role of identification, credibility, and Product-Endorser fit. In *Leveraged marketing communications* (pp. 208–231). Routledge.

Scorrano, P., Fait, M., Iaia, L., & Rosato, P. (2018). The image attributes of a destination: An analysis of the wine tourists' perception. *EuroMed Journal of Business, 13*(3), 335–350. https://doi.org/10.1108/EMJB-11-2017-0045

Seyedimany, A., & Koksal, M. H. (2022). Segmentation of Turkish wine consumers based on generational cohorts: An exploratory study. *Sustainability, 14*(5), 3031. https://doi.org/10.3390/su14053031

Sigala, M. (2019). The synergy of wine and culture: The case of Ariousios wine, Greece. In M. Sigala & R. N. S. Robinson (Eds.), *Management and marketing of wine tourism business* (pp. 295–312). Springer International Publishing. https://doi.org/10.1007/978-3-319-75462-8_15

Sigala, M., & Dimopoulou, M. (2017). *Does terroir matter for wine and wine destination marketing? The case of Greek wines and wine consumers*, 25–28.

Skuras, D., & Vakrou, A. (2002). Consumers' willingness to pay for origin labelled wine: A Greek case study. *British Food Journal, 104*(11), 898–912. https://doi.org/10.1108/00070700210454622

Smith Maguire, J., & Charters, S. (2021). Aesthetic logics, *terroir* and the lamination of grower champagne. *Consumption Markets & Culture, 24*(1), 75–96. https://doi.org/10.1080/10253866.2020.1730823

Souza Gonzaga, L., Bastian, S. E. P., Capone, D. L., Danner, L., & Jeffery, D. W. (2022). Consumer perspectives of wine typicity and impact of region information on the sensory perception of Cabernet Sauvignon wines. *Food Research International, 152*, 110719. https://doi.org/10.1016/j.foodres.2021.110719

Stavridou, K., Soufleros, E. H., Bouloumpasi, E., & Dagkli, V. (2016). The phenolic potential of wines from French grape varieties Cabernet Sauvignon, Merlot and Syrah cultivated in the region of Thessaloniki (Northern Greece) and its evolution during aging. *Food and Nutrition Sciences, 07*(02), 122–137. https://doi.org/10.4236/fns.2016.72014

Stergiou, D. P. (2019). Generation Z as young winery visitors in Greece. In M. Sigala & R. N. S. Robinson (Eds.), *Management and marketing of wine tourism business* (pp. 63–79). Springer International Publishing. https://doi.org/10.1007/978-3-319-75462-8_4

Tait, P., Saunders, C., Dalziel, P., Rutherford, P., & Driver, T. (2019). Examining generational preferences for sustainability attributes of wine: A discrete choice experiment in California (No. 2229-2019-1933). https://doi.org/10.22004/ag.econ.289680

Teagle, J., Mueller, S., & Lockshin, L. (2010). *How do millennials' wine attitudes and behaviour differ from other generations?* In 5th International Academy of Wine Business Research Conference, 8–10 February 2010 Auckland (NZ).

Thach, L., Riewe, S., & Camillo, A. (2021). Generational cohort theory and wine: Analyzing how gen Z differs from other American wine consuming generations. *International Journal of Wine Business Research, 33*(1), 1–27. https://doi.org/10.1108/IJWBR-12-2019-0061

Thrassou, A., Katsioloudes, M. I., & Hadjidakis, S. (2007). Doing business in the industrialized countries. In *International business* (pp. 439–482). Routledge.

Thrassou, A., Uzunboylu, N., Efthymiou, L., Vrontis, D., Weber, Y., Riad Shams, S. M., & Tsoukatos, E. (2022). Editorial introduction: Business under crises: Organizational adaptations. In D. Vrontis, A. Thrassou, Y. Weber, S. M. R. Shams, E. Tsoukatos, & L. Efthymiou (Eds.), *Business under crisis, Volume II: Organisational adaptations*. Palgrave Studies in Cross-disciplinary Business Research, in Association with EuroMed Academy of Business. Palgrave Macmillan. https://doi.org/10.1007/978-3-030-76575-0_1

Troiano, S., Marangon, F., Tempesta, T., & Vecchiato, D. (2016). Organic vs local claims: Substitutes or complements for wine consumers? A marketing analysis with a discrete choice experiment. *New Medit, 2*, 14–21.

Tziolas, E., Karapatzak, E., Kalathas, I., Karampatea, A., Grigoropoulos, A., Bajoub, A., Pachidis, T., & Kaburlasos, V. G. (2023). Assessing the economic performance of multipurpose collaborative robots toward skillful and sustainable viticultural practices. *Sustainability, 15*(4), 3866. https://doi.org/10.3390/su15043866

Van Leeuwen, C., Roby, J.-P., Pernet, D., & Bois, B. (2010). Methodology of soil-based zoning for viticultural terroirs. *Bulletin de l'OIV, 83*(947), 13.

Van Leeuwen, C., & Seguin, G. (2006). The concept of terroir in viticulture. *Journal of Wine Research, 17*(1), 1–10.

Vaudour, E. (2002). The quality of grapes and wine in relation to geography: Notions of terroir at various scales. *Journal of Wine Research, 13*(2), 117–141. https://doi.org/10.1080/0957126022000017981

Vaudour, E. (2003). *Les terroirs viticoles: Définitions, caractérisation et protection.* Dunod.

Vrontis, D., Bresciani, S., & Giacosa, E. (2016). Tradition and innovation in Italian wine family businesses. *British Food Journal, 118*(8), 1883–1897. https://doi.org/10.1108/BFJ-05-2016-0192

Vrontis, D., Makrides, A., Christofi, M., & Thrassou, A. (2021). Social media influencer marketing: A systematic review, integrative framework and future research agenda. *International Journal of Consumer Studies, 45*(4), 617–644. https://doi.org/10.1111/ijcs.12647

Vrontis, D., & Paliwoda, S. J. (2008). Branding and the Cyprus wine industry. *Journal of Brand Management, 16*(3), 145–159. https://doi.org/10.1057/bm.2008.1

Vrontis, D., Thrassou, A., & Czinkota, M. R. (2011). Wine marketing: A framework for consumer-centred planning. *Journal of Brand Management, 18*(4–5), 245–263. https://doi.org/10.1057/bm.2010.39

Vrontis, D., Thrassou, A., Efthymiou, L., Weber, Y., Shams, R., & Tsoukatos, E. (2022). Editorial introduction: Business under crisis—Avenues for innovation, entrepreneurship and sustainability. In D. Vrontis, A Thrassou., Y. Weber, S. M. R. Shams, E. Tsoukatos, & L. Efthymiou (Eds.), *Business under crisis, Volume III: Avenues for innovation, entrepreneurship and sustainability*. Palgrave Studies in Cross-disciplinary Business Research, in Association with EuroMed Academy of Business. Palgrave Macmillan. https://doi.org/10.1007/978-3-030-76583-5_1

Vrontis, D., Thrassou, A., Weber, Y., Shams, R., Tsoukatos, E., Efthymiou, L. (2022). Business under crisis, Volume III: Avenues for innovation, entrepreneurship and sustainability. Book series: Palgrave Studies in Cross-Disciplinary Business Research, in Association with EuroMed Academy of

Business, Palgrave Macmillan (Springer), Cham, Switzerland. https://doi.org/10.1007/978-3-030-76583-5

Warman, R. D., & Lewis, G. K. (2019). Wine place research: Getting value from terroir and provenance in premium wine value chain interventions. *International Journal of Wine Business Research, 31*(4), 493–508. https://doi.org/10.1108/IJWBR-09-2018-0052

Wiedmann, K.-P., Behrens, S., Klarmann, C., & Hennigs, N. (2014). Customer value perception: Cross-generational preferences for wine. *British Food Journal, 116*(7), 1128–1142. https://doi.org/10.1108/BFJ-01-2013-0027

CHAPTER 11

Leading Factors in Women Migrant Entrepreneurial Success in Bavaria

Simona Mihail-Yiannaki and Sofia Bakirli

11.1 Introduction

Within the framework of constant socio-political changes due to unforeseen circumstances, like the coronavirus, and ongoing situations, such as immigration and financial instabilities, the role of women in business is promoted (GEM, 2020). Despite the low ratio of professional engagement (World Bank, 2019) female entrepreneurship has an increased tendency in the last decade (GEM, 2018). At a European level, to foster women's entrepreneurship in all European countries a running project between 2018 and 2021, named "Peer-learning activities in entrepreneurship education and women's entrepreneurship" led to a list

S. Mihail-Yiannaki · S. Bakirli (✉)
European University of Cyprus, Nicosia, Cyprus
e-mail: sb201423@students.euc.ac.cy

S. Mihail-Yiannaki
e-mail: s.mihai@euc.ac.cy

D. Vrontis et al. (eds.), *Business in Uncertainty*, Palgrave Studies in Cross-disciplinary Business Research, In Association with EuroMed Academy of Business, https://doi.org/10.1007/978-3-031-65587-6_11

of recommendations. The thematically oriented framework of recommendations referred to European media campaigns for women's entrepreneurship promotion, funding methods, lifelong entrepreneurial learning, and support of empirical studies around the topic.

From a managerial perspective, it remains crucial to examine how women interact in business communities, their academic or professional experiences that help to develop the family business, their cultural background regarding the concept of the family affects the business strategies, and how digitalization has impacted the improvement of the family firms. When digitalization is a decisive factor in competition, it is observed that not all countries worldwide are well equipped to support technological advancements referred to as digitalization (Göll & Zwiers, 2018; Vrontis et al., 2023). On the contrary, and zooming in on Europe, Germany has issued a set of national strategies that outline a roadmap for digital transformation concerning all types of businesses (BMBF, 2018; Dengler & Gundert, 2021). According to recent research at the Technical University of Munich (TUM) (Deutschinstitut, 2023), women's proportion in supervising bodies and leading positions showed a slight increase between 2015 and 2020, and indeed in the public sector at 22%. However, the gender pay gap has remained constant at 20% for the last decade, demonstrating Germany's low performance. In West Germany, the gap is higher than in East Germany, hence one of the reasons behind selecting Bavaria in our study. The same research provides evidence of less developed networks in female start-up initiatives and shows that the male start-up territory receives more capital than the female one.

In a country where 60% of start-ups with a valuation of around 1€ billion have at least one migrant founder (Existenzgründungsportal des BMWK, 2023), and the Bavarian state had one the highest share of migrant founders from 2020 to 2022 among other western federal states, the German government has designed and launched integrating approaches for migrants' labor integration . Nevertheless, there has been observed a low proportion of women in leadership positions in the country, due to unconscious biases and gender stereotypes, such as assertiveness and independence as common personality traits for men, and friendliness or sensitivity for women. These gender stereotypes also affect social groups, such as ethnic or religious groups, which refer to migrants or minorities of a host country (TM & Joseph, 2021).

Migrants tend to use technologies based on their social needs, and only a limited proportion establish networks to support local businesses to break into the global competition. Entrepreneurship in developing and developed countries differ institutionally, socially, and economically (Acs et al., 2011). In Germany, where one in five citizens has a migration background, around 14% of all registered entrepreneurs have a migration background, and female entrepreneurs count for 29.1% of the working population. Although women have a high potential for establishing new companies and becoming entrepreneurs in the country, among migrant founders the female team composition reaches only 12.7%, but compared to founders with no immigrant background, migrant founders are most likely to be part of female or mixed teams at the proportion of 44% (BMWK, 2023).

The German start-up ecosystem faces many challenges, such as diversity and openness, and considers the interrelated aspects of migration in the job arena. Cultural aspects such as language, education, and family background, signify the business performance of entrepreneurs worldwide, as well as in Germany, where 25% of first-generation migrant founders arrived in the country as a child (BMWK, 2023). National cultural dimensions like respect to hierarchies and authorities, traditional roles, and long-term orientation plans indicate high or low potentials within the market arena (Hofstede & Hofstede, 2005), alongside funding conditions and access to funding.

In collectivistic European countries, such as Greece, Romania, and Portugal, it is more likely for women to inherit or get involved in the family business. Family in such cultures is the core of all life activities, and there might not be a distinction between the personal and professional aspects, which leads to limited time dedicated in general for entrepreneurship. Considering this, women entrepreneurs, who have taken over family enterprises or established their own, have carried on with their cultural background in the host country. On the other hand, Germany is an individualistic society (Arrak et al., 2020) that has welcomed many foreigners from different cultures and nations and has managed several situations with migrant founders dealing with local authorities, searching for investors, or establishing social networks. It is interesting to investigate how women entrepreneurs, from different ethnicities, operate and manage their inherited family business or start-up company, regarding digital and innovative products or services and cultural variety.

11.2 Literature Review

Female Entrepreneurs in Germany

Although entrepreneurship remains heavily dominated by the male population (Dileo & Garcia-Pereiro, 2018) due to work-family conflict, entrepreneurial norms, or financial resources, the importance of female entrepreneurship for economic prosperity is beyond doubt (Lewis et al., 2014). In the OECD countries, Greece, Italy, and the Netherlands score the highest rate while Hungary and Malta appear to have the lowest rate (Eurobarometer, 2012). In the same study, it is remarkable the gap in percentage between West and East Germany. In the East of Germany, the percentage is at 9.3% compared to 4.6% in the West of Germany.

Germany scored the lowest rate of entrepreneurial intentions in 2014 among all European country members (GEM, 2020), and the female population didn't feel it had the capabilities to start a business.

However, the recent pandemic has affected entrepreneurs, and indeed immigrant ones, due to digital globalization and the multiple embeddedness. A recent study in Bremen (Harima, 2022), regarding entrepreneurs coming from Western and non-western countries but located in Germany, demonstrates that government supports bilateral relationships between home and host countries and the transnational network communities, while during the pandemic Germany reported the highest increase in income from 21 to 32% (GEM, 2020).

In a country where one in five German citizens have a migration background, German states prevent failed entrepreneurs from starting a new business six years after they have gone bankrupt to avoid business and social uncertainty (Audretsch & Lehmann, 2016). At the same time, founder competitions as a political intervention, and programs that target entrepreneurs with a racial background, such as INTEGRA in Munich (Deutschinstitut, 2023) and EXIST (Existenzgruender, 2023), promote entrepreneurial initiatives. The German Institute Integra currently provides formal vocational language courses to support employment at a local level, the state of Bayern, and the Existenzgründsportal of the Federal Ministry for Economic Affairs and Climate Action supports start-ups regardless of gender, ethnicity, age, or other aspects of workforce diversity.

Germany scored 87.5 out of 100 in the innovation capability pillar, as one of the influential factors of a country's productivity, at a global level (WEF, 2018), while also during the pandemic the country reported the highest increase in income from 21 to 32% (GEM, 2020). Success is tightly connected to the Federal Ministry of Education and Research which aims to the effective collaboration between science and industry under the guidance of the High-Tech designed strategy (Research in germany.org, 2023).

In Munich, the Deutscher Start-up Monitor highlights the role of the LMU EC Accelerator, a platform that empowers entrepreneurs based in Munich, and in 2020 the proportion of women was higher than that of men. Other activities of one of the two public universities in the city, Ludwig University, include the Munich Global Impact Club, the Spin-off Service, and the LMU Innovation Incubator. The Federal Ministry of Economic Affairs and Climate Action funds and supports all activities (iec. Uni-Muenchen, 2023). The question is how much the federal programs regarding digital innovation have supported immigrant entrepreneurial initiatives and indeed female businesses in the Bavarian state. Therefore, the first research question (RQ) is formulated as RQ1: How has digital innovation affected female immigrant businesses in Bavaria?

Migrant Female Entrepreneurship in Germany

Germany has been a country with a long tradition of migration. The first wave of labor migrants occurred in the 1960s, with immigrants from Spain, Italy, Greece, Turkey, and Tunisia, to reinforce the national Industry. These first ethnic communities created the first entrepreneurship (Leicht & Langhauser, 2014). The second wave of migrants arrived in the 1990s from the former state of Yugoslavia (BAMF, 2016), and the latest wave was just in 2015 with asylum seekers from Syria, Afghanistan, Eritrea, and Kosovo. Also, domestic migrants within the EU member states, Bulgaria, Romania, Poland, and Croatia arrive for professional reasons.

National infrastructure with funding banks, governmental programs, European programs, competition, policy efforts for the integration of immigrants in the job arena, and trade unions are beneficial for both natives and immigrants. Especially immigrants and women have started having a higher potential for becoming entrepreneurs, and the share of entrepreneurs with an ethnic background has increased (Statistisches Bundesamt, 2015).

Female migrant entrepreneurship remains less representative, and women are less willing to start up their own companies not only because of gender discrimination but of ethnicity as well. Cultural barriers related to religion and family values, educational background, labor regulations in the host country, and gender differences are often met and framed in studies (Statistisches Bundesamt, 2015). Therefore, the second research question (RQ) is established RQ2: How has the cultural background affected immigrant female entrepreneurs' managerial role and competencies to lead in Bavaria?

Digital Innovative Strategies in Germany

Digitalization has brought new developments to entrepreneurs who transform existing models into digital ones (Niemand et al., 2017). Digital ventures grow rapidly and promise to increase social welfare and employment rates (Kurz, 2017). Organized digital innovation is carried out from processes to practices by entrepreneurial employees through interconnected webs of workforce, tools, and resources (Ciriello, 2017). For the implementation of digital innovation, specialists, user representatives, and frequent researchers are needed. User needs are explored to provide respective services accordingly.

Based on OECD data (2020), in Germany, only 16% of the firms use cloud services compared with Finland's percentage (57%), and high-speed internet to all corners of the country reaches only 2% while Sweden's is at 58% or Latvia's at 62%. The country counts on the development of infrastructure to succeed in the digitalization of the economy. Therefore, the High-Tech Strategy 2025 (HTS 2025) is one of the several governmental programs and enhancers, to support the innovation of firms in collaboration with the public (BMBF, 2020). The Ministry for Economic Affairs and Energy promotes innovative digital practices. A good example is the Digital Summit (www.de.digital), a platform that aims to enhance digitally and innovatively companies of different industries, especially regarding artificial intelligence strategies. The third established research question has been formulated as: RQ3: In which ways do women entrepreneurs of Western countries differ from those of Eastern countries based on entrepreneurial skills?

Although Germany intends to upgrade the skills of its labor workforce and endorse entrepreneurship, to align with the European digital powering, research shows that only 19% of European ICT entrepreneurs are women (EC, 2019). The current share of women entrepreneurs in the German start-up scene is just 16% since only 7.7% of female-led firms can find investors (GEM, 2020). The first hypothesis has been established. H1: Governmental support ensures a safety net for female immigrant firms in Bavaria for the development of entrepreneurial skills.

Family Business and Migrant Women in Germany

Taking into consideration the firms' vulnerability due to the threat of digital disruption, technology is a key challenge for family and non-family businesses (Buhalis et al., 2024; Thrassou et al., 2022; Vrontis et al., 2024). Innovative firms are those with a more diverse and inclusive workforce and those that count on technology. And even if the family business needs more time to change its mindset and reconsider the old way of its success story, digitalization has to be a central aspect in every communication and marketing strategy, to tackle financial capital, resources, and innovation (Wenzel et al., 2020). Moreover, cultural changes raise difficulties in digital transformation. The women's cultural background shape unconsciously their decisions and initiatives regarding entrepreneurship (Roy et al., 2018).

In Germany, family values have shaped the structure of giant corporations (Kocka, 1975). From the 1980s onwards, family firms started contributing to economic growth (Dore, 2000). Research on women in the family business is still limited and conceptual (Bjursell & Bäckvall, 2011; Danes & Olson, 2003; Sonfield & Lussier, 2012).

Women entrepreneurship in family firms is driven by national culture, spousal support, family tradition (Pearson et al., 2008; Robinson & Stubberud, 2012; Welsh et al., 2013), personal characteristics (Barrett et al., 2015), previous entrepreneurial experience and father's role as self-employed that increases the likelihood of the daughter to become an entrepreneur (Hoffmann et al., 2015). Studies of women entrepreneurs in the family business, particularly in Germany, are scarce (Hopp & Martin, 2017). Therefore, the second hypothesis is formulated as H2: Female entrepreneurs from diverse cultural backgrounds face more challenges in developing their managerial competencies and entrepreneurial skills in their family firms in Bavaria. And accordingly, the last research question: RQ4: How do they differ in terms of family value(s) that impact job engagement Western from non-Western women entrepreneurs?

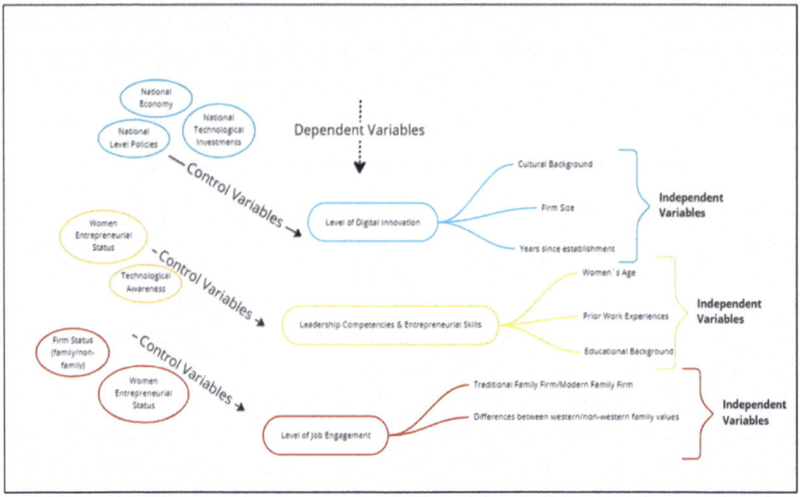

Fig. 11.1 Conceptual framework compiled by the author

Conceptual Framework

Based on the literature review summary, the purpose, and the research questions of this study, a conceptual model has been developed as illustrated in Fig. 11.1.

Theoretical Framework

Entrepreneurial Theories

Psychological Entrepreneurial Theory

Individuals can innovate and tolerate ambiguity regardless of the community context due to personal characteristics (Coon, 2004). In the personality traits theory, personality traits are defined as stable qualities and are related to the high level of innovation, creativity, lifelong learning, and emotional intelligence of entrepreneurs.

Sociological Entrepreneurial Theory

Social contexts, such as social networking, ethnic identification, life experiences, and population ecology regarding environmental, political, and legal influential factors, are related to entrepreneurial opportunities in any country (Reynolds, 1991). Individuals are often depended on their social background to function and make decisions.

Resource-Based Entrepreneurial Theory
Financial, social, and human resources are determinants of the success of entrepreneurs (Aldrich, 1999). Although empirical research is not associated with a tight relationship between high financial capital and new venture growth, access to financial capital is highly appreciated and considered an opportunity for growth exploitation (Anderson & Miller, 2003).

Entrepreneurs with a larger social network benefit more from business growth opportunities, while education and work experiences increase the potential for successful entrepreneurship (Anderson & Miller, 2003).

Hofstede's Theory
Individuals exhibit professional behavior influenced by their cultural background. Key cultural elements such as language, religion, values, and norms play a significant role in shaping one's personality within both social and business contexts. According to Hofstede's theory, countries and regions are categorized into larger groups, such as the Germanic group, based on their national culture. This theory introduces six cultural dimensions that form the fundamental model: power distance, individualism, masculinity, indulgence, long-term orientation, and uncertainty avoidance. These dimensions assess the degree to which people accept authority structures, seek certainty in decision-making, prioritize individual or community benefits, control their desires, focus on relationships or materials, and adhere to values related to long or short-term orientation. These cultural factors deeply impact organizational culture, business relationships, communication, as well as professional achievements and growth (Hofstede, 2005) (Fig. 11.2).

Literature Gap

The literature review provides an understanding of all themes that need to be investigated and analyzed. Influential factors have been studied by several authors and the importance of the topic in the business context has been highlighted. However, prior research studies related to the combination of all themes are limited to a global level and do not appear at a local or national level in Germany. Research studies were mainly focused

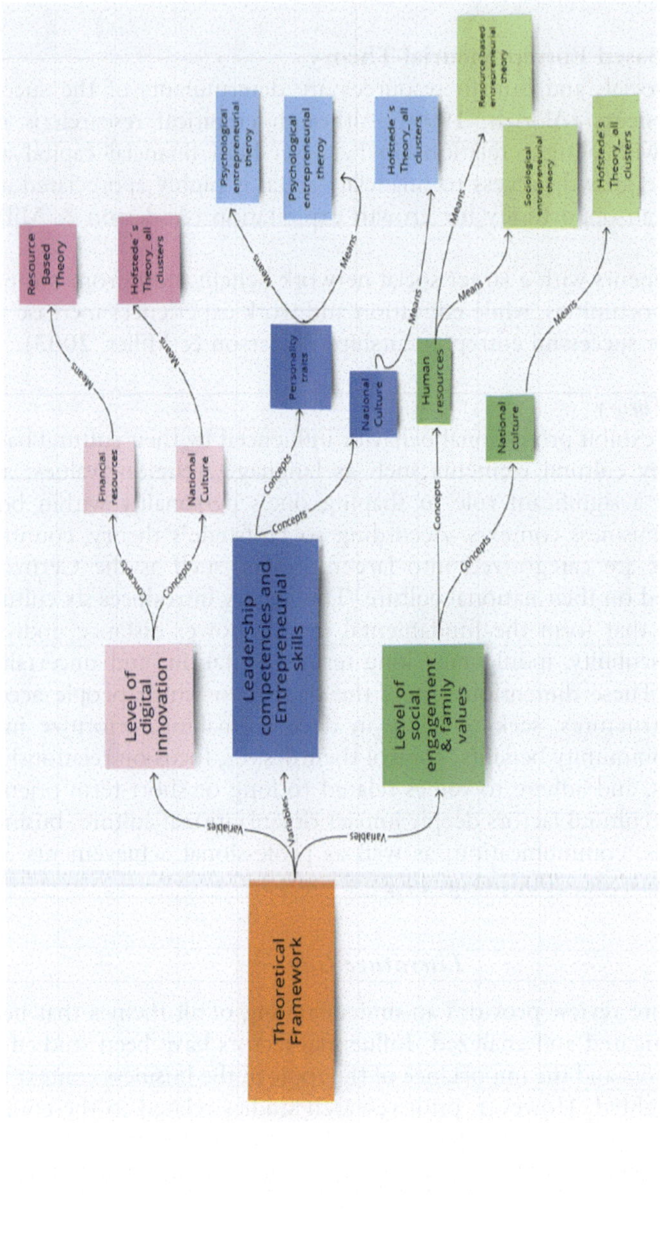

Fig. 11.2 Theoretical framework compiled by the author

on migrant female entrepreneurs and the influential factors of business performance, but not on the topic of the family business (Hopp & Martin, 2017; OECD, 2014; Rath & Swagerman, 2016; Sahin et al., 2014; Zahra & Wight, 2016).

11.3 Research Design

The study employed a mixed research method with an exploratory and narrative research design, grounded in interpretive and positivist epistemology. Using an inductive approach, primary qualitative data were collected through an online survey and semi-structured interviews featuring open-ended questions. The research adopted a cross-sectional approach, examining various population groups at a single point in time. The pilot survey involved 9 first- or second-generation migrant female entrepreneurs managing family businesses in Bavaria, with diversity in various aspects. The online survey targeted women entrepreneurs from different cultural backgrounds in Bavaria, spanning various industries and company sizes.

The online survey used convenient non-probability sampling, while snowball sampling was employed for interviews. The pilot survey aimed for a sample size adhering to various opinions, settling on 12 participants, striving to follow the thumb rule. Originally scheduled for a week in April 2023, the pilot survey was extended to May 23, 2023, due to limited participation. The number of pilot interviews was related to the richness and trustworthiness of data, the saturation indicator, and the fact that people are not solely numbers.

Data Collection Instruments

An online survey of 43 questions was designed in Microsoft Forms and distributed online mainly via LinkedIn with an invitation to women entrepreneurs' groups, located or activated in Bavaria. Online semi-structured interviews were employed with descriptive, structural, and contrast questions connected to the research questions and hypotheses and participants were contacted via email.

The first questions of the survey were screening questions, questions 11–15 referred to research question 1, questions 16–24 to research questions 2–4, questions 25–33 to hypothesis 1, and questions 34–43 to hypothesis 2. All questions collected ordinal data based on Likert-scale, 1–5, questions, excluding demographics.

Regarding the qualitative data, four categories of interview questions were designed to investigate in depth the research questions and hypotheses and look for potential patterns derived from entrepreneurs' perspectives. The interviewees were contacted via email and the process was run online.

Data Analysis Procedures

The study employed a qualitative approach to analyze interview data both narratively and thematically. Narrative analysis focused on coherence, examining stories or events with a sense of movement and contextual connections to support researcher interpretations. Thematic analysis via NVivo 14 software, was used to code and analyze factors related to digital innovation, family values, and management skills.

For the online survey, descriptive data were analyzed using frequency distribution analysis, and the reliability of the questionnaire was tested with Cronbach's Alpha. Excel was used for result calculations.

11.4 Analysis of Findings

Frequency Distribution Analysis

Screening Questions

A group of 43 questions were made to participants, the first ten questions were related to demographics, and based on statistics there was an age distribution from 18 to 55 and above, half the participants were self-employed, and the others were either students or full-time employees, the field of expertise entails general management, human resources, branding, marketing, business administration, retails, and studies, half of the participants were MBA graduates, only one has completed doctorate studies, and less than the half have studies at an undergraduate level. Participants come from African countries, the States, Europe, and Asia, 77% are second-generation immigrants, 44% come from a western country, and 66% are family firm owners and managers.

Digital Innovation

Almost half of them often update the delivered services, the access to scientific resources varies mostly from very often to sometimes, very often or often KPIs regarding operational efficiency and employee engagement are reviewed, and at 88% there is satisfaction due to launch of new products or services. Governmental support hasn't worked with all entrepreneurs' decision-making for launching new products or services since 22% were very much supported, 22% much supported, 22% had a neutral opinion, 22% were not much supported, and 11% of participants were not supported at all.

Cultural Background

A rate of 44% of participants has been supported from governmental initiatives for their entrepreneurship due to their diverse cultural background, 22% of participants had been definitely supported, 22% probably, and 11% of participants were not supported.

Nearly half of the surveyed, 44%, attributed German governmental support to their diverse cultural background. About 55% linked employees' innovative ideas to firm success, with a majority (88%) emphasizing the importance of empathy. Regular communication with employees is reported by 88%, and 89% highly value employee competencies. The cultural background is seen as influential in employee communication (89%) and client communication (77%). A significant majority, 89%, trust colleagues at a high or very high level.

Governmental Support for Skills Development

Almost 90% find evidence-based practices important in the workplace, 55% increased their working hours in the last two years, similarly requested an increase of working hours from the staff members at 55%, many new hires have been done in the last two years at 33%, entrepreneurial skills impacted the sales profit at 99%, strategic orientation has been increased since establishing at 58% of participants, while in the last two years increased strategic orientation has not been observed much for 11% of participants with 88% of participants to have observed it. A definite positive impact of entrepreneurial skills on the market access has been seen by 88% of respondents, and a possible positive impact by 11% of them. At a percentage of 88%, respondents name the cultural background as an influential factor of their entrepreneurial career.

Skills Growth Challenges Due to Diverse Cultural Backgrounds

1. Approximately 80% of participants are satisfied with the company's turnover.
2. All participants express loyalty to their clients.
3. 77% of participants consider gender and age workforce diversity meaningful, while 22% are neutral on this aspect.
4. Employee absenteeism occurs sometimes for 44%, rarely for 44%, and not at all for 11% of participants.
5. Focus on performance appraisals is definite for 44% of participants, probable for 22%, and possible for 11%.
6. All participants provide training and development sessions, with 44% doing it often and 55% doing it sometimes.
7. 88% believe that cultural background significantly influences employees' performance, both individually and as a team.
8. The same ratio of participants regards cultural background as meaningful for organizational performance.
9. 66% of participants spot differences between Western and non-Western mindsets regarding professional values like honesty, trust, and fairness, while 11% probably and 22% possibly.

Cronbach's Alpha Reliability

In our online survey, we conducted the Cronbach's Alpha reliability test using Microsoft Excel, and Table 11.1 displays the calculated value, which exceeds 0.90 (>0.90). We assessed the reliability of 37 questions in the instrument, revealing redundancy in certain added items.

Thematic Analysis of Qualitative Data

The interviews were split into four themes based on the research questions and the formulated hypotheses. Several codes were automatically identified per transcribed part on NVivo 14 software application, as presented in Table 11.2.

Digital Innovation

Both participants employ digital applications to ease job activities, depending on the industrial field.

Table 11.1 Cronbach's Alpha reliability test results

Total score	39	40
63		
69		
66		
91		
54		
65		
79		
70		
104		
239.7777778		
		α = 1.09361
30		

Participant 1 (P1): I use Microsoft 365 Applications including Outlook, OneDrive, SharePoint, and the other office programs. In addition to these applications, I use Teams to connect with the students who cannot attend the class, and to record the classes too.

Participant 2 (P2): Canva, Zoom, Teams, Trello, Notion, Google Workspace, Planoly

The pandemic has changed needs and probably prioritized virtual communication when the discussion goes to business growth and sales.

P1: The ones that I started to use with the pandemic are OneDrive, SharePoint, and Microsoft Teams.

P2: Notion, Trello and Canva were relatively new to me and I explored them much more.

Customer communication has been achieved via LinkedIn and through emails, as well as by using personal recommendations.

P2: DMs on LinkedIn and personal recommendation. This is more related to the culture in Germany that is against cold calling to the point of making it illegal. So, personal recommendation and personal contact work best.

It is interesting to have received contradictory information concerning innovative practices delivered by the federal authorities.

Table 11.2 Codes derived from the thematic analysis

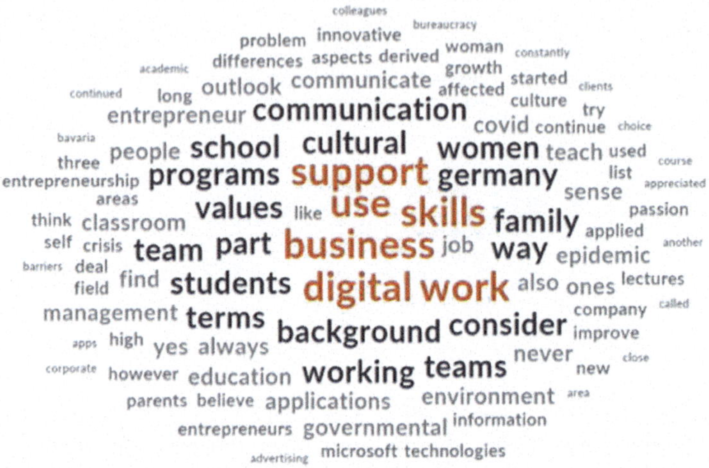

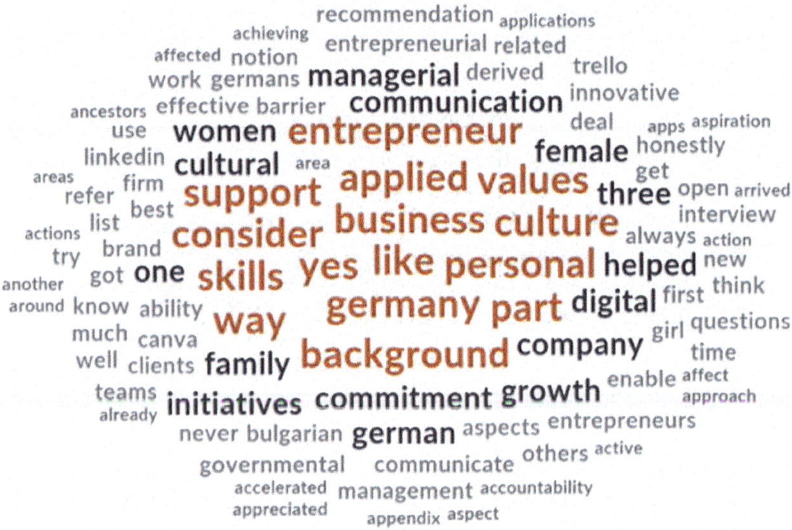

P1: Unfortunately, I do not have an information about the governmental support in digital innovative practices.
P2: There are such programs like EXIST but all in German which is my barrier.

Both participants provided a list of three entrepreneurial values.

P1: Determination, passion on higher education, self-improvement.
P2: I am a problem-solver, action- and speed-oriented with aspirations to help others, or enable them by sharing my knowledge.

National Culture and Management
The second domain of the interview questions investigated the third research question: ***In which ways do women entrepreneurs of Western countries differ from those of Eastern countries based on entrepreneurial skills?*** Participants were called to list the managerial skills they would like to improve.

P1: Stress management, Delegation, Coaching.
P2: I'd like to sharpen the ability to delegate.

Individual cultural values derived from their ancestors were the following ones.

P1: I believe the values delivered by my parents affected me a lot in terms of having a sense of judgement and a healthy skepticism, integrity in the sense of being honest and trustworthy, the value of reading and writing and finally an endless curiosity and eagerness to learn to understand the society.
P2: Emotional intelligence and empathy. The ability to connect to people on a personal level faster.

When they were asked to describe any identified differences on the way they manage workforce compared to German entrepreneurs the answers below were given.

P1: I see some differences, especially in terms of flexibility and efficiency. My working style is more flexible, and communication based. Additionally, I work very quickly when necessary and I am result-oriented. On the other hand, the way of working in Germany is, with some exceptions, slower, bulky, and much more bureaucratic. I should also say that most businesses are still reluctant or worried about adapting to digital technologies. Fortunately, great steps were taken in digitalization during the epidemic period.

P2: Yes, most definitely. I use humor in my managerial style which is unheard of by the Germans.☺

Entrepreneurial Skills and Cultural Background & Family Background and Entrepreneurship

The last two domains of the semi-structured interview questions were seen together. The first interviewee finds governmental initiatives in Bavaria *ineffective, inadequate, and immature with exception of the KOSGEB program, which includes financial support, training programs, and mentoring to encourage women's participation in entrepreneurship.* The second interviewee referred to some private initiatives "*I know of private such initiatives, like Businettes, 10 more in, Nushu,* etc."

As women migrant entrepreneurs and not risk takers or at a moderate at least level, they faced a few challenges in Germany "*Language barriers, high bureaucracy, and insufficient income despite high living expenses*" and "*Language barrier, bureaucracy.*"

They so far developed skills they needed to have for their business success are

> Work responsibility, hard work and passion for my job are the most important ones. I believe that motivation derived from passion.

as well as communication and networking

> I always try to give first, without immediate expectations to gain something out of it. I communicate a lot on LinkedIn, and I network at events.

Corporate culture and cultural background are interconnected for both participants. P1 mentions

> I think that almost all aspects of my cultural background interact with the corporate culture of my business. My cultural background, in terms of my identity, family values and my education are a part of my business.

and P2

> Bulgaria has a rich history of resilience, community spirit, and a commitment to fostering inclusivity, and these values are deeply ingrained in the fabric of Brand Like A Girl. My commitment to transparency and open communication is another aspect influenced by Bulgarian culture. I try to encourage open dialogue, active listening, and a flat organizational structure that promotes collaboration at all levels.

The addressed values that are related to business ethics and adhere to their business mindset is

> a sense of judgement and a healthy skepticism, integrity in the sense of being honest and trustworthy, the value of reading and writing and finally an endless curiosity and eagerness to learn to understand the society.

and

> Integrity (commitment to honestly, openness, trust), Accountability (taking responsibility for my actions and how they affect others), Togetherness (achieving more by being together and helping each other).

Only one of the two participants gave her insights regarding the concepts of individualism and long-term orientation as cultural dimensions in Germany "*Since the job I have is in the field of education, individualism (in the sense of having weak ties with the society in which I live) would be negative for me. However, as a woman who settled in Germany only 6 years ago, it would not be an honest answer to say that my social ties are very tight. I must say that I am lonelier and more individualistic here compared to my life in my homeland. However, I try to establish close relationships with people and communities that I feel close to. I must add that I have come a long way. Now my sense of belonging is stronger, and I don't feel as lonely in terms of socializing as I did in the beginning.*"

Family background plays a remarkable role in the business choices of one interviewee.

P1 mentions "*My parents always taught me and my sister the importance of financial independence. I also think that my family had an influence on my choice of academic field, because when I was growing up, our house was full of books, and we were constantly talking and discussing about literature and history*".

While P2 focused on more on her latest family

> Well, being a mom of two girls helped my decision to get involved in female empowerment.

Aspiration for entrepreneurial growth derives from *obligation* for P1, and from *unemployment* for P2 "*I've always had it in me, it's how I am built, but I think Germany helped as I never got the chance to get employed here. I applied to hundreds of places, and never got invited to an interview. So, I became an entrepreneur.*"

The last interview question dealing with attitudes and uncertainty as one of the cultural dimensions in Hofstede's theory was answered more descriptively by P1

> I try to focus on what I can control and to have realistic, short-term objectives. But it is not easy. The feeling of uncertainty comes with anxiety and stress

and rather diplomatically by P2 "*By believing that there isn't such thing as certainty ☺.*"

11.5 Conclusions and Recommendations

Due to the type of data collection, there cannot be any generalizations regarding women migrant entrepreneurs in Bavaria. However, there is evidence in the target population of a tight connection between family and professional values. The cultural background has shaped intangible professional values and has played a significant role in the career decision-making.

Management and entrepreneurial skills are being adjusted because of the immigrant status, the needs in the market arena, and the entrepreneurial experience. Employees' voice has been highlighted, while it is remarkable that delegation is a pending entrepreneurial skill to be developed by participants.

Governmental support is indicated in the discussed business initiatives but not evident. Private initiatives seem to interplay and rather gain ground. Although there hasn't been any distinguishment between entrepreneurs come from Western and non-Western countries concerning governmental support, the study's interviewees coming from non-Western countries faced difficulties in requesting this type of support due to the German language.

Extended research of the study is recommended to test hypotheses and generate validated conclusions. A reflection in participants' characteristics is required. The study's sample population will contribute to the field of female entrepreneurs in Germany, and the study's results will be available for future studies in the field. At a deeper level, participants' insights will be wrapped to support locally women migrant entrepreneurs for social networking, expanding business growth, and mentoring newcomers in business.

Practical Implications

The data analysis will be the backbone of a digital platform as the Launchpad for new research in Entrepreneurship, starting at a local standard and navigating virtually to reach out to women migrant entrepreneurs. The same digital platform would host mentoring programs offered to young or recently joined the field women entrepreneurs. Programs may begin running locally and continue across European or non-European countries as per demand and available mentors. Locally and nationally, at a socio-political stage, the study's results will provide learning support to firms either by contributing to the employees' training and skills development or by promoting governmental financial incentives based on entrepreneurs' insights and a list of implemented programs. At a theoretical status, a sample population that hasn't been examined yet can provide us with perceptions in the area of female entrepreneurs.

References

Acs, J., Bardasi, E., Estrin, S., & Svejnar, J. (2011). Introduction to a special issue of Small Business Economics on female entrepreneurship in developed and developing economies. *Small Business Economics, 37*(4), 393–396.

Aldrich, H.E. (1999) *Organizations evolving.* Sage Publications.

Anderson, A., & Miller, C. (2003). Class matters: Human and social capital in the entrepreneurial process. *The Journal of Socioeconomics, 32*, 17–36.

Arrak, K., Kaasa, A., & Varblane, U. (2020). Regional cultural context as a determinant of entrepreneurial behaviour: The case of Germany. *The Journal of Entrepreneurship, 29*(1), 88–118.

Audretsch, D. B., & Lehmann, E. E. (2016). *The seven secrets of Germany: Economic resilience in an era of global turbulence.* Oxford University Press.

Audretsch, D., Lehmann, E., & Wirsching, K. (2017). Female immigrant entrepreneurship. In A. N. Link (Ed.), *Gender and entrepreneurial activity* (pp. 46–68). Edward Elgar Publishing

Barrett, M., Davidson, E., Prabhu, J., & Vargo, S. L. (2015). Service innovation in the digital age: Key contributions and future directions. *MIS Quarterly, 39*(1), 135–154.

Bjursell, C., & Bäckvall, L. (2011). Family businesswomen in media discourse: The business role and the mother role. *Journal of Family Business Management, 1*(2), 154–173.

BMBF. (2018). *The High-Tech Strategy 2025.* Available at: Research and innovation that benefit the people—The High-Tech Strategy 2025 (bmbf.de). Accessed 2 January 2021.

BMBF. (2020). *The High Tech Strategy 2025* (Progress Report). Available at: The_High_Tech_Strategy_2025.pdf (bmbf.de). Accessed 2 January 2021.

Buhalis, D., Efthymiou, L., Uzunboylu, N., & Thrassou, A. (2024). Charting the progress of technology adoption in tourism and hospitality in the era of Industry 4.0. Tourism & Hospitality in the Digital Era: Technology and its (im)Possibilities special issue in *Euromed Journal of Business.*

Bundesamt für Migration und Flüchtlinge (BAMF). (2016). *Das Bundesamt in Zahlen 2015* – Asyl. http://www.bamf.de/SharedDocs/Anlagen/DE/Publikationen/Broschueren/bundesamt-inzahlen-2015-asyl.html?nn=1694444. Accessed 28 December 2020.

Bundesamt für Migration und Flüchtlinge. (2015). *Migrationsbericht 2014.* http://www.bamf.de/SharedDocs/Anlagen/DE/Publikationen/Migrationsberichte/migrationsbericht-2015.html;jsessionid=11D4632CD08941797C2D8FC9E5333520.1_cid359?nn=1663558. Accessed 30 December 2020.

Bundesamt für Migration und Flügtlinge (BAMF). (2017). Wanderungsmonitoring: Erwerbsmigration nach Deutschland,Bericht für das erste Halbjahr 2017 *[Migration monitor, Economic migration to Germany, report on first half of 2017].* http://www.bamf.de/SharedDocs/Anlagen/DE/Publikationen/Broschueren/wanderungsmonitoring-halbjahr-2017.pdf?__blob=publicationFile. Accessed 8 January 2021.

Ciriello, R. F. (2017). *Digital innovation: People, practices, tools* (Doctoral dissertation). University of Zurich

Coon, D. (2004). *Introduction to psychology* (9th ed.). West Publishing Company.

Danes, S. M., & Olson, P. D. (2003). Women's role involvement in family businesses, business tensions, and business success. *Family Business Review, 16*(1), 53–68.

Dengler., K., & Gundert, S. (2021, October). Digital transformation and subjective job insecurity in Germany. *European Sociological Review, 37*(5), 799–817. https://doi.org/10.1093/esr/jcaa066

Deutschinstitut INTEGRA. (2023). https://www.deutschinstitut.de/en/our-german-courses/. Accessed 7 February 2023.

Dileo. I., & Garcia-Pereiro, T. (2018). The moderate impact of gender egalitarianism on nascent entrepreneurship at the individual level. Evidence from GEM data on some European Countries. *L'industria, Rivista di Economia e Politica Industriale, 39*(3), 405–428.

Dore, R. (2000). *Stock market capitalism: Welfare capitalism: Japan and Germany versus The Anglo-Saxons*. https://doi.org/10.1093/prof:oso/9780199240623.001.0001

Eurobarometer. (2012). Entrepreneurship in the EU and beyond. *Flash Eurobarometer, 354*.

European Commission. (2019) Available at Women in Digital|Shaping Europe's digital future (Europa.eu). Accessed 29 December 2020.

Existenzgründungsportal des BMWK. (2023). Available at: https://www.existenzgruender.de/EN/Home/inhalt.html. Accessed 6 February 2023.

Female immigrant entrepreneurship in Germany. Available at: https://www.researchgate.net/publication/318787872_Female_immigrant_entrepreneurship_in_Germany. Accessed 8 February 2023.

Global Entrepreneurship Monitor. (2018). *Global report*. https://www.babson.edu/media/babson/assets/blank-center/GEM-2018-2019-Women's-Report.pdf. Accessed 10 May 2020.

Global Entrepreneurship Monitor. (2020) *Global report*. https://www.gemconsortium.org/economy-profiles. Accessed 10 October 2021.

Göll, E., & Zwiers, J. (2018). *Technological trends in the MENA region: The cases of digitalization and information and communications technology (ICT)*. (MENARA Working Papers, (23)). Available at: Technological Trends in the MENA Region: The Cases of Digitalization and Information and Communications Technology (ICT) (iai.it). Accessed 29 December 2020.

Harima, A. (2022). Transnational migration entrepreneurship during a crisis: Immediate response to challenges and opportunities emerging through the COVID-19 pandemic. *Business and Society Review, 127*(S1), 223–251. https://doi.org/10.1111/basr.12266

Hoffmann, A., Junge, M., & Malchow-Møller, N. (2015). Running in the family: Parental role models in entrepreneurship. *Small Business Economics, 44*(1), 79–104.

Hofstede, G., & Hofstede, G. J. (2005). *Cultures and organizations. Software of the mind* (2nd ed.). McGraw-Hill.

Hopp, C., & Martin, J. (2017). Does entrepreneurship pay for women and immigrants? A 30 year assessment of the socio-economic impact of entrepreneurial activity in Germany. *Entrepreneurship and Regional Development, 29*(5–6), 517–543.

Kocka, J. (1975). Sozialgeschichte - Strukturgeschichte - Gesellschaftsgeschichte, *Archiv für Sozialgeschichte,* ISSN 0066–6505. *Verlag Neue Gesellschaft, Bonn-Bad Godesberg, 15*, 1–42.

Kurz, M. (2017). *On the formation of capital and wealth.* Stanford University Working Paper.

Leicht, R., & Langhauser, M. (2014) Ökonomische Bedeutung und Leistungspotenziale von Migrantenunternehmen in Deutschland: Studie im Auftrag der Abteilung Wirtschafts-und Sozialpolitik, *Arbeitskreis Mittelstand und Gesprächskreis Migration und Integration der Friedrich-Ebert-Stiftung,* Friedrich-Ebert-Stiftung.

Lewis, K. V., Henry, C., Gatewood, E. J., & Watson, J. (Eds.). (2014). *Women's entrepreneurship in the 21st century. An international multi-level research analysis.* Edward Elgar.

Ludwig-Maximilians Universität München – LMU Innovation and Entrepreneurship Center. (2023). https://www.iec.uni-muenchen.de/impact-readiness-program/index.html. Accessed 7 February 2023.

Ludwig-Maximilians-Universität München—LMU. (2023). *News overview.* https://www.lmu.de/en/newsroom/news-overview/news/female-start-up-entrepreneurs-in-the-limelight.html. Accessed 7 February 2023.

Niemand, T., Rigtering, C., Kallmünzer, A., Kraus, S., & Matijas, S. (2017). Entrepreneurial orientation and digitalization in the financial service industry: A contingency approach. In *Proceedings of the European Conference on Information Systems (ECIS)*, Guimarães, Portugal, June 5–10, 2017 (pp. 1081–1096).

OECD. (2014). *Matching economic migration with labour market needs.* OECD Publishing. https://doi.org/10.1787/9789264216501-en. Accessed 7 January 2021.

OECD. (2020). *Digital Economy Outlook 2020.* Chapter 9. Digital innovation|OECD Digital Economy Outlook 2020|OECD iLibrary (oecd-ilibrary.org). Accessed 2 January 2021.

Pearson, A., Carr, J., & Shaw, J. (2008). Toward a theory of families: A social capital perspective. *Entrepreneurship Theory and Practice, 32*, 949–969. https://doi.org/10.1111/j.1540-6520.2008.00265.x

Rath, J., & Swagerman, A. (2016). Promoting ethnic entrepreneurship in European cities: Sometimes ambitious, mostly absent, rarely addressing structural features. *International Migration Review, 54*(1), 152–166.

Research in Germany. (2023). https://www.research-in-germany.org/en/our-service/publications.html. Accessed 7 February 2023.

Reynolds, P. D. (1991). Sociology and entrepreneurship: Concepts and contributions. *Entrepreneurship: Theory & Practice, 16*(2), 47–70.

Robinson, S., & Stubberud, H. A. (2012). All in the family: Entrepreneurship as a family tradition. *International Journal of Entrepreneurship, 16*, 19–30.

Roy, R., Lampert, C. M., & Stoyneva, I. (2018). When dinosaurs fly: The role of firm capabilities in the 'avianization' of incumbents during disruptive technological change. *Strategic Entrepreneurship Journal, 12*(2), 261–284.

Sahin, M., Nijkamp, P., & Suzuki, S. (2014). Contrasts and similarities in economic performance of migrant entrepreneurs. *IZA Journal of Migration, 3*(7). https://doi.org/10.1186/2193-9039-3-7. Accessed 7 January 2021.

Sonfield, M. C., & Lussier, R. N. (2012). Gender in family business management: A multinational analysis. *Journal of Family Business Management, 2*(2), 110–129.

Statistisches Bundesamt. (2015). *Statistisches Jahresbuch. Deutschland und Internationales 2015.* https://www.destatis.de/DE/Publikationen/StatistischesJahrbuch/StatistischesJahrbuch2015.pdf?__blob=publicationFile. Accessed 3 January 2021.

Thrassou, A., Vrontis, D., Efthymiou, L., & Uzunboylu, N. (2022). An overview of business advancement through technology: Markets and marketing in transition. In A Thrassou, D. Vrontis, L. Efthymiou, Y. Weber, S. M. R. Shams, & E. Tsoukatos (Eds.), *Business advancement through technology Volume I*. Palgrave Studies in Cross-disciplinary Business Research, in Association with EuroMed Academy of Business. Palgrave Macmillan. https://doi.org/10.1007/978-3-031-07769-2_1

TM, A., & Joseph, R. P. (2021). Gender and firm innovation—A systematic literature review and future research agenda. *International Journal of Entrepreneurial Behavior & Research, 27*(2), 301–333. https://doi.org/10.1108/IJEBR-08-2019-0480

Vrontis, D., Thrassou, A., Uzunboylu, N., & Efthymiou, L. (2023). An overview of business for sustainability: Strategic avenues and managerial approaches. In D. Vrontis, A. Thrassou, L. Efthymiou, Y. Weber, S. M. R. Shams, & E. Tsoukatos (Eds.), *Business for sustainability, Volume I*. Palgrave Studies in Cross-disciplinary Business Research, in Association with EuroMed Academy of Business. Palgrave Macmillan. https://doi.org/10.1007/978-3-031-37361-9_1.

Vrontis, D., Thrassou, A., Efthymiou, L., Weber, Y., Shams, S. M. R., & Tsoukatos, E. (2024). *Business for sustainability, Volume II: Contextual evolution and elucidation.* Springer Nature. https://doi.org/10.1007/978-3-031-37365-7

Welsh, D. H. B., Memili, E., Kaciak, E., & Ahmed, S. (2013). Sudanese women entrepreneurs. *Journal of Developmental Entrepreneurship, 18*(2), 1350013 (18 p.).

Wenzel, M., Stanske, S., & Lieberman, M. B. (2020). Strategic responses to the crisis. *Strategic Management Journal*. https://doi.org/10.1002/smj.3161

World Bank. (2019). https://data.worldbank.org/indicator/SL.TLF.CACT.FE.ZS. Accessed 11 December 2020.

World Economic Forum. (2018). *The global competitiveness report*. https://www.weforum.org/reports/the-global-competitveness-report-2018. Accessed 7 February 2023.

Zahra, S., & Wright, M. (2016). Understanding the social role of entrepreneurship. *Journal of Management Studies, 53*(4), 610–629.

CHAPTER 12

Investigating the Dual Moderated Mediation of Work Autonomy and Supervisor Support in the Relationship Between Workload and Turnover Intentions Through Burnout

Sherwin Ignatius Chia

12.1 Introduction

This study empirically investigates the mediation of burnout on the relationship between the job demand of workload and turnover intentions and the first-stage dual moderated mediation of two job resources of work autonomy and supervisor support. The COVID-19 pandemic crisis resulted in governments enforcing the requirement of work from home (WFH) and social distancing to curb the spread of the virus (Foucault & Galasso, 2020; Thrassou et al., 2022). These regulations

S. I. Chia (✉)
S R Nathan School of Human Development, Singapore University of Social Sciences, Singapore, Singapore
e-mail: sherwinchiatm@suss.edu.sg

D. Vrontis et al. (eds.), *Business in Uncertainty*, Palgrave Studies in Cross-disciplinary Business Research, In Association with EuroMed Academy of Business, https://doi.org/10.1007/978-3-031-65587-6_12

have led employees to feel overworked and overwhelmed that has been observed not just in the healthcare industry but in other industries (Wang et al., 2021; Zhang & Kowalczuk, 2023). Mainstream media also reported that many workers have resigned as a result (Cai, 2021; Morgan, 2022). This was corroborated by the report from the 2021 Microsoft Trend Index which polled about 30,000 employees across 31 countries (Microsoft, 2021). The report found that 54% of the global workforce were feeling overworked, 39% were feeling exhausted, and 41% were considering changing employers that year. This study develops these relationships using Job Demands-Resources theory and Conservation of Resources theory on employees who have been required to WFH in Singapore during the pandemic. Although past studies have supported the buffering effects of two important job resources of work autonomy and supervisor support on burnout (Bakker & Demerouti, 2017; Bakker et al., 2023), these were conducted during times of normality rather than during times of crisis (Demerouti & Bakker, 2022). Thus, this study answers this call to investigate these relationships especially on testing the buffering effects of these two important job resources during the COVID-19 pandemic crisis and on working adults who have been required to WFH in Singapore where studies have been few.

12.2 Literature Review

Job Demands-Resources Theory

Job Demands-Resources (JD-R) theory is an established and well-validated theory that proposes that job demands and job resources can impact employee and organisational outcomes (Bakker et al., 2023). Job demands are defined as physical, social, or organisational aspects of the job that require sustained physical or mental effort that associates with certain physiological and psychological costs whereas job resources are defined as physical, social, or organisational aspects of the job that help one achieve work goals, alleviate job demands and its associated costs, and/or stimulate personal growth and development.

JD-R theory proposes that the impact on employee and organisational outcomes can be through two processes (Bakker et al., 2023). The first process is the health-impairment process where chronic job demands consume employees' resources which results in burnout. The second process is the motivational process where job resources enable achievement of work goals and foster growth and development which results in improved functioning. JD-R theory also proposes that job demands and job resources can have a moderating impact on employees and organisational outcomes (Bakker et al., 2023). Thus, job resources can buffer the impact of job demands on strain (e.g. burnout) while job demands can enhance the impact of job resources on work engagement.

Conservation of Resources Theory

Conservation of Resources (COR) theory proposes that "individuals strive to obtain, retain, foster, and protect those things they centrally value" (Hobfoll et al., 2018, p. 104). The COR theory has four principles (Hobfoll et al., 2018). The primacy of loss principle postulates people are affected more by resource loss than by resource gain. The resource investment principle postulates that investment of resources can protect against resource loss. The gain paradox principle postulates that when people face resource loss, resource gains become more important. The desperation principle postulates that when individuals are unable to do so due to a lack of resources, they will try to protect themselves even if such actions are irrational such as conserving their resources or finding alternative strategies to survive.

The Indirect Effect of Burnout Between Workload and Turnover Intentions

The COVID-19 pandemic has forced all employees around the world to work differently such as the requirement to WFH because of government regulations to curb the spread of the virus (Foucault & Galasso, 2020). As a result, the pandemic has posed significant changes in job demands faced by employees globally (Kniffin et al., 2021). This has led to increased workload not just for healthcare workers but also for workers in other industries during the pandemic (Wang et al., 2021; Zhang & Kowalczuk, 2023). Similarly, media reports in Singapore have found that majority of employees polled in Singapore felt overworked (Chee, 2021) and employees were struggling to balance both their work and home (Ang, 2020).

While workload is a complex construct with no widely accepted definitions, workload can be measured using several factors (Jacobs et al.,

2013). These factors can include the quantitative aspects of the job such as the work pressure, the cognitive aspects of the job such as the amount of information processing required to complete work tasks, and the emotional aspects of the job such as managing emotions involved in completing work tasks (Estes, 2015; Hart & Staveland, 1988; Karasek et al., 1985). WFH as a mandatory requirement during the COVID-19 pandemic has seemed to increase these aspects of workload (Wang et al., 2021). First, balancing both work and non-work is challenging for most employees (Ramarajan & Reid, 2013). While WFH during the pandemic, many employees reported clocking more work hours as they must manage family commitments during regular hours (Osborne, 2021; Yang, 2022). Second, the predominant use of virtual communications to collaborate and complete work tasks due to WFH requirements (Kniffin et al., 2021) can increase cognitive workload as employees have to engage in higher cognitive effort to process information possibly due to a lack of non-verbal cues (Hammond et al., 2000). Third, social isolation due to social distancing during the pandemic (Kniffin et al., 2021) can create negative emotions such as anxiety and frustration (Cacioppo et al., 2006). Thus, prolonged WFH periods can increase workload that can lead to burnout through the health-impairment process based on the JD-R theory. Indeed, this pattern between workload and burnout was reported among workers in various industries during the pandemic (Wang et al., 2021; Zhang & Kowalczuk, 2023).

Burnout is also associated with turnover intentions. According to COR theory, health and well-being are things that are commonly valued by people and people will seek to protect them (Hobfoll et al., 2018). When these valued things are being threatened and individuals lack or have exhausted the resources to protect them, according to the desperation principle in COR theory, individuals can engage in irrational actions by finding alternative strategies just to survive even if it may not be adaptive. For instance, when employees face a high level of burnout, such employees may look for an exit strategy by finding more sustainable jobs (Vrontis et al., 2023a, 2023b). Past studies have also supported this positive association between burnout and turnover intentions (Hansung & Stoner, 2008; Lu & Gursoy, 2016). However, it may not be prudent for individuals to switch jobs during times of uncertainty such as during the pandemic when global economy is in a recession (World Bank, 2020). Yet, the desperation principle appears to align with media reports of people quitting their jobs (Cai, 2021; Morgan, 2022). Therefore, it is hypothesised that:

Hypothesis 1: There will be a positive indirect effect between workload and turnover intentions through burnout, such that workload will be positively related to burnout which, in turn, will be positively related to turnover intentions.

The Conditional Indirect Effects of Work Autonomy and Supervisor Support

According to the buffering hypothesis in JD-R theory, work autonomy and supervisor support are two important job resources that have been widely investigated and can reduce the negative impact of job demands on strain (Bakker & Demerouti, 2017). Autonomy is defined as "the extent to which a job allows freedom, independence, and discretion to schedule work, make decisions, and choose the methods used to perform tasks" (Morgeson & Humprey, 2006, p. 1323). As work autonomy gives employees flexibility to choose when and how work gets done, this resource can help employees to buffer the impact of workload on burnout while WFH during the COVID-19 pandemic, thereby reducing turnover intentions. There was evidence of these relationships found in employees with similar work modes before the COVID-19 pandemic. Previous studies done on telework provide some support on the buffering effects of autonomy. For instance, Kossek and her colleagues (2008) found that employees who telework experience lower turnover intentions when they perceived higher work autonomy. Perry and her colleagues (2018) found support for autonomy as a moderator between the amount of remote work on burnout.

Supervisor support can also help to buffer the negative effects of work overload. Supervisors represent the organisation and manage resources and their subordinates (Eisenberger et al., 2002). Supervisors can help subordinates' task completion by mobilising resources when required and helping them cope with negative emotions arising from work (Avanzi et al., 2018). This can be an important social resource for employees who may have to deal with high workloads and social isolation while WFH during the COVID-19 pandemic. For example, supervisor support reduces burnout in young adult Korean workers by improving their resilience and self-efficacy during the COVID-19 pandemic (Kim et al.,

2022). A study before the COVID-19 pandemic on remote workers who received supervisor support was also associated with less social isolation which was related with less psychological distress (Bentley et al., 2016). Hence, it is hypothesised that:

Hypothesis 2: There will be a first-stage condition indirect effect for work autonomy (Hypothesis 2a) and Supervisor Support (Hypothesis 2b) on the relationship between workload and turnover intentions through burnout such that when the respective job resource is high, the indirect effect will be reduced as compared to when the respective job resource is low.

12.3 Research Design

Procedure

A cross-sectional research design was used. Survey measures were designed using Qualtrics and were distributed to working adult participants from September 2021 to October 2021 in Singapore. As this period was after a lockdown, safe distancing and workplace capacity limits were still enforced which limited access to participants. Hence, participants were recruited through personal contacts as well as through online evening classes consisting of working adults. A snowball approach was then used to increase participation by asking participants to forward the survey to their colleagues (Biernacki & Waldorf, 1981). At the start of the survey, a description of the study was provided. Informed consent with confidentiality and anonymity emphasised was sought from participants before proceeding with the survey. As an eligibility check, participants were asked about their WFH requirements for the past six months. This was followed by the study measures and demographic information consisting of age, gender, marital status, and people-manager role.

Participants

Two hundred and five participants provided complete responses. Thirty-six participants were excluded from the analysis as they reported WFH was not required. The final sample included 169 participants comprising 73% females and 22% males who are mostly young working adults (Reported average age was in the age category between 26 and 30 years old). All six industry clusters (Ministry of Trade and Industry, n.d.) were represented in the final sample (22% Manufacturing cluster, 8% Built Environment cluster, 7% Trade and Connectivity cluster, 11% Essential Domestic Services cluster, 40% Professional Services cluster, 11% Lifestyle cluster).

Measures

There are seven measures used in this study: Turnover intentions, burnout, work overload, autonomy, supervisor support, supervisor feedback, and employee engagement.

Turnover intentions are measured using two items adapted from Hom and Griffeth (1991). A 7-point Likert scale is used (1–Strongly disagree to 7–Strong agree). The two items are: "I frequently think about quitting this job" and "I will probably look for a new job next year". Cronbach's alpha is 0.82 suggesting adequate reliability.

Burnout is measured using 16 items from the Oldenburg Burnout Inventory (OLBI) (Demerouti et al., 2010). OLBI consists of two dimensions. Exhaustion consists of eight items and measures "the general feelings of emptiness, overtaxing from work, a strong need for rest, and a state of physical exhaustion" (Demerouti et al., 2001, p. 503). An example item is, "After my work, I usually feel worn out and weary". Disengagement consists of eight items and measures the perception of "distancing oneself from the object and the content of one's work and to negative, cynical attitudes and behaviours towards one's work in general" (Demerouti et al., 2001, p. 503). An example item is, "sometimes I feel sickened by my work tasks". Participants are asked to rate each statement based on whether they had these feeling about their job in the past six months on a 7-point Likert scale (1–Never to 7–Always). All 16 items are aggregated to measure burnout. Cronbach's alpha is 0.85 suggesting adequate reliability.

Workload is taken from the Questionnaire sur les Ressources et Contraintes Professionnelles (Lequeurre et al., 2013). Three dimensions of work overload consisting of four items each are used. Pace and amount of work measures "the sense of having too much work to do in the time available" (Lequeurre et al., 2013, p. 100). An example item is, "Do you have too much work to do?". Mental workload measures "the cognitive demands that primarily impinge on the brain processes involved in information processing" (Lequeurre et al., 2013, p. 100). An example item is, "Does your work demand a lot of concentration?". Emotional workload measures "the effort needed to deal with job inherent emotions" (Lequeurre et al., 2013, p. 100). An example item is, "Does your work put you in emotionally upsetting situations?". A 5-point Likert scale is used (1–Never to 5–Always). All 12 items are aggregated to measure workload. Cronbach's alpha is 0.86 suggesting adequate reliability.

Work Autonomy is taken from the Leiden Quality of Work Questionnaire (van der Doef & Maes, 1999). Two dimensions of work autonomy consisting of four items each are used. Decision authority measures the degree to which employees can make work decisions on their own. A sample item is, "My job allows me to make a lot of decisions on my own". Task Control measures the degree to which employees control how and when they work. A sample item is, "If I want to, I can leave my workplace for a short while". A 5-point Likert scale is used (1–Strongly disagree to 5–Strongly agree). All eight items are aggregated to measure work autonomy. Cronbach's alpha is 0.74 suggesting adequate reliability.

Supervisor Support is based on an adapted Karasek's Job Content Survey (Karasek et al., 1985) from Baruch-Feldman et al. (2002). Ten items measure the participant's perceptions of the supervisor as caring, supportive, and absence of hostility. A sample item is, "My supervisor cares about me". A 5-point Likert is used (1–Not at all to 5–Very much). Cronbach's alpha is 0.90 suggesting adequate reliability.

The study controlled for work engagement which is measured using nine items from the shortened Utrecht Work Engagement Scale (UWES) (Schaufeli et al., 2006). Three dimensions of work engagement consisting of three items each were used. Vigour measures the participant's "high levels of energy and resilience while working" (Schaufeli et al., 2006, p. 702). A sample item is, "At my work, I feel bursting with energy". Dedication measures the participant's "strong involvement in work and experiencing a sense of significance, enthusiasm, inspiration, pride, and challenge (Schaufeli et al., 2006, p. 702). A sample item is, "My job inspires me". Absorption measures the participant experience of "fully concentrated and happily engrossed in one's work" (Schaufeli et al., 2006, p. 702). A sample item is, "I feel happy when I am working intensely". Participants are asked to rate each statement based on whether they had these feeling about their job in the past six months on a 7-point Likert scale (1–Never to 7–Always). All nine items are aggregated to measure work engagement. Cronbach's alpha is 0.92 suggesting adequate reliability.

The study also controlled for demographic variables such age (Coded in 5 year increments with 1–21 to 25 years old to 11–More than 70 years old), gender (Coded as 0–Male and 1–Female), and marital status (Coded as 0–Not married and 1–Married) as well as whether participant work position involves people management (Coded as 0–No and 1–Yes).

A 5-item Family to Work Conflict scale (Netemeyer et al., 1996) was used as a marker variable to test for the risk of common method bias. A sample item is "the demands of my family or spouse/partner interfere with work-related activities". Participants are asked to rate the agreement of each statement based on a 5-point Likert scale (1–Strongly Disagree to 5–Strongly Agree). Cronbach's alpha is 0.94 suggesting adequate reliability.

12.4 Results

Confirmatory factor analysis (CFA) using Lisrel 8.80 is conducted on turnover intentions, burnout, workload, work autonomy, supervisor support, and work engagement. As the sample size is small, parcels are used to increase the power of the latent variable models (Little et al., 2013). Burnout, workload, work autonomy, and work engagement are parcelled using the domain-representative approach. Supervisor support is parcelled using the balancing approach. The overall fit of the CFA model shows acceptable fit ($\chi^2(194) = 350.74$, RMSEA = 0.07, 90% CI [0.06, 0.08], SRMR = 0.06, CFI = 0.97, NNFI = 0.96, AIC = 465.38, EVCI = 2.77).

The risk of common method variance (CMV) is tested following the procedure of the comprehensive CFA marker technique (Williams et al., 2010). The presence of CMV associated with the marker variable compares the Method-C model with the Baseline Model. The χ^2 test is not significant ($\Delta\chi^2(1) = 3.120$, $p = 0.077$) which suggests that the presence of CMV does not significantly impact the measurement variables and the risk of CMV is minimal.

The descriptive statistics and correlations are presented in Table 12.1. The correlations between the independent variables and dependent variable and among the independent variables are in the expected directions.

Multiple regression analysis with the PROCESS macro (Version 4.0) in SPSS (Version 26) is used to test for indirect and conditional indirect effects (Hayes, 2022). The PROCESS macro provides bootstrapped (k =

Table 12.1 Descriptive statistics and correlations

Variables	M	SD	*1*	*2*	*3*	*4*	*5*	*6*	*7*	*8*	*9*
1. Turnover Intentions	3.62	1.69	0.82								
2. Burnout	3.10	0.52	0.52^{***}	0.85							
3. Workload	3.19	0.69	0.31^{***}	0.35^{***}	0.86						
4. Work Autonomy	3.56	0.63	-0.36^{***}	-0.41^{***}	-0.16^{*}	0.74					
5. Supervisor Support	3.89	0.76	-0.47^{***}	-0.38^{***}	-0.18^{*}	0.45^{***}	0.90				
6. Work Engagement	4.24	0.90	-0.39^{***}	-0.68^{***}	−0.05	0.42^{***}	0.48^{***}	0.92			
7. Age[a]	2.24	1.92	-0.21^{***}	0.29^{***}	−0.03	0.22^{**}	0.04	0.31^{***}	–		
8. Gender[b]	0.73	0.45	0.00	0.01	−0.05	0.01	0.02	0.05	−0.13	–	
9. Marital Status[c]	0.22	0.42	−0.14	-0.24^{**}	−0.08	-0.16^{*}	−0.04	0.22^{**}	0.68^{***}	−0.09	–
10. People Manager[d]	0.26	0.44	0.00	−0.11	0.26^{**}	0.07	−0.03	0.19^{*}	0.34^{***}	−0.03	0.26^{**}

Note Cronbach's alpha represented in the diagonals

[a]Age is coded with 1–21 to 25 years old, 2–26–30 years old, 3–31 to 35 years old, 4–36–40 years old, 5–41 to 45 years old, 6–46–50 years old, 7–51 to 55 years old, 8–56 to 60 years old, 9–61 to 65 years old, 10–66 to 70 years old, and 11–More than 70 years old

[b]Gender is dummy coded with 0 representing males and 1 representing females

[c]Marital Status is dummy coded with 0 representing not married and 1 representing married

[d]People manager is dummy coded with 0 represening not a people manager and 1 representing people manager. n = 169. $^{*}p < 0.05$; $^{**}p < 0.01$, $^{***}p < 0.001$

5,000) percentile confidence intervals (BootCI) for the conditional indirect effects. The indirect and conditional indirect effects are significant if these intervals do not include zero. Results for Hypothesis 1 and Hypothesis 2 are calculated using Model 4 and Model 9 from the PROCESS macro, respectively. For the conditional indirect effects, all continuous independent variables are centred (Aiken & West, 1991).

Hypothesis 1 proposes that there will be a positive indirect effect between workload and turnover intentions through burnout such that workload will be positively related to burnout which, in turn, will be positively related to turnover intentions. Results from the multiple regression analysis suggest that workload is significantly and positively related with burnout ($B = 0.24$, $SE = 0.04$, $t(160) = 5.737$, $p < 0.001$) and burnout is significantly and positively related to turnover intentions ($B = 1.12$, $SE = 0.31$, $t(159) = 3.625$, $p < 0.001$). After burnout is added into the regression model with age, gender, marital status, people manager, work engagement, work autonomy, and supervisor support as controls, the relationship between workload and turnover intentions became not significant ($B = 0.29$, $SE = 0.17$, $t(159) = 1.626$, $p = 0.106$). A significant index of mediation (Index = 0.27, Boot*SE* = 0.10, BootCI [0.0930, 0.4802]) confirms the positive indirect of burnout in the relationship between workload and turnover intentions. Thus, Hypothesis 1 is supported.

Hypothesis 2 proposes a first-stage conditional indirect effects for work autonomy (Hypothesis 2a) and supervisor support (Hypothesis 2b) on the relationship between workload and turnover intentions through burnout such that when the respective job resource is high, the indirect effect will be reduced as compared to when the respective job resource is low. Results are presented in Table 12.2.

From Table 12.2, the interaction of workload and work autonomy on burnout is significant ($B = 0.15$, $SE = 0.07$, $t(158) = 2.153$, $p = 0.033$) but not for the interaction of workload and supervisor support on burnout ($B = -0.03$, $SE = 0.05$, $t(158) = -0.521$, $p = 0.603$). There is only one significant index of partial moderated mediation which confirms the moderated mediation involving work autonomy (Index = 0.18, Boot*SE* = 0.10, BootCI [0.0143, 0.3884]) but not for supervisor support (Index = −0.03, Boot*SE* = 0.06, BootCI [−0.1782, 0.0808]). For work autonomy, the conditional indirect effect is positive and significant when participants rate having lower work autonomy (−1 SD) (Index

Table 12.2 Results for the hypothesised moderated mediation model

Outcome	*Burnout*		*Turnover Intentions*	
Variables	B(SE)	t	B(SE)	t
(Constant)	4.54(0.16)	28.641***	1.00(1.61)	0.622
Workload	0.23(0.04)	5.554***	0.41(0.19)	2.187*
Work Autonomy	−0.10(0.05)	−1.981*		
Workload x Work Autonomy	0.15(0.07)	2.153*	–	–
Supervisor Support	−0.01(0.04)	−0.193	–	–
Workload x Supervisor Support	−0.03(0.05)	−0.521	–	–
Burnout	–	–	1.20(0.32)	3.710***
Age[a]	−0.00(0.02)	−0.164	−0.09(0.08)	−1.153
Gender[b]	0.08(0.06)	1.323	0.00(0.25)	0.012
Marital Status[c]	−0.04(0.09)	−0.412	0.17(0.36)	0.473
People Manager[d]	−0.08(0.07)	−1.204	0.20(0.28)	0.698
Work Engagement	−0.34(0.03)	−9.210***	−0.23(0.18)	−1.286
F	22.485***		10.305***	
R^2	0.59		0.31	

[a]Age is coded with 1–21 to 25 years old, 2–26–30 years old, 3–31 to 35 years old, 4–36–40 years old, 5–41 to 45 years old, 6–46–50 years old, 7–51 to 55 years old, 8–56 to 60 years old, 9–61 to 65 years old, 10–66 to 70 years old, and 11–More than 70 years old

[b]Gender is dummy coded with 0 representing males and 1 representing females

[c]Marital Status is dummy coded with 0 representing not married and 1 representing married

[d]People manager is dummy coded with 0 represening not a people manager and 1 representing people manager. $n = 169$. $^{*}p < 0.05$; $^{**}p < 0.01$, $^{***}p < 0.001$

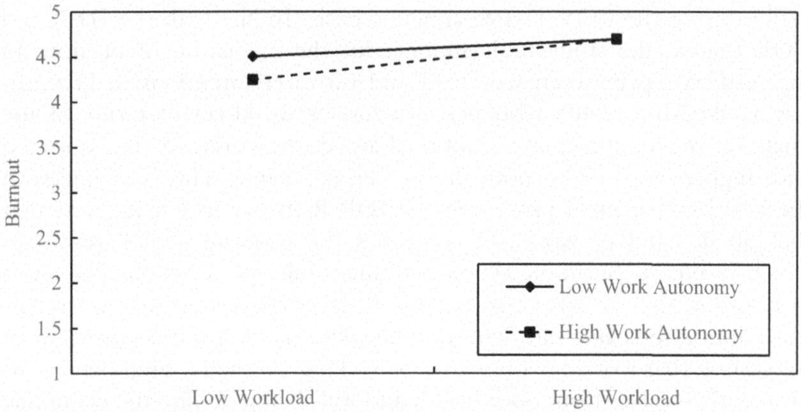

Fig. 12.1 Interaction plots of workload and work autonomy on burnout

= 0.16, Boot*SE* = 0.08, BootCI [0.0311, 0.3463]). However, the conditional indirect effect is significantly stronger (Contrast Index = 0.22, Boot*SE* = 0.12, BootCI [0.0179, 0.4881]) when participants rate having higher work autonomy (+1 SD) (Index = 0.39, Boot*SE* = 0.14, BootCI [0.1419, 0.6684]) in contrast to Hypothesis 2a. To further interpret this effect, a simple slope analysis is conducted (Aiken & West, 1991) and the results of the interaction are plotted in Fig. 12.1.

From Fig. 12.1, the simple slope analysis suggests that when participants rate having lower work autonomy (− 1 SD), the relationship between workload and burnout is positive and significant (B = 0.14, SE = 0.06, $t(165)$ = 2.167, p = 0.032) However, when participants rated having higher work autonomy (+1 SD), the relationship between workload and burnout appears stronger (B = 0.32, SE = 0.06, $t(165)$ = 5.719, $p < 0.001$) in contrast to Hypothesis 2a. Thus, Hypothesis 2a and Hypothesis 2b are not supported.

12.5 Discussion

This study empirically investigates the mediation of burnout on the relationship between the job demand of workload and turnover intentions and the first-stage dual moderated mediation of two job resources of work autonomy and supervisor support on working adults in Singapore while

WFH during the COVID-19 pandemic crisis. In line with the JD-R and COR theory, the study finds support for the mediation of burnout in the relationship between workload and turnover intentions in Hypothesis 1. Working adults who perceive higher workload in terms of the quantitative, cognitive, and emotional aspects of workload are associated with higher levels of burnout during the pandemic. This is in line with the health-impairment process in the JDR-R theory which suggests that the job demand of workload consumes the working adults' resources which results in burnout. When working adults perceived higher levels of burnout, they are also associated with higher levels of turnover intentions during the pandemic. This is in line with the desperation principle in suggesting that working adults may be seeking alternative employment to protect themselves from poor health and well-being despite the economic uncertainty.

Interestingly, there is only one moderated mediation for work autonomy but it is in the opposite direction of Hypothesis 2a. Among working adults who perceive higher work autonomy during the pandemic, workload is more positively related to burnout which, in turn, is positively related to turnover intentions as compared to working adults who perceived lower work autonomy. While the hypothesis is not supported in the proposed direction, the interaction plot in Fig. 12.1 does suggest that work autonomy may still buffer the relationship between workload and burnout but only at lower levels of workload. This may indicate that work autonomy can be a job resource that buffers the relationship between workload and burnout when employees view work to be manageable. The failure to find support for the proposed direction for this hypothesis may also be due to a ceiling effect. The ratings of burnout are close to the upper limit of the rating scale among employees who perceive lower work autonomy. Note that this data was collected when the pandemic was already into its 18th month and participants have already endured another lockdown in Singapore. At that juncture, working adults who perceived lower work autonomy may find work to be overwhelming having to again deal with challenges of mandatory WFH requirements such as increased work pressures, cognitive, and emotional aspects of work. In line with the health-impairment process in JD-R theory, the occurrence of another lockdown in a long-drawn battle against COVID-19 pandemic may have pushed them towards their limits.

The study did not support the moderated mediation for supervisor support in Hypothesis 2b. As representatives of the organisation, supervisors can rally resources and provide care and concern to their subordinate especially during times of crisis such as the pandemic. However, the results did not indicate any significant conditional indirect effects for supervisor support. There can be several possible reasons. One possible reason can be that supervisors may not provide adequate support. Supervisors face the same predicament as their subordinates and may also be overwhelmed at this stage of the pandemic given the added responsibility to look after their subordinates. Past study suggests that managing virtually has its challenges (Birchall & Giambona, 2008). This might become more acute when supervisors must manage virtually during another lockdown and thus may also limit their care and concern for their employees to protect their own health and well-being in line with COR theory. Another possible reason can be that supervisor support may not be perceived to be crucial at this stage of the pandemic as compared to the beginning. Since these participants have endured more than 18 months of the pandemic, organisational policies and procedures regarding resources and routines during this crisis may have been more established. Therefore, subordinates may be aware of the expectations required of them at this stage of the pandemic.

Limitations

However, there are several limitations for this study. CMV can threaten the validity of this study's results due to the self reported cross-sectional design. However, this threat is likely to be minimal. First, CMV is not found to be significant using the comprehensive CFA marker technique (Williams et al., 2010). The observed conditional indirect effect also suggests that this result as an artefact of CMV is less likely (Siemsen et al., 2010). Convenience sampling and self-selection bias also reduce the ability to generalise the results to a wider population. In this study, the percentage of females are oversampled, hence this result may not generalise to males in Singapore. Also, given the cross-sectional design of the study, casuality cannot be established. However, given that the COVID-19 pandemic is over, other studies conducted during that period may support the results of this study as it will be difficult to imitate the intense work conditions of the pandemic in future research.

Implications and Recommendations

There are some implications for human resource management. First, the study suggests that people may still have intentions to quit when they face higher workloads and burnout even when the future economic conditions are uncertain or gloomy. Recent media report suggests that resignations have increased towards the tail end of the COVID-19 pandemic (Morgan, 2022). Given that past meta-analysis has shown that turnover intentions is the strongest predictor of actual turnovers (Griffeth et al., 2000), management are reminded to pay attention to the work demands on their people. When workload becomes overwhelming, employees will seek alternative employments even when the economic outlook and job market are bleak. The phenomenon of the Great Resignation reiterates this finding that management should take care of their people or risks losing their talents when a crisis is over (Fuller & Kerr, 2022). Thus, managers need to be cognisant of their employees' working conditions, especially their work demands and work stress. During a crisis, managers should consistently monitor the work demands and work stress of their employees either through regular meetings or through regular measurements using employee pulse surveys so that early interventions can help reduce turnovers.

Second, the role of supervisor support buffering the relationship between workload and turnover intentions through burnout was not supported in this study. However, recent meta-analysis has supported the role of supervisor support in the development of burnout (Aronsson et al., 2017), although this effect size is smaller as compared to work autonomy. This suggests that limitations or boundary conditions exist in the relationship between supervisor support and burnout. One boundary condition can be temporal. The study did not find support for supervisor support at the later stage of the pandemic for working adults who are required to WFH in Singapore but supervisor support may be more critical at crucial earlier stages of the crisis. Another boundary condition can be spatial. Both supervisors and subordinates are physically distant from their workplace and each other. While employees may feel that their supervisor provides support, the physical distance and perhaps psychological distance may have diluted the impact of the supervisor support. This physical distance can also be helpful when employees face unsupportive supervisors based on a recent study on telecommuting where the amount of telecommuting boost job performance only when there was low supervisor support (Golden & Gajendran, 2019). Testing these boundary conditions can provide interesting and important future research directions.

Lastly, the study suggests that not all job resources buffer the health-impairment process equally during a crisis such as the COVID-19 pandemic. Comparing the two important job resources that were highlighted in past research, work autonomy but not supervisor support buffers the health-impairment process between workload and turnover intentions through burnout but only when working adults who are required to WFH in Singapore perceived higher work autonomy and at lower levels of workload (i.e. manageable workload) during this stage of the pandemic in this study. Managers should not be too quick to jump to conclusion that their support for their employees can always alleviate their employees' burnout. This study's finding suggests that employees may value work autonomy more especially when they are required to WFH during a crisis where the boundaries between work and home are blurred and the flexibility in how, when, and where one works matters more. Perhaps, giving employees autonomy may just be the space they appreciate most from their managers when faced with similar situations brought about by the COVID-19 pandemic.

Acknowledgements The author would like to thank Tan Hui Shan, Felicia Ley, and Sharalyn Ng for their efforts in the collection of the data.

References

Aiken, L. S., & West, S. G. (1991). *Multiple regression: Testing and interpreting interactions*. Sage Publications, Inc.

Ang, J. (2020, April 8). Parents struggle to juggle working from home and supervising kids' home-based learning amid Covid-19 crisis. *The Straits Times*. https://www.straitstimes.com/singapore/juggling-working-from-home-and-supervising-kids-home-based-learning-is-a-struggle-for-some

Aronsson, G., Theorell, T., Grape, T., Hammarström, A., Hogstedt, C., Marteinsdottir, I., Skoog, I., Träskman-Bendz, L., & Hall, C. (2017). A systematic review including meta-analysis of work environment and burnout symptoms. *BMC Public Health*, *17*, 264–277. https://doi.org/10.1186/s12889-017-4153-7

Avanzi, L., Fraccaroli, F., Castelli, L., Marcionetti, J., Crescentini, A., Balducci, C., & van Dick, R. (2018). How to mobilze social support against workload

and burnout: The role of organizational identification. *Teaching and Teacher Education*, *69*, 154–167. https://doi.org/10.1016/j.tate.2017.10.001
Bakker, A. B., & Demerouti, E. (2017). Job demands-resources theory: Taking stock and looking forward. *Journal of Occupational Health Psychology*, *22*(3), 273–285. https://doi.org/10.1037/ocp0000056
Bakker, A. B., Demerouti, E., & Sanz-Vergel, A. (2023). Job demands-resources theory: Ten years later. *Annual Review of Organizational Psychology and Organizational Behavior*, *10*, 25–53. https://doi.org/10.1146/annurev-orgpsych-120920-053933
Baruch-Feldman, C., Brondolo, E., Ben-Dayan, D., & Schwartz, J. (2002). Sources of social support and burnout, job satisfaction, and productivity. *Journal of Occupational Health Psychology*, *7*(1), 84–93. https://doi.org/https://doi.org/10.1037/1076-8998.7.1.84
Bentley, T. A., Teo, S. T. T., McLeod, L., Tan, F., Bosua, R., & Gloet, M. (2016). The role of orgaisational support in teleworker wellbeing: A socio-technical systems approach. *Applied Ergonomics*, *52*, 207–215. https://doi.org/10.1016/j.apergo.2015.07.019
Biernacki, P., & Waldorf, D. (1981). Snowball sampling: Problems and techniques of chain referral sampling. *Sociological Methods & Research*, *10*(2), 141–163. https://doi.org/10.1177/004912418101000205
Birchall, D. W., & Giambona, G. (2008). The impact of ICT on the work patterns of managers and their organisations. *EuroMed Journal of Business*, *3*(3), 244–262. https://doi.org/10.1108/14502190810906428
Cacioppo, J. T., Hawkley, L. C., Ernst, J. M., Burleson, M., Bernston, G. G., Nouriani, B., & Spiegel, D. (2006). Loneliness with a nomological net: An evolutionary perspective. *Journal of Research in Personality*, *40*(6), 1054–1085. https://doi.org/10.1016/j.jrp.2005.11.007
Cai, C. (2021, February 6). I quit without a new job despite the Covid-19 pandemic, and I'm not alone. *Asiaone*. https://www.asiaone.com/lifestyle/i-quit-without-new-job-despite-covid-19-pandemic-and-im-not-alone
Chee, K. (2021, May 24). Rising digital workloads contributing to worker burnout in S'pore. *The Straits Times*. https://www.straitstimes.com/tech/tech-news/rising-digital-workloads-contributing-to-worker burnout
Demerouti, E., & Bakker, A. B. (2022). Job demands-resources theory in times of crises: New propositions. *Organizational Psychology Review*, *0*(0), 1–28. https://doi.org/10.1177/20413866221135022
Demerouti, E., Bakker, A. B., Nachreiner, F., & Schaufeli, W. B. (2001). The job demands-resources model of burnout. *Journal of Applied Psychology*, *86*(3), 499–512. https://doi.org/10.1037/0021-9010.86.3.499
Demerouti, E., Mostert, K., & Bakker, A. B. (2010). Burnout and work engagement: A thorough investigation of the independency of both constructs.

Journal of Occupational Health Psychology, *15*(3), 209–222. https://doi.org/10.1037/a0019408

Eisenberger, R., Stinglhamber, F., Vandenberghe, C., Sucharski, I. L., & Rhoades, L. (2002). Perceived supervisor support: Contributions to perceived organizational support and employee retentiion. *Journal of Applied Psychology*, *87*(3), 565–573. https://doi.org/10.1037/0021-9010.87.3.565

Estes, S. (2015). The workload curve: Subjective mental workload. *Human Factors*, *57*(7), 1174–1187. https://doi-org.suss.remotexs.co/10.1177/0018720815592752

Foucault, M., & Galasso, V. (2020). Working during VOID-19: Cross-country evidence from real-time survey data. In OECD (Ed.), *OECD Social, Employment and Migration Working Papers*. Paris, France.

Fuller, J. B., & Kerr, W. R. (2022). The great resignation didn't start with the pandemic. *Harvard Busines Review*. https://hbr.org/2022/03/the-great-resignation-didnt-start-with-the-pandemic

Golden, T. D., & Gajendran, R. S. (2019). Unpacking the role of telecommuter's job in their performance: Examining job complexity, problem solving, interdependence, and social support. *Journal of Business and Psychology*, *34*, 55–69. https://doi.org/10.1007/s10869-018-9530-4

Griffeth, R. W., Hom, P. W., & Gaertner, S. (2000). A meta-analysis of antecedents and correlates of employee turnover: Update, moderator tests, and research implications for the next millennium. *Journal of Management*, *26*(3), 463–488. https://doi.org/10.1177/014920630002600

Hammond, J., Harvey, C. M., & Koubek, R. J. (2000). Effect of communication medium on virtual design teams' workload. *Proceedings of the Human Factor and Ergonomics Society Annual Meeting*, *44*(1), 77–80. https://doi.org/10.1177/154193120004400121

Hansung, K., & Stoner, M. (2008). Burnout and turnover intention among social workers: Effects of role stres, job autonomy and social support. *Administration in Social Work*, *32*(3), 5–25. https://doi.org/10.1080/03643100801922357

Hart, S. G., & Staveland, L. E. (1988). Development of NASA-TLX (Task Load Index): Results of empirical and theoretical research. In P. A. Hancock & N. Meshkati (Eds.), *Human mental workload* (pp. 139–183). Elsevier Science Publishers B.V. (North-Holland).

Hayes, A. F. (2022). *Introduction to mediation, moderation, and conditional process analysis* (3rd ed.). Guilford Press.

Hobfoll, S. E., Halbesleben, J., Neveu, J.-P., & Westman, M. (2018). Conservation of resources in the organizational context: The reality of resources and their consequences. *Annual Review of Organizational Psychology and Organizational Behavior*, *5*, 103–1028. https://doi.org/10.1146/annurev-orgpsych-032117-104640

Hom, P. W., & Griffeth, R. W. (1991). Structural equations modeling test of a turnover theory: Cross-sectional and longitudinal analyses. *Journal of Applied Psychology*, *76*(3), 350–366. https://doi.org/10.1037/0021-9010.76.3.350

Jacobs, K., Hellman, M., Markowitz, J., & Wuest, E. (2013). Workload. In M. D. Gellman & J. R. Turner (Eds.), *Encyclopedia of behavioral medicine* (pp. 2068–2069). Springer. https://doi.org/10.1007/978-1-4419-1005-9_934

Karasek, R., G., G., Pietrokovsky, C., Frese, M., Pieper, C., Schwartz, J., Fry, L., & Schirer, D. (1985). *Job content instrument: Questionnaire and user's gudie*. Unviersity of Southern California, Department of Industrial and Systems Engineering.

Kim, H., Mattson, L. D., Zhang, D., & Cho, H. J. (2022). The role of organizational and supervisor support in young adult workers' resilience, efficacy and burnout during the COVID-19 pandemic. *Journal of Applied Communnication Research*, *50*(6), 691–710. https://doi.org/10.1080/00909882.2022.2141070

Kniffin, K., Narayanan, J., Anseel, F., Antonakis, J., Ashford, S. P., Bakker, A. B., & Johns, G. et al. (2021). COVID-19 and the workplace: Implications, issues, and insights for future research and action. *American Psychologist*, *76*(1), 63–77. https://doi.org/10.1037/amp0000716

Kossek, E. E., Lautsch, B. A., & Eaton, S. C. (2008). "Good tele-working": Under what conditions does teleworking enhance employees' well-being. In Y. Amichai-Hamburger (Ed.), *Technology and psychological well-being* (pp. 148–173). Cambridge University Press. https://doi.org/10.1017/CBO9780511635373.007

Lequeurre, J., Gillet, N., Ragot, C., & Fouquereau, E. (2013). Validation of a French questionnaire to measure job demands and resources. *Revue Internationale De Psychologie Sociale*, *26*(4), 93–124.

Little, T. D., Rhemtulla, M., Gibson, K., & Schoemann, A. M. (2013). Why the items versus parcels controversy needn't be one. *Psychological Methods*, *18*(3), 285–399. https://doi.org/10.1037/a0033266

Lu, A. C. C., & Gursoy, D. (2016). Impact of job burnout on satisfaction and turnover intention: Do generationaal differences matter? *Journal of Hospitality & Tourism Research*, *40*(2), 210–235. https://doi.org/10.1177/1096348013495696

Microsoft. (2021). *2021 Work Trend Index: Annual Report*. Microsoft.

Ministry of Trade and Industry. (n.d.). *Industry transformation map overview*. Retrieved 16 June, 2023 from https://www.mti.gov.sg/ITMs/Overview

Morgan, K. (2022). The great resignation was triggered by the pandemic - so why aren't resignations slowing down now as it wanes? *BBC*. https://www.bbc.com/worklife/article/20220817-why-workers-just-wont-stop-quitting

Morgeson, F. P., & Humprey, S. E. (2006). The work design questionnaire (WDQ): Developing and validating a comprehensive measure for assessing job design and the nature of work. *Journal of Applied Psychology, 91*(6), 1321–1339. https://doi.org/10.1037/0021-9010.91.6.1321

Netemeyer, R. G., Boles, J. S., & McMurrian, R. (1996). Development and validation of work-family conflict and family-work conflict scales. *Journal of Applied Psychology, 81*(4), 400–410. https://doi.org/10.1037/0021-9010.81.4.400

Osborne, H. (2021, February 4). Home workers putting in more hours since Covid, research shows. *The Guardian*. https://www.theguardian.com/business/2021/feb/04/home-workers-putting-in-more-hours-since-covid-research

Perry, S. J., Rubino, C., & Hunter, E. M. (2018). Stress in remote work: Two studies testing the demand-control-person model. *European Journal of Work and Orgnizational Psychology, 27*(5), 577–593. https://doi.org/10.1080/1359432X.2018.1487402

Ramarajan, L., & Reid, E. (2013). Shattering the myth of separate worlds: Negotiating nonwork identities at work. *Academy of Management Review, 38*(4), 621–644. https://doi.org/10.5465/amr.2011.0314

Schaufeli, W. B., Bakker, A. B., & Salanova, M. (2006). The measurement of work engagement with a short questionnaire: A cross-national study. *Educational and Psychological Measurements, 66*(4), 701–716. https://doi.org/10.1177/0013164405282471

Siemsen, E., Roth, A., & Oliveira, P. (2010). Common method bias in regression models with linear, quadratic, interaction effects. *Organizational Research Methods, 13*(3), 456–476. https://doi.org/10.1177/1094428109351241

Thrassou, A., Uzunboylu, N., Efthymiou, L., Vrontis, D., Weber, Y., Riad Shams, S.M. & Tsoukatos, E. (2022b). Editorial Introduction: Business Under Crises: Organizational Adaptations. In D. Vrontis, A. Thrassou, Y. Weber, S. M. R. Shams, E. Tsoukatos, & L. Efthymiou, L. (Eds.), *Business under crisis, Volume II: Organisational adaptations*. Palgrave Studies in Cross-disciplinary Business Research, In Association with EuroMed Academy of Business. Palgrave Macmillan, Cham. https://doi.org/10.1007/978-3-030-76575-0_1

Vrontis, D., Thrassou, A., Efthymiou, L., Weber, Y. Shams, SMR, Tsoukatos, E. (2023a). *Business for sustainability, volume I: Strategic avenues and managerial approaches,* Springer Nature.

Vrontis, D., Thrassou, A., Uzunboylu, N., Efthymiou, L. (2023b). An overview of business for sustainability: Strategic avenues and managerial approaches. In D. Vrontis, A. Thrassou, L. Efthymiou, Y. Weber, S. M. R. Shams, & E. Tsoukatos (Eds.), *Business for sustainability, volume I*. Palgrave Studies in Cross-disciplinary Business Research, In Association with EuroMed Academy of Business. Palgrave Macmillan. https://doi.org/10.1007/978-3-031-37361-9_1

van der Doef, M., & Maes, S. (1999). The Leiden Quality of Work Questionnaire: Its construction, factor structure, and psychometric qualities. *Psychological Reports*, *85*(3), 954–962. https://doi.org/10.2466/pr0.1999.85.3.954

Wang, B., Liu, Y., Qian, J., & Parker, S. K. (2021). Achieving effective remote working during the COVID-19 pandemic: A work design perspective. *Applied Psychology: An International Review*, *70*(1), 16–59. https://doi.org/10.1111/apps.12290

Williams, L. J., Hartman, N., & Cavazotte, F. (2010). Method variance and marker variables: A review and comprehensive CFA marker technique. *Organizational Research Methods*, *13*(3), 477–514. https://doi.org/10.1177/1094428110366036

World Bank. (2020). COVID-19 to plunge global economy into worse recession since World War II. https://www.worldbank.org/en/news/press-release/2020/06/08/covid-19-to-plunge-global-economy-into-worst-recession-since-world-war-ii

Yang, C. (2022, January 24). Overworked in S'pore: Study shows one in two logs extra hours since Covid-19 pandemic started. *The Straits Times*. https://www.straitstimes.com/singapore/jobs/overworked-in-spore-one-in-two-works-extra-hours-daily-since-covid-19-pandemic-started

Zhang, S. X., & Kowalczuk, K. (2023). New evidence on psychological impacts and consequences of COVID-19 on mental workload healthcare workers in diverse regions in the world. *Frontiers in Psychiatry*, *14*. https://doi.org/10.3389/fpsyt.2023.1226793

CHAPTER 13

Crowdsourcing in Management Studies: A Systematic Literature Review

Niccolò Fiorini, Valerio Natale, Alberto Massacci, and Tommaso Pucci

13.1 Introduction

The introduction of new technologies and, above all, the changes in the technological paradigm have always prompted management scholars to question themselves about the changes that these phenomena produce on the way of doing business (especially in terms of effectiveness and efficiency: the possibility of new processes, improvements, performances, etc.). In the wake of the importance of the fourth industrial revolution and the digitization processes that companies are going through, this work questions how a specific aspect considered in Industry 4.0 has been studied and analysed in the past years. More specifically, given the importance that platforms have assumed in society and particularly in business, we believe it is appealing to examine how the growth of this technology

N. Fiorini (✉) · V. Natale · A. Massacci · T. Pucci
Department of Business and Law, University of Siena, Siena, Italy
e-mail: niccolo.fiorini@unisi.it

D. Vrontis et al. (eds.), *Business in Uncertainty*, Palgrave Studies in Cross-disciplinary Business Research, In Association with EuroMed Academy of Business, https://doi.org/10.1007/978-3-031-65587-6_13

has affected innovation and problem-solving solutions through crowdsourcing. As a matter of fact, crowdsourcing involves, and it is made possible by a well-functioning and coordinated system which involves several business operations and actors which has strongly benefited from the advancement of technologies. The purpose of this research is twofold: to record the development of the works related to crowdsourcing and to propose new potential directions for future research.

The debate about crowdsourcing in all areas of business management (management, marketing, accounting, finance) has been present for many years, concerning many aspects and taking place in different ways. Already 20 years ago, Patterson et al. (2003) say that technology changes almost every day and its applications in business as well, the companies need to adopt these new technologies in many areas of the business to avoid the loss of competitive advantage.

This debate has had a dividing line with the advent of Industry 4.0 (Peter & Mbohwa, 2018): a paradigm that, in fact, uses technologies that existed previously.

With the advent of Industry 4.0, studies regarding new technologies in management have multiplied (Buhalis et al., 2024). One of the most important articles about the topic says that, after the creation of IoT, governments and companies will launch an evolutionary journey (Shrouf et al., 2014). It predicts that industrial production of the new era will be highly flexible, and it consists of extensive integration between customers, companies, and suppliers, and above all sustainable (Vrontis et al., 2023, 2024).

However, all this debate always focused on the use and impact of new technologies in companies. For example, Flavian et al. (2019) analysed the impact on the customer experience; Guo and Liang (2016) analysed the impact in the banking industry and Zhu et al. (2012) analysed the managerial applications in different industries. New technologies and paradigms are not only changing how companies are managed and their strategies, but also relations and collaborations between them (Messeni Petruzzelli et al., 2022). Furthermore, firms' relations and technologies adoption and related effects also influence industrial districts (Fiorini et al., 2023).

Consistent with the growing attention towards the 4.0 paradigm, the importance of crowdsourcing has also increased over the last decade, starting as early as the 2010s (Afuah & Tucci, 2012; Stieger et al., 2012) and becoming more relevant in recent years, as also highlighted in recent reviews of the literature that have focused on specific aspects related to the topic, such as in the case of Ataur Rahman and Masudur Rahman (2023) who analysed the impact of crowdsourcing in formal organisations.

Therefore, when talking about new technologies in the last years, many works enlighten the importance and the role of crowdsourcing in both capturing and creating value, for the company, for the users, and for all the players in general (Brem et al., 2023).

13.2 Literature Review

Many studies focus their attention on how interactions between companies have changed with the development of crowdsourcing and the benefits that derive from it. The first author using the term crowdsourcing was Howe (2006a, 2006b, 2008) as a new word deriving from outsourcing and crowd. There are many studies that link crowdsourcing to open innovation. Among the most recent literature reviews in this field, we find the research published in 2022 by Cricelli et al.. In their work, the authors analysed the scientific production connecting open innovation and crowdsourcing. In addition to the findings of Cricelli et al. (2022), several studies have investigated similar topics. The work by Liu et al. (2018) proposes a review on the concepts, mechanisms, and interactions between players concerning open innovation. They provide an interpretation of the "value co-creation mechanism of idea generation", and they identify three types of crowdsourcing: Cooperative crowdsourcing, Competitive crowdsourcing, and Candidate crowdsourcing. Moreover, they suggested considering the perspective of value co-creation for future academic works.

Another interesting literature review is the one published by Ghezzi et al. (2018), which represents one of the first systematic reviews published in management journals. They pointed out that crowdsourcing can not only be related to open innovation, but also, as mentioned in many studies they cited, as a co-creation support tool. Through an Input-Process-Output framework, they identified the existent (in 2018) research, and they identified important aspects to be considered: the scenario and the field in which crowdsourcing can be applied; the required skills and capabilities to succeed, as well as the rules and policies involved in the process. Finally, they point their attention to the possible frictions that may emerge during the crowdsourcing process.

Few years after the introduction of the term crowdsourcing, the academic debate has moved on to the less traditional aspects that derive from it. Afuah and Tucci (2012) focused their attention on the use of crowdsourcing as an alternative process for problem solving, exploiting the capabilities of individuals outside the firm's boundaries. Moreover, crowdsourcing has been proven to be of great importance in marketing, too. Gassenheimer et al. (2013) pointed out that the research interest in this topic can encompass various aspects: design choice, creation of promotions, price choice, and offer testing.

The systematic review carried out by Maroufkhani et al. (2018) is more wide-ranging. Although the study does not specifically tackle crowdsourcing, it represents a fundamental element of the entrepreneurial ecosystem. Indeed, crowdsourcing is therefore very much linked to the creation, and to the very existence, of ecosystems and collaborative networks even between the companies themselves.

In the wake of reviews that propose analyses related to value creation, it is also interesting to mention the work published in 2020 by Pavlidou et al. Their paper identifies 4 main themes related to crowdsourcing: innovation, performance, operational aspects, and motivation. In addition, the authors also propose notions for managers and practitioners to organise a successful crowdsourcing project.

Some authors, on the other hand, analyse crowdsourcing from aspects that, although linked to management, are less oriented to business studies. As an example, Kamel Boulos et al. (2011) analyse the effects of crowdsourcing in the geographical context and, specifically, for public and environmental health surveillance and crisis management.

Richter (2015) reports in his study some academic works in which he emphasises the increase in efficiency and effectiveness related to crowdsourcing in the processes of: idea creation, draft design, and procedure creation. In this way, according to the work analysed in the review, it is possible to reduce costs thanks to the use of a global workforce.

Although crowdsourcing is often linked to connections between different firms, or between companies and consumers and, more generally, to network dynamics, Stieger et al. (2012) instead focus their study on the applications of crowdsourcing within companies.

Finally, after the large debate on the various impacts of crowdsourcing as a system, there is a stream of studies that have focused their attention on specific aspects or fields related to it.

Interest in crowdsourcing platforms has been particularly relevant in recent years. A study conducted by Humayun et al. in 2023 reviews the literature on motivation to participate in crowdsourcing activities, also considering the role of platforms in increasing motivation in crowd participation. Platforms and open collaborative projects are also used for scientific collaborations (Franzoni & Sauermann, 2014). Interest about crowdsourcing and science has been pointed out also by Beck et al. (2022) in their study about crowd-generated research questions. Love and Hirschheim (2017) analyse crowdsourcing in the field of information systems. In this context, crowdsourcing plays a key role in technology-mediated mass collaboration. Alnaggar et al. (2021), as part of their operations research, carried out a review of the literature focusing on the use of crowdsourcing in logistics, also providing a classification of the platforms that allow matching and therefore the efficiency of delivery.

Although there have been many studies that, over the last few years, have analysed crowdsourcing from various research perspective, without neglecting managerial repercussions, the aim of this research is to propose an analysis of the literature that proposes an holistic analysis of the academic contributions in the major journals of business and management in order to identify the macro-themes studied so far and to propose some hints for future research directions. In fact, from the analysis of the existing reviews in the field of business and management, and accounting we noticed the need to propose an up-to-date review of the literature on crowdsourcing that proposed a bibliometric and systematic analysis.

13.3 Research Design

As for many studies with similar purposes, we decided to use the bibliometric analysis (e.g. Casprini et al., 2020) and a systematic literature review (REF). We are interested in analysing the research about crowdsourcing that has been published so far in the field of Management. We used the bibliographic coupling analysis and performed it throughout VOSviewer 1.6.20 software (Van Eck & Waltman, 2010).

SCOPUS has been chosen as the database, choosing "Crowdsourcing" as the keyword to perform the extraction from the database. We included contributions (articles and reviews) in the English language from 2006 to 2022. In this way, we were sure that we covered the fourth industrial revolution whose birth is traced back to 2011 (Kagermann, 2013), since it includes crowdsourcing within the examined technologies (Bonaccorsi et al., 2020). We have considered 5 more years because some technologies were already being used. At first, we limited our analysis to the business journals according to Scopus database and, therefore, the query entered in the database was the following:

> TITLE-ABS-KEY ("crowdsourcing") AND PUBYEAR > 2005 AND PUBYEAR < 2023 AND (LIMIT-TO (SUBJAREA, "BUSI")) AND (LIMIT-TO (DOCTYPE, "ar") OR LIMIT-TO (DOCTYPE, "re")) AND (LIMIT-TO (LANGUAGE, "English"))

We, first, obtained a total of 1,107 documents, with 39.164 total citations. We then restricted the analysis to top journals of management and strategy identified as 4* ranked by the Academic Journal Guide-ABS 2021: Academy of Management Annals; Academy of Management Journal; Academy of Management Review; Administrative Science Quarterly; Journal of Management; Journal of International Business Studies; Research Policy; Journal of Consumer Psychology; Journal of Consumer Research; Journal of Marketing; Journal of Marketing Research; Journal of the; Academy of Marketing Science; Marketing Science; Journal of Operations Management; Management Science; Operations Research; Organization Science; Strategic Management Journal. Furthermore, we decided to include Journal of Management Studies which, despite being ranked 4, appears to the authors to be an essential journal in the management debate. The number of documents obtained after this restriction was 78, while citations were 6,424.

Finally, we manually screened the articles, selecting those consistent with our research goal. The final number of documents obtained after this step was 54, while the overall number of citations was 5,360.

13.4 Presentation and Analysis of Findings/ Results

We then proceeded to perform a bibliometric analysis in order to have an initial overview of the topics covered in the articles of the database, before proceeding with the systematic analysis by examining the details of all of them. The first analysis performed with the software showed that all the 54 articles were bibliographically connected to each other.

Starting from the sources, we found that some journals published a relevant number or paper; Research Policy (14 papers, representing 25,9%

of the share) and Management Science (12 papers, representing 22,2% of the share) published almost half of the paper in our analysis. Other articles have been published in various journals, among them it is worthy to mention: Journal of Marketing (4 publications); Journal of Marketing Research (4 publications); Journal of Operations Management (4 publications); Organization Science (4 publications); Academy of Management Review (3 publications).

We found a similar result by analysing the citations in the articles of each journal: more than half of the total citations were in the two mentioned journals and Academy of Management Review. The citations were divided as following: Management Science (1212 citations, representing 22,6% of the share); Research Policy (982 citations, representing 18,4% of the share) and Academy of Management Review (930 citations, representing 17,4% of the share). Other journals with a relevant number of citations are: Marketing Science (405 citations); Organization Science (393 citations); Academy of Management Journal (384 citations); Journal of Consumer Research (355 citations); Journal of Marketing (173 citations); Journal of Marketing Research (159 citations); Journal of Operations Management (146 citations); Journal of Management Studies (132 citations).

We subsequently analysed the number of publications per year, obtaining the following result: the majority of publications (29, representing 53,7% of the share) were made starting from 2019 and the first publication on the topic dates back to 2011. This is the complete result: 1 publication in 2011; 2 publications in 2012; 4 in 2013, 2014, and 2015; 2 publications in 2016; 4 publications in 2017, and 2018; 9 publications in 2019; 4 in 2020; 6 in 2021; 10 in 2022.

After these first descriptive analyses, we made use of aforementioned software for performing the Authors' Countries Bibliographic Coupling, the Author keywords Co-occurrence and, above all, the Documents Bibliographic Coupling for clustering documents in thematic groups.

Authors' Countries Bibliographic Coupling analysis is a bibliometric analysis technique that examines, based on the shared references in the publications, the scholars' collaboration patterns among authors emphasises their country of provenance (Van Eck & Waltman, 2010). This was useful to explore the collaborative networks across different countries within the academic literature of our topic. For doing this, we set the software with a full counting method and these thresholds: 1 as the minimum of documents for a country and 1 as the minimum number of citations for a country, obtaining 16 countries. The countries were grouped in five clusters: the first, very heterogeneous, included the United States (at least one author in 32 articles, representing 59.2% of the share), China (authors involved in 4 articles), Canada (authors involved in 2 articles), and New Zealand (authors involved in 1 article); the second was Northern European with Germany (authors involved in 9 articles), Austria (authors involved in 3 articles), and Denmark (authors involved in 2 articles); the third one included two Commonwealth countries, UK (authors involved in 11 articles) and Australia (authors involved in 1 article) plus Israel (authors involved in 1 article), the fourth included France (authors involved in 4 articles) and South Korea (authors involved in 1 article) and the fifth the Netherlands (authors involved in 8 articles) and Spain (authors involved in 1 article). Scholars from Italy (involved in 2 articles) and Switzerland (involved in 2 articles) were, for this topic, outside international networks.

The Author keywords Co-occurrence analysis is a bibliometric technique that identifies and analyses the frequency with which specific keywords appear together in publications (the more frequently two keywords appear together, the stronger the connection between them) (Van Eck & Waltman, 2010). This method reveals associations and thematic relationships between topics or concepts. For this purpose, we set the software with a full counting method and 1 as the minimum number of occurrences of a keyword and we obtained 193 keywords. We decided to exclude the keyword "crowdsourcing", present in 36 articles, obtaining 11 as a number of keywords used in at least 3 articles. These keywords are the following: "open innovation" (13); "innovation", "creativity" and "new product development" (5); "idea generation". "problem solving" and "innovation contests" (4); "user-generated content", "citizen science", "sharing economy" and "ideation" (3). Of these 193 keywords, 167 were related to each other and were divided into 23 clusters. We then set the overlay visualisation with the purpose to see for each cluster, based on the colour, in which period it falls: we noted some older clusters (2014–2016) with keywords such as "open source", "community", "performance", "knowledge sharing", "knowledge community", "funding", "dynamic learning". Some clusters from an "middle era" (2016–2020) where we move from "open source" concept to "open innovation" concept; and keywords such as "creativity", "idea generation" and "problem solving". Finally, some clusters of the "contemporary era" (2020–2022) where they talked about "consumer empowerment", "sharing economy" and "crowd-logistics".

The last analysis we performed was the bibliographic. This analysis groups the documents on the basis of shared references (the higher the overlap between the shared sources between two works, the more likely the two articles will be allocated to the same thematic group) (Van Eck & Waltman, 2010). This helped us in clustering documents in thematic groups that emphasise the different aspects about crowdsourcing debate in management journals. The result of the analysis is shown in Fig. 13.1.

As we can see from the image, the articles were closely linked to each other based on references and the software grouped them into 6 clusters:

Cluster 1 (red) included 12 articles and we found that the main topics in this cluster are about marketing and customer engagement (in particular, consumer behaviour and perception) and the main

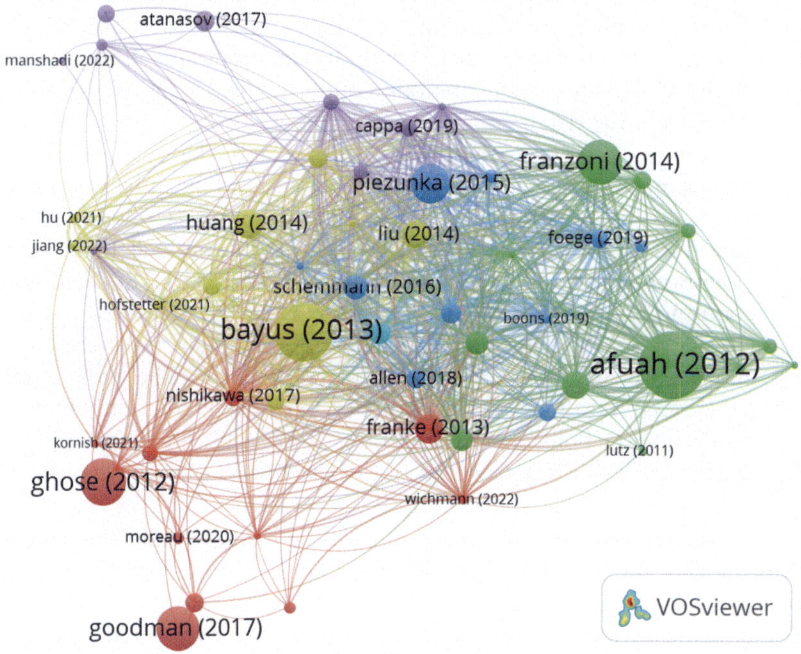

Fig. 13.1 Bibliographic coupling (*Source* Authors' own)

dimensions were firm and individual level. The most cited article is "Designing Ranking Systems for Hotels on Travel Search Engines by Mining User-Generated and Crowdsourced Content" (Ghose et al., 2012) with 403 citations and the all clusters have 1.212 citations for 22,6% of the share.

Cluster 2 (green) included 12 articles mainly about a theoretical dimension of crowdsourcing. The main dimensions analysed were at network and firm level and the period of the publications in this cluster was quite far in time (2011–2018) except for two articles that were about a debate introduced by the article of 2012 "Crowdsourcing As a Solution to Distant Search" (Afuah & Tucci, 2012), which with 826 citations was the most cited paper of the cluster and also of the all database. The whole cluster has 1.716 citations counting for 32,1% of the total database citations.

Cluster 3 (blue) included 10 articles with prevalent topics crowdsourcing for idea generation and form problem solving. The most cited article was "Distant Search, Narrow Attention: How Crowding Alters Organizations' Filtering of Suggestions in Crowdsourcing" (Piezunka & Dahlander, 2015) with 300 citations and all the papers in the cluster had 814 citations counting for 15,2% of the total citations in the database.

Cluster 4 (yellow) included 10 articles and the main topic is participants engagement, including feedback and incentives systems. The most cited article, with 636 citations was "Crowdsourcing New Product Ideas over Time: An Analysis of the Dell IdeaStorm Community" (Bayus, 2013). The whole cluster had 1.187 citations, counting for 22,1% of the total citations of our database.

Cluster 5 (purple) included 9 articles and the main topic area was about optimal method and problem recognition. The most cited paper was "Distilling the Wisdom of Crowds. Prediction Markets vs. Prediction Polls" (Atanasov et al., 2017) with 86 citations. The cluster has 340 citations (6,3% of the share).

The software created a sixth cluster which includes only the article "Motivations and solution appropriateness in crowdsourcing challenges for innovation" (Acar, 2019), which had 91 (1,7%) citations and it was bibliographically linked to all the other clusters. We considered that, for the topic, it falls within the scope of cluster 5.

From this analysis, we noted that 76.8% of the articles belong to clusters 1 + 2 + 4, namely marketing and customer engagement, participant engagement and theoretical dimension of crowdsourcing and only the small remaining part deals with crowdsourcing for idea generation and form problem-solving optimal method and problem recognition.

The intermediate conclusion we arrived at after this first analysis was that most of the articles deal, in addition to the general theoretical part of crowdsourcing in management, the concept of engagement and less how this new technology has changed management processes and theories.

As previously mentioned, the literature on crowdsourcing in the Management field has been increasing in the last 10 years. Crowdsourcing activity has been shown to provide several positive effects; however, optimal design and strategy are crucial to maximise the efficiency of the efforts generated by all the stakeholders involved in the innovation process.

While part of the analysed literature has aimed at investigating the overall utility of crowdsourcing as a form of innovation, the majority of the papers analysed in this work have been focusing on specific phases or actors of the process.

In order to provide a better understanding, we provide a framework that aims to encompass the main phases and actors involved in crowdsourcing projects.

While there is a limited body of literature examining the role of crowdsourcing in addressing community problems (Porter et al., 2020), the majority of these studies have focused on the conventional model wherein a singular actor, typically a firm, employs crowdsourcing as a tool for research and innovation. Hence, the framework we provide attempts to synthetically describe the main contributions, dividing the main results in the different phases involving the standard crowdsourcing process.

A crucial phase in any crowdsourcing project is related to the possibility of embracing a large and valid pool of contributors. We define the first phase as "engagement". Although the engagement phase is part of a unidirectional process in which the company should implement a design capable of attracting the necessary resources, the implications of these works can also prove relevant for those who undergo the process.

Once each member of the community has been engaged into the process, the validity of their contributions is affected by a huge variety of exogenous and endogenous factors. As a matter of fact, a large share of the management literature has attempted to highlight how creativity and value propositions are affected, and affect, the crowd and the seekers. We define this phase as "Source management".

Finally, once the process of idea generation is over, the whole community needs to digest the mass of value generated by the crowd and optimise its use. This phase, that we define as "exploitation", includes all the potential implications that can derive from the use of crowdsourcing as an innovation mechanism, both internally and externally.

The two main journals investigating the phase of engagement during the crowdsourcing process are "Management science", "Research Policy" and "Journal of Operations Management". The journal of Operations Management mainly tackles the role of incentives in determining the size of the crowd (Castillo et al., 2022; Liu et al., 2021). Research Policy has put more effort on how to optimally design crowdsourcing context. Pollock et al. (2019) and Foege et al. (2019) tackle the issue related to the trade-off between disclosing personal information and the quality and quantity of feedback received from the crowd. On the quality side, Martinez (2015) shows that emotional and cognitive engagement is positively correlated to creativity. Finally, Management Science is mainly devoted to comprehending the behaviour of the crowd. The experiment of Liu et al. (2014) sheds light on the aversion to competition among the best competitors when other ideas are disclosed, despite monetary incentives benefiting the average quality of the submissions. At the same time, when the crowd is allowed to provide comments on their peers' projects, bad inventors are discouraged from submitting their own ideas, providing an endogenous self-selection mechanism within the platform (Huang et al., 2014).

These results show that the engagement process is strongly dependent on multiple characteristics, some of which are in control of the firms and others that mainly depend on the population. Most of the time, the optimal design depends on the desired trade-off that should be defined as the result of a holistic analysis that considers managerial and political aspects.

In a crowdsourcing context, the engagement phase is crucial to draw on a valid user base capable of responding to the needs of the organisers. However, once the challenger pool has been established, an adequate setting is crucial to get the most out of them.

In the phase that we define as "source management" we attempt to identify the main key findings and the actions that sourcers and crowds can take to define a win–win strategy.

A stream of literature has been focusing on the relationship between performance and the idiosyncratic characteristics of the individual. The work of Boons et al. (2019) studies the relationship between background knowledge and performance; their paper shows that despite educational proximity to the task tends to over perform, a related perspective to the idea domain in the crowd is needed to achieve the best results. Acar (2019) focuses on the motivations that drive competitors' best ideas. Through a quantitative study, he shows that although intrinsic and extrinsic motivations are essential, prosocial and learning stimuli tend to lead to inadequate ideas.

Despite the prosocial motive may not be beneficial for firms in a competition, the environment is crucial to generate innovation and avoid ideas' redundancy. Bockstedt et al. (2015) show that the characteristics of the environment have an impact on the average contribution, with increasing levels of GDP reducing the effort of participants.

Indeed, a further line of research has attempted to understand the collective dynamics that are capable of fostering innovation and the actions that firms can take to positively contribute to the generation of good ideas.

Stephen et al. (2016) highlight that a high level of networking in projects with interdependent ideation tasks is likely to generate redundant ideas and low degree of innovations. Similar results were found by Hofstetter et al. (2021) where, in a field experiment, they show that displaying other competitors' ideas reduces the generation of innovative proposals. Conversely, over a long-time horizon, the possibility to learn from others improves individual performance, provided that participants are sufficiently capable of distinguishing good ideas from bad ones (Riedl et al., 2018; Schemmann et al., 2016).

Jiang et al. (2022) aim to test the role of feedback during the crowdsourcing context. They show that providing feedback in the second half of the competition seems to be the most effective strategy. On a similar focus, Camacho et al. (2019) highlight that negative feedback performs better than positive or no feedback at all; their results are proven to be valid for both the intensity and the quality of the contributions.

Further, the information disclosure, which has been said to be crucial in the engagement phase, is proven to be a critical aspect also in the second phase of the crowdsourcing process. In particular, Althuizen et al. (2022) focus on the type of invention, showing that when the seeker is looking for functional design an high level of information is important to boost the quality of the ideas but, on the other hand, it may reduce creativity and, hence, it is not preferable for aesthetic design.

Hence, the literature seems to prove that engaging the right individual only partially fulfils the complete task of achieving innovation. An adequate management of the available resources, a valid infrastructure and the right mix of competition and coopetition are needed to exploit the potential of this organisational form.

Finally, to conclude the crowdsourcing process, idea seekers need to exploit the mass of ideas generated by the crowd. Exploitation, as we have defined in the last phase, is a multi-level and multi-dimensional process that must be implemented by all company departments.

The literature has looked less deeply into this part of the process, probably assuming that it can be treated similarly to the more standard internal innovation or problem-solving processes. However, 3 main lines of research have highlighted why and how more attention should be paid to this topic.

Piezunka et al. (2019) try to understand the functioning of the management of human resources that, despite being taken from outside the usual boundaries, could contribute to the growth process over a long period of time. Regarding this, their paper shows that rejection letters strongly impact the submission of future ideas and the relation is amplified when those include explanations.

However, crowdsourcing has also been shown to provide a viable strategy to build loyalty with customers. The work of Wichmann et al. (2022) provides several insights on how traditional brands could benefit from their own platform to crowdsource and crowdsend with third parties. Because of this, they highlight the importance of designing a platform that reflects the firm's goals and strategies.

Indeed, crowdsourcing may be also exploited as a marketing tool. As a matter of fact, 20% of the literature lies in the Marketing field. Among those, Allen et al. (2018) show that design crowdsourcing is positively related to unit sales. More deeply, Nishikawa et al. (2017) find that labelling crowdsourced products can improve the performance up to 20%. However, Moreau et al. (2020) further exploit the topic and they show that consumer preferences with respect to crowdsourcing (in the form of product personalization) are inversely correlated to the brands' value.

13.5 Concluding Discussion and Recommendations

From this literature review, it is possible to draw some implications for managers and lines for future research. In Fig. 13.2, we propose a framework that comprehends all the analyses of the previous paragraph which may be useful for both practitioners and academics. The outcomes underlined in the systematic analysis (i.e. engagement, source management, and exploitation) are here disclosed together with the levels deriving from the bibliographic analysis. From this, the areas of intervention and analysis discussed in the documents of the dataset are reported. Then we individuated the topics involved (also thanks to the bibliographic coupling) to depict a comprehensive framework of analysis of the literature and the debate around crowdsourcing.

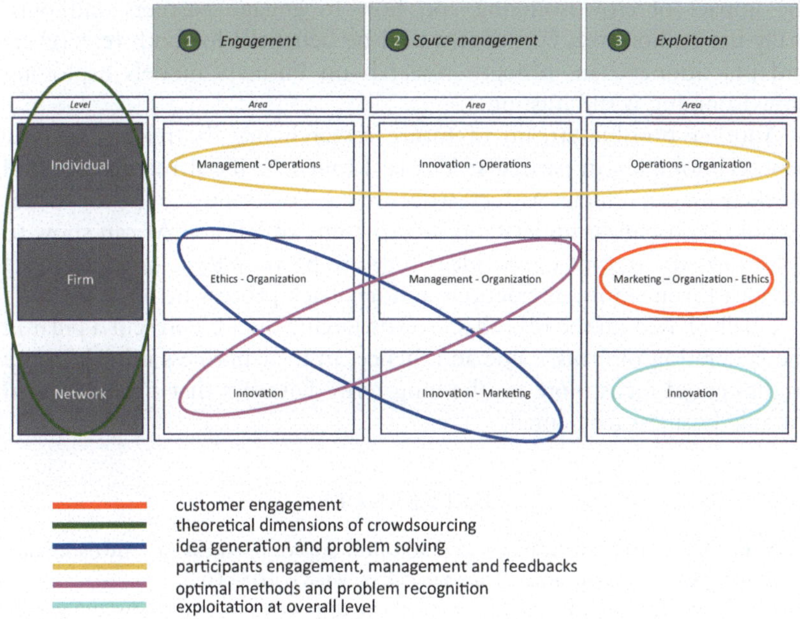

Fig. 13.2 Interpretative Framework (*Source* Authors' own)

Figure 13.2 synthesises the main areas analysed by the academic literature and, furthermore, it provides a tool for understanding and interpreting the intersections between all the levels involved in crowdsourcing and the various opportunities that arose from it. For those who are new in this field, this research can be useful to start understanding the potentialities and different uses of crowdsourcing. For managers and consultants already familiar with it, this chapter gives help for an advantageous use of crowdsourcing and the potential challenges that they may be required to face during the implementation.

Given the framework and the analysis performed, it was possible to provide academics with an immediate and effective representation of the state of the art of the academic literature. Furthermore, this allowed us to identify some hints for future research directions.

From the analysed works, there is still needed to research on the business models for incentivising crowdsourcing. Some studies analysed the impact of crowdsourcing and how to engage partners and optimally use it; however, even if it would be beneficial for both researchers and practitioners, an in-depth research on business models exploiting crowdsourcing is still missing.

Another possible stream of future research may be related to how new technologies, in particular Virtual Reality, Artificial Intelligence and blockchain, can interact with crowdsourcing. For example, we believe that it could be useful to understand how the mix of VR and AI can show to the crowd the output of the ideas they are proposing, in order to make the idea formulation, interactions and feedback process better.

Finally, based on the idea that crowdsourcing could represent a pillar in the generation of firms' value and, hence, in their business model, future studies could focus more on the long-term dynamics that a crowd-based durable business may entail.

References

Acar, O. A. (2019). Motivations and solution appropriateness in crowdsourcing challenges for innovation. *Research Policy, 48*(8), 103716.

Afuah, A., & Tucci, C. L. (2012). Crowdsourcing as a solution to distant search. *Academy of Management Review, 37*(3), 355–375.

Allen, B. J., Chandrasekaran, D., & Basuroy, S. (2018). Design crowdsourcing: The impact on new product performance of sourcing design solutions from the "crowd." *Journal of Marketing, 82*(2), 106–123.

Alnaggar, A., Gzara, F., & Bookbinder, J. H. (2021). Crowdsourced delivery: A review of platforms and academic literature. *Omega, 98*, 102139.

Ataur Rahman, M., & Masudur Rahman, M. (2023). Impact of crowdsourcing in organizations: A Systematic Literature Review (SLR) and future research directions. *Journal of Technology Management & Innovation, 18*(2), 81–90.

Althuizen, N., & Chen, B. (2022). Crowdsourcing ideas using product prototypes: The joint effect of prototype enhancement and the product design goal on idea novelty. *Management Science, 68*(4), 3008–3025.

Atanasov, P., Rescober, P., Stone, E., Swift, S. A., Servan-Schreiber, E., Tetlock, P., Ungar, L. H., & Mellers, B. (2017). Distilling the wisdom of crowds: Prediction markets vs. prediction polls. *Management Science, 63*(3), 691–706.

Bayus, B. L. (2013). Crowdsourcing new product ideas over time: An analysis of the Dell IdeaStorm community. *Management Science, 59*(1), 226–244.

Beck, S., Brasseur, T. M., Poetz, M., & Sauermann, H. (2022). Crowdsourcing research questions in science. *Research Policy, 51*(4), 104491.

Bockstedt, J., Druehl, C., & Mishra, A. (2015). Problem-solving effort and success in innovation contests: The role of national wealth and national culture. *Journal of Operations Management, 36*, 187–200.

Bonaccorsi, A., Chiarello, F., Fantoni, G., & Kammering, H. (2020). Emerging technologies and industrial leadership. A Wikipedia-based strategic analysis of Industry 4.0. *Expert Systems with Applications*, 160: 113645.

Boons, M., & Stam, D. (2019). Crowdsourcing for innovation: How related and unrelated perspectives interact to increase creative performance. *Research Policy, 48*(7), 1758–1770.

Brem, A. M., Tucci, C. L., Brown, T., & Chen, J. (2023). Guest editorial: The age of crowdsourcing and crowdfunding for technological innovation: Where we are, and where to go? *IEEE Transactions on Engineering Management, 70*(9), 3015–3020.

Buhalis, D., Efthymiou, L., Uzunboylu, N., & Thrassou, A. (2024) Charting the progress of technology adoption in tourism and hospitality in the era of industry 4.0. *Tourism & Hospitality in the Digital Era: Technology and its (im)Possibilities special issue in Euromed Journal of Business, 19*(2).

Camacho, N., Nam, H., Kannan, P. K., & Stremersch, S. (2019). Tournaments to crowdsource innovation: The role of moderator feedback and participation intensity. *Journal of Marketing, 83*(2), 138–157.

Casprini, E., Dabic, M., Kotlar, J., & Pucci, T. (2020). A bibliometric analysis of family firm internationalization research: Current themes, theoretical roots, and ways forward. *International Business Review, 29*(5), 1–18.

Castillo, V. E., Mollenkopf, D. A., Bell, J. E., & Esper, T. L. (2022). Designing technology for on-demand delivery: The effect of customer tipping on crowdsourced driver behavior and last mile performance. *Journal of Operations Management, 68*(5), 424–453.

Cricelli, L., Grimaldi, M., & Vermicelli, S. (2022). Crowdsourcing and open innovation: A systematic literature review, an integrated framework and a research agenda. *Review of Managerial Science, 16*(5), 1269–1310.

Fiorini, N., Pucci, T., Casprini, E., & Zanni, L. (2023). The actors' role in industrial districts facing the challenge of technologies 4.0 between absorption and dissemination. *European Planning Studies, 31*(7), 1377–1396.

Flavián, C., Ibáñez-Sánchez, S., & Orús, C. (2019). The impact of virtual, augmented and mixed reality technologies on the customer experience. *Journal of Business Research, 100*, 547–560.

Foege, J. N., Lauritzen, G. D., Tietze, F., & Salge, T. O. (2019). Reconceptualizing the paradox of openness: How solvers navigate sharing-protecting tensions in crowdsourcing. *Research Policy, 48*(6), 1323–1339.

Franzoni, C., & Sauermann, H. (2014). Crowd science: The organization of scientific research in open collaborative projects. *Research Policy, 43*(1), 1–20.

Frey, K., Lüthje, C., & Haag, S. (2011). Whom should firms attract to open innovation platforms? The role of knowledge diversity and motivation. *Long Range Planning, 44*(5–6), 397–420.

Gassenheimer, J. B., Siguaw, J. A., & Hunter, G. L. (2013). Exploring motivations and the capacity for business crowdsourcing. *AMS Review, 3*, 205–216.

Ghezzi, A., Gabelloni, D., Martini, A., & Natalicchio, A. (2018). Crowdsourcing: A review and suggestions for future research. *International Journal of Management Reviews, 20*(2), 343–363.

Ghose, A., Ipeirotis, P. G., & Li, B. (2012). Designing ranking systems for hotels on travel search engines by mining user-generated and crowdsourced content. *Marketing Science, 31*(3), 493–520.

Guo, Y., & Liang, C. (2016). Blockchain application and outlook in the banking industry. *Financial Innovation, 2*, 1–12.

Hofstetter, R., Dahl, D. W., Aryobsei, S., & Herrmann, A. (2021). Constraining ideas: How seeing ideas of others harms creativity in open innovation. *Journal of Marketing Research, 58*(1), 95–114.

Howe, J. (2006a). Crowdsourcing: A definition. [WWW Document].https://ww.crowdsourcing.typepad.com/cs/2006/06/crowdsourcing_a.html

Howe, J. (2006b). *The rise of crowdsourcing, Wired*. http://www.wired.com/wired/archive/14.06/crowds.html

Howe, J. (2008). *Crowdsourcing: Why the power of the crowd is driving the future of business*. Crown Publishing Group.

Huang, Y., Vir Singh, P., & Srinivasan, K. (2014). Crowdsourcing new product ideas under consumer learning. *Management Science, 60*(9), 2138–2159.

Humayun, H., Ghazali, M., & Malik, M. N. (2023). Is sustained participation a myth in crowdsourcing? A review. *European Journal of Innovation*

Management, Vol. ahead-of-print No. ahead-of-print. https://doi.org/10.1108/EJIM-10-2022-0589

Jiang, Z., Huang, Y., & Beil, D. R. (2022). The role of feedback in dynamic crowdsourcing contests: A structural empirical analysis. *Management Science, 68*(7), 4858–4877.

Kagermann, H., Wahlster, W., & Helbig, J. (2013). *Recommendations for implementing the strategic initiative Industrie 4.0: Final report of the Industrie 4.0 Working Group*. Forschungsunion: Berlin, Germany.

Kamel Boulos, M. N., Resch, B., Crowley, D. N., Breslin, J. G., Sohn, G., Burtner, R., Pike, A. W., Jezierski, E., & Chuang, K. Y. S. (2011). Crowdsourcing, citizen sensing and sensor web technologies for public and environmental health surveillance and crisis management: trends, OGC standards and application examples. *International journal of health geographics, 10*(1), 1–29.

Liu, Q., Zhao, X., & Sun, B. (2018). Value co-creation mechanisms of enterprises and users under crowdsource-based open innovation. *International Journal of Crowd Science, 2*(1), 2–17.

Liu, T. X., Yang, J., Adamic, L. A., & Chen, Y. (2014). Crowdsourcing with all-pay auctions: A field experiment on taskcn. *Management Science, 60*(8), 2020–2037.

Liu, Z., Hatton, M. R., Kull, T., Dooley, K., & Oke, A. (2021). Is a large award truly attractive to solvers? The impact of award size on crowd size in innovation contests. *Journal of Operations Management, 67*(4), 420–449.

Love, J., & Hirschheim, R. (2017). Crowdsourcing of information systems research. *European Journal of Information Systems, 26*(3), 315–332.

Maroufkhani, P., Wagner, R., & Wan Ismail, W. K. (2018). Entrepreneurial ecosystems: A systematic review. *Journal of Enterprising Communities: People and Places in the Global Economy, 12*(4), 545–564.

Martinez, M. G. (2015). Solver engagement in knowledge sharing in crowdsourcing communities: Exploring the link to creativity. *Research Policy, 44*(8), 1419–1430.

Messeni Petruzzelli, A., Murgia, G., & Parmentola, A. (2022). How can open innovation support SMEs in the adoption of I4. 0 technologies? An empirical analysis. *R&D Management*, *52*(4), 615–632.

Moreau, C. P., Prandelli, E., Schreier, M., & Hieke, S. (2020). Customization in luxury brands: Can Valentino get personal? *Journal of Marketing Research, 57*(5), 937–947.

Nishikawa, H., Schreier, M., Fuchs, C., & Ogawa, S. (2017). The value of marketing crowdsourced new products as such: Evidence from two randomized field experiments. *Journal of Marketing Research, 54*(4), 525–539.

Patterson, K. A., Grimm, C. M., & Corsi, T. M. (2003). Adopting new technologies for supply chain management. *Transportation Research Part e: Logistics and Transportation Review, 39*(2), 95–121.

Pavlidou, I., Papagiannidis, S., & Tsui, E. (2020). Crowdsourcing: A systematic review of the literature using text mining. *Industrial Management & Data Systems, 120*(11), 2041–2065.

Peter, O., & Mbohwa, C. (2018, March). Correlation between future energy systems and industrial revolutions. In *Proceedings of the International Conference on Industrial Engineering and Operations Management* (pp. 1953–1961).

Piezunka, H., & Dahlander, L. (2015). Distant search, narrow attention: How crowding alters organizations' filtering of suggestions in crowdsourcing. *Academy of Management Journal, 58*(3), 856–880.

Piezunka, H., & Dahlander, L. (2019). Idea rejected, tie formed: Organizations' feedback on crowdsourced ideas. *Academy of Management Journal, 62*(2), 503–530.

Pollok, P., Lüttgens, D., & Piller, F. T. (2019). Attracting solutions in crowdsourcing contests: The role of knowledge distance, identity disclosure, and seeker status. *Research Policy, 48*(1), 98–114.

Porter, A. J., Tuertscher, P., & Huysman, M. (2020). Saving our oceans: Scaling the impact of robust action through crowdsourcing. *Journal of Management Studies, 57*(2), 246–286.

Richter, C. (2015). Crowdcreation as a dimension of crowdsourcing: Conditions for entrepreneurs. *International Journal of Entrepreneurial Venturing, 7*(4), 324–340.

Riedl, C., & Seidel, V. P. (2018). Learning from mixed signals in online innovation communities. *Organization Science, 29*(6), 1010–1032.

Schemmann, B., Herrmann, A. M., Chappin, M. M., & Heimeriks, G. J. (2016). Crowdsourcing ideas: Involving ordinary users in the ideation phase of new product development. *Research Policy, 45*(6), 1145–1154.

Shrouf, F., Ordieres, J., & Miragliotta, G. (2014, December). Smart factories in Industry 4.0: A review of the concept and of energy management approached in production based on the Internet of Things paradigm. In *2014 IEEE international conference on industrial engineering and engineering management* (pp. 697–701). IEEE.

Stephen, A. T., Zubcsek, P. P., & Goldenberg, J. (2016). Lower connectivity is better: The effects of network structure on redundancy of ideas and customer innovativeness in interdependent ideation tasks. *Journal of Marketing Research, 53*(2), 263–279.

Stieger, D., Matzler, K., Chatterjee, S., & Ladstaetter-Fussenegger, F. (2012). Democratizing strategy: How crowdsourcing can be used for strategy dialogues. *California Management Review, 54*(4), 44–68.

Van Eck, N. J., & Waltman, L. (2010). Software survey: VOSviewer, a computer program for bibliometric mapping. *Scientometrics, 84*(2), 523–538.

Vrontis, D., Thrassou, A., Uzunboylu, N., & Efthymiou, L. (2023). An overview of business for sustainability: Strategic avenues and managerial approaches. In D. Vrontis, A. Thrassou, L, Efthymiou, Y. Weber, S. M. R. Shams & E. Tsoukatos (Eds.), *Business for sustainability, volume I*. Palgrave Studies in Cross-disciplinary Business Research, In Association with EuroMed Academy of Business. Palgrave Macmillan. https://doi.org/10.1007/978-3-031-37361-9_1

Vrontis, D., Thrassou, A., Efthymiou, L., Bozat, M. (2024). Delineating business for sustainability: Contextual evolution and elucidation. In D. Vrontis, A. Thrassou, L, Efthymiou, Y. Weber, S. M. R. Shams & E. Tsoukatos (Eds.), *Business for sustainability, volume II*. Palgrave Studies in Cross-disciplinary Business Research, In Association with EuroMed Academy of Business. Palgrave Macmillan. https://doi.org/10.1007/978-3-031-37365-7_1

Wichmann, J. R., Wiegand, N., & Reinartz, W. J. (2022). The platformization of brands. *Journal of Marketing, 86*(1), 109–131.

Zhu, X., Mukhopadhyay, S. K., & Kurata, H. (2012). A review of RFID technology and its managerial applications in different industries. *Journal of Engineering and Technology Management, 29*(1), 152–167.

Index

D. Vrontis et al. (eds.), *Business in Uncertainty*, Palgrave Studies in Cross-disciplinary Business Research, In Association with EuroMed Academy of Business, https://doi.org/10.1007/978-3-031-65587-6

The manufacturer's authorised representative in the EU is Springer Nature Customer Service Centre GmbH, Europaplatz 3, 69115 Heidelberg, Germany. If you have any concerns regarding our products, please contact ProductSafety@springernature.com

Printed and bound by CPI Group (UK) Ltd, Croydon, CR0 4YY
01/10/2026
02225913-0004